Understanding China

The series will provide you with in-depth information on China's social, cultural and economic aspects. It covers a broad variety of topics, from economics and history to law, philosophy, cultural geography, and regional politics, and offers a wealth of materials for researchers, doctoral students, and experienced practitioners.

Wu Jinglian

China's Economic Reform Process

CTPH

Springer

Wu Jinglian
Development Research Center of the State Council, China Europe International Business School (CEIBS)
Beijing, China

ISSN 2196-3134 ISSN 2196-3142 (electronic)
Understanding China
ISBN 978-981-96-9606-2 ISBN 978-981-96-9607-9 (eBook)
https://doi.org/10.1007/978-981-96-9607-9

Jointly published with China Translation & Publishing House
The printed edition is not for sale in Chinese Mainland. Customers from Chinese Mainland please order the print book from China Translation & Publishing House.
ISBN of the Co-Publisher's edition: 978-7-5202-1229-8

This Springer imprint is published by the registered company Springer Nature Singapore Pte Ltd.
The registered company address is: 152 Beach Road, #21-01/04 Gateway East, Singapore 189721, Singapore

Preface to the Second Edition

This book was first published in 2018 to commemorate the fortieth anniversary of China's reform and opening. In the blink of an eye, four years have passed, and the economic situation in China has changed. The external environment has become more complex and uncertain, while economic development at home has encountered multiple risks and challenges, particularly during the last two years. The economy still faces "three overlapping challenges of slowing economic growth, pending structural adjustments, and the consequences of the 2008 stimulus program." At the same time, the economy is also facing "three overlapping pressures in terms of contracted demand, supply impacts, and weakened expectations." Within and outside the government, people are focused on addressing current problems under the government policy aimed to "stabilize the overall economy." In this context, why are we reprinting an old book on the forty-year history of reform and opening?

I believe urgent responses are necessary to cope with the current situation. Ad-hoc response measures are insufficient because the state of an economy is the product of a historical process. Take the present difficulties as an example. It is true that some incidental factors, such as the Covid-19 pandemic, have exacerbated the challenges, but, as the saying goes, "It takes more than one day for the river to freeze three feet deep." If we retain the traditional contempt for theoretical thinking, indulge in only looking at the colorful and ever-changing exterior, and address the so-called "hot topics" in a superficial manner, or if we attempt to alleviate the contradictions by treating only the symptoms, it will be impossible to grasp the constant nature and permanent law of motion, leading to a failure to address the ultimate reasons for the economic problems. This is like trying to stop water from boiling over in a pot by constantly scooping it out and then pouring it back into the pot rather than removing the firewood from under the cauldron.

China's economy has been facing two fundamental challenges for a long time. The first challenge is to shift from the past economic growth model of high targets, giant inputs, and low efficiency to an efficiency-driven model to achieve sustained and quality development. The second challenge is to change the outdated, isolated, and ossified system into a new system characterized by full vitality. *China's Economic*

Reform Process systematically introduces the theoretical debates and the evolution of the policy surrounding these two challenges from the mid-1970s to the mid-2010s.

After the fall of the Gang of Four that followed the end of the Cultural Revolution, the first problem China had to deal with was that of the outdated growth mode that was hindering growth of the economy. In the 1981 "Ten Principles of Economic Construction," proposed in the Government Work Report to the National People's Congress, the central focus is on improving the economic returns. The principles highlight the need to "explore a new path that allows realistic speed and better economic returns and that gives the people more material benefits." Unfortunately, one year later, some theoreticians and politicians, calling themselves "advocates of Marxist reproduction theory," attacked these principles, to some extent leading to a reemergence of the traditional growth model.

Extensive growth resulted in two rounds of economic overheating and inflation, in 1984–85 and 1992–93. In this context, during preparations for the 1995 Ninth Five-year Plan, the State Planning Commission proposed a shift from investment-driven extensive growth to an efficiency-driven intensive mode. After detailed discussions, the national leadership decided to realize two overarching and fundamental transformations, as stated in the CCP Central Committee's Recommendations on the Ninth Five-year National Socioeconomic Development Plan (1996–2000) and Vision 2010. The first transformation was to be "economic system transformation, from the traditional planned economy to a socialist market economy." The second was an "economic growth mode transformation, from extensive growth to intensive growth." After 1995, progress in these two fundamental transformations ushered in a new economic development phase of faster growth and higher efficiency. As a result, by 2010 China's GDP surpassed that of Japan, and China became the world's second-largest economy.

However, the outstanding GDP growth during the Ninth Five-year Plan period gave an illusion that the two tasks of improving economic efficiency and changing the growth mode had been accomplished. Beginning with the Tenth Five-year Plan period (2001–5) and onward, the expansionary fiscal and monetary policies returned. Massive investments supported overambitious projects, a rush to introduce new projects, and "building-big-city" projects in succession. For certain senior officials, these "political showcase" and "boosting-the-city-image" projects were the best way to enhance their achievements and status. The adverse effects of these extensive growth methods quickly accumulated, leading to another round of economic overheating and inflation in 2005–7.

Against this backdrop, the Third Plenary Session of the 16th Party Central Committee in 2006 criticized the "incorrect view of political achievements," and the 17th Party Congress in 2007 called for "accelerated implementation of the strategic task to transform the economic development mode." Furthermore, in 2010 the CCP Central Committee Recommendations on the Twelfth National Socioeconomic Development Plan, adopted by the Fourth Plenary Session of the 17th Party Central Committee, stressed that "based on a comprehensive assessment of the economic situation at home and abroad, the economic development mode should be transformed without delay," thereby underscoring the requirement that such a transformation be accelerated.

Unfortunately, people tended to analyze long-term growth issues with a Keynesian short-term approach that was biased toward the consumption side. Moreover, the 2007 subprime mortgage crisis in the U.S. triggered a global financial crisis. To cope with the impact of the crisis on China and to maintain relatively rapid growth, the Chinese government again turned to expansionary fiscal and monetary policies and increased investments to expand domestic demand. However, using expansionary macroeconomic policies to stimulate high growth resulted in excessive leverage on the national balance sheet. The government and many enterprises were heavily indebted, and financial risks were increasing significantly. Given this situation, in 2013 the central leadership announced that the Chinese economy was entering a "new normal" phase with three overlapping challenges due to the deceleration of economic growth, the pending structural adjustments, and the consequences of the stimulus program.

The challenges of this "new normal" phase prompted considerable debate about which development concept and growth model China should adopt for the mid-2010s. As a result, the Thirteenth Five-year Plan (2016–20) attempted to clarify the basic conceptual framework for economic development, requiring future reforms to center on improving supply-side efficiency to realize a transformation from rapid growth to quality development.

However, as the first thirty-plus years of reform demonstrated, making decisions and thoroughly implementing them are two entirely different things. *China's Economic Reform Process* summarizes the decision-making and implementation processes leading up to adoption of the basic conceptual framework in the mid-2010s. The book points out that if the conceptual framework is not followed to overcome the difficulties, the macroeconomy will face a dilemma and further economic development will be like playing a teeter-totter game, or as the Chinese idiom goes: "pushing the gourd down in the water only to see the ladle floating on the top" [tr.: a situation whereby solving one problem immediately gives rise to another problem]. In such a situation, if fiscal and monetary stimuli are weakened to prevent financial risks, the economic growth rate will decline further. Conversely, maintaining a relatively high growth rate will require more potent policy stimuli, which will quickly lead to a higher leverage ratio, and systemic financial risks will be more likely to materialize. Moreover, if stimulus policies are repeatedly used to promote economic growth through increased investments, the leverage ratio in the national economy and the accumulation of financial risks will increase. In a worst-case scenario, a balance-sheet recession might be induced.

Historical experiences in choosing an economic development mode are worth studying today. In addition, there is also a lesson to be learned regarding short-term measures, such as relaxing credit and increasing investments, i.e., reliance on expansionary fiscal and monetary policies to stimulate growth, which will cause an excessive leverage ratio and a balance-sheet crisis. Instead, priority should be placed on improving efficiency for high-quality development.

Another challenge to China's economic development is probably more fundamental: economic system reform. In essence, economic system reform involves choosing between two resource allocation models: one that allows a market pricing mechanism to allocate resources, and one that supports administrative command and state planning. This is an issue about who is decisive in resource allocations, the market or the government?

At the beginning of the reform and opening in the late 1970s, enlightened people both within and outside the government reached a consensus in support of a market-oriented reform, which included introducing market mechanisms and letting the law of value play its role. Later, a socialist market economy and rule of law were solemnly adopted by the CCP national congresses and written into Central Committee decisions.

However, achieving the objective of a market-oriented and rule-of-law–based reform was not all smooth sailing. The significant reforms in the late twentieth century spurred continuous rapid growth by the turn of the twenty-first century, propelling China to become the world's second-largest economy. Despite these achievements, advocates of a government-led resource allocation model repeatedly attacked the market-oriented reforms. They advocated a strengthening of control of resource allocations. Their resistance to a market economy obstructed the reforms and sometimes even led to a reversal of economic policy, preventing a return to the proper course until their backpedaling was abandoned.

The reform and opening process has experienced many rounds of confrontation between advocates of the market-led resource allocation model and the opposing camp. *China's Economic Reform Process* provides a brief review of five major confrontations that ended with victories for reform and opening. The book also explores the conflicts between the opposing ideas underlying these confrontations and presents this author's assessments from a historical perspective.

The pro–government-dominance camp launched its most vicious assault in the early twenty-first century. After the 14th Party Congress in 1992 set the socialist market economy as the reform objective, China began establishing a uniform, open, competitive, and orderly market. However, the transitional economy was characterized by a "semi-controlled and semi-market" system due to a lack of reform progress in some areas and the government's ongoing dominance in others. Under this dual-track system of both plan and market and both administrative command and free pricing, administrative interventions in microeconomic activities were widespread, providing a broad institutional basis for rent-seeking. In addition, development of the rule of law was delayed significantly. These drawbacks resulted in rampant corruption and a widening gulf between the rich and the poor. Naturally, the general public became resentful due to the lack of reform progress in the direction of the market, democracy, and rule of law. In contrast, opponents of the market economy took the opportunity to attack the reform. They demanded that the government's control over society, its allocation of resources, and its interventions in enterprises be reinforced. Following the slogan "taking class struggle as the key link," they even called for a return to an ultra-leftist political line together with its representatives, the Gang of Four. These people were in favor of "launching another round in the Cultural Revolution."

Due to this ideological trend, populism and "narrow nationalism" [chauvinism] skyrocketed. Reform measures to develop a market system were attacked. In some areas, the state sector advanced and the private sector retreated.

Fortunately, the 18th CCP Congress in 2012 met the people's expectations by standing fast against this revisionist trend. It decided to "timely deepen the reform in the major areas with greater political courage and wisdom." In 2013, the Third Plenary Session of the 18th Party Central Committee adopted the Decision of the Central Committee of the Communist Party of China on Some Major Issues Concerning Comprehensively Deepening the Reform, which provides a top-down design and an overarching plan for the reform. This decision points out, "comprehensively deepening the reform should focus on the economic system, and the central task is to improve the relationship between the government and the market to let the market play a decisive role in resource allocations and to let the government better carry out its role." In addition, the decision extends the reform to other aspects of society. It states that "the overall objective of comprehensively deepening the reform is to improve and develop socialism with Chinese characteristics and to promote modernization of the country's governance system and capability." This important Party document indicates the future direction of the economic and political reforms, with specific reform requirements for China to move out of its transitional economic system and to establish a rule-based modern market economy with rule of law.

After the top-down design, road map, and timetable for the comprehensive reform were set, the key was to implement them effectively.

The 2018 edition of *China's Economic Reform Process* succinctly discusses the various obstacles to comprehensively deepening the reform and, in its final paragraphs, it explains how these hurdles might be overcome. However, the implementation period had not yet lasted long enough for the book to thoroughly analyze the reform's progress and its shortcomings after the Third Plenary Session of the 18th Party Central Committee. Nevertheless, in looking for solutions to the existing challenges, one may still learn from the book's observations and ideas about China's reform and opening process.

Take the most critical of the "three overlapping pressures," the weakened expectations, as an example. This problem has now become more pronounced due to the pandemic. However, underlining the problem is the lack of confidence among businesspeople to establish a sound business and policy environment, a worry that has been growing over an extended period.

Recall the excitement of various market entities in 2013, when the decisions of the 18th Party Congress and the Third Plenary Session of the 18th Party Central Committee were about to be implemented. At the time, businesspeople were eager to invest, open new firms, or expand existing firms. According to the National Bureau of Statistics, from 2013 to 2019 the number of sole proprietorships and private enterprises reached 118 million, an increase of 107 percent, of which 35.16 million were firms having more than eight employees, a rise of 183 percent. The private sector has since significantly contributed to China's robust economic development.

Unfortunately, opinions opposing these decisions soon emerged. At the beginning of 2018, a well-known professor at a prestigious university claimed, "the shared development of multiple forms of ownership is a unique phenomenon during the initial phase of socialism, and it should not be solidified and perpetuated," "Every measure undertaken based on the on-the-ground situation should represent a step toward communism," and "Private ownership should gradually be eliminated."[1] Later, a senior professional in the financial sector offered his view: "China's private sector has accomplished its role of supplementing the public economy, and it should gradually exit the scene."[2] While the mainstream press negated the call for the private sector to exit, the ideological trend against the market-oriented reform continued. The capitalist class was condemned, and private businesses were disparaged. In such an atmosphere, many businesspeople became anxious and confused, and thus they lacked the motivation to invest or to start new firms.

Historical experiences show that promoting government support and soothing businesspeople's pains can help somewhat, but they are inadequate in restoring and strengthening the confidence of market entities. Therefore, in my view, the most critical measure is to implement further reforms in the direction of a market economy, rule of law, and democracy to create an enabling business environment for autonomous operations and a policy habitat for fair competition where everything not forbidden is allowed.

To sum up, I hope the observations in this book on the history of reform and opening, along with my reflections on critical related issues, can serve as a reference for readers who are studying China's economic development and are exploring solutions to its current challenges. This is the goal that this new reprint hopes to achieve. If it succeeds, I, as the author, will indeed be genuinely gratified.

Beijing, China
June 2022

Wu Jinglian

[1] Zhou Xingcheng, "Communists Can Sum Up Their Theory in One Sentence: Eliminate Private Ownership," www.qizhiwang.org.cn, January 11, 2018.

[2] Wu Xiaoping, "The Private Sector Should Gradually Exit the Scene As It Already Supplements Public-Sector Development," www.toutiao.com, September 12, 2018.

Preface

Beginning in the late 1970s, China embarked on what has now been almost forty years of reform and opening. The process brought huge socioeconomic changes that enabled the country to become the world's second-largest economy in 2010. This book aims to offer a concise commentary on this significant and eventful historical period.

In my view, the most critical factor in China's economic rise has been the expansion of the market, which has provided space both to individuals and to enterprises to exercise their decision-making rights. Although constraints still exist, firms now enjoy freedom to choose the organization of production and the pricing of products. Individuals are free to make decisions about the provision of labor and the consumption of goods. This would have been unimaginable in the pre–reform and opening era. The expansion of such market-based freedoms has resulted in an effective combination of labor, capital, and technology within a given time and place, thereby releasing China's potential for significant economic growth.

From this perspective, China's economic reforms can be summarized as a process in which the market has continuously expanded in both reach and scope. However, given the previous existence of a planned economy, the emergence of the market has not been a linear process. The view that the reform and opening was a rational policy choice based on Pareto optimality is, to say the least, a simplistic interpretation. This view fails to explain why China adopted a cautious approach to reviving a market economy while still grappling with the legacy of the planned economy. Nor does it explain why the transition from a planned economy to a market economy faced so many twists and turns or why there were moments when the reform process risked coming to a halt or even being reversed

The economic reforms were first envisaged and implemented when China's traditional industrialization model was breaking down and the society was on the verge of collapse. The reforms, as a replacement for the command economy, were essentially a response to this situation. Because of the exploratory nature of the reforms, the market was initially introduced to only a few sectors where state control was less tight (e.g., agriculture, and general services in the urban areas) or to some standalone regions (e.g., the coastal special economic zones). The model of East European market socialism influenced early thinking on reform of the traditional planned, state-sector-dominant economy in China. It was hoped that a partial introduction of market pricing and incentive mechanisms would raise economic efficiency, while the basic framework of a Soviet-style socioeconomic system could be maintained. The result was constant vacillation between rampant insider control followed by strict state control in the state-owned enterprises (SOEs). This early stage of reform clearly reveals that the establishment of a market economy was not the ultimate objective at that time. Instead, practical and adaptive economic measures were undertaken to escape the predicament caused by both the rigid command economy and the ideology that supported a strong omnipotent state.

The pragmatism that guided the reform was a double-edged sword, with far-reaching influence and long-term effects on the path of *China's Economic Reform Process*. On the one hand, by "crossing the river by feeling for the stones," China could bypass any obstacles and foster an economic model characterized by "incremental reforms." This model was hugely successful in the general goods and services sectors, and it increased demand for further development of a market economy and rule of law. On the other hand, due to the lack of thorough critiques on the root causes of the defects in the command economy and the lack of a broad-based consensus about the reform, the state-dominated economy model that placed a priority on state control of the economy gained both explicit or implicit support in theoretical circles. From time to time, temporary difficulties and problems during the reform process, such as the social divide between the rich and the poor and the flagrant corruption, were used as justifications for an excessive expansion of state power over enterprises and the market, and they generated enormous resistance to those reforms that sought to establish a market economy and rule of law. In particular, in the early twenty-first century, when the economy and society were becoming increasingly complex, reform of the factors markets (land, capital, etc.) stagnated. There was even a so-called "*guojin mintui*" phenomenon in industry whereby the SOEs were advancing while the private sector was retreating.

However, as the saying goes, "Good fortune follows upon disaster." The issues arising from the stagnating reforms resulted in a broad-based consensus on the only viable solution: deepening the reforms. Consequently, the 18th Chinese Communist Party (CCP) Congress of 2012 adopted the historic decision to "lose no time in deepening reform in key sectors and to resolutely discard all notions and systems that hinder efforts to pursue development in a scientific way." The 2013 Third Plenary Session of the 18th Central Committee formulated an overall plan, a top-down design, and a road map for deepening the reform. The Decision of the Party Central Committee on Some Major Issues Concerning Comprehensively Deepening the Reform reaffirmed the Party's determination to "deepen economic system reform by centering on the decisive role of the market in allocating resources." Furthermore, the decision extended the reform to the social and political arenas, establishing an overall objective "to step up efforts to form a scientific and effective social management system, … to promote the modernization of the national governance system and capacity, … and to accelerate socialist democracy in a systematic way." Hence, China's reform and opening entered a new phase.

The course of the economic reforms demonstrates that when the dominant policy stance shifted toward a market economy and market mechanisms were implemented for resource allocations, the quality and speed of economic growth improved. Innovations and business startups in the non-state sector prospered. These, in turn, provided a better external environment for reform of the SOEs. This causality was repeatedly confirmed by the success of the rural household contracting system and the emergence of the township and village enterprises during the early phase of the reform; by the visible results in development of the private sector and external capital inflows due to the holistic reforms of government finance and tax, the financial sector, and foreign trade in the mid-1990s; and by the vast market and institutional dividends resulting from accelerated integration with the global economy after China joined the World Trade Organization (WTO) in 2001. However, whenever thinking that favored a state-dominated economy influenced economic policymaking, the market-based non-state economy contracted, SOE reforms were stalled, macroeconomic risks increased, and microeconomic returns declined. The most fitting examples of this observation can be found in the anti-market bias of 1989–92 after the political turmoil of 1989 and in the unintended economic consequences of the government's powerful stimulus package adopted after the 2008 global financial crisis. These positive and negative examples reveal that the solution to the various problems that emerged during the reform process was not increased state intervention; instead, the solution entailed comprehensively deepening the reform in the direction of a market economy and rule of law and allowing the market to play a greater role in resource allocations.

Drawing on the above argument and a historical perspective on changes in China's economic policy, this book combs through the evolution of the reform causalities by subject matter. By so doing, the book reveals the long-existing contradictions and conflicts between market and controlled economies. It points to the significant risks to socioeconomic development if market and rule-of-law–oriented reforms are halted. Although "letting the market play a decisive role" has been incorporated into the Decision of the Third Plenary Session of the 18th Party Central Committee, the conflict between moving further in the direction of a market economy or returning to a state-dominated economy will persist. China's reform and opening will continue to be characterized by its immense complexity and massive problems. Without clearly recognizing the challenges, it will be difficult to "comprehensively deepen the reforms" in the direction of a market economy and rule of law. There is also a possibility that the reforms could be abandoned in mid-course.

The book is structured as follows. Chapters 1 and 2 provide background on the socioeconomic conditions during the pre-reform period and China's state of preparedness for reform in terms of theoretical research. The chapters then discuss the inevitability of the reforms and the historical constraints in selecting a reform path during the initial stages. Chapters 3, 4, and 5 introduce, chronologically and in line with economic logic, the early "incremental reform model," exploration of the reform objectives in the mid-1980s, and the context for the decision in the 1990s to implement the reforms holistically, along with the significant impact of the relevant policies for the non-state sector and the national economy. Chapters 6 and 7 focus on the strong driving force for growth generated by access to the outside world and the removal of ownership barriers at home. Due to these market-based reforms, including China's accession to the WTO, Chinese firms enjoyed a vast and increasingly integrated market both within and outside the country. The role of the market in resource allocations was strengthened, paving the way for the monumental rise of China's economic power at the turn of the twenty-first century.

However, a major problem continued to trouble policymakers, i.e., the relatively low quality of growth. This problem can be found in the SOEs' high leverage ratio and low efficiency. It can also be found in the extensive growth mode that has led to heavy pollution and high energy consumption. Chapters 8, 9, and 10 discuss, respectively, the bias toward a controlled economy during the SOE reform and the distribution of the state sector in the economy, and the penchant for excessive investment caused by price distortions in land and capital markets and local protectionism, and the consequent macroeconomic fragility. The chapters thus reveal the shortcomings of the system and the significant risks facing the Chinese economy. Chapter 11 further analyzes the severe rent-seeking activities and corruption caused by the defects and distortions in the economic system. If corruption spreads unchecked to become a social cancer, the greatest casualty will be the much-needed public support for market-economy reforms and the rule of law.

The final chapter discusses the prospects for "comprehensively deepening the reform." The chapter shows that the guiding principles and policies adopted since the 18th Party Congress have laid a solid political foundation for further reforms. However, the existing obstacles and resistance should not be overlooked. Consequently, the key to achieving sustained and steady development lies in steadfast adoption and implementation of the reform program.

Beijing, China
August, 2018

Wu Jinglian

Contents

Chapter 1
The End of the Cultural Revolution and the Beginning of the Post-Mao Era

On September 9, 1976, Chairman Mao Zedong passed away. Just twenty-seven days later, another pivotal event occurred: the arrest of the Gang of Four, led by Mao's widow, Jiang Qing. This marked the end of the Great Proletarian Cultural Revolution, which Mao had initiated a decade earlier. Thereafter, China entered a new stage of development, marked by the creation of a new economic system.[1]

The transition from the former system to the new system would not be a straightforward road like Beijing's Chang An Avenue. Instead, it was destined to be full of twists and turns, nearly reversing course on a number of occasions. As Marx wrote, "In addition to the modern calamities, those of the past are also oppressing us. This is because the ancient legacy modes of production, with their accompanying outdated social and political relations, are still lingering. We suffer not only from the living but also from the dead. The deceased have captured the living!"[2]

The Resolution on Certain Questions in the History of our Party Since the Founding of the People's Republic of China describes the period from the arrest of the Gang of Four in October 1976 to the eve of the Third Plenary Session of the 11th Central Committee in December 1978 as one in which progress was made by taking hesitant steps.[3] This period actually extended beyond the 1978 Third Plenary Session and continued into the early 1980s. The correct direction of the reform and opening was determined only after many ups and downs.

---

[1] The 1981 Resolution on Certain Questions in the History of Our Party, adopted by the Sixth Plenary Session of the 11th Party Central Committee, points out that the "victory in overthrowing the counterrevolutionary Jiang Qing clique in October 1976 saved the Party and the revolution from ruin and enabled our country to enter a new historical period of development."

[2] Karl Marx, "Preface to Book One," *On Capital,* in *Complete Works of Marx, Engels, Lenin, and Stalin* (Chinese translation. Beijing: People's Publishing House, 1972), vol. 23, p. 11.

[3] Resolution on Certain Questions in the History of Our Party, adopted at the Sixth Plenary Session of the 11th Party Central Committee on June 27, 1981.

W. Jinglian, *China's Economic Reform*, Understanding China,
https://doi.org/10.1007/978-981-96-9607-9_1

1.1 Retaining the "Two Whatevers" or Exploring a New Path?

The period following the overthrow of the Gang of Four was marked by social disorder and a crumbling economy. Despite this predicament, the national leadership under Hua Guofeng was eager to reestablish social stability and accelerate economic development, reaffirming the economic development goal first proposed by Premier Zhou Enlai prior to the Cultural Revolution: to build China into a strong socialist power within the twentieth century.[4] The leaders announced that "in the next 23 years, the main task of the Communist Party of China and of the proletariat is to lead our people in continuing to implement Chairman Mao's teachings, adhering to the basic line of the Party, taking class struggle as the key link, upholding the theory of continuous revolution under proletarian dictatorship, and building our country into a great and strong socialist power."[5]

While both Party cadres and the general public sought to accelerate realization of the Four Modernizations, Hua Guofeng and other national leaders at the time failed to recognize the gravity of China's social crisis, and they did not seriously analyze the root ideological and institutional causes of the crisis. With the removal of the

[4] The objective of "building China into a strong socialist power with modern agriculture, industry, defense, and science and technology" was presented by Premier Zhou Enlai in his Report on the Work of the Government to the National People's Congress in December 1964. However, shortly thereafter this objective was replaced by "class struggle" and the "two-line struggle." As a result, China descended into the ten turbulent years of the Cultural Revolution.

[5] Hua Guofeng, "Speech at the National Conference on 'Industry Learning from Daqing,'" May 7, 1977. In his Political Report to the 11th National Congress of the Communist Party of China on August 12, 1977, Hua reiterated this slogan, making it the political line of the 11th Party Congress. The "theory of continuous revolution under the dictatorship of the proletariat" was the Cultural Revolution–era description of the essence of Mao Zedong Thought. A joint editorial in the *People's Daily*, *People's Liberation Army Daily*, and *Red Flag* on November 6, 1967, drafted by Chen Boda and Yao Wenyuan and cleared by Mao Zedong, states: "Comrade Mao Zedong has carried on, defended, and developed Marxism and Leninism. He proposed the great innovative theory of continuous revolution under the dictatorship of the proletariat. Furthermore, he launched the extraordinary Great Proletarian Cultural Revolution. This was an important landmark in a new phase in the development of Marxism, that is, the phase of Mao Zedong Thought." The editorial summarizes the theory of continuous revolution as follows: "[in] the current historical stage of socialism, there exist classes, class contradictions, and class struggle. There also exists the struggle between the socialist road and the capitalist road and the danger of the restoration of capitalism.... In essence, class struggle under the dictatorship of the proletariat is a struggle for political power.... The proletariat must impose full dictatorship over the bourgeoisie in all the superstructures, including the cultural sphere.... The struggle between the two classes and the two roads in the society will inevitably be reflected in the Party.... The handful of capitalist roaders represents the bourgeoisie within the Party.... To strengthen the proletarian dictatorship, we must pay full attention to see through 'the Khrushchev-like figures at our bedside' to fully expose and denounce them, and to overthrow them, so they can never be reestablished…. The most important part of the continuous revolution is to carry on the Great Proletarian Cultural Revolution." The editorial also states that "this theory of continuous revolution proposed by Comrade Mao Zedong represents a genius and innovative advancement of the Marxist and Leninist idea about proletarian dictatorship. It is both epoch-making and a second great milestone."

Gang of Four, their power base was strengthened, however, and they began to feel that they could continue to follow Mao's governing philosophy of his later years to realize the goal of "Great Order Under Heaven." But this belief was still out of touch with reality.

The main problem was due to the political limitations of the leadership under Hua Guofeng. With the support of the old generation of revolutionaries, such as Ye Jianying, the Jiang Qing clique was overthrown, an event that won widespread support. The leaders under Hua believed that China's problems had been due to the conspiracy of the Jiang Qing clique to seize the highest powers. However, they did not recognize that the root causes of the problems were due to China's long-term pursuit of the ultra-leftist political line, including "the policy of taking class struggle as the key link," "the theory of continuing the revolution under the dictatorship of the proletariat," and "all-round dictatorship over the bourgeoisie."[6] In accepting such ultra-leftism, the leaders insisted that it was a core principle for governing the country.

On the second day after Mao's death, the CCP Central Committee, the Standing Committee of the National People's Congress, the State Council, and the Central Military Commission issued an Open Letter to All the Members of the Party, the Army, and the People, calling for the country to "carry on Chairman Mao's legacy and uphold the policy of taking the class struggle as the key link, the Party's basic political line, and continuing the revolution under the dictatorship of the proletariat." Even though the Gang of Four had been overthrown, their tone, as reflected in this statement, was retained in Party and government documents until December 1978, when the Third Plenary Session of the 11th Party Central Committee rejected the ultra-leftist political line.

Influenced by this ideology, the CCP Central Committee, led by Hua Guofeng, adopted a program of "running the country by grasping the key link." On February 7, 1977, the *People's Daily*, *People's Liberation Army Daily*, and *Red Flag* issued a joint editorial entitled "*Study* the *Documents Well* and *Grasp* the *Key Link*" which formally put forward the "strategic decision on running the country by grasping the key link." The joint editorial explained that the goal of this strategy was to "realize stability and unity, to strengthen the dictatorship of the proletariat amid the fierce class struggle, and to strengthen our socialist country." As instructed by Wang Dongxing, a member of the Party leadership, the editorial proposed a fundamental principle called the "two whatevers." In the editorial, it is stressed that "whenever we complied with Chairman Mao's revolutionary line and implemented his instructions, the revolution was successful; and whenever we departed from Chairman Mao's revolutionary line, the revolution suffered defeat and setbacks.... we will resolutely uphold *whatever* policy decisions Chairman Mao made and unswervingly follow *whatever* instructions Chairman Mao gave." Although at the time this proposition

[6] Even after the fall of the Gang of Four, Hua Guofeng reiterated this point on several occasions. For example, at a meeting of senior officials on October 8, 1977, he stressed that the Cultural Revolution should be fully affirmed. According to Hua, when dealing with Gang of Four problems, attention should not be focused on what they did during the Cultural Revolution. For Hua, the core of the Gang of Four's problems was their scheme to seize Party and state power. See Tong Qinglin, *1978 in Retrospect: A Turning Point in History* (Beijing: People's Publishing House, 2008), p. 23.

was questioned both within and outside the Party, it nevertheless was confirmed as official CCP Central Committee policy.[7]

In March 1977, the leadership held a Central Committee Work Conference to facilitate policy implementation. The conference summarized the work that had been done following the overthrow of the Gang of Four, and it adopted the Outline on Several Issues Related to the 1977 National Economic Plan, submitted by the State Planning Commission.

At this work conference, views that differed from mainstream thinking were voiced.

There were demands to remove the ultra-leftist line from all political policies and discourse. For instance, Hu Yaobang, then a vice president of the Central Party School, pointed out that "overall, the situation is good, but there are difficulties and unfavorable factors. The biggest unfavorable factor is that the lingering influence of the Gang of Four is far from being eliminated in the political, ideological, and organizational spheres. Therefore, great efforts should be made to correct this ideological and political confusion."[8] However, these suggestions were not accepted. Although Hua Guofeng had not proposed that the "two whatevers" be included in the joint editorial, he nevertheless did agree with the general proposition of the "two whatevers." His speech at this Central Committee Work Conference merely proposed some editorial changes to the principle: "We must defend all the policy decisions Chairman Mao made and suppress all words and actions that tarnish Chairman Mao's image."

Another view pointed out that the prolonged economic structural contradictions had been exacerbated during the Cultural Revolution and that readjustment and stabilization should take priority over economic development.

However, the national leaders did not accept this proposal. Instead, the work conference judged that "1977 should be the year in which we move toward great order," and it decided to take an "active marching forward" approach under the annual national economic plan. On July 30, the Party Central Committee issued a State Council report on industrial production for the first half of 1977, stating that "a new leap forward in the national economy is emerging."[9] On August 15, Hua Guofeng reaffirmed this position in his Report to the Eleventh Party Congress.

In December 1977, the State Council issued the Outline of the National Economic Development Program, 1976–85 (Revised). The State Planning Commission had prepared this ten-year plan based on the 1975 Outline on Developing the National

---

[7] For instance, when told to publish the editorial in *People's Daily*, *PLA Daily*, and *Red Flag* monthly, Geng Biao, then in charge of the Party Central Committee's propaganda organs, told several subordinates that publication of the article would negate the overthrow of the Gang of Four. He reportedly said, "If we follow this article's 'Two Whatevers,' nothing can be achieved" (quoted in Tong Qinglin, *1978 in Retrospect*, p. 29). See also Shen Baoxiang, *The Complete Story of the Truth Criterion Debate* (Beijing: China Youth Publishing House, 1997), p. 4.

[8] Huang Yibing, "A Study on the 1977 Central Committee Work Conference," *CCP History Research*, no. 2 (2010).

[9] "State Council Report on Industrial Production in the First Half of 1977," issued by the Party Central Committee on July 30, 1977.

Economy (Draft) that had been prepared under the guidance of Deng Xiaoping. The 1977 plan set the ten-year average annual growth rate for total industrial and agricultural output at 9.5 percent. The value of agricultural output was expected to reach 4.7 percent, and the value of industrial output was expected to reach 11 percent.

In fact, the reality proved that the central leadership at the time had seriously underestimated the damage to Chinese society caused by the ultra-leftist line. Nevertheless, Hua Guofeng was confident that "great order across the land" could be achieved. In his July 1977 Opening Remarks at the Third Plenary Session of the tenth Party Central Committee, he reported that "since the overthrow of the Gang of Four more than nine months ago, the Party Central Committee has raised high the great banner of Chairman Mao, upheld the principle of taking class struggle as the key link and as the basic line of the Party, and has carried on the continuous revolution under the dictatorship of the proletariat. We have also made a strategic decision to run the country by grasping the key link and to lead the Party, the People's Liberation Army, and all ethnic groups in a great political revolution against the Gang of Four. Hence, much work has been done in all fields, and a great victory has been achieved."[10]

On the issue of the "two whatevers," Deng Xiaoping, who had recently returned to the central leadership but had not yet been officially reinstated, disagreed with the dominant view as represented by Hua Guofeng.

In Hua Guofeng's view, "all victories of the Chinese revolution should be attributed to Chairman Mao's thought and practice. The glorious Mao Zedong Thought is like a great beacon in the darkness, lighting the path of our revolution and guiding us to advance forward."[11]

Having lived through the turbulent years of the Great Leap Forward and the Cultural Revolution, Deng Xiaoping completely understood the desires of ordinary people. While also seeking to maintain Mao's paramount stature, Deng realized that there would be little hope for China in developing the economy if the ultra-leftist practices, as promoted in the "two whatevers" doctrine, were not abandoned and if the institutional defects of the system were not corrected.[12]

In February 1977, shortly after the "two whatevers" slogan was put forward, Deng Xiaoping shared his opposition to the slogan with Wang Zhen during a visit by the latter: "This is not Marxism, nor is it Mao Zedong Thought,"[13] Deng said.

---

[10] Hua Guofeng, "Opening Remarks at the Third Plenary Session of the tenth Party Central Committee," July 16, 1977.

[11] Hua Guofeng, "Speech at the Ceremony upon Completion of the Chairman Mao Memorial Hall," September 9, 1977.

[12] Deng Xiaoping strongly opposed the ultra-leftist principle of socialist construction. For instance, at a meeting with Ted Hill, at the time the chairman of the Communist Party of Australia (Marxist/Leninist), Deng pointedly commented: "What is the advantage of socialism? Is it that people do not have to go to school or do not have to work? Is it worsening instead of improving the people's living standards? If these are the advantages, we do not want socialism" (*Chronicle of Deng Xiaoping's Life [1975–1997)]* (Beijing: Central Party Literature Press, 2004), vol. 1, p. 250.

[13] Ibid., p. 155.

The March 1977 Central Committee Work Conference arranged for Deng Xiaoping to return to power. On April 10, he wrote to Hua Guofeng, Ye Jianying, and the Party Central Committee to thank them for clarifying that he had not been involved in the April 1976 Tiananmen Incident. In his letter, he proposed that [the central leadership] "should forever use the precise and holistic Mao Zedong Thought to guide our Party, the army, and the people."[14] Deng later noted that this proposal was targeted at the "two whatevers" slogan, and he had put it forward after long deliberation.[15]

Later on, Wang Dongxing and Li Xin, director and deputy director of the General Office of the Party Central Committee, visited Deng Xiaoping to brief him on the distribution of his two letters, dated respectively October 10, 1976 and April 10, 1977. On this occasion, Deng made it clear to his visitors that "the two whatevers will not work."[16] In his May 24 talk with Vice Premier Wang Zhen and Party theoretician Deng Liqun, Deng Xiaoping again pointed out that the "two whatevers" did not make sense. He said, "Comrade Mao Zedong himself admitted that he could make inappropriate remarks, noting that anyone who works always runs the risk of making mistakes. Mao said that 'Marx, Engels, Lenin, and Stalin[17] had also made mistakes. If this were not the case, then why were their manuscripts often subject to modification and revision? The revisions indicate that some of their viewpoints had not been entirely correct or complete.' … It is impossible for any human to be absolutely correct all of the time and for every sentence uttered to be completely accurate. There is no such thing as always being correct. If what a person does in his life is said to be 70 percent right and 30 percent wrong, this will already be an excellent assessment. After my death, if I can receive such an assessment, I will be thrilled and completely satisfied.... This is an important theoretical issue related to whether to uphold historical materialism. Marx and Engels never maintained that everything they said should always be upheld, nor did Lenin or Stalin say such a thing, and neither did Comrade Mao Zedong either.... In my April 10 letter to the Party Central Committee, I proposed that we should forever use the precise and holistic Mao Zedong Thought to guide our Party, army, and people, to carry out the socialist cause of the Party as well as that of the international communist movement. This proposition was made after several rounds of contemplation. Mao Zedong Thought is a system.... If we are to hold high this banner, we must learn and implement the entire system."[18]

The "two whatevers" implied continuing to follow the disastrous ultra-leftist line and the related policies. This was thus a significant obstacle to ending the ultra-leftist political line and seeking an optimal development path, and many people,

---

[14] Ibid., p. 157.

[15] Deng Xiaoping, "Adhere to the Two Whatevers," 1977, in *Selected Works of Deng Xiaoping* (Beijing: People's Publishing House, 1994), vol. 2, pp. 38–39.

[16] *Chronicle of Deng Xiaoping's Life (1975–1997),* vol. 1, p. 157.

[17] Joseph Stalin (1878–1953) was general secretary of the Communist Party of the Soviet Union (Bolshevik) when Lenin died in 1924. After purging the other members of the Party leadership, Stalin served as supreme leader of the Communist Party of the Soviet Union until his death in 1953.

[18] Deng Xiaoping, "Adhere to the Two Whatevers," 1977, in *Selected Works of Deng Xiaoping*, vol. 2, pp. 38–39.

both inside and outside the Party, believed that some Party leaders were entirely incorrect in suppressing any attempts to re-examine the ultra-leftist line. People longed for a change. Against this backdrop, *Guangming Daily*, on May 11, 1978, with the support of Hu Yaobang, director of the Party Organization Department and executive vice president of the Central Party School, allowed for publication of the commentary "Practice is the Sole Criterion for Testing Truth." Publication of this article led to a great wave of debate that eventually emancipated the people's minds.[19] The article maintained that the standard of truth is to be tested by practice. Therefore, "irrefutable theories," such as "taking class struggle as the key link" and "continuing the revolution under the dictatorship of the proletariat," might be subject to doubt. This also meant that "sacred and inviolable economic and political systems," or an economy in which the state "commands everything under the sky" and holds a total dictatorship over the bourgeoisie (including those in senior positions who were said to have taken the capitalist road as well as the bourgeois intellectuals) can be challenged. But such a prospect was intolerable to the guardians of the former political line, and, as a result, some leaders used their positions at the center of power to retaliate against those who were advocating the "criterion of truth," accusing them of making a strategic error by abandoning the banner of Mao Zedong Thought.

However, after the Great Leap Forward and the Cultural Revolution, people understood that any return to the old system and the old political line would also bring back the hardships of those years. The proposal to examine past practices by the "truth criterion" won broad-based support both inside and outside the Party. Even many senior leaders, notably Deng Xiaoping, who was already a vice chairman of the Party Central Committee, and Luo Ruiqing, who was chief of staff of the People's Liberation Army, supported this proposal, Self-examination using the truth criterion as a basis gained the upper hand during these debates within the leadership. At the December 1978 Central Committee Work Conference, Hua Guofeng, chairman of the Party Central Committee, made a self-criticism for his opposition to the truth criterion.

The truth criterion debate marked the beginning of the movement to emancipate people's minds that paved the way for the reform and opening of the 1980s and for a national revitalization.

1.2 Revelations from "Seeing the Outside World"

The reform and opening was not only the result of analyzing China's past experiences, as discussed above, but also an outcome of a cross-country comparison of various development models.

Hua Guofeng attached great importance to bringing in foreign equipment, technology, and funding, as well as expanding and accelerating imports. He also called

[19] Wu Jiang, "My Experience with the Truth Criterion Debate," *Tongzhou gongjin*, no. 9 (2001).

for studying foreign experiences and adopting their successful practices. He therefore favored "going abroad" and "opening our eyes."

In May 1978, at Hua Guofeng's request, Gu Mu led a government delegation to France, Switzerland, Belgium, Denmark, and the Federal Republic of Germany to "study from the Western capitalist countries." On June 30, during a debriefing meeting on Gu Mu's trip, Hua said: "The study findings are illuminating. Foreign enterprise management offers us a valuable experience from which to learn.... If we do not learn from these positive overseas experiences, we will easily become self-congratulatory, just like the arrogant King of Yelang [tr.: referring to someone who thinks too highly of himself and who is ignorant of the rest of the world]. Hua felt deeply that self-complacency "is not an isolated or limited phenomenon. It is widespread. So then, how can we accelerate economic growth?" He realized that "the sources of the problem are our backward guiding principles.... These principles constrain us. To accelerate economic construction, we should overcome our unwillingness to learn..... We should emancipate our minds a little more." At a discussion meeting on implementing the Outline of the Ten-year Development Program, passed by the First Session of the fifth National People's Congress in March 1978, Hua proposed learning from other countries' experiences and paving a new road to development.[20] In his July 4 meeting with Hu Yaobang and other leaders, Hua again pointed out, "Now the problem is that our high-level cadres are lagging [in terms of accepting new thinking]. What should we do? We should send those people abroad more often to learn from other countries."[21]

In the face of adversity during the Cultural Revolution, Deng Xiaoping had thoroughly reflected on China's past failures, paying close attention to development trends in the outside world. In December 1977, he pointed out that "we have enormous potential. We should now begin seriously studying foreign experiences and making innovations. Such prospects will energize us. But there are also many problems that we need to solve." A first step in finding a new path was to send people to study abroad and to visit the European and Asian-Pacific countries.

During a meeting with Ministry of Education officials on June 23, 1978, Deng proposed that more students should be sent abroad to study. He said, "I support significantly increasing the number of overseas students, mainly to study the natural sciences. There should be hundreds and thousands of them.... This is an important way to quickly achieve results in raising our level of science and education within five years."[22] On July 11, the Ministry of Education submitted to the Party leadership its report on increasing the number of students to be sent overseas to study, and on December 26 of that year, the first group of students to be sent abroad during the era

[20] Fang Weizhong, comp., *Marching through Storms: Chronicle of China's Development and Reform (1977–89)*, vol. 1 (1977–78), unpublished draft, dated 2004, pp. 127–130.

[21] Han Gang, "Several Historical Facts about Hua Guofeng," *Wangshi*, no. 74 (November 14, 2008).

[22] *Chronicle of Deng Xiaoping's Life (1975–1997)*, vol. 1, p. 331.

of reform and opening set off for the United States. In the 22 years between 1978–2000, about 350,000 Chinese students engaged in study abroad,[23] with 70 percent of them returning to China after graduation. Today, many of these former students hold key positions in various fields, significantly contributing to China's economic, cultural, and social development.

At the urging of Hua Guofeng, Deng Xiaoping, and other senior leaders, government agencies, institutions of higher education, and scientific research organizations all proceeded to send delegations abroad. As a result, a wave of study abroad tours began at the end of 1977.

Beginning at that time, central and local government officials also embarked on several dozen overseas study tours. The most important include:

> In December 1977, an enterprise management study tour, led by Yuan Baohua, chairman of the State Economic Commission, and Minister of Foreign Trade Li Qiang, visited the UK and France.
>
> In February-March 1978, a Party Central Committee delegation led by Li Yimang, executive vice minister of the International Department of the CPC Central Committee (head of the delegation), Yu Guangyuan, vice president of the Chinese Academy of Social Sciences (deputy head of the delegation), and Qiao Shi, vice minister of the International Department of the CPC Central Committee (deputy head of the delegation), visited Yugoslavia.
>
> In March–April 1978, an economic delegation, led by Lin Hujia, Party secretary of Shanghai, visited Japan to study Japan's post-war development experience; and a State Planning Commission and Foreign Trade Ministry delegation, led by Duan Yun, vice chairman of the State Planning Commission, visited Hong Kong and Macao.
>
> In May-June 1978, a State Economic Commission delegation, led by Vice Premier Gu Mu, visited the five Western European countries of France, Switzerland, Belgium, Denmark, and West Germany.
>
> In October–December 1978, an industrial enterprise management study tour by the State Economic Commission visited Japan.

Upon their return, all of the delegations provided reports on their visits and briefed the Politburo members.

The overseas study tours and the visits by national leaders peaked in 1978, when there were 20 visits to 51 countries made by 12 senior leaders (including vice premiers and vice chairmen of the Standing Committee of the National People's Congress). Hua Guofeng made two trips to four countries, and Deng Xiaoping made four trips to eight countries.

What these senior leaders saw during their visits shocked them. After living in an isolated environment for so long, they were finally witnessing with their own eyes the huge development gap between China and the outside world. The delegation to the five West European countries led by Gu Mu reported:

> In West Germany, an open pit with a capacity of 50 million tons of brown coal per year only employs 2,000 workers, whereas we require 160,000 workers to produce the same quantity of brown coal, an eightfold difference.

---

[23] According to Ministry of Education statistics, in 1978, 860 students were sent abroad to study. This number reached 84,000 in 2001, and by 2013, the number of Chinese students studying overseas exceeded 400,000.

> In Bern, Switzerland, a hydroelectric plant with an installed capacity of 25,000 kilowatts employs only 12 people, whereas a hydropower plant in Jiangxi province with an installed capacity of 26,000 kilowatts employs 298 people
>
> A Salmer steel plant in Marseillė, France, employing 7,000 workers, produces 3.5 million metric tons annually. In contrast, 67,000 workers are required for the Wuhan Iron and Steel Plant to achieve an annual steel output of 2.3 million metric tons.
>
> At Charles de Gaulle Airport in Paris, 60 planes take off and land per hour, that is, one plane per minute. However, at Beijing's International Capitol Airport two planes per hour, or one plane every 30 minutes, either takes off or lands. Still, the airport is often in a state of chaos.

Years later, Wang Quanguo, a former vice governor of Guangdong province, was still excited about his visit abroad. He recalled, "The study tour, lasting over a month, opened our eyes. As our minds suddenly became clearer, what we saw truly shocked us. But it was also inspiring. When our doors were closed to the outside world, we believed that China was a strong power. We loved to provide aid to Third World countries, and we thought that capitalism was rotten to the core and on the verge of collapse. But after stepping foot abroad, we realized that our previous ideas had been completely wrong: China belonged to the lagging two-thirds of the countries of the world."[24]

Deng Liqun, a Party theoretician who had worked on policy research and also had served as a political aide to several Party leaders, and who at the time was a vice president of CASS, was a member of the economic delegation to Japan. Upon returning to Beijing, he wrote a lengthy report entitled "Takeaways from the Study Tour to Japan." Here are some excerpts:

> A department store in Tokyo carries more than 500,000 pieces of merchandise of all types and sizes. Our Wang Fujing Department Store [in Beijing] only offers about 22,000 pieces of merchandise.... Marxism believes that without abundant products, the idea of 'to each according to his needs' cannot be realized. It seems that such a goal is not beyond reach in Japan. Capitalist Japan is much more abundant in products than we are.... Our goal is to eliminate the Three Major Differences [i.e., workers vs. peasants, urban vs. rural, and mental vs. manual labor]. This can only be achieved when the socialist productive forces are maximized. A few executive directives will by no means be able to accomplish this goal. Although capitalist, some more economically advanced countries are gradually reducing the Three Major Differences, particularly the worker-peasant and the urban-rural differences.... Personal ethics will gradually improve with advances in the productive forces and the abundance of products. In a capitalist society, bicycles do not need to be locked up, auction items are displayed in the open, and people are very polite. All these phenomena show that ethical standards have risen in Japan.... A more advanced social system and the educational effects of an advanced ideology are all based on development of the productive forces. Therefore, the improved public ethics in Japan has not been achieved merely by preaching but rather by developing the productive forces and raising the people's living standards.

The impact of the overseas study tours and the cross-national comparisons went beyond economic development and management. They also touched upon some ideological concepts and social norms that had been considered taboo in the past.

---

[24] Cao Pu, "The Impact of the 1978 Overseas Study Tours by Senior Leaders," *Study Times* (December 8, 2008).

For instance, Deng Liqun, in observing the advanced economic development, the people's psychological state, the social order, and personal ethics in Japan, noted the decline in the Three Major Differences between the urban and rural areas, industry and agriculture, and manual and mental labor. Based on these observations, Deng Liqun felt that communism and the ideal of "to each according to his needs" was not beyond reach. Therefore, he was confident that "our cause is promising."

Deng Liqun admits in the above-mentioned report that Japan was more advanced than China in many ways, and he suggests bringing such advances to China and using them as tools for socialist construction. For that purpose, he wrote a section in his report on "the law of value and the nature of the plan," in which he questions some of Stalin's sayings, such as "the means of production is not a commodity under socialism, and "the law of value and planned, proportionate development are mutually exclusive"—ideas that were considered to be a fundamental part of the principles of Marxism. Deng Liqun voices his support for learning from Japanese practices: "the plans of the state, the ministries, and the enterprises (i.e., indicative economic planning) should be premised on the law of value, or they should be fully adapted to the requirements of the law of value." But Deng's views changed by the second half of 1982, when he became a supporter of establishing a commodity economy in China.[25]

Among the stories about the senior leaders' overseas visits, that of Wang Zhen's visit to the UK was quite widespread. Wang had visited the UK on November 6–17, 1978, and Yu Ri, commercial attaché at the Chinese embassy in London, helped with his itinerary. In his memoirs "Ten Years in the UK: Re-understanding Capitalism," Yu Ri recalls that Vice Premier Wang Zhen had surprised everyone when he was asked about his impressions of the visit and he replied: "I think Britain has done a good job: it has plenty of material goods; the Three Major Differences are gone; there is social equity; and social welfare is valued. If the Communist Party were in power, Britain would be an ideal Communist society."[26]

The overseas trips were a revelation for the senior leaders, who before then had had little chance to know anything about the real West, and the tours significantly impacted their mindset. They found that China's productive forces and the people's living standards were lagging considerably behind those in the neighboring market economies. For years, China had relied on the policy of class struggle and the theory of continuing the revolution under the dictatorship of the proletariat to enhance government and promote economic development, while Japan, Singapore, and Hong Kong had seized the opportunity provided by the post-World War II economic and technological boom to achieve an economic takeoff. It became obvious that China needed to abandon its old ways and seek a new path forward.

---

[25] Deng Liqun, "The Law of the Commodity Economy and the Plan," speech at the Enterprise Management Seminar organized by the State Economic Commission, March 12, 1970, in *Selected Works of Deng Liqun* (Beijing: Contemporary China Publishing House, 1998), vol. 1, pp. 189–222.

[26] Yu Ri, "Ten-Years in the UK: A Re-Understanding of Capitalism," *Chen Duxiu Studies*, nos. 3, 4 (2002), http://www.chenduxiu.net/ReadNews.asp?NewsID=335

When meeting Kim Il-Sung in North Korea on September 12, 1978, Deng Xiaoping said: "Recently, our comrades have visited some foreign countries. The more they saw, the more they came to realize how backward we are. What is modernization? The 1960s differed from the 1950s, and the differences are even greater now in the 1970s."[27] On his return to Beijing, Deng met with local leaders of the Northeast provinces and Tianjin municipality. At these meetings, he reiterated that China must seriously study the experiences of the advanced world and reform its backward system. He pointed out, "Our system, including our institutions, have been copied from the Soviet Union.... Our system has not adapted to modernization, and our superstructure cannot meet the new requirements.... Our development should be based on the scientific and technological advances of the world. We should have such an ambition. Once introduced, we should manage the imported equipment and technologies through international management, operations, and allotment practices. In other words, we should follow the laws of economics. In brief, we need a systemic revolution, not incremental improvements or mere patch-ups."[28]

In October, during a visit to Japan Deng Xiaoping took a ride on the Shinkansen high-speed train and visited Nippon Steel Corporation, Nissan Motor Corporation, and Panasonic Corporation. Then, on November 5–14, he visited Thailand, Malaysia, and Singapore. During these trips, he was deeply impressed by Japan's rapid post–World War II economic growth and the role of external capital in contributing to Singapore's economic development.

In June 1978, the Politburo held three meetings to hear briefings by the delegations that had visited Japan, Hong Kong, Macao, and the five West European countries, respectively. Many Party and government officials came to realize that China had fallen far behind many nations, and following the old path would no longer be sufficient to realize the Outline of the Ten-Year Plan for National Economic and Social Development and the Twenty-Three Year Vision, typically referring to the longer-term strategic goals set by the Chinese government. Therefore, it was felt that China should take the experience of the foreign countries as an example and study their respective development paths.

The Party leadership unanimously confirmed the significance of the overseas study tours and of learning about the benefits of the foreign experiences. Hua Guofeng had originally believed that as long as the Gang of Four was no longer wielding its influence, China's current development model had the potential to create a stable and prosperous nation, leading to "great order across the land." But after being briefed on the findings from the study tours, Hua commented: "We are self-conceited and like a toad at the bottom of a well who believes that what he sees above is the whole sky. China is not only the homeland of Mao Zedong Thought but also the homeland of the absurd King of Yelang. … The study tours are enlightening.... Our existing superstructure is indeed unsuitable and it must be reformed."[29]

[27] *Chronicle of Deng Xiaoping's Life (1975–1997)*, vol. 1, pp. 372–373.

[28] Ibid., pp. 376, 386.

[29] Han Gang: "Several Historical Facts About Hua Guofeng (Continued)," *Yanhuang chunqiu*, no. 3 (2011).

The second step in finding a new path was to hold a unique State Council retreat in July 1978 to brainstorm about accelerating the Four Modernizations.

After the June 30 debriefing meeting, Hua Guofeng requested that Vice Premier Gu Mu "organize the overseas study tour participants to prepare proposals for a State Council retreat. The proposals should be conceptual and specific.... The retreat should be held as early as July. Discussions and decisions can proceed in parallel. Once we know what to do, we should immediately take action."[30]

The State Council brainstorming retreat lasted two months and four days, from July 6 to September 9. The sessions were presided over by Vice Premier Li Xiannian, and the participants included Gu Mu, several other vice premiers, and the heads of all 44 State Council departments.

On the first day of the retreat, Li Xiannian set out the objectives of the retreat in his opening remarks. The objectives included summarizing the positive and negative experiences of the past and making improvements to the Ten-Year Program to accelerate the Four Modernizations.

During the retreat, two speeches transcended simple discussions on specific matters. These speeches provided critiques of the old system and the political line both inside and outside the Party. They also put forward a vision for a future system of economic development. These speeches had a far-reaching influence on the formulation of a reform strategy.

The first speech was a report entitled "Following the Laws of Economics to Accelerate Realization of the Four Modernizations," drafted by Hu Qiaomu, Yu Guangyuan, and Ma Hong and presented at the retreat by Hu Qiaomu, who was then president of CASS and head of the State Council Research Office. A Party theoretician and politician, Hu Qiaomu had also been an aide to Mao Zedong. Yu Guangyuan was a deputy head of the State Council Research Office, and Ma Hong was director of the CASS Institute of Industrial Economics (he would later become president of CASS).[31]

The speech mainly consisted of the following:

First, it criticized the widespread view that denied the existence of laws of economics, and it equated the will of society, the government, and senior officials to these natural laws, maintaining that the laws could be arbitrarily changed based on political whim. The speech emphasized that to expedite the Four Modernizations, it was crucial to evaluate both the positive and negative experiences from the past

---

[30] Ibid.

[31] Yu Guangyuan, *I Witnessed the Great Turning Point in History in 1978* (Beijing: Central Compilation and Translation Press, 2008), p. 55. As a leading proponent of Mao Zedong Thought, Hu Qiaomu introduced new ideas into this speech. Yu Guangyuan recalled that the reason he had drafted the part of the speech on the need to comply with the basic economic laws of socialism and the necessity of realizing that the purpose of production was not production per se but to meet the needs of the society and the statement on the objectivity of the fundamental laws had come from another book he had written. Yu Guangyuan also mentioned that the part of the speech on the law of value in commodity production had been drafted by Ma Hong, with editorial changes by Hu Qiaomu. The excerpts in this chapter are from the part of the speech that appeared in the *People's Daily* on October 6, 1978, which was a revised version published under Hu Qiaomu's byline.

thirty years since the founding of the People's Republic. It also urged adherence to the objective laws of economics.

Second, the speech criticized the notion that the law of value could not regulate production within a socialist system. Instead, it highlighted the importance of upholding the law of value, emphasizing that commodities must be traded at their exchange value. Although up until that point the law of value had been excluded from the socialist economy, the speech raised its importance to that of the law of planned and proportional development, pointing out that the latter could not be strictly implemented without acknowledging the former.

Third, the speech advocated learning from the capitalist countries. It called for a "combination of the strengths of a socialist system with the advanced science, technology, and management model of the capitalist countries. Only by integrating all positive foreign experiences with China's unique conditions and successes will the country swiftly enhance its ability to adhere to objective laws."

Fourth, the speech envisaged several reforms, including: (a) adopting contracting not only between enterprises but also between the central government and the local governments, between various local governments, and between different levels within the local governments; (b) expanding enterprise autonomy based on the clearly identified economic responsibilities of the state and the enterprise; (c) abandoning the industrial organization model based on "large and all-encompassing" or "small and all-encompassing" enterprises, and instead establishing specialized companies or companies in related industries at the national, local, or sectoral levels; (d) rehabilitating the banks and significantly enhancing their role in effectively monitoring enterprise activities through bank credits and appropriations; and (e) developing economic legislation and jurisdictions to codify the respective interests of the state, the enterprises, and the employees, as well as relations among these interests, so that the judicial agencies are able to handle relevant cases according to the law.

The second speech consisted of the concluding remarks by Li Xiannian on September 9, 1978.[32] The central theme of his speech was how to accelerate economic development and speed up realization of the Four Modernizations. He stressed the importance of further opening to the outside world, highlighting the need to accelerate imports of cutting-edge equipment and to quickly adopt state-of-art technologies. For this purpose, the Party Central Committee made the major strategic decision to increase funding for technology imports to USD 80 billion within the next ten years.

[32] Li Xiannian's concluding remarks at the retreat include the following six parts: (a) seeking favorable opportunities to accelerate the Four Modernizations; (b) under the uniform plan, bringing the role of the central government, the local government, and the enterprise into full play; (c) importing technology and expanding exports; (d) issues related to agriculture; (e) issues related to industry; and (f) realigning the leadership and improving the leadership style. "The first part was the key link, and the remainder consisted of the specific components. The central theme was high-speed economic development. Consolidating comments by various participants at the retreat, the remarks were cleared by the Politburo Standing Committee. The speech marked a prelude to the reform and opening because it systematically proposed new views and measures" (Zhu Yu, "Li Xiannian and the 1978 State Council Retreat Meetings," *Party History Research*, no. 1 [2005]). Note that the *Selected Works of Li Xiannian* (Beijing: People's Publishing House, 1989) only contain Parts (b) and (c) of the speech.

More importantly, Li commented on the system and policy necessary for accelerated economic development. Like Hu Qiaomu's speech, Li Xiannian's speech stressed that the government's economic work should strictly follow the objective laws of economics rather than obeying the diktats of those from above. He called for courage to reform all relations of production that were unsuitable for development of the productive forces and the superstructure and that could not meet the demands of the economic base. He advocated breaking up the former framework that strictly followed administrative hierarchies, divisions, and means but ignored economic accounting, results, efficiency, and responsibility. He urged changing those management practices characterized by craft production, a peasant economy, and a feudal bureaucratic style and instead adopting the capability to manage large-scale modern industrial production.

Li Xiannian criticized the earlier economic management reforms because they usually started with the transfer of administrative power and then got stuck in a vicious cycle of decentralization and centralization. He therefore called for reforms in the planning, fiscal, material supply, enterprise management, and domestic and external trade sectors to establish modern economic organizations and to manage a modern economy with modern means and tools.

Li's concluding remarks also touched upon the characteristics of a modern economic system. His description of China's [future] economic system as a market economy that "combines a planned economy with a market economy" was warmly received by the retreat participants.[33] This was the first time that a Chinese Party or government document had used the term "market economy" to describe the nature of the country's economic system. Although Li Xiannian did not elaborate on the term in his speech, traditionally Marxism had always considered a "market economy" as a synonym for capitalism. Therefore, the appearance of this term in the CCP's description of the reform objectives attracted wide attention and led to heated discussions among economists. Although neither the authorities nor academia later described the reform objective as a "combination of the planned economy and the market economy,"[34] the fact that the term "market economy" appeared in official

[33] Zhu Jiamu, who had been an aide to Chen Yun, recalled that "in his concluding remarks at the September 1978 State Council retreat, Li Xiannian mentioned "a combination of a planned economy and a market economy." While this phrase was excluded from the documents on the retreat that were distributed, the participants at the retreat took note of these remarks and included them in their oral briefings.... I think the phrase was coined by Comrade Chen Yun, and Comrade Li Xiannian made it public" (Zhu Jiamu, "Chen Yun's Thoughts on Relations between Plan and Market," *Party Literature Bimonthly*, no. 3 [2000]). As recorded at a meeting of branch presidents of the People's Bank of China on February 22, 1979, Li Xiannian mentioned that he had spoken with Chen Yun. The latter agreed to use the phrase "the combination of the planned economy and the market economy, with the planned economy as the mainstay." Chen Yun had said, "the market economy is a complement. It is a major rather than a minor complement" (*Chronicle of Chen Yun's Life* [Beijing: Central Party Literature Press, 2000], vol. 2, p. 236).

[34] There were two views about this proposition. Some people felt that combining the two economies would be logically impossible, while others, from a Marxist perspective, could not accept the idea of including a "market economy" as the reform objective. Because a member of this latter group held a leading position in Party ideological work, in published official documents, the expression

remarks by a national leader represented a kind of prologue to the market-oriented economic reforms that were to take place in 1990s.

1.3 The Third Plenary Session of the 11th Party Central Committee: A Critical Turning Point in History

The Third Plenary Session of the 11th Party Central Committee, which opened on December 28, 1978, was a significant milestone in the history of the People's Republic of China. Advocating finding a new path, it marked a victory for the forces within the CCP that supported a departure from the ultra-leftist political line.

For an extended period in the past, propaganda had led many to believe that people in other countries were living in dire conditions and that only those living under "continuing revolution under the dictatorship of the proletariat" were enjoying a "beautiful life." After the Gang of Four was overthrown and China opened to the outside world, people could finally compare the state of development in China with that in other countries, and they came to the realization that what Chinese propaganda had been describing was entirely false. As the country was finally emerging from isolation, many felt like the character in a fable who went to a mountain for a week only to discover that a millennium had passed in the outside world. These revelations shocked both the cadres and the masses into reflecting on the old political line and economic system, prompting them to begin to learn from the experiences of other countries. Although those who continued to follow the "two whatevers" condemned such activities for "being in violation of Chairman Mao's instructions" and for "damaging Chairman Mao's image," the tide of history was unstoppable. The shared desire of most Chinese was to embark upon change. At the Central Committee Work Conference held November 10–December 15, 1978, a heated debate between the two factions holding differing political ideas ended with the defeat of the "two whatevers" group.

The original agenda for the 36-day Work Conference's was (a) to further take agriculture as the foundation to increase agricultural production, (b) to make arrangements for the national economic plan for the next two years (1979–80), and (c) to discuss Li Xiannian's concluding remarks at the State Council brainstorming retreat.

Shortly after the opening of the Work Conference, the discussions proceeded beyond these three topics, and they concluded with disavowing the political line of

"the combination of a planned economy and a market economy" is often replaced by the phrase "the combination of a planned economy with market adjustments." For instance, in his March 1979 manuscript outlining the article "On Plan and Market," Chen Yun uses the term "market economy." But when the article was included in the *Selected Important Works Since the Third Plenary Session of the 11th Party Central Committee* (compiled by the Party Literature Research Center and published in 1982), the term was changed to "market adjustments." In 1995, based on a request from Chen Yun, the term "market economy" was reinserted in the second edition of the *Selected Works of Chen Yun* (see Zhu Jiamu, "Chen Yun's Thoughts on Relations between Plan and Market," *Party Literature Bimonthly*, no. 3 [2000].)

"the theory of continuing the revolution under the dictatorship of the proletariat." In addition, they confirmed the need for a policy pivot from "taking class struggle as the key link" to "focusing on the central task of economic construction." At the Work Conference, CCP Chairman Hua Guofeng, who formerly had been a supporter of the "two whatevers," made a self-criticism. This paved the way for the Third Plenary Session of the 11th Party Central Committee to usher in a momentous historical change.

At the concluding session of the Work Conference, Deng Xiaoping delivered a speech entitled "Emancipate the Mind, Seek Truth From Facts, and Unite As One In Looking to the Future."[35]

In his speech, Deng Xiaoping emphasized the importance of liberating thought, seeking truth from facts, and uniting to look forward, with the primary focus on liberating thought. He noted that the issue of liberating thought had not been fully resolved among Party cadres, especially among leading cadres. Many remained in a state of rigidity or semi-rigidity, leading to the emergence of numerous problematic phenomena due to their "rigid thinking and widespread superstition."[36]

In such a situation, "if we do not break the rigidity of thought and significantly liberate the ideas of the cadres and the masses, Four Modernizations will have no hope." The vitality of the Party and the state would cease, leading to the demise of both.

The debate over the standards of truth, which essentially revolved around whether to liberate thought, was indeed a question of ideological direction and political significance, affecting the future and the fate of the Party and the country. "Only with liberated thought can we correctly use Marxism-Leninism and Mao Zedong Thought as guides to address past issues and new problems, and to reform production relations and the superstructure that are mismatched by rapidly developing the productive forces, and determining the specific paths, policies, methods, and measures to achieve the Four Modernizations according to our national conditions."

Addressing the past situation when "democracy was disregarded in favor of centralization" and when many were reluctant to speak up, Deng stressed that "democracy is a crucial condition for liberating thought." In political life within the Party and among the people, democratic methods must be used rather than repressed or suppressed. The rights guaranteed by the Constitution and the Party Charter must be resolutely upheld, and any infringement must be prevented. Deng criticized the

[35] Deng Xiaoping, "Emancipate the Mind, Seek Truth From Facts, and Unite As One In Looking to the Future," December 13, 1978, in *Selected Works of Deng Xiaoping*, vol. 2, pp. 140–153. On the Third Plenary Session of the Eleventh Party Central Committee, see Yu Guangyuan, *I Witnessed the Great Historical Turning Point in 1978*.

[36] The curious phenomena to which Deng Xiaoping was referring included: "(a) increased restrictions.... For instance, 'strengthening the role of Party leadership' became having the Party do everything and intervening everywhere.... 'Centralizing Party leadership' became mingling the role of the Party with that of the government, or having the Party replace the government.... 'Upholding Party leadership' became allowing only one voice for everything; (b) more people became opportunistic.... [For instance,] ignoring Party ethics and principles, responding to the person speaking rather than what was being said; and (c) book worship [dogmatism].... [People] dared not say or do anything not written in books or documents or mentioned by the leaders."

negative practice of investigating "political backgrounds" or "political rumors" in response to any public criticism, stressing that such malicious practices must be resolutely stopped.

Deng called for research into the new situations and solutions for the new problems, focusing particularly on management methods, systems, and economic policies. He advocated bold decentralization of the overly concentrated management powers to unleash the initiative of the state, localities, enterprises, and workers. He proposed an "overall policy" that would allow some regions, enterprises, and workers to improve their incomes and living standards sooner than others due to their hard work and achievements, which would "impact and drive the entire national economy" and accelerate the overall prosperity of the people.

This speech by Deng Xiaoping was the de facto keynote report of the Third Plenary Session of the 11th Party Central Committee, and it marked a historic turning point in establishing the CCP's guiding principles for running the country. The conference called for the Party and the people to turn their focus to socialist modernization and to abandon the slogans of "taking class struggle as the key link,"[37] "continuing the revolution under the dictatorship of the proletariat," and asserting "full dictatorship over the bourgeoisie within and outside the Party."[38] Although the ultra-leftist theories and political line continued for a long time, this decision by the Party in power implied an official ending of the era that took "class struggle as the key link," just as was foreseen by Nobel Economics prize winner Ronald Coase.[39]

The communiqué of the Third Plenary Session did not dwell on any specific reform measures. Furthermore, it did not mention the "market orientation," which would later become the main thrust of the reform. However, the communiqué highly praised the debate on "Practice is the Sole Criterion for Testing the Truth." It called

---

[37] At the Third Plenary Session of the eighth Party Central Committee, held in October 1958, Mao Zedong had stressed that "the contradictions between the proletariat and the bourgeoise, and between the socialist path and the capitalist path, remain the main contradictions in our society." At the Tenth Plenary Session of the eighth Party Central Committee in 1962, he emphasized the need to remind the people of "class struggle year after year and month after month." At the Central Work Conference in February 1963, Mao suggested several solutions to effectively grasp and address class struggle. These "supreme instructions," addressing the political and ideological challenges facing the Chinese Communist Party, became part of the CCP's general political line to govern the country.

[38] During the Cultural Revolution, class struggle was elevated to the status of a theory and a political line, or, in other words, to the status of "continuing the revolution" and "full dictatorship over the bourgeoisie." The Constitution of the Communist Party of China, passed at the ninth Party Congress, adopted this political line. In his article "Full Dictatorship Over the Bourgeoisie" (*Red Flag*, no. 4 [1975]), Zhang Chunqiao, a Standing Committee member of the Party Politburo and of the Central Military Commission cum vice premier, advocated that the proletariat should exert full dictatorship over the bourgeoisie and carry on the continuous revolution under the dictatorship of the proletariat through to the end, until all class differences, all relations of production born from these differences, and all social relations adapted to these relations of production are eliminated and until all the exploiting classes, including the bourgeoisie, can no longer exist or reemerge. Zhang claimed this was the only way for the proletariat to liberate mankind.

[39] R. H. Coase and Ning Wang, et al., *Transforming China: The Road to a Market Economy in China* (Beijing: CITIC Publishing House, 2013), p. 55.

on all Party members to "emancipate their minds, seriously study the new situations, new things, and new issues; and uphold the principle of 'seeking truth from facts,' 'starting everything from reality,' and 'combining theory with practice.'... [Only by so doing can the Party] successfully change the focus point, correctly develop the specific path, principles, and the ways and means for the 'Four Modernizations' and reform the relations of production and the superstructure that are not suited for rapid development of the productive forces." Thus, people's minds were freed from the old ideological shackles, opening the door for a serious examination of past mistakes and exploration into the right way to achieve China's revitalization.

At the onset of the reform when there was a critical sense of urgency, the national leadership adopted an approach characterized by "crossing the river by feeling for the stones,"[40] or "regardless of whether it is a white cat or a black cat, it is a good cat if it catches mice."[41] In parallel with exploring the right way to reform theory and policy, this approach, on the one hand, encouraged local governments to make systemic and policy adjustments to provide more room for enterprises and individuals to play an active role in the economy. But, on the other hand, it also adapted existing institutions and policies to allow for some private-sector innovation and entrepreneurship.

The essential institutional and policy adaptations included the following:

The first institutional policy adaptation: Although collective ownership of land was kept intact, farmers could work land contracted (leased) from the collectives under the household contract management system.

During the 1955 agricultural collectivization movement, a campaign was launched to denounce the so-called "right-wing–leaning, conservative thinking" under which most Chinese farmers were forced to join collectively owned agricultural production cooperatives. As a result, land allocated to individual farmers during land reform

[40] At the Central Work Conference held on December 16, 1980, Chen Yun's important speech, "On the Current Situation and the Tasks for Economic Work," called for further readjustments to the national economy. He described the appropriate approach for the reform and opening from a historical perspective, pointing out: "We should reform, but our steps should be cautious. This is because the reform faces complex problems and cannot be rushed. Of course, theoretical research, statistics, and economic forecasting are important. However, most essential is to start from pilots to gain timely insights, i.e., 'crossing the river by feeling for the stones', with small initial steps to move forward slowly." *Selected Works of Chen Yun* (Beijing: People's Publishing House, 1995), vol. 3, p. 279.

[41] Deng Xiaoping first mentioned the "white cat and black cat" (although at the time it was a yellow cat rather than a white cat) in two July 1962 talks: the first talk, a July 2 meeting of the Secretariat of the Party Central Committee, set the stage for a more pragmatic approach to agricultural development. At the other talk, which took place on July 7 when receiving the participants at the Seventh Plenary Session of the third Central Committee of the Communist Youth League, Deng said, "The relations of production are determined by the level of the productive forces. If the relations of production do not match the level of the productive forces, then the relations of production will restrict development of the productive forces. ... What is the best form of production relations? Perhaps the answer to this question should be a form that can relatively easily and quickly restore agricultural production or a form that will be preferred by the masses; if the form is not legal, make it legitimate.... Be it a yellow cat or a black cat, a cat that can catch mice is a good cat" ("Restore Agricultural Production," *Selected Works of Deng Xiaoping* [Beijing: People's Publishing House, 1994], vol. 1, p. 323). This principle was used by Deng as a basis for China's economic reforms.

became part of the "indivisible property of the collective." Then, in July 1958, Mao Zedong called for the merger of individual higher-stage cooperatives into the people's communes, which were renowned for their "large size and public ownership." Land, labor, and other means of production were all to be uniformly allocated by the commune, which combined both government and society. In this way, except for the state not being responsible for wage distribution, the "collective economy" did not differ significantly from state-owned enterprises.

Even after the agricultural collectivization and the people's commune movements, farmers still wanted to rebuild their family farms. Whenever there was a chance, e.g., a poor harvest year, farmers would seek to lease farmland for independent farming under the name of "production responsibility." There were cases of "household output contracting," small "household plots" for farmers, and "free markets" where farmers could sell household products. In some places, household-owned small businesses were also allowed to manage their profits and losses. However, Mao Zedong criticized these practices (that is, freedom to decide what to plant, freedom to manage production, freedom to trade the surplus produce, and contracting production to households, or the "*sanzi yibao*") for backpedaling to restore capitalism. Any requests to restore household contracting were harshly denounced and forcibly stopped.

After the end of the Cultural Revolution, farmers in various regions again sought to restore household contracting. This "household contract responsibility system" had two primary forms: household output contracting and production contracting. The former was similar to piecework wages: the collective set output quotas per land lot for each household; after the harvest, the collective distributed the output within the quota. Under the latter, the collective (usually represented by the village committee), as the landowner, allocated land lots to households based on the number of family members or able laborers. The farmers paid taxes to the state, fulfilled unified government procurement quotas or contract orders, and contributed to the provident fund and welfare fund of their production team. Whatever remained of the output belonged to the farmers for their own disposal. This practice ended the uniform production and distribution by the production team. As long as what was due to the state and the collective was remitted, the remainder was left for the farmers. Although collective land ownership was retained, household production contracting changed the system from collective farming to family farming on contracted land. This represented a fundamental transformation.

In addition to Anhui province, the household contract responsibility system gained momentum in Sichuan, Guizhou, Gansu, Henan, and Inner Mongolia. It was a vital force to improve agricultural development in these areas. However, the Party leadership at the time did not accept this institutional change and insisted on retaining the "two whatevers" principle. It was not until the 1979 Fourth Plenary Session of the 11th Party Central Committee that household output contracting was introduced, thereby allowing "dividing up the farmland for family farming."[42]

[42] Decision on Issues Concerning the Reform of Agricultural Production Relations, adopted by the Fourth Plenary Session of the 11th Party Central Committee on September 28, 1979.

In September 1980, a provincial First Party Secretaries Forum was held, during which the political line of the "two whatevers" was terminated, and Deng Xiaoping's de facto leadership was restored. The forum's summary proceedings, entitled "On a Few Questions Related to Further Strengthening and Improving the Agricultural Production Responsibility System," proposed that "in the remote mountainous areas and poor and backward regions, production teams may adopt the household output contract responsibility system if for a long time they had been forced to rely on state-resold grains for their supply of food and on loans for agricultural production and livelihood relief, and if they had lost all confidence in the collective. After the Party Central Committee forwarded this document to Party and government organizations, the various forms of contract responsibility expanded rapidly throughout the country, among which household output and production contracting were the most popular.

In January 1982, the CCP Central Committee and the State Council issued the first "Number One Document" regarding rural economic policy, namely the National Agricultural Work Summary. This document explicitly states: "Contracting work, contracting output, and contracting responsibilities primarily reflect different methods of distributing labor results. Contracting responsibilities mainly involve 'contracting output with retention,' which eliminates the allocation of work points, simplifies the process, and is welcomed by the masses." This provided formal policy support for the responsibility contracting system, mainly in the form of contracting responsibilities, thus transforming this bottom-up spontaneous system into a top-down recognized system, and it won top-down support throughout Party and government organizations.

By early 1983, the share of production teams adopting the household responsibility system (mainly production contracting) reached 98 percent of the national total. This meant that under the condition of maintaining public ownership of land, Chinese agriculture allowed farmers to establish family farms through contracting.

Expansion of the household contracting systems significantly facilitated the recovery and development of agriculture, bringing about considerable changes to the agricultural sector and the rural areas. Compared with 1978, total agricultural output in 1985 had increased nearly three times.[43] In 1984, total grain output reached 407.31 million tons, a rise of 33.6 percent from 1978.[44] In addition, the industrial structure in the rural areas became more logical, and forestry, animal husbandry, side-line occupations, and fishery production all increased. As a result, farmers saw their incomes rise by a large margin: in 1984, net per capita income of rural households reached RMB 355, an increase of 85.5 percent from 1978.[45]

The second institutional policy adaptation: while public and enterprise finance functions remained mixed, the authorities adopted a fiscal system called "eating

---

[43] National Bureau of Statistics of China, *China Statistical Yearbook 1989* (Beijing: China Statistics Press, 1989), p. 228..

[44] Zhu Rong, et al., eds., *Contemporary China's Agriculture* (Beijing: Contemporary China Publishing House, 1992), p. 375.

[45] National Bureau of Statistics, *China Statistical Yearbook 1981* (Beijing: China Statistics Press, 1981), and National Bureau of Statistics, *China Statistical Yearbook 1985* (Beijing: China Statistics Press, 1985).

from separate kitchens," giving local governments incentives to develop the local economy.

Under the planned economy, the entire country was a massive company, and there was no distinction between public and enterprise finance. Fiscal power was centralized in the central government, and public finance organizations were structured like a nationwide unitary enterprise. Under this economic system, the localities did not have their own economic interests nor did local governments have any enthusiasm to develop the local economy.

Following the end of the Cultural Revolution and beginning from 1980, the central government decentralized part of its resource allocation authority and granted decision-making power for revenue and expenditures to local governments to mitigate the problems caused by the extensive budget deficits in 1979 and to encourage the local governments to increase revenue and to reduce expenditures. The fiscal and budget system shifted from a "uniform revenue and expenditure regime" of the central government to contracting with lower-level governments, i.e., the so-called "eating from separate kitchens" approach. While the three municipalities directly under the central government, Beijing, Shanghai, and Tianjin, generally remained under the centralized system, the new practice was extended to the rest of the provinces and autonomous regions. Revenue was allocated between the central and local governments based on a prior set ratio or amount. As a result, provincial, prefectural, and county governments each became economic entities with independent economic interests, and China's economy changed from a unitary enterprise for to a multidivision form.[46] It is more appropriate to describe this economic form as similar to a holding enterprise.[47] After local governments gained power within a specific limit to manage the economy, local output increased, leading to higher local-government revenue and higher incomes for officials. This motivated local officials to protect and support local entrepreneurs in the market, and it can be considered an unexpected outcome of the "eating from separate kitchens" reform.

The third institutional policy adaptation: in parallel with the "planned track," whereby the state plan allocated materials, and prices were set administratively, a second track, or a "market track," was created to allow for the trading of materials at negotiated prices.

Lenin believed that "small-scale production is still widespread in the world, and small-scale production *engenders* capitalism and the bourgeoisie continuously, daily, hourly, spontaneously, and on a mass scale." He also said that petty commodity production is a "very sound, deep-rooted basis for capitalism, a basis upon which capitalism persists or arises anew in a bitter struggle against communism.[48] According to these teachings, China strictly restricted and even banned

---

[46] Qian Yingyi and Xu Chenggang, "Why China's Economic Reforms Differ: The M-Form Hierarchy and Entry/Expansion of the Non-State Sector," *The Economics of Transition* 1, no. 2 (June 1993), 135-170.

[47] This is probably the origin of the local government corporatization in recent years.

[48] Vladimir Lenin, "Left-Wing Communism: An Infantile Disorder," 1920, *Selected Works of Lenin* (Chinese translation. Beijing: People's Publishing House, 1972), vol. 4, p. 181; Vladimir Lenin, "Economics and Politics in the Era of the Dictatorship of the Proletariat," in ibid., p. 86.

peasant sideline production and related commodity exchanges under its centralized planned economy. The planning authorities allocated production materials (the means of production) to state-owned entities through administrative command, and prices were merely a tool for economic accounting. There was no real market except for limited trading of "third category materials"[49] in rural markets that accounted for only a tiny share of the economy. At the beginning of the reform and opening, township and village enterprises, sole proprietor enterprises, and other non-state entities suddenly emerged and grew. However, the state plan did not cover the means of production for these firms, and they would not have been able to survive, to say nothing of grow further, without market transactions.

In 1979, the State Council issued Regulations on Expanding Operational Auto2nomy of State-Owned Industrial Enterprises, allowing SOEs to sell above-the-plan products at negotiated prices as long as the prices did not exceed 20 percent of the plan price. Meanwhile, as individuals were allowed to open and develop their businesses, they needed a"second [market] track" for the means of production and product pricing. The dual-track pricing system enabled non-state enterprises to purchase production materials and sell products through the market. This institutional arrangement created a business environment and market condition for the non-state economic sector to survive and grow. Initially, there were restrictions on outside-the-plan products' prices. However, by 1984, the total output of non-state industrial enterprises had reached 31 percent of the national total, and the outside-the-plan production and transactions by the SOEs were increasing. In this context, in January 1985, the National Price Bureau and the National Bureau of Materials Management jointly issued the Notice on Price Deregulation for the-Above-the-Plan Means-of-Production Sold by Industrial Enterprises, removing the restrictions on the pricing of outside-the-plan products. This was the official establishment of the dual-tract system for the supply and pricing of the means of production. Under this system, SOEs with the right to receive materials within the state plan before 1983 continued to receive supplies at the plan price up to the 1983 quotas (the 1983 base). However, they had to purchase the supplies for any production exceeding the base at the market price.

The fourth institutional policy adaptation: in the absence of a developed domestic market environment, creating a localized "microclimate" for opening up to connect with the international market was proposed.

[49] During the period of the planned economy, the state divided products into three categories for administrative purposes. Products critical to the national interest and the people's livelihood were in the first category. "Relatively significant products" belonged in the second category. Finally, the remainder was grouped in the third category, for example, scissors, hairpins, toothbrushes, cold creams, gloves, handkerchiefs, sock suspenders, straw ropes, dustpans, brooms, waxberries, loquats, dried radishes, kohlrabi, various small hardware items, small household goods, some chemical products, electrical goods, and some traditional Chinese medicinal materials were all considered Category 3 goods. These materials were numerous, widespread, small-scale, diverse in variety, and complex in specifications, but they were all necessary for people's production and daily life. Because it was impossible to fully incorporate these goods into the planned economy under centralized management, the state adopted various measures, such as opening market trading, organizing material exchanges, and signing production and sales contracts, to meet market demand.

As early as 1972, when the Cultural Revolution was still underway, China began to change its closed-door policy by developing trade relations with and learning from the Western countries and by importing foreign technologies and equipment. In December 1978, the Third Plenary Session of the 11th Party Central Committee officially adopted the opening policy to actively develop equal and mutually beneficial economic cooperative relations with other countries.

In the early stages of reform and opening, it was completely impossible to form a domestic market and integrate comprehensively with the international market within a short period of time. Therefore, China drew lessons from other countries' experiences in establishing export processing zones and free ports. Leveraging the advantages of the coastal regions, which are close to Hong Kong, Macau, and Taiwan, and have large overseas Chinese populations, China created regional "microclimates" as bases for opening up to the outside world. In May 1980, the Chinese government decided to put into effect "special policies" in Guangdong and Fujian provinces for opening up. In August 1980, it approved the pilot establishment of Special Economic Zones in Shenzhen, Zhuhai, Shantou, and Xiamen, featuring "market-oriented regional export-oriented economic forms."

These pragmatic institutional arrangements allowed entrepreneurs to engage in productive activities.

During the pre-reform era, China followed a Leninist economic model, and the economy was organized as an all-inclusive state corporation. Under this system, the only way for talented people to gain maximum returns (be it wealth, power, or reputation) was to join the Party and become a government official, or, in other words, to become a member of the bureaucracy. Within the SOEs, one first had to reach a certain position within the bureaucratic system. But even then, it was difficult for talented people to play a direct role in production. Not all gifted people could enter those government entities that gave the highest returns for their skills. Due to political reasons and the household registration system, many people could not bring their talents into full play to maximize returns. But under the pragmatic institutional arrangements in the post–Cultural Revolution period, private business startups were allowed, and their productive activities generated higher remunerations. Therefore, some capable members of society left their jobs and became entrepreneurs. First, farmers, in the rural areas, who formerly faced the greatest uncertainties and who received the lowest returns under the command economy , made their move. Next, among the urban population, people who were capable but could not join state entities because of their class backgrounds or for other reasons were motivated to engage in private business. Last, when the entrepreneurs' innovative activities began to show better returns, some government officials and state enterprise employees left the bureaucracy to join the private sector.

Thus, while the state sector, as the foundation of the command economy, continued to operate by the logic of the command economy, the emerging private sector was given more room for market-oriented activities. As a result, China's private enterprises proliferated. By 1990, the number of private enterprises reached 98,141, and the number of sole proprietorships exceeded 13.28 million.[50]

However, creating room for the growth of the non-state sector alongside the powerful state economy differed from a systematic transformation of the national economy. The economy as a whole was in a situation whereby the old command economic system had broken down, but the new market economy system had not yet been established, and economic growth was unstable.

1.4 Preliminary Exploration for a Target Model of Economic Reform

As early as the beginning of the 1980s, some Party/government officials and economists were becoming dissatisfied with the piecemeal reforms, and they hoped to find a systematic solution for China's economic problems.

As a first step, they took "catch-up classes" in modern economics and began to learn from the reform experiences of other socialist countries.

Given the similarities between China and the Soviet Union and the East European countries, and because Chinese economists already had some knowledge of these countries' reform processes, China's exploration into its overall reform objectives began with learning about these countries' reform theories and practices. First, at the end of 1979 and then into early 1980, and again in March–April 1981, CASS invited exiled Polish economist Włodzimierz Brus[51] and Czech economist Ota Šik[52] to give a series of lectures in China, which attracted large audiences of researchers

[50] Cheng Siwei, comp., *China Non-State Economy Yearbook 2007* (Beijing: Democracy and Construction Publishing House, 2007), pp. 748, 754.

[51] Władysław Brus (1921–2007), a proponent of the school of market socialism, had been director of the Research Department of the State Planning Commission and vice chairman of the State Economic Commission in Poland. In his 1961 book *The General Problems of the Functioning of the Socialist Economy*, Brus argues on in favor of a decentralized model for economic reform under state ownership (i.e., a planned economy with market mechanisms). In 1972 he became a professor at Oxford University and he later assumed British citizenship. In 1989, together with Kazimierz Laski, another Polish economist, Brus published *From Marx to the Market*. In this book, Brus revisits the propositions in his 1961 book and argues that market socialism contains institutional defects that result in inefficiencies. He thus came to the realization that the only solution for these economies is to adopt a full market economy.

[52] Ota Šik (1919–2004) was a famous Czech politician and Marxist economist. He argued in favor of an organic combination of plan and market and a "third way," i.e., "macro-level planning and a micro-level market." In 1968 he became a vice premier, and he led the reform in Czechoslovakia during the Prague Spring. After Warsaw Pact military forces occupied his country, Sik went into exile in Switzerland, where he continued advocating on behalf of socialist political and economic reforms, becoming a spiritual leader of dissidents and the Charter 77 group in Czechoslovakia. He died in 2004 in Switzerland.

and government officials.[53] Their introduction to the reform experiences in Poland, Czechoslovakia, and Hungary expanded the horizons of the Chinese researchers. Those who were supportive of market-oriented reforms highly praised the ideas of market socialism, as advocated by Brus and Šik, such as greater SOE autonomy, the market under state control, and enterprise operational decisions guided by a government-regulated market. Such propositions would have a profound and lasting influence on the trajectory of China's future reforms.

These lectures also had an unexpected side effect: the concepts and tools of modern economics, as used by Brus and Šik, opened the eyes of the Chinese economists. As a result, Chinese scholars wanted to more systematically learn about modern economics to improve their ability to solve China's problems.

In the early 1980s, an upsurge in learning "Western economics," that is, modern economics, emerged among Chinese economists. Within one year, from the summer of 1980 to the summer of 1981, the Institute of Economics of CASS held three large workshops on quantitative, foreign, and development economics.[54]

As a result of further research on reform and of learning from outside experiences, the focus of studies on reform gradually exceeded the motivations and measures of the late 1970s to research on the new type of economic system that should replace the old planned economy. As a result, three models for economic reform were proposed in political, economic, and academic circles.

The first model that influenced Chinese economists was the market socialism model (the Soviet Union/East European model), based on the reform theories and practices in the Soviet Union and Eastern Europe. Scholars like Sun Yefang and Jiang Yiwei proposed an expansion of enterprise autonomy under the planned economy. Their proposal, similar to the 1950s' enterprise self-management movement in Yugoslavia and Liberman's proposals in the Soviet Union in the 1960s, was adopted as part of a nationwide reform at the end of the 1970s to enlarge enterprise autonomy. Even after encountering difficulties, enlarging enterprise autonomy continued to be used to revitalize enterprises. Thereafter, scholars like Yu Guangyuan, Su Shaozhi, Liu Guoguang, and Dong Fureng, after carrying out profound comparative studies of the East European countries' reform processes, systematically introduced their theories and practices, which led to the popularity of the Yugoslav and Hungarian experiences. But with the reforms in the Soviet Union and the East European countries bogging down in difficulties beginning in the second half of the 1980s, the influence of their reform model declined. Nevertheless, the model's proposals to grant enterprise managers more autonomy and to establish a government-regulated market had a significant impact on China's future economic reforms.

---

[53] Edwin Lim, "Preface: Beginning to Think about the Outside World during the Process of China's Reform and Opening," *Fifty Economists Look at Thirty Years of Reform and Opening* (Beijing: Economic Press, 2008), p. 29; Library of the Institute of Economic Research, CASS, comp., *Socialist Economic System Reform: Minutes of the Brus and Sik Lectures in China* (Beijing: China Legal Publishing House, 1982).

[54] Wu Jinglian, "Economics and the Rise of the Chinese Economy: Speech at the 16th World Congress of the International Economic Association," *Works of Wu Jinglian* (Beijing: Central Compilation and Translation Press, 2013), 1530–1547.

The second model was the East Asia model. After World War II, Japan, South Korea, Singapore, and some other East Asian economies combined their authoritarian governments with a market economy, developing a mercantilist economy model.[55] Under this model, the market is allowed to play a certain role, but the government uses a selective industrial policy[56] and administrative guidance to control industrial development and enterprise decision-making. These economies operated within the overall framework of a state-dominated economy.[57] Such a model was very attractive to some Chinese officials who focused on economic affairs. At the beginning of the reform and opening, many officials who had taken the study tours to Japan and other East Asian countries had become deeply impressed with their economic system, development policy, and the role of government in their countries. The resultant recommendations from these officials became influential at the time. In 1980, with Deng's consent, Gu Mu and Saburo Okita, the renowned Japanese economist and politician, organized and established an annual Forum of the China-Japan Society for the Exchange of Economic Information. When visiting Singapore in November 1978, Deng Xiaoping praised the country for its well-kept social order under an authoritative government. Even during his 1992 southern tour, Deng recalled his earlier visit to Singapore, saying: "Thanks to a strict administration, Singapore has good public order. We should learn from its experience and surpass it in this respect."[58]

The third model was a free-market economy (the European and U.S. model). Many scholars, particularly economists, believed that the essential role of government was to provide public goods rather than to offer commodities and services for private use. They felt that excessive government intervention would affect market efficiency and would breed corruption. Therefore, they preferred a European-U.S. type of free-market economic system. After the second half of the 1980s, with an increasing

---

[55] Mercantilism, which had been popular in Western Europe in the 1500 and 1600s, supports substantial government intervention in economic activities to accumulate monetary wealth so as to achieve the objective of becoming a rich country with a strong army. In his famous *The Wealth of Nations*, Adam Smith critiques the theory and policy of mercantilism.

[56] In general, there are two basic types of industrial policy. The first type is selective and differential, or vertically targeted; the second is functional, or horizontally targeted. Under the former, the government uses direct or indirect adjustment means to support selected industries while suppressing other industries. Under the latter, the government applies policy tools to correct market failures, restricts harms to competition caused by company market power, strengthens market functionality, and thus improves efficiency. In the post–World War II period, Japan and some other East Asian economies adopted the former industrial policy to boost high economic growth and to manage economic development.

[57] The state-dominated economy model originated from the Principal Industries Control Act, passed by the Imperial Diet of Japan in April 1931. At the time, the government exerted control directly or through cartel agreements among firms. After World War II, some people in the Ministry of International Trade and Industry sought to retain this practice. However, under a tide of liberalization, such control became indirect through "policy inducements." See Chalmers Johnson, *MITI and the Japanese Miracle: The Growth of Industrial Policy, 1925–1975* (Stanford: Stanford University Press, 1982).

[58] Deng Xiaoping, "Excerpts from Talks Given in Wuchang, Shenzhen, Zhuhai and Shanghai,"January 18-February 21, 1992, in *Selected Works of Deng Xiaoping* (Beijing: People's Publishing House, 1993), vol. 3, pp. 378–379,

number of scholars becoming equipped with backgrounds in modern economics, such thinking became more influential. However, the command economy remained dominant, and the market only existed in a rudimentary form. Under these circumstances, scholars recognized the need for the government to assume more coordination responsibilities, thus their differences with the supporters of the East Asia model did not surface. Moreover, many advocates of free market economics as the ultimate goal of the reform were also influenced by development economists such as Alexander Gerschenkron. They believed that a strong government would be more beneficial than harmful for the rapid development of backward economies.

Chapter 2
Initial Experimentations with Market Socialism

At the end of the 1970s, China for the first time embarked on an economic reform with a clear systemic objective rather than targeting individual policies. To a large extent, this reform was a copy of the reforms in the Soviet Union and the Eastern European countries in the 1960s that sought to increase the role of the market and to expand enterprise autonomy. The economic model for the reform was based on visions of a socialist system known as market socialism.

In the debates among Western academics in the 1920s–30s, proponents of socialism had suggested that the efficiency of a socialist economy can be improved by allowing the planning authorities to simulate a market pricing mechanism and allowing a certain degree of competition among the state-owned enterprises (SOEs). This proposition eventually evolved into market socialism. From the 1960s to the 1980s, market socialism was critical to the modification of Soviet-style socialism during the economic reforms in the Soviet Union and the Eastern European countries. After the onset of China's reforms, thinking about market socialism and similar ideas gave birth to a widespread Chinese experiment to enlarge enterprise autonomy in the state sector. As the approach began to wane in its original countries and when the negatives of this move became apparent, enlarging enterprise autonomy was no longer the primary focus of the reform.

However, market socialism principles continued to have an important influence on China's reform.

2.1 The Origins of Market Socialism

In the view of classical Marxist authors, any attempt to combine the market and socialism is flawed because market transactions between independent economic entities cannot seamlessly be integrated in a socialist system where wealth is collectively owned by all members of the society. Marx writes: "Imagine a community of free

W. Jinglian, *China's Economic Reform*, Understanding China,
https://doi.org/10.1007/978-981-96-9607-9_2

individuals who work with common means of production and consciously use their individual labor as a collective social labor. There, the regulations of Robinson's labor are replayed, not on an individual basis but rather within a social context. The total products of this community are social products. A portion of these products is used again as a means of production, and this portion remains social. The other portion is consumed as living materials by the members of the community."[1] In his "Critique of the Gotha Program," Marx points out that "within a collective society founded on common possession of the means of production, the society does not exchange its products. The labor employed to produce these products is not shown as the products' value or their material quality. Unlike in capitalist society, individual labor no longer needs to go through twists and turns to show its existence; it exists directly as a component of total labor."[2]

Engels held a similar view. In *Anti-Duhring*, he writes: "Once the society possesses the means of production, the production of commodities will be done away with, and domination of the product over the producer will be done away with as well. A conscious and planned organization will replace the disorderly state of social production. ... From the beginning, the labor of each person directly becomes social labor, regardless of its specific useful nature. At that point, the amount of social labor in a product can be determined without first taking any roundabout way. ... People will be able to manage all this very simply, without the need for the so-called "value" to intervene."[3]

Lenin fully agreed with the views of Marx and Engels on this issue. His "state syndicate" was a monopolistic, mega-corporation covering the whole of society under a state monopoly. In this model, elements of a market economy, such as commodity, value, money, and competition, do not exist. In his important work, "The State and Revolution," written before the October Revolution, Lenin points out that in the first stage of communist society, that is, socialist society, "all citizens become employees of the state (armed workers). All citizens become employees and workers of one nationwide state 'syndicate,' and "the whole society will become one office and factory, with equal work and equal pay."[4] Before the October Revolution, Lenin repeatedly proclaimed that "socialism requires the eradication of all private ownership of the means of production and the eradication of the commodity economy.[5]

---

[1] Karl Marx, *Das Capital*, vol. I, 1876, in *Selected Works of Marx and Engels* (Chinese translation. Beijing: People's Publishing House, 1995), vol. 2, p. 141.

[2] Karl Marx, "Critique of the Gotha Program," 1875, in *Selected Works of Marx and Engels* (Chinese translation. Beijing: People's Publishing House, 1995), vol. 3, p. 303.

[3] Friedrich Engels, *Anti-Duhring*, in ibid., pp. 660–661.

[4] See *Selected Works of Lenin*, vol. 3 (Chinese translation. Beijing: People's Publishing House, 1995), pp. 202–203.

[5] Vladimir Lenin, "Inserts to V. Kalinin's Article 'The Peasant Congress,'" in *Complete Works of Lenin* (Chinese translation. Beijing: People's Publishing House, 1987), vol. 12, p. 75.

After the Communist Party of the Soviet Union (CPSU) took power, Lenin immediately announced that "the Russian Communist Party strives to abandon money as soon as possible."[6]

In early 1921, when "war communism" caused devastating difficulties, the Russian Communist Party adopted the New Economy Policy and the "economic type of a market."[7] At that time, the Party's leftist clique feared this policy change would threaten the country's socialist future and rule by the Communist Party. In November 1922, Lenin, in a report in response to concerns at the Fourth Congress of the Communist International, used the German term "*komandohohen*," i.e., commanding heights, to refer to the key national economic sectors. He said what was being implemented in Russia was "special state capitalism," the meaning of which differed from its usual meaning.[8] This type of state capitalism was described as: "We control all the commanding heights. ... The proletarian state holds land and controls all crucial industrial sectors.... Only part of the small and medium-sized enterprises are leased out in the first step. The rest are still in our hands.... In the future, [the private sector's] activities will be within this limit." Furthermore, he argued that the state could adjust its policies at any time. Thus, this type of state capitalism was by no means a threat to the Russian Communist Party.[9]

Nevertheless, Lenin reminded his followers that the purpose of the new policy was to "make economic preparations for the socialist economy." The policy was a breathing spell under exceptional circumstances, or "a temporary retreat to prepare better for another offensive on capitalism."[10]

The New Economy Policy was hugely successful in the economic arena. Meanwhile, inner-Party struggles concerning the life and death of the market economy intensified. After defeating and purging the so-called "right opportunistic anti-Party group" that favored a continuation of the New Economy Policy, Stalin decisively declared: "Let the New Economy Policy 'go to hell,'"[11] and 1929 became "the year

---

[6] Vladimir Lenin, "The 1919 Lenin Program of the CPSU (Bolsheviks),"1919, in *Selected Works of Lenin*, vol. 3 p. 749.

[7] Twelfth Congress of the Communist Party of the Soviet Union (Bolshevik), "Revolution About Industry," 1923, *Compilation of Congress, Representative Conference, and Central Committee Plenary Session Resolutions of the Soviet Communist Party* (Chinese translation. Beijing: People's Publishing House, 1964), pp. 259–261.

[8] In the Chinese translation of Lenin's book, *komandohohen* is translated as "*mingmai*" (lifeline). Thus, "tightly controlling the national economic lifelines" is considered a fundamental Leninist principle. See Lenin, "Five Years of the Russian Revolution and the Prospects of World Revolution," 1922, *Selected Works of Lenin* (Chinese translation. Beijing: People's Publishing House, 1972), vol. 4, p. 667.

[9] Twelfth Congress of the Communist Party of the Soviet Union (Bolshevik), "Revolution About Industry," 1923, *Compilation of Congress, Representative Conference, and Central Committee Plenary Session Resolutions of the Soviet Union Communist Party*, pp. 259–261.

[10] Vladimir Lenin, "Draft Theses on the Role and Functions of the Trade Unions Under the New Economy Policy," 1921–22, in *Thematic Collections of Lenin: On Socialism* (Chinese translation. Beijing: People's Publishing House, 2009), p. 298.

[11] Josef Stalin, "Concerning Questions of Agrarian Policy in the U.S.S.R.,"1929, *Complete Works of Stalin* (Chinese translation. Beijing: People's Publishing House, 1955), vol. 12, pp. 150–151,

of great changes." By the mid-1930s, the Soviet Union had established a central planning system that excluded the market through such political movements as forced collectivization.

Ideas about market socialism first appeared in the early 1900s in arguments among some Western neoclassical economists about the feasibility of a central planned economy. Vilfredo Pareto (1848–1923), the grandmaster of neoclassical economics, first proposed in his *Les Systèmes Socialistes* (1902–3) and his *Manual on Political Economy* (1906) that an optimal allocation of resources could be realized by having a "socialist production department" formulate and implement the plan based on scientific calculations. Thereafter, Enrico Barone (1859–1924), a follower of Pareto, elaborated on Pareto's thinking in his famous 1908 article "The Minister of Production in the Collectivist State."[12]

Decades later, the theoretical design of market socialism emerged from the debates on socialist calculations.

Oskar Lange (1904–65), a Polish economist who immigrated to America, was the first supporter of market socialism. In 1936, he published *On the Economic Theory of Socialism*[13] in response to the criticisms of the socialist planned economy by Ludwig von Mises (1881–1973) and Friedrich von Hayek (1899–1992). Mises and Hayek had believed that a socialist planned economy could not efficiently allocate resources due to its lack of a market pricing mechanism. In his response, Lange, following the thinking of Pareto, argued in support of the effectiveness of a socialist economy. However, there was a technical problem: before invention of the computer, it was impossible to quickly solve an equation with thousands of unknown variables. To overcome this difficulty, Lange significantly modified the planning methodology suggested in Barone's 1908 paper. He assumed that the planning authority would no longer formulate and allocate plan targets; instead, it would adjust product prices

163. See also *Selected Works of Stalin,* vol. 2 (Chinese translation. Beijing: People's Publishing House, 1979), p. 232. The relevant sentences are translated as "We adopted the New Economy Policy because it served socialism. When it no longer serves socialism, we must reject it" *Buharin Manuscripts* (Chinese translation by Zhang Yifan. Beijing: Central Compilation and Translation Press, 1997), p. 410.

[12] The title of Barone's article here uses the translation by Gu Zhun. See Joseph Schumpeter, *Capitalism, Socialism, and Democracy*, 1942 (Chinese translation by Gu Zhun. Beijing: Commercial Press, 1979). Neoclassical economics assumes that institutional arrangements are irrelevant to efficiency under complete information and zero transaction costs. Based on this premise, Barone shows that, in principle, resource allocations under a planned economy and under a market economy are identical, thereby solving a system of resource allocation equations. The solution, i.e., a group of price vectors, may provide a relative valuation of the resources that balance supply and demand. He points out that the solution can be arrived at by hundreds of thousands of market transactions, or by direct calculations by the "Ministry of Production," i.e., the central planning authority. As long as the Ministry of Production can solve the economic equilibrium equations and set the prices of scarce resources based on the solution, and as long as production units can organize production based on the principle that a market price is equal to its marginal cost, the planned economy can achieve the same results as market competition. Given these arguments, Barone finds that a socialist planned economy is entirely achievable.

[13] Oskar Lange, *On the Economic Theory of Socialism*, 1936 (Chinese translation. Beijing: China Social Sciences Press, 1981), p. 10.

through market simulations, i.e., a trial-and-error process like the market pricing mechanism. In other words, when the planning authority found that supply of a commodity exceeded demand, it would lower the price of the commodity, and vice versa. If the relative price reflected the relative scarcity, a Pareto efficiency equilibrium would be achieved when the enterprise in such a transaction responded to the price signal. In this case, a socialist planned economy founded on public ownership could allocate resources as efficiently as a market economy.

The market socialism economic model proceeded from these arguments. This model attempted to improve the efficiency of a socialist economy by combining adjustments to the plan and the market while maintaining public (state) ownership of the means of production, the state plan, and other characteristics of Soviet-style socialism.

An economy under market socialism would have three primary levels of decision-making. The first was the central government. At this level, the planning authority would have three functions: (a) to set the prices of the means of production based on a balance of supply and demand; (b) to make investment decisions; and (c) to allocate net income (rent and profits) earned by using the state-owned means of production. The second level was the SOEs. At this level, enterprises would organize production based on two principles: (a) that output should reach a level whereby the product price equals the marginal cost, and (b) that, at this output level, production costs should be minimized. The third decision-making level was composed of families and individuals who would be free to decide how much labor input they want to provide and would be free to dispose of individual income. Individuals would make decisions according to their personal preferences and market conditions.

In 1935–45 Hayek published some articles showing that Lange's propositions were not feasible.[14] In these articles, Hayek points out that socialism's biggest problem is not whether it can set the price equilibrium. Instead, the biggest problem is that socialism, unlike a market economy, cannot establish an incentive mechanism to utilize valuable information from many different places.

It should be noted that this debate took place in countries outside of the Soviet Union where the economies had become bogged down in the worldwide crisis that began in 1929. Compared to the countries in the West, the Soviet Union's planned economy, despite its various problems, did demonstrate certain advantages. At the time, the debates in the West had almost no influence on domestic affairs in the Soviet Union. However, in the second half of the twentieth century when the Soviet Union and the East European countries urgently needed reform, these discussions became attractive to the socialist reformers. János Kornai pointed out that for those who still adhered to Marxism politically but had abandoned Marxist economics in favor of neoclassical economics, market socialism provided an easy, straightforward solution.[15] The socialist reformers believed that the successful practices in the market

[14] Friedrich Hayek, *Individualism and Economic Order*, 1940 (Chinese translation. Beijing: SDX Joint Publishing Company, 2003), pp. 175–302.

[15] János Kornai, *The Socialist System*, 1992 (Chinese translation. Beijing: Central Compilation and Translation Press, 2006), p. 445.

economies should be studied, even though the entire system of classical socialism had to be maintained.

At the beginning of this systemic change, market socialism was often regarded as a first choice.

Włodzimierz Brus, a leading exponent of Lange's propositions and an important representative of market socialism, had participated in Poland's reforms in the 1950s.[16] He has recalled that after the mid-1950s, several market-socialism–based reforms had taken place in East Europe. Despite some differences, these reforms all sought to strengthen the role of the market. In 1958, Czechoslovakia began preparing for reform. In 1963, the German Democratic Republic implemented the New Economic System. In 1965, the Soviet Union began the Kosygin Reforms, and Bulgaria followed suit. In 1968, Czechoslovakia started economic reforms during the Prague Spring. In January 1968, Hungary introduced the New Economic Mechanism. Poland experimented with two small-scale reforms in the 1960s and a large-scale reform in the mid-1970s. But by the early 1980s, except for the Hungarian New Economic Mechanism, all the other reform experiments had been abandoned and they only had made some secondary modifications within the framework of the command economy.

Although differing in detail, these countries' economic reforms followed the market socialism model. First, they partially opened the market, particularly the consumer goods market. But the overall market remained under government control and subject to government policy adjustments, including price controls. Second, they provided the SOEs with varying degrees of operational autonomy and increased the material incentives for managers.

(1) The Reform and Its Failure in the Soviet Union

Stalin died in 1953. In 1957, Soviet leader Nikita Sergeyevich Khrushchev (1894–1971) launched the Sovnarkhoz reform, characterized by regional decentralization of economic decision-making power. The Union and Republic agencies in charge of the economy were abolished, and their former functions were delegated to 105 newly established regional economic councils. Union and Republic control of 15,000 SOEs was decentralized to these councils. Material supplies under the plan were balanced by the regions rather than by the central government. Thus, sectoral administration of the Soviet economy (vertical control) was replaced by regional administration (spatial control). However, by default, a planned economy requires centralized resource allocations by the national government. Instead of solving the problems caused by the administrative allocation of resources, the regional decentralization broke up the

[16] Włodzimierz Brus, like Oskar Lange and Michal Kalecki, was an internationally known Polish economist. When working as vice chairman of the Polish Economic Commission in the mid-1950s (at the time both Lange and Kalecki were also working there), Brus put forward a series of economic reform proposals that represented his most significant contribution to the Polish economy. After *Władysław Gomułka,* the government leader, lost interest in reform, Brus resigned from the Economic Commission. In 1972, he was also fired by Warsaw University for expressing sympathy with students who had staged a play mocking Russian chauvinism to protest the political repression. Thereafter, he immigrated to the UK and taught at Oxford University.

existing pattern of economic relationships, aggravating regional divides and leading to economic chaos.

The Sovnarkhoz reform failed. In 1961, a new program, adopted at the 22nd Congress of the Communist Party of the Soviet Union (CPSU) proposed reforms that centered on enlarging enterprise autonomy, utilizing the commodity-money relationship, and applying economic leverages to enhance economic incentives. This signaled a shift in the reform direction toward market socialism. In 1962, the CPSU organized a debate on the so-called Liberman proposals. In a *Pravda* article, titled "Plan, Benefit, and Prisms," Evsei Liberman (1897–1981), a professor at the Kharkiv Institute of Engineering and Economics, put forward the following proposition: except for the output plan and the delivery date plan, enterprises should be left alone to formulate their own business plans; control over enterprise plans should focus on profit incentives, and enterprises should receive bonuses based on fulfillment of their profit targets. However, before the market-socialism–style proposals were implemented, Khrushchev was overthrown during a 1964 coup.

After the removal of Khrushchev, Alexei Nikolayevich Kosygin (1904–80), an industrial management expert, became chairman of the Soviet Council of Ministers. Upon his appointment, Kosygin restored the centralized, sectoral (vertical) administration system, but in 1965 he began to push for market socialism reforms. The centerpiece of these reforms was relaxation of control by the plan, enlargement of enterprise autonomy, and implementation of "full economic accounting" for enterprises. This reform resulted in short-term increases in production and revenue. But, after one or two years, the effects of the incentives weakened and the fiscal situation worsened. By the end of the 1960s, the Kosygin reforms were abandoned.

After the failure of Kosygin's full economic accounting reform experiment, Soviet leaders no longer attempted to fundamentally alter the economic system. Instead, they sought improvements within the framework of a centralized planned economy. They called for a "shift in the mode of economic growth, full application of modern computing technology, and scientific management of planning work."

(2) "Self-Management Socialism" in Yugoslavia

The reform in Yugoslavia constituted a particular case in the market socialism experiments, centering on enterprise autonomy.

In the early 1960s, Yugoslavia removed plan control over wages, investment, foreign trade, and prices. Enterprises had complete freedom to decide on the product mix, supplies, marketing, income distribution, and investment. As a result, the economy gained a new vitality, but it continued to suffer from severe defects. First, "social ownership" was an ambiguous institutional property rights arrangement. According to Edvard Kardelj (1910–79), a prominent leader of the League of Communists of Yugoslavia and designer of self-management socialism, social ownership was a no-owners system because property rights were owned by the whole people, but they belonged to no one. Thus, it was a system of group ownership by all employees of an enterprise. Furthermore, because of attempts to maximize employee income, this system suffered from the "Illyria short-term behavior syndrome," named after the Illyria model.[17] The model, created by Benjamin Ward, professor at University of California at Berkeley, describes behaviors that seek less profit retention and more distribution, debt-financed investments, and high-tech components. With the lack of effective macroeconomic management, these institutional defects would lead to accelerating inflation, an increase in the unemployment rate, and a widening of the income gap. Social unrest would follow. The anti-reform faction used this opportunity to blame all unrest on the expansion of the role of the market.

Under these circumstances, in the early 1970s the Yugoslav leadership began a policy readjustment. On the one hand, managerial personnel and technical experts who advocated a free market-economy approach were forced out of economic circles and decision-making agencies. On the other hand, constraints on enterprises by the social contract and government rules and regulations were strengthened. In the 1974 constitution, the enterprise, as a statutory body, was replaced by a basic organization of associated labor. Several such basic organizations of associated labor could be organized into a commercial entity called a "composite association of labor." Self-management agreements and social contracts were used to adjust the relationships between the commercial organizations and between the organizations and the government. A self-management agreement, a contract among organizations of associated labor, covered prices, supply terms, credit, and investment. However, it was difficult to enforce such agreements, and the economy fell into a state of chaos, with neither plan nor market. Administrative means were commonly used to address economic issues, and various government agencies issued a massive number of administrative rules and directives to steer the behavior of economic entities.

This social contract type of socialism was a strange mixture of market forces and administrative authority. Aleksander Bajt (1921–2000), a Yugoslav/Slovenian economist, called this social contract system "quasi-feudal–style economic management."[18] The reform inevitably led to low economic efficiency, macroeconomic turbulence, and social instability. Moreover, expanding the administrative powers of the republics and the autonomous provinces led to segmentation in the domestic market and polycentric nationalism. By the 1980s, Yugoslavia entered a period of severe economic and political crisis.

(3) Czechoslovakia's Short-Lived Prague Spring

In 1962, Czechoslovakia's economy plunged into crisis, and there was strong dissatisfaction among workers. Hence, the Czech leadership appointed reformist economist Ota *Šik* to preside over the design of a reform program. In 1967, under *Šik*'s leadership, the country adjusted the prices of the means of production, using shadow prices

[17] Benjamin Ward, "The Firm in Illyria: Market Syndicalism," *American Economic Review* 48, no. 4 (1958), 566–589. Illyria refers to the northeast Balkan peninsula, roughly where the former Yugoslavia republics of Slovenia, Croatia, Bosnia, and Herzegovina exist today. Hence, Ward named his economic self-management socialism model the "Illyria model."

[18] Alexander Bajt, "The Experience of Yugoslavia's Economic System Reform," 1985, *Macroeconomic Management and Reform: Selected Speeches at the International Symposium on Macroeconomic Management,* comp. China Society of Economic Reform (Beijing: Economic Daily Press, 1986), pp. 95–102.

based on input and output tables. On January 1, 1968, it began a market-oriented reform that was more thorough than that in Hungary. Price controls were liberalized, and enterprises were granted operational autonomy. Together with democracy-oriented political reforms, the economic reforms were enthusiastically supported by people of varying social statuses. This period was called the famous 1968 Prague Spring. In August of the same year, the Warsaw Pact[19] countries, led by the Soviet Union, invaded the country. Czech leaders were taken to Moscow and under pressure they were forced to sign the Moscow protocol denouncing the reforms. The reforms ended and the old system was restored.

(4) Hungary's New Economic Mechanism

Hungary advanced the furthest among the countries that undertook market socialism reforms. On January 1, 1968, Hungary, led by veteran Communist Party leader János Kádár (1912–89), began the New Economic Mechanism reform. Direct interference with enterprises was replaced by indirect government control. Short-term decisions, adjusted and supported by the government to maximize profits, were left to the enterprises. Influenced by the market socialism idea of combining the strengths of both the plan and the market, the New Economic Mechanism did not wholly abandon plan institutions or government interventions. The central planning authorities still made decisions on significant development and structural adjustment plans, price subsidy policies for consumer goods, and principles of public services. Specifically, the following are the main characteristics of the new mechanism: (a) The most critical projects were subject to central planning and were financed by state investments. The central government and the relevant enterprises jointly made other investment decisions and shared funding responsibilities. (b) Market and fixed prices coexisted. Market-determined prices of commodities did not become dominant until after 1987, and factors prices were never liberalized. (c) Financial suppression remained. Restrictions on small non-state enterprises were gradually relaxed, and small-scale private enterprises were allowed to be established within strictly controlled limits. However, large-scale private enterprises were not allowed. (d) Imports were subject to licensing controls.

Hungary's gradual reform did not overcome the existing institutional defects, nor was it able to prevent the collapse of the political system at the start of the 1990s. However, the reform helped Hungary avoid severe social upheavals, and it facilitated a smooth transition to a market economy after the dramatic changes in the Soviet

[19] The Warsaw Pact was a political and economic alliance established in 1955 to counter the United States–led North Atlantic Treaty Organization. In addition to the Soviet Union, the Warsaw Pact countries included the People's Republic of Albania, the People's Republic of Bulgaria, the People's Republic of Hungary, the Democratic Republic of Germany (East Germany), the People's Republic of Poland, the People's Republic of Romania, and the Republic of Czechoslovakia. The People's Socialist Republic of Vietnam, the People's Democratic Republic of Laos, and the People's Republic of Mongolia had observer states. Albania withdrew from the alliance after the Warsaw Pact's military invasion of Czechoslovakia in 1968. East Germany announced its withdrawal after German unification in 1990. The Warsaw Pact was officially dissolved after the collapse of the Soviet Union in 1991.

Union and the other Eastern European countries in the final decade before the turn of the twentieth century.

After the overthrow of the Gang of Four, China turned to the outside world to find new ways to revitalize itself. The East European countries were the first to attract attention because the reform of their Soviet-style economies resonated with the Chinese. In the spring of 1978, a Party Central Committee delegation, led by Li Yimang, Yu Guangyuan, and Qiao Shi, visited Yugoslavia. Upon returning home, the delegation submitted a report the central leadership arguing that Yugoslavia could still be considered a socialist country. Based on this report, the Party leadership decided to recognize Yugoslavia as a socialist country and to restore relations with the League of Communists of Yugoslavia, thereby establishing a precedence for studying the reform experiences in socialist Eastern Europe. Thereafter, concerted efforts were made to understand economic development and reform in Yugoslavia and Hungary. In 1979–81, reformer economists Włodzimierz Brus and Oto *Šik* visited China to give a series of lectures. Their systematic introduction to the economic reforms in their countries generated further interest in the East European reforms among Chinese scholars. The published reports on the study tours to Eastern Europe were in high demand.[20]

2.2 The Domestic Source of Market Socialism

At the 20th Party Congress of the CPSU in February 1956, Khrushchev made a secret report, "On the Cult of Personality and Its Consequences," revealing Stalin's disregard for human life and repression of dissidents. The report shocked the Chinese, who had regarded the Soviet system as a socialist economic model. Khrushchev's speech coincided with the Chinese government's review of its own economic development process after the First Five-year Plan. As a result, the Soviet-style centralized economic planning system was increasingly questioned. In response, in 1956 Mao Zedong and his aides prepared a report, On the Historical Experience of the Dictatorship of the Proletariat. In addition, at a Politburo meeting Mao gave the speech "On the Ten Major Relationships," in which, for the first time, he urged that the problems of the Soviet Union be seen as a warning, and he advocated for a reassessment of China's own experience to forge its unique path of socialist construction.[21]

"On the Ten Major Relationships" proposed institutional reforms to decentralize central powers and to share certain benefits with local governments, production entities, and employees.

[20] For example, Liu Guoguang, *The Plan and the Market in Yugoslavia* (Changchun: Jilin People's Publishing House, 1981); Yu Guangyuan, Su Shaozhi, and Liu Guoguang, *Report of a Study Tour on Hungary's Economic System* (Beijing: China Social Sciences Press, 1981).

[21] Bo Yibo, *A Review of Major Strategic Policy Decisions and Events* (Beijing: Central Party School Press, 1993), vol. 1, p. 486.

At the same time, most academics and government officials favored increasing the role of the market and enlarging enterprise autonomy. The leading proponent of this view was Sun Yefang (1908–83), a veteran communist and a well-known Marxist economist.[22]

In the fall of 1956, Sun Yefang, then deputy director-general of the State Statistics Bureau, delivered a lengthy speech at the National Statistics Conference.[23] He criticized the ossified and inefficient Soviet-style planned economy, and he called for systemic reforms to increase the role of the law of value in economic activities.[24] Thereafter, Sun began to develop his own socialist economic model based on anchoring the plan to the law of value. This model, called "*daquan dulan, xiaoquan fensan*" (centralized control for major decisions, decentralized control for minor decisions) proposed decentralization benchmarks based on funding levels and control of the big/key powers and decentralization of the small/specific powers. "*Daquan,*" or major powers, refers to the decision-making powers within the scope of expanded reproduction, such as investment decision-making power over supply, production, and sales arrangements of newly added production capacity. "*Xiaoquan,*" or small powers, refers to decision-making powers within the scope of "simple reproduction," for example, powers to adjust various specifications. The government was to make the former decisions, and the enterprises could make the latter decisions. In other words, Sun Yefang's model gave enterprises more autonomy in day-to-day operations (simple reproduction), while, at the same time, maintaining state ownership and the planned management of enterprise supply and sales relationships by the state.

Sun Yefang's model is similar to the decentralization model proposed by Włodzimierz Brus, the leading exponent of Polish market socialism. It is also called a "model of a planned economy with regulated markets."[25]

---

[22] Sun Yefang (original named Xue Eguo, 1908–83) joined the Chinese Communist Party at age 16 in 1924. In 1925, he was sent to study at Moscow's Sun Yatsen University (where the CPSU had established a training program for Asian revolutionaries). After graduation, he remained in the Soviet Union and worked as a translator in classes on political economy until 1930, when he thereupon returned to China. Although an active Marxist economist as early as the 1930s, by the mid-1950s Sun became increasingly skeptical about the Soviet-style centrally planned economy. He thus developed his own socialist economic model, for which he was criticized as a revisionist. After the Cultural Revolution, Sun actively participated in the economic reform efforts.

[23] Sun Yefang, "About Total Value" and "The Plan and Statistics Should Be Based on the Law of Value," 1956, *Selected Works of Sun Yefang* (Taiyuan: Shanxi People's Publishing House, 1984), pp. 117–146.

[24] In China, the concept of the law of value and the law of the market are often confused. The former is a Marxist theorem, arguing that the average quantity of socially necessary human labor to produce a commodity determines the value of the commodity, and commodity exchanges are based on these values. The latter indicates that supply and demand for a commodity determine its price. Sun called the law of value the number one value, and he once remarked that "there may be one-thousand or ten-thousand natural laws, but the law of value is always the first value," thus making it clear that he was referring to the Marxist law of value. See Sun Yefang, "The Plan and Statistics Should Be Based on the Law of Value," *Economic Research*, no. 6 (1956).

[25] In 1979, during his lecture tour in China, Brus visited Sun Yefang in the hospital. It was their first meeting, but chatting in Russian, they immediately became good friends.

During his 1979 lectures in Beijing, Brus explained his classification of the various types of economies and his decentralization model. Under his model, economic decision-making consists of three levels. The top level involves national economic strategies, i.e., macroeconomic decision-making. The middle level involves individual enterprises and associated companies, i.e., day-to-day operational decision-making. The bottom level involves families and individual economic activities, i.e., decision-making regarding choice of jobs and consumer goods. Based on the degree of centralization (the administrative means) and decentralization (the economic means), Brus listed four economic types: (a) centralization at all three levels, i.e., the economic system under war communism; (b) centralized decision-making at the top and middle levels but decentralization at the bottom level, i.e., the centralized model, or the Soviet model; (c) centralized decision-making at the top level, and decentralization at the second and third levels, i.e., the decentralization model, i.e., the target of the reform in Hungary and the other East European countries; and (d) dispersed decision-making at all three levels, i.e., Adam Smith's laissez-faire economy. Brus believed the first and fourth models should never be adopted, leaving a choice between the second and third models. Ultimately, he proposed adoption of the decentralization model.

Under Brus's decentralization model, the government determines the prices of the means of production and makes investment decisions. In addition, the government adjusts market conditions based on price, wage, credit, and tax parameters to set limits for enterprise and individual activities. Enterprise-level decision-making aims to maximize profits. For this purpose, enterprises carry out production based on prices set by the state planning commission and on other economic parameters. Among the enterprises, buyers and sellers independently establish contractual relations. At the lowest decision-making level, residents are free to decide where to work and how to dispose of their income.

Brus believed the decentralization model would allow market mechanisms to play a role while, at the same time, state control and the planned nature of the national economy would be maintained. Instead of weakening the planned economy, utilizing market mechanisms with state adjustments would actually improve the planned economy. Brus argued: "Under the decentralization model, use of an adjusted market does not mean abandoning the plan. On the contrary, its use will improve the plan with market mechanisms. Here a market mechanism is not a tool that subjects production and exchanges to a spontaneous process. Instead, it is a tool to subject the activities of individual enterprises to the social preferences embodied in the plan."[26]

During the Hundred Flowers Campaign (China's policy of "letting one hundred flowers bloom and a one hundred schools of thought contend") in the mid-1950s, Sun Yefang elaborated on his propositions. Because he still emphasized the importance of the law of value and the profit indicator as calculation tools, he became the first victim of an anti-revisionist crackdown in the 1960s. Kang Sheng (1898–1975), who

---

[26] The content of Włodzimierz Brus' lectures can be found in *On the Socialist Economic System Reforms*, comp. Economic Academic Information Office of the Chinese Academy of Sciences (Beijing: China Law Press, 1982), pp. 1–44.

was in charge of Party ideological work at the time, called Sun "a revisionist who is more revisionist than Liberman." Sun Yefang was arrested in April 1968 and jailed in Qincheng prison until 1975.

Upon his release from prison, Sun Yefang announced that he not changed his ambitions, his profession, or his views," and he proceeded to enthusiastically promote reform after the fall of the Gang of Four. Most economists and government officials who experienced the turmoil of the Cultural Revolution realized that Sun's criticism of the centrally planned economy was correct. His ideas that enlarging enterprise autonomy and increasing enterprise vitality should be the core of the reform profoundly influenced Chinese scholars, economists, and the vision of the national leadership regarding reform.

Many economists provided theoretical arguments for enterprise autonomy. The most prominent idea was the "theory of an enterprise-based economy," advocated by Jiang Yiwei, who at the time was deputy director of the CASS Institute of Industrial Economics, as opposed to the "theory of a state-based economy" (the centralization approach) or the "theory of a region-based economy" (an administrative decentralization approach). Jiang believed that "the base unit of the socialist economy should be an independent enterprise....[The national economy] is like a consortium of countless base units....An enterprise is an association of all employees, ... [and] the entire employee body controls the rights of the enterprise." He proposed that under state leadership and oversight, an enterprise, as an independent commodity producer, should be independent in terms of operations and financial accounting, responsible for profits and losses and business development, and enjoy "its rights while fulfilling its duties to the state."[27]

These propositions, modeled after the Yugoslav reforms on enterprise autonomy, were supported by other economists. For instance, Dong Fureng, at the time deputy director of the CASS Institute of Economic Research, summarized the core content of enterprise reform as "changing the form of state ownership within the system of public ownership." Public ownership enterprises "should have independence under unified leadership and should implement comprehensive, independent, and strict economic accounting." "Workers in each economic organization have the right to directly participate in management, considering the interests of their own units and themselves under the premise of maintaining and enhancing the common interests of all workers and under the guidance of a unified plan."[28]

The proposal to enlarge enterprise autonomy also reflected the wishes of a significant interest group in the socialist countries, i.e., the SOE managers, who wanted the government to relax controls and to decentralize power. Given these external and internal factors, some influential economic leaders supported introduction of the role of the market to a certain extent and expansion of enterprise autonomy.

As early as September 1978, in his concluding remarks at a State Council retreat, Vice Premier Li Xiannian pointed out: "A major drawback of the economic system

---

[27] Jiang Yiwei, "The Theory of an Enterprise-Based Economy," *Social Sciences in China*, no. 1 (1981).

[28] Dong Fureng, "On Our Country's Socialist Ownership Forms," *Economic Research*, no. 1 (1979).

reforms during the last twenty years or more has been their focus on separation and transfer of administrative powers, resulting in a cycle of centralization and decentralization. In the future, the reforms should provide enterprises with the necessary independence so that they will actively rather than passively implement economic accounting and improve comprehensive economic efficiency."[29]

When recalling his visit to Japan to study Japanese enterprise management in October–December 1979, Yuan Baohua, at the time a vice chairman of the State Economic Commission, said that during the visit "the issue he and other delegation members discussed most often was why Japanese firms had been able to develop so rapidly and why Chinese enterprises were so far behind. We all felt that reform is needed to provide more autonomy to enterprises.... Developing a commodity economy should start at a theoretical level. Implementing planned proportional principles cannot be separated from the development of a commodity economy and commodity exchanges. Development of a commodity economy cannot be achieved without letting enterprises organize production based on market needs."[30] Upon returning to China, the delegation briefed Hua Guofeng and Li Xiannian about their visit, and their findings were well received. After the briefing, Li Xiannian instructed the State Economic Commission to take the lead in drafting a regulation on expanding enterprise autonomy. He reasoned: "It appears that the first step in improving the economy should be improving the performance of enterprises and enlarging enterprise autonomy.

For a long time, Chen Yun was the most authoritative and influential among the primary leaders responsible for economic work.

In 1955–56, China had carried out a socialist transformation movement that affected agriculture, handicrafts, industry, and commerce, establishing a planned economy based on public ownership and with state ownership in the dominant position. However, the resultant rapid transformation led to a loss of initiative on the part of enterprises, a mismatch between supply and marketing, a decline in product quality, and an economic downturn. Against this background, Chen Yun was asked to lead efforts to implement economic adjustments.

At the September 1956 Eighth Party Congress, Chen proposed a flexible economic policy to overcome the drawbacks of the excessively centralized economy. He said there should be mainstay and supplemental forces in three areas (*san weizhu, san weifu*), i.e., (a) in industry and commerce, state and collective enterprises should be the dominant force, with a certain number of sole proprietorships as the supplement; (b) in production planning, industrial and agricultural production under the plan should be the dominant force, supplemented by free (non-plan) production based on market changes within the permissible scope of the plan; and (c) in the uniform socialist market, the state-run market should be the dominant force, but to a specific

---

[29] Li Xiannian, "Speech at the State Council Retreat, September 9, 1978," in *Selected Works of Li Xiannian* (Beijing: People's Publishing House, 1989), p. 330.

[30] Yuan Baohua, "An Unforgettable Experience and a Great Practice: Recalling Enterprise Reform After the Third Plenary Session of the 11th Party Central Committee," *Enterprise Management*, no. 12 (2008).

limit a free market under state leadership would be allowed to supplement the state-run market.

In 1978 after the overthrow of the Gang of Four, Chen Yun backed Li Xiannian's proposal at the State Council retreat that advocated "combining a planned economy with a market economy, but with the former as the dominant force. While the market economy would be supplementary, it would be a large, rather than a small, supplement." In a 1979 speech outline, Chen Yun formally proposed that the two economies should coexist throughout the socialist period, with the planned economy as the central part and the market economy as the supplemental part. In 1982, when meeting some State Planning Commission officials, he summarized his thinking as a "dominant planned economy with supplemental market adjustments." This thinking became an influential model for China's reforms. Under this model, the SOEs enjoyed a certain degree of autonomy within a permissible scope under the plan.

In September 1979, the Finance and Economy Committee of the State Council, led by Chen Yun, submitted to the Party Central Committee a report on state plan arrangements for 1980–81. Enlarging enterprise autonomy was listed as the centerpiece of the reforms.

2.3 Large-Scale Experiments with Enlarging SOE Operational Autonomy

At the end of the 1970s, China began a large-scale SOE reform that expanded enterprise autonomy.

The December 1978 Third Plenary Session of the 11th Party Central Committee established the basic principles for the SOE reform. The plenary session's communiqué pointed out: "One of the serious shortcomings in the structure of economic management in our country is the over-concentration of authority, and it is necessary boldly to shift it under guidance from the leadership to lower levels so that the local authorities and the industrial and agricultural enterprises will have greater power of decision-making in management under the guidance of unified state planning".[31]

In April 1979, a Central Work Conference was held to arrange for formulation of the principle of "readjusting, restructuring, consolidating, and improving" the economy, resulting in the Ten Regulations on the Enlargement of State-owned Enterprise Autonomy.

In October 1978, even before the official onset of the reforms, the Sichuan provincial government was experimenting with reform in six different SOEs, such as the Chengdu Cutting and Measurement Tools Plant. The pilot program successfully increased production and revenue, leading the Provincial Party Committee to expand the number of pilots to 100 SOEs.

[31] "Communiqué of the Third Plenary Session of the 11th Party Central Committee," December 22, 1978, in Party Literature Research Center, comp. *Selected Important Articles After the Third Plenary Session* (Beijing: People's Publishing House, 1982), pp. 1–16.

After the Ten Regulations were issued, the State Council began to prepare guidelines for nationwide experimentation. However, during preparation of the document, the Ministry of Finance felt that the intended decentralization and revenue sharing went too far, and it disagreed with the State Economic Commission that was in charge of drafting the guidelines. Under these circumstances, the State Economic Commission held an on-site national industrial work conference in July 1979 in Chengdu and invited the Sichuan provincial officials to introduce their experience with the 100 pilots. At the meeting, Kang Shien, at the time a vice premier of the State Council and chairman of the State Economic Commission, pointed out that "enlarging enterprise autonomy is a major policy that must be implemented. The reform will solve the problem whereby all enterprises receive the same treatment no matter how different their profits, losses, or performance." Du Xingyuan, then Party secretary in charge of industry in Sichuan, also presented a report at the conference (in early 1980, Du would accompany Zhao Ziyang, then Party secretary of Sichuan, to Beijing to become secretary-general of the State Council). Tian Jiyun, then director of the Provincial Finance Bureau, spoke on how the Finance Bureau supported industrial production and reform (Tian would later become vice premier in charge of finance). He noted that the goal of the reform was "to gradually adjust allocative relations among the state, the enterprises, and the individuals, to modify the uniform revenue and expenditure regime, and to restore the due rights and interests of socialist enterprises as relatively independent commodity producers. This direction is unalterable."[32]

After rounds of debate and bargaining,[33] the central government ministries agreed on the extent of decentralization and revenue sharing. In addition, they produced five State Council documents on SOE management system reform, including the Regulations on the Enlargement of Operational Autonomy of State-owned Industrial Enterprises.[34]

The State Council officially issued these documents and required local governments and line ministries to select pilot enterprises.

[32] Yuan Baohua, "An Unforgettable Experience and a Great Practice." Also see Tian Jiyun, "How Did the Economic Reforms Begin," *Yanhuang chunqiu*, no. 1 (2008).

[33] Yuan Baohua has recalled that "at the conference, comrades from the enterprise sector and from Sichuan province spent several hours debating with comrades from the Ministry of Finance." See He Yaomin, "Expanding Power and Profit: The Breakthrough Point of State-owned Enterprise Reform—An Interview with Comrade Yuan Baohua," *Bainianchao*, no. 8 (2003).

[34] The four other State Council documents are: the Regulations on Profit Retention of State-owned Enterprises, the Provisional Regulations on Raising the Fixed Asset Depreciation Rate and Improving the Use of Depreciation in State-owned Industrial Enterprises, the Provisional Regulations on Levying a Fixed Asset Tax on State-owned Industrial Enterprises, and the Provisional Regulations on the Full Amount of Working Capital Loans to State-owned Industrial Enterprises. Due to the numerous compromises, the documents drafted at the meeting only provided "limited expansion of authority and limited profit-sharing." As Feng Lanrui, a researcher at the State Council Research Office, stated, overall the rights granted to enterprises were quite limited, and essentially they amounted to minor adjustments within the original system (Feng Lanrui, "Several Issues on Expanding Enterprise Autonomy," *Economic Research Reference Materials*, no. 367 [November 1, 1980]).

By the end of 1979, the number of pilot enterprises had reached 4200 nationwide; by June 1980, it reached 6600. These enterprises accounted for 60 percent of total output generated by industrial enterprises under the budget, and their profits accounted for 70 percent of the national industrial total.

This reform was quite similar to the 1965 "full economic accounting" reform in the Soviet Union. The similarity was mainly in the following two areas: first, relaxing controls by the plan to give enterprise managers considerable operational autonomy, and second, increasing the amount of incentive funds to enhance the material incentives for enterprises and workers. Specifically, enterprises were granted autonomy in the following areas:

(a) Provided they fulfilled the state plan, enterprises could increase production to respond to market demand, and they could sell the output produced beyond the plan on their own.
(b) The enterprise fixed asset depreciation rate and profit retention ratio were gradually increased, and the enterprise could arrange on its own use of production development funds, collective welfare funds, and employee incentive funds financed by the retained profits.
(c) Enterprises were given more power to appoint and to dismiss middle- and low-level managers.
(d) Enterprises had the right to apply for central or local government permission to export their products, and they could retain their foreign exchange earnings.

In the first few months, the reform mobilized workers' enthusiasm for increasing production and income, and for a time, enterprise revenue and workers' livelihood subsidies and bonuses rose significantly. For the first time in years, the market was booming. However, the limitations of the market socialism reforms soon appeared. On the one hand, enterprises were still attached to the administrative authorities and could not make operational decisions independently or take full responsibility for profits and losses. Furthermore, they had limited operational autonomy, and they failed to significantly improve efficiency. On the other hand, enterprise autonomy was not subject to ownership or market constraints. As a result, so-called enterprise enthusiasm often led to an inefficient allocation of resources. Similar to what had occurred with the 1965 full economic accounting reform in the Soviet Union, the enterprise autonomy reform in China soon led to runaway aggregate demand, sharply increased budget deficits, high inflationary pressures, and economic chaos.

Varying views surfaced about the economic situation and how the national leadership should respond.

From August 30 to September 10, 1980, the third annual meeting of the Fifth National People's Congress (NPC) reviewed two reports, the Report on Fulfillment of the National Economic Plan of 1980 and 1981 and the Report on the Final State Accounts for 1979, the Draft State Budget for 1980, and the Financial Estimates for 1981. The NPC was quite optimistic about the economic situation, concluding that the 1979 national economic plan had been well implemented, and the economy had grown steadily during the adjustments. The meeting considered the proposed main plan and budgetary indicators for 1980 and 1981 to be appropriate and the implementation measures effective. On September 2, the State Council issued the State Economic Commission's Report on Expanding Enterprise Autonomy Pilots and the Next-Step Proposals. This report summarized the year-long experiment and confirmed its direction and results. According to the report, the pilot program had raised enterprise and worker enthusiasm and had facilitated enterprise rectification and management, resulting in expanded production and increased profits. The production, output, and profit handovers of the pilot enterprises had increased significantly from the pre-reform period. The increases were also significant compared to the performance of the non-pilot enterprises. All involved parties were rewarded with higher profits and revenue: the state saw its revenue increase, the pilot enterprises retained more profits, and workers' income increased. The main identified drawback of the experiment was the limited enlargement of autonomy and profit-sharing. Calling for expanding the pilot program, in 1981 the program was extended nationwide to all industrial enterprises, giving enterprises more autonomy in human, financial, and material resource utilization and with respect to production, supplies, and marketing.

At a State Council plenary meeting held at the same time, Zhao Ziyang, who was newly appointed as premier and chairman of the Central Party Leading Group for Financial and Economic Affairs, commented that "the experience of the last year and more shows that our economic reform is moving in the right direction with good results. The entire economic system reform is based on enlarging enterprise autonomy and recognizing the relative independence of enterprises....In 1981, a further step should be undertaken to expand and deepen the experiment: the enlargement of enterprise autonomy should be extended to the entire country and pilots should begin to experiment with a tax-for-profits handover, independent accounting, and responsibility for their own profits and losses....Administrative and enterprise functions should be separated, decision-making power decentralized, and enterprise autonomy expanded. Individual enterprises will be organized based on these principles. ... In addition, the economic authorities will continue overseeing the overall planning, coordination, monitoring, and services, thereby providing vitality to our economic structure. This is our train of thought and a sketch of our vision for the economic reforms."[35]

But shortly after the State Council meeting, the situation on the ground appeared to be quite different. The fiscal system and the economy were in trouble: budget deficits had expanded, and prices were increasing rapidly. The original plan had been to have a balanced budget in 1979, but in the end, there was a massive deficit of RMB 17.06 billion, accounting for 4.2 percent of GDP.[36] To finance the deficit, RMB 4 billion from past surpluses was used, and the Ministry of Finance borrowed

---

[35] China Society of Economic Reform, comp., *Major Events in China's Economic Reform, 1978–2008* (Beijing: China Financial and Economic Publishing House, 2008), pp. 40–41.

[36] In his Report on the Final State Budget Outcome of 1979, the Draft State Budget of 1980, and the Estimated State Budget of 1981 to the third annual meeting of the Fifth NPC on August 3, 1980, Finance Minister Wang Bingqian said that in certain areas, there had been lapses in cutting enterprise costs and losses, a lack of fiscal discipline, and waste and squandering, which were the leading causes of the vast unbudgeted deficits (*People's Daily*, September 13, 1980).

RMB 6 billion from the central bank. In 1980, although the plan continued to fix the prices of most means of production and consumer goods were still rationed at government-set prices, the retail price index shot up by 6 percent due to excessive currency issues. There was growing dissatisfaction among the general public.

From October 7 to October 10, 1980, the Central Leading Group for Financial and Economic Affairs held a meeting to discuss the economic situation. On the occasion, Yao Yilin, a vice premier and vice chairman of the State Planning Commission, said, "The various parts of the economy did not come together; we have studied the situation after the annual NPC meeting and have found that this situation was enormously challenging." On October 23, Chen Yun agreed with this assessment.[37]

On November 15–30, 1980, the State Council held a meeting of provincial leaders and a National Planning Conference, in which the economic situation and the adjustments to the 1981 national plan were discussed. The meeting issued the State Council document, On the Current Economic Situation and the Important Adjustment Measures to Ensure Stable Economic Growth. The document criticized the ineffective implementation of the 1979 adjustment policy, noting that "after local governments and enterprises had more financial power, they initiated many repetitive construction projects." At the meeting, Yao Yilin forwarded the views of Deng Xiaoping, Chen Yun, and Li Xiannian about the need to adjust the 1981 national plan. The leaders thereupon emphasized that infrastructure projects should be withdrawn and that there should be no fiscal deficits or increases in the issuance of currency. In addition, they stressed the need to centralize powers in order to overcome these difficulties.[38]

Based on a suggestion from Deng Xiaoping, the Party Central Committee held a work conference on December 16–25, 1980, to arrange for further economic adjustments. On December 16, Chen Yun gave a long speech on the need to slow down the reform and to prioritize the adjustment. He said that the negative side of the economic situation should not be overlooked, even though the situation was more favorable than it had ever been since the establishment of the People's Republic. Still, the prices of many commodities were rising, thereby affecting the people's livelihoods. If the price hikes were not stopped, public resentment would grow. The reform of the economic system had achieved unprecedented positive results, but still there were drawbacks: repetitive projects were started without careful study, small projects squeezed out big projects, projects with backward technology squeezed out projects using advanced technology, and new factories squeezed out existing projects. It was beneficial to follow the laws of economics, but China was taking the planned economy as the dominant force. In many areas, state intervention would be necessary for a certain period. The prices of SOE and collectively owned enterprise products needed to be frozen for at least half a year, and expenditures of the central and local governments needed to be significantly cut for the next several years. Chen

---

[37] Jiang Yongqing, "Chen Yun and the Two Major Economic Adjustment Decisions in the New Era," *Xiangchao*, no. 5 (2015).

[38] China Society of Economic Reform, comp., *Major Events in China's Economic Reform, 1978–2008*, p. 43.

Yun then quoted a policy proposal in a letter that four young people had sent to him: "suppress demand and stabilize prices; place stability over development; slow down reform to focus on adjustment; and centralize at the overall level and decentralize in specific areas." Chen Yun reported that he found this proposal made sense, although he suggested modifying the phrase "put stability over development" to "seek stability with controlled development." He said that because the reform was complex, it should be slowed down and not be carried out hastily. He then recommended the approach of "crossing the river by feeling for the stones, with small and slow initial steps." Based on these arguments, Chen Yun explained the need for "a clearheaded and healthy adjustment."[39]

While proposing that adjustments to the national economy must center on a substantial contraction of fixed-asset investments and capital construction projects, Chen Yun once again emphasized that "our country takes the planned economy as the mainstay." All departments and all sectors, including agriculture, must be primarily guided by the planned economy, and they must act in accordance with the state plan; market-based adjustments can only play a supplementary role within the limits permitted by the plan. Therefore, this round of national economic adjustments was carried out within an institutional environment that emphasized the primacy of the planned economy. The reform to enlarge enterprise autonomy was halted and replaced by a "responsibility system" under which SOEs would be held accountable for achieving the plan targets.

2.4 The Legacies of Market Socialism on China's Reforms

The setback in enlarging enterprise autonomy led to an unexpected result: it was used as a reason to counter the market-oriented reforms, leading to the first pushback in the reform and opening era. At the time, some officials and economists blamed the weakening of the state plan for the economic difficulties. They believed the role of the market and enterprise operational autonomy had been exaggerated.

The first reform advocate to be attacked was Xue Muqiao, a veteran economist who had been a proponent of a commodity economy.[40]

In the early summer of 1980, Xue Muqiao, at the time an advisor to the State Council System Reform Office, drafted a document entitled "Preliminary Proposals for Economic System Reform," in which he suggested: "At present, China's socialist

---

[39] Chen Yun, "The Economic Situation and the Lessons Learned: Speech at the Central Work Conference on December 16, 1980," in Fang Weizhong, comp., *Marching through Storms: Chronicle of China's Development and Reform (1977–89)*, vol. 3 (1980), unpublished draft dated 2004, pp. 203–209. In the *Selected Works of Chen Yun*, the policy proposal from the four young people is omitted.

[40] A "commodity economy" is a Russian term for a market economy. At the beginning of the reform and opening when the mainstream view equated a market economy with capitalism, the phrase was often used to refer to a market economy to avoid any political trouble during discussions on the reform's target model.

economy is a commodity economy where public ownership of the means of production is dominant over other coexisting ownerships. While upholding the dominant position of public ownership of the means of production, the authorities should consciously utilize the law of value as required by a commodity economy and move from adjusting the economy only by the plan to letting the market play an adjustment role under guidance of the plan. This should be the policy and direction of the reform." When elaborating on this draft document at the September 1980 meeting of provincial first Party secretaries, Xue pointed out: "Economic system reform is about solving the problem of what form of a socialist economy should be established in China. This is the fundamental direction of socialist construction. The future reform plan for systemic economic management to be drafted in the future will be an 'economic constitution.'"[41] Xue Muqiao's views were supported by Hu Yaobang and some other leaders, but they did not become official policy.

Organized criticism of the "theory of a socialist commodity economy" began in early 1981. According to Xue Muqiao, in April 1981 the Research Office of the Secretariat of the Party Central Committee prepared an internal report, Several Opinions About Adjustment by the Plan or Adjustment by the Market, grouping the opinion holders into four categories based on their attitudes toward the plan and the market. The first group included economists upholding the planned economy. The second group was made up of people whose support for the planned economy was not firm. The third group included economists whose support of the commodity economy was weak, and the fourth group consisted of those who favored development of a commodity economy. Xue Muqiao and Lin Zili were grouped in the fourth category because they believed that a socialist economy should be a commodity economy, highlighting the role of the market in economic adjustments. Beginning in the second quarter of 1981, some people openly criticized this proposition. According to these people, the proposal to "combine the roles of the plan and of the market in the economic adjustment and to let the market play a role under guidance of the state plan" should not be the guiding principle of the economic reforms. A socialist economy should be a planned economy, not a commodity economy. They also opposed the "planned commodity economy" proposition, saying it was anchored on a commodity economy and it removed the substance of a planned economy. According to this view, mandatory planning symbolized the planned economy and was an essential component of socialist whole-people ownership in the organization and management of production. Therefore, the reform would be incompatible with a socialist system if it were to follow the principles of a commodity economy and ignored or negated mandatory planning. They attributed the lack of progress in implementing the 1979–80 economic adjustment program to the excessive weakening of the mandatory plan

[41] Xue Muqiao, "Recommendations on Economic System Reform," and "Explanation of the Preliminary Proposals for Economic System Reform,"1980, in *On China's Economic System Reform* (Tianjin: Tianjin People's Publishing House, 1990), pp. 211–255; *Memoirs of Xue Muqiao* (Tianjin: Tianjin People's Publishing House, 1996), p. 357.

that had shaken the foundations of the planned economy as well as to the extensive use of the indicative planning and market regulation.[42]

When preparing the Central Committee draft report to the Twelfth Party Congress, to be held in September 1982, Hu Qiaomu, leader of the drafting team, organized several members of the team to write a letter criticizing the view that advocated establishment of a commodity economy in China. The letter suggested that "although commodity production and exchange exist in our country, we should never define our economy as a commodity economy. If such a generalization is made, it would mean that the relations of collective ownership and joint labor among people under socialism is equivalent to relations of commodity exchange. It would suggest that the main force governing our economic activities is the law of value rather than the basic economic laws of socialism and the laws of planned development. This would inevitably blur the distinctions between the planned development of a socialist economy and the anarchic state of a capitalist economy as well as the essential differences between socialist and capitalist economies....Therefore, describing a socialist economy as a commodity economy or as a planned commodity economy.... limiting the role of the state plan in governing the macro economy and letting the market adjust the microeconomy, i.e., all operational activities of enterprises.... [and] turning enterprises into independent economic entities are all considered undesirable."[43]

The editorial department of *Red Flag* Publishing House collected articles written in 1981–82 to publish in the first volume of *Selected Works on the Planned Economy and the Market Adjustment.* In the preface to this work, the editors write, "mandatory planning is the basic hallmark of a socialist planned economy and an important embodiment of socialist whole-people ownership in economic organization and management.... Completely abandoning the mandatory plan.... [and] removing direct state command of the backbone enterprises.... will inevitably lead to social and economic chaos. We would then be unable to maintain the socialist direction of economic development."[44]

In the final report of the Central Committee to the Twelfth Party Congress, the objective of China's reform of the economic system is expressed as having the planned economy play the main role, supplemented by the market economy. The report states that "China has a planned economy based on public ownership. Planned production and circulation cover the main body of our national economy. At the same time, the production and circulation of some products are allowed to be regulated through the market without being planned, that is, by letting the law of value spontaneously play a regulatory role, within the limits circumscribed by the state's unified plan and in light of the specific conditions during different periods. This serves as a

[42] *Memoirs of Xue Muqiao*, p. 376.

[43] Letter from Lin Jianqing, Yuan Mu, Wang Renzhi, You Lin, and Gui Shiyong to Hu Qiaomu, dated August 25, 1982 (circulated printout).

[44] Editorial Department of Red Flag Publishing House, comp., *Selected Works on the Planned Economy and the Market Adjustment* (Beijing: Red Flag Publishing House, 1983), vol. 1.

supplement to planned production and circulation, subordinate and secondary to it but essential and useful nonetheless."[45]

The retreat of market socialism in China took place against the backdrop of the following international situation.

First, by the mid-1980s all the East European countries that had attempted market socialism reforms were facing dire situations. In Hungary, considered the best reform trailblazer, there was a stalemate between inflation and reform. In the USSR, after coming to power in 1985, Gorbachev had attempted to revitalize the reform in the Soviet Union, but there was nothing he could do. In 1989, dramatic political changes occurred in Eastern Europe, and in 1991, the Soviet Union was dissolved. After these events, most Central and East European countries no longer mentioned reform as they transitioned to a free-market economy under their new political systems.

Second, the East European economists who had significantly influenced China's economic strategy began to examine their previous views on market socialism. For instance, after having immigrated to London in 1972, Włodzimierz Brus' ideas changed significantly. In their 1989 book *From Marx to the Market*, Brus and his co-author Kazimierz Łaski (also an economist and a Polish emigrant) admitted the existence of the following problems: a planned economy with a controlled market is a defective model, the controlled market is used merely as a planning tool and, to a large extent, it is reduced to a new form of administrative coordination. The controlled market uses different means, but it has the same objective and similar results to an administrative command market.[46] In addition, they reexamined other basic principles of market socialism, questioning whether the principles applied to enterprises (self-responsibility for profits and losses, self-funding, and self-governance) can be reconciled with the traditional dominant state ownership. They realized that market socialism might not require giving up public ownership, but it had to abandon all ownership principles. In this book, Brus also criticizes his previous suggestion of using the market to strengthen the planned economy, and he advocates a transition from the early partial market socialism to market socialism in the strictest sense. Nevertheless, the two authors maintain that they still favored market socialism. What made them initially fall for such ideas was no longer the dominance of state ownership or the planned economy but rather the fundamental values of socialism: equal opportunity, full employment, and social safety nets. They point out that if socialism still contained the doctrines of public ownership dominance, centralized planning,

---

[45] Hu Yaobang, "Strive to Create a New Situation in All Fields of Socialist Modernization, Report to the Twelfth National Congress of the Communist Party of China," September 8, 1982. https://d37djvu3ytnwxt.cloudfront.net/assets/courseware/v1/ffb6d9f9df769dca4f09d795358 5996c/asset-v1:TsinghuaX+ZG001x+3T2016+type@asset+block/12_%E8%8B%B1_.pdf

[46] Włodzimierz Brus and Kazimierz Łaski, *From Marx to the Market: Socialism in Search of an Economic System*, 1989 (Chinese translation. Shanghai: SDX Joint Publishing Company, 1998), pp. 101–115. In this book, Brus criticizes his earlier idea of using the planned economy model with a built-in market mechanism to intervene in the market, in particular because it omits the operations of capital markets. He also identifies similar defects in Sun Yefang's model.

and "to each according to his contribution," this would run counter to every pillar in their beliefs.[47]

After the waning of the 1979–81 reforms, the foreign-born ideas of market socialism no longer played any leading role in China's reforms. However, it appears that Chinese reformers did not have much exposure to the lessons of the failed market socialism reforms in the Soviet Union and the other East European countries, nor did they know much about the reexamination of the market socialism reforms by scholars in those countries. Later, some market socialism ideas with local characteristics reappeared in China. For example, ideas about "decentralization and profit-sharing" to turn SOEs into commodity producers with operational autonomy, and SOEs being "self-responsible for profits and losses," "self-developing," and "self-constrained" had a lasting influence on China's SOE reforms.

Furthermore, the goal of the Chinese reforms in the late 1980s became "the state guiding the market, and the market guiding the enterprises," a modified form of a "planned economy with a controlled market." The following chapters will further discuss this issue.

[47] Włodzimierz Brus, "From Revisionism to Pragmatism: Sketches toward a Self-Portrait of a 'Reform Economist,'" 1988, in *Comparative Economic and Social Systems*, no. 2 (1989); Brus and Laski, *From Marx to the Market.*

Chapter 3
Development of the Private Sector Led by Incremental Reforms

The reform to enlarge enterprise autonomy in the state sector did not achieve the desired results, so the reform policy reverted back to strengthening the plan, and, as a result, the first round of market-oriented reforms in China failed. Fortunately, as the saying says, "When the sun sets in the east, it rises in the west." The reform found a new path outside of the system (*tizhiwai*),[1] i.e., outside the state sector. In the rural areas where most Chinese resided, a household contracting system reestablished family farming, offering new hope for reform. Unlike in the Soviet Union and the Eastern European countries where the reforms began in the state sector, China found a new path through breakthroughs in the non-state sector.

In his memoirs, Xue Muqiao, an important theorist and reform practitioner, points out that two steps were successful during the initial stage of the reform in the 1980s. The first step was the prioritization of the rural reforms. As agriculture emerged from a period of prolonged stagnation, it became an important driving force behind the economic adjustments and systemic reforms. The second step was the accelerated development of the collective economy, fostering growth of the non-public sector, including the *getihu*, or individual businesses (sole proprietorships), private-owned firms, and enterprises consisting of three different foreign investment modes. In this new model, multiple forms of ownership co-existed while the "dominance of state ownership with the public economy as the mainstay"[2] was maintained.

The early stage incremental reform strategy facilitated the gradual growth of market forces beginning from scratch. However, this strategy on its own could not establish a full market economy. The coexistence of a primary planned economy and a secondary market economy led to various problems. The most severe was the profiteering activities by certain government officials and by those connected to the authorities (*guandao*) under the dual-track system for resource allocations and

---

[1] *Tizhiwai* is a Japanese term meaning outside the dominant system. In China, the term refers to the non-state sector.

[2] *Memoirs of Xue Muqiao* (Tianjin: Tianjin People's Publishing House, 1996) pp. 351–352.

W. Jinglian, *China's Economic Reform*, Understanding China,
https://doi.org/10.1007/978-981-96-9607-9_3

pricing. In the mid- and late 1980s, it became clear that shifting from incremental changes to a comprehensive reform strategy would be necessary.

3.1 The Choice in the Rural Areas: Family Farms or Large-Sized, Public-Owned Communes?

After completion of land reform in 1952, peasants began to establish family farms on the land that had been allocated to them. However, the lifeline of this mode of agricultural production, i.e., a free market, did not adhere to the principles of Soviet-style industrialization. Therefore, in 1953 China established a uniform (planned) procurement and marketing system for the government to obtain sufficient grain and cotton to develop heavy industry, which at the time was a policy priority. Because grain and cotton were in short supply and the official prices were substantially lower than the market prices, uniform procurement encountered strong resistance from among the farmers. In 1954, there was widespread unrest among the population, mainly due to problems in food supply and uniform procurement. But if the more than 120 million rural households had not been organized into collectives under the control and command of the state, the state would have encountered difficulties obtaining sufficient grain and agricultural raw materials. Therefore, in the summer of 1955, Mao Zedong criticized "right deviation thinking" and launched the agricultural collectivization movement, during which farmers were organized into agricultural production cooperatives.

The movement started by criticizing Deng Zihui, at the time the director of the Rural Work Department of the CCP Central Committee, who had proposed voluntary membership in the collectives. But thereafter, the family farming was abolished under substantial political pressures, and collectivization was thus completed within one year. By the end of December 1956, the 120 million rural households had been organized into 760,000 agricultural production collectives, of which 540,000, or 71%, were higher-level collectives. On average, each higher-level collective consisted of 200 households. The socialist transformation of "*geti nongye,*" or family farming, was considered to have been completed.[3]

The higher-level collectives consolidated the property of farmers into indivisible collective property. Farmers could not freely withdraw from the collectives, and government officials had authority over management and allocations to the collectives. Except for the absence of government-paid wages, the collectives, in fact, were not very different from the state-run enterprises. Since the government controlled the distribution of grain and other products, government concerns that farmers would not sell their produce to the state were alleviated. However, in order to ensure uniform state administration, these collectives were considered to be too

[3] National Statistics Bureau of China, comp., *China's Economic Construction and the People's Livelihood* (Beijing: China Statistics Press, 1958), p. 184.

small and too dispersed. In addition, it was difficult for the state to manage the collectives directly because they were not part of the local government structure. In order to alleviate this problem Mao Zedong proposed consolidating the small collectives into larger collectives. In March 1958, the CCP Central Committee Work Conference (the Chengdu conference) adopted a proposal calling for consolidation of the small collectives. This marked a prelude to establishment of the people's communes in the rural areas.

But the purpose of the transformation from agricultural collectives to people's communes was not only to facilitate governance. It was also related to Mao Zedong's idealized vision of the future basic social unit, i.e., the commune. At the May 1958 Second Plenary Session of the 8th Party Central Committee, Lu Dingyi, then director of Propaganda of the CCP Central Committee, delivered a speech entitled "Marxism is Still Evolving." He said: "When Chairman Mao described to Comrade Liu Shaoqi what our country would look like several decades from now, he said that by that time the rural areas will have many communist communes; each commune will have its own industry, agriculture, educational and science research institutions, hospitals, shops, and other service entities, including transportation, kindergartens, canteens, leisure clubs, as well as police to maintain public security. This will signify the achievement and enhancement of the utopian ideals held by our predecessors."

In July 1958, the CCP Central Committee's *Red Flag* journal published the article "Under the Banner of Comrade Mao Zedong," written by its then editor-in-chief Chen Boda, who also served as Mao's assistant. In the article, Chen discusses Mao's remarks to several central-level leaders in June of that year about establishing the communes: "Our objective should be to gradually and orderly consolidate the functions of industry, agriculture, commerce, culture, education, and the militia (the "entire nation in arms") into large communes, which will be the primary social units in in the country." Furthermore, Chen writes, "It is evident that under the guidance of Mao Zedong Thought, and under the banner of Comrade Mao Zedong, at a time when the national economy and culture are rapidly advancing as if 'one day equals twenty years,' people can already foresee that our country will gradually transition from socialism to communism in the not-too-distant future."[4]

Responding to Mao's call, local governments competed to establish communes that combined both administrative and production functions and that included all five sectors, i.e., agriculture, commerce, culture, education, and the military, all under the same roof. Mao famously proclaimed, "people's communes are good" on August 6–8 when he was visiting Qiliying commune in Xinxiang county, Henan province and again on August 9 when he toured Licheng county in Shandong province.[5]

---

[4] Chen Boda, "Under the Banner of Comrade Mao Zedong: Speech at the Peking University Gathering to Celebrate the CCP's 37th Anniversary," *Red Flag*, no. 4 (1958).

[5] During his August 9, 1958, tour of the rural areas in Shandong province, Mao Zedong pointed out: "The People's communes are better because they consolidate industry, agriculture, commerce, education, and the military into one unit, making it easier to command" (Xinhua News Agency, "Chairman Mao Tours Shandong Villages, August 12, 1958," *People's Daily*, August 13, 1958, p. 1).

On August 29, an expanded meeting of the Politburo (the Beidaihe meeting) adopted the Resolution on the Establishment of People's Communes in the Rural Areas. The resolution pointed out that "under current circumstances, our basic policy is to establish people's communes that will achieve the comprehensive development of agriculture, forestry, animal husbandry, sideline production, and fishery and that will combine industry, agriculture, commerce, culture, education, and the military. This will be the guiding policy for farmers to accelerate socialist construction so that the country will reach its goal of achieving socialism ahead of schedule and gradually transition to a communist society. ... At present, it is appropriate for one township to have one commune with 2000 households. ... After the size of the collective is expanded, the roles of the government and of the agricultural collectives should be merged: the township Party committee shall concurrently become the commune Party committee, and the township people's committee shall become the commune people's committee." Finally, the resolution proclaimed that "the realization of communism is no longer in a distant future in China. Therefore, we should diligently use the people's commune organizational form to discover the way to transition to communism."

As a result, a campaign to establish people's communes was rapidly rolled out throughout the country. By October of the same year, the 760,000 agricultural collectives had been replaced by 26,600 people's communes. After the people's communes were established throughout the country, almost all rural households (99.1%) had joined a commune, with the average number of households in each commune about 4500.[6]

Initially, the communes were the sole ownership tier and accounting unit. Land and other means of production that were previously owned by the higher-level collectives were transferred, with no compensation, to the communes. The communes managed agricultural production, distributed output, and were responsible for profits and losses. Farmers were organized into this quasi-military organization; eating together in public canteens and their labor input was allocated by the commune.

The people's commune movement was disastrous. In 1958, food production throughout the country was 200 billion kilograms; in 1959, it decreased by 30 billion kilograms to 170 billion kilograms; in 1960, it fell to 143.5 billion kilograms, below the 1951 level (143.7 billion kilograms). In 1960, nationwide per capita grain consumption in the urban and rural areas decreased from 203 kg in 1957 to 163.5 kg, a decline of 19.5%, with rural per capita consumption decreasing by 23.4%. The per capita annual consumption of vegetable oils contracted by 23%, from 2.4 kg in 1957 to 1.85 kg in 1960, and the consumption of vegetable oils in the urban areas decreased by 31%. Annual per capita pork consumption dropped 70%, from 5.1 kg in 1957 to 1.65 kg in 1960, and annual pork consumption in the urban areas declined by 78%.[7] Hence, agriculture suffered the most under the planned economy. When the widespread famine occurred, news about it was censored, and there was a lack

---

[6] Su Mu, "The People's Commune Is Like a Magnificent Rising Sun," *People's Daily*, December 31, 1958.

[7] Lin Yunhui and Gu Xunzhong, *The Rhapsody of the People's Communes* (Zhengzhou: Henan People's Publishing House, 1995), p. 339.

of relief measures. In the urban areas, many people suffered from edema caused by malnutrition. In the rural areas, the number of unnatural deaths was 10 million.[8]

Given the economic and social disasters caused by the decline in production and the food shortages, the government began to readjust its economic policy in early 1959. After the February 1959 Politburo meeting in Zhengzhou, ownership of the people's communes was converted to a tiered structure based on the production team. As a result, the basic accounting unit was gradually decentralized. In February 1962, the Party Central Committee issued the Instructions on Changing the Basic Accounting Unit of the Rural People's Communes." The new structure had three ownership tiers, with the production team (formerly known as the sub-production team), the lowest tier, becoming the basic accounting unit. This system lasted until the end of the Cultural Revolution in 1976.

Most farmers still hoped for a further transformation of the economic system. Since it was impossible politically to change the collective ownership of land, they hoped that a form of family farming could be implemented, similar to the ancient tenancy system. After collectivization, farmers attempted to return to the familiar tenant farming after the political controls were lifted a bit, and there were spontaneous attempts to sign farmland contracts to reestablish family farming. However, following harsh political criticism, each attempt to establish household contracting was brought to an end (until the period of reform and opening). There were three such attempts between 1956 and 1962.[9]

In the face of the severe famine, beginning in 1961 many local cadres and farmers across the country began to demand the implementation of a household-based contract system to secure their livelihoods. Their demands were supported by some local Party and government leaders. For example, the Anhui Provincial Committee of the Chinese Communist Party, based on investigations and research, confirmed and encouraged the farmers' spontaneous responsibility system, which included contracting out labor and production to households. By August 1961, the number of

---

[8] According to estimates by scholars, the number of unnatural deaths in China during the Great Leap Forward and after the people's commune movement was between 10 and 40 million. See Sun Yefang, "Strengthening Statistical Work, Reforming the Statistical System," *Economic Management*, no. 2 (1981); Jiang Zhenghua and Li Nan, "Methods and Results of Estimating China's Population Dynamics," *China Population Statistics Yearbook 1987*, comp. Office of Population Research, Chinese Academy of Social Sciences (Beijing: Economy and Management Publishing House, 1988); Lin Yunhui and Gu Xunzhong, *The Rhapsody of the People's Communes*; Li Chengrui, "Population Change Caused by the Great Leap Forward," *Studies on CCP History Bi-monthly*, no. 2 (1997); Cao Shuji, "The Great Famine: Chinese Population, 1959–61," *Population Science of China*, no. 5 (2005); Yang Jisheng, *Tombstone* (Hong Kong: Cosmos Books, 2008). However, some people denied that a famine was taking place. For instance, Professor Sun Jingxian, at the School of Mathematics of Xuzhou Normal University, has said, "It is a groundless allegation to claim that there were widespread unnatural deaths in China during 1959–61 because there is no scientific evidence." Sun believes there were 2.5 million malnutrition-related deaths, with deaths from starvation accounting for only a small share (Sun Jingxian, "Fact Check: 30 Million People Starved to Death," *Chinese Social Sciences Today*, August 23, 2013).

[9] Chen Xiwen, *Rural Reforms in China: Retrospect and Prospects* (Tianjin: Tianjin People's Publishing House, 1993), pp. 39–49. In this book, Chen describes the three attempts to introduce household output responsibility contract practices in 1956–62.

production teams implementing responsibility fields in Anhui accounted for 74.8% of the total number of production teams in the province, and by October, this figure had increased to 84.4%. However, the views of the local Party and government leaders were not accepted by the central leadership. In November 1961, the Central Committee of the Chinese Communist Party issued the Instructions on Launching a Socialist Education Movement in the Rural Areas, stating: "The current practices of contracting out production to households and other forms of disguised individual farming that have emerged in some areas are not in line with the principles of a socialist collective economy and are therefore incorrect. We must gradually steer farmers away from these practices."[10]

But the grave situation in the rural areas led some senior leaders with a sense of reality to realize that these instructions were not in line with the wishes of the people and would lead to unimaginable disasters. Therefore, at the July 1962 Central Work Conference and the Tenth Plenary Session of the 8th Party Central Committee, several senior leaders proposed making Concessions to the farmers to achieve a quick recovery in the agricultural sector.

Based on extensive research, Deng Zihui, at the time director of the Rural Work Department of the Party Central Committee who had long been in charge of agriculture and forestry, expressed his support for farmland contracting. In May 1962, he submitted the Suggestions on Several Policy Issues related to the People's Communes to the Party Central Committee stating, "Agricultural production is at the stage of manual labor and animal power. Currently, limited freedoms and small-scale private ownership are the best way to generate enthusiasm for production among the farmers and to give them a sense of responsibility."

In July, at a meeting of the Secretariat of the Party Central Committee when receiving the participants at the Seventh Plenary Session of the 3rd Congress of the Communist Youth League, Deng Xiaoping, a member of Politburo Standing Committee and secretary general of the Party Central Committee, repeatedly pointed out that "attitudes regarding choosing the best form of production relations should be thus: choose the form that will facilitate a quick recovery and development of agricultural production and choose a form that the masses prefer. If the form is not legal, make it legal. In Sichuan, we say, 'whether it is a yellow cat or a black cat, a cat that catches mice is a good cat'".[11]

That same month, Chen Yun, another long-time economic leader and a member of the CCP Politburo Standing Committee, personally suggested to Mao Zedong that dividing the land among households would be a more effective way to stimulate farmers' enthusiasm and restore agriculture. He believed that contracting production

---

[10] Party Literature Research Center, ed., *Selected Literature since the Establishment of the People's Republic* (Beijing: Central Party Literature Press, 1997), vol. 14, pp. 765–770.

[11] Deng Xiaoping, "Restore Agricultural Production," *Selected Works of Deng Xiaoping* (Beijing: People's Publishing House, 1994), vol. 1, p. 323.

to households was not thorough enough and that dividing the land directly among households would be a better approach.[12]

At the same time, Tian Jiaying, Mao Zedong's assistant, reported to Mao that about 30% of the country's farmers were already engaged in household output contracting, or the "*fentian daohu*" system, and this number was still growing. Under such circumstances, Tian suggested that it might be better to officially implement these practices and then to guide the farmers back to collective farming once production had recovered.[13]

Endorsement of these practices by senior Party leaders angered Mao. He sharply criticized "*dangan feng*" (the family farming trend) and once again, at the Beidaihe Central Work Conference held from July 25 to August 24, 1962, he stressed class struggle. In his speech at the Tenth Plenary Session of the 8th Party Central Committee on September 24, 1962, Mao said: "Therefore, from now on we must talk about this [i.e., class struggle] every year, every month, every day. We will talk about it at congresses, at Party delegate conferences, at plenums, [and] at every meeting we hold, so that we will follow a more enlightened Marxist-Leninist line regarding this problem."

Due to the dominance of the ultra-leftist line, from the 1958 establishment of the People's Communes through to 1978, although there were significant improvements in agricultural production conditions, such as farmland water conservancy, agricultural production efficiency did not improve. In fact, it declined. According to statistics, during these twenty years, average grain output per laborer decreased from 1030 kg in 1958 to 962 kg in 1978, a reduction of 7.6%. The production cost per 100 yuan of agricultural income increased from 36 to 55 yuan, an increase of 53%. The average net output value per laborer dropped from 355 to 317 yuan, a decline of 10.7%. Agricultural production remained stagnant for a long time. despite the significantly improved farmland conditions and irrigation facilities.[14]

After total food production reached 200 million tons in 1958, it took twenty years to reach 300 million tons in 1978, and the average annual growth rate was only 2% despite the yearly emphasis on "taking grain production as the key link." For many years, cotton production remained at about 2 million tons.[15]

As a result, any increase in farmers' incomes was extremely slow. In 1976, production teams with an average annual income per capita of less than 60 yuan accounted for 38% of the total production teams; those with an income below 50 yuan made up 27%; and those with less than 40 yuan comprised 16%. The average per capita grain consumption decreased by 4 *jin* compared to 1957. In drought-prone areas, 19% of production teams had per capita grain consumption below 300 *jin*, while in

---

[12] Party Literature Research Center, comp., *Chronicle of Mao Zedong's Life (1949–76)* (Beijing: Central Party Literature Press, 2013), vol. 5, pp. 108–111.

[13] Ibid., pp. 110–111.

[14] "References for Economic Research and Political Participation," April 30, 1989, p. 66, in Lin Yunhui and Gu Xunzhong, *The Rhapsody of the People's Communes*, pp. 361–362.

[15] National Statistics Bureau, comp., *35 Glorious Years* (Beijing: China Statistics Press, 1984), p. 49.

rice-growing regions, 18% of the production teams reported per capita consumption below 400 *jin*. This means that approximately 140 million people across the country were living in a state of near starvation.[16]

3.2 The Victory of the Household Responsibility System

Agricultural recovery and growth remained slow, even after the overthrow of the Gang of Four, because the old political line and policies had not yet been fully eradicated. As a result, the struggle between the two agricultural development paths intensified.

The senior leaders who adhered to the "two whatevers" policy continued promoting the "movement to learn from Dazhai in agriculture."[17] In December 1976, two months after the downfall of the Gang of Four, the Second National Conference on Learning from Dazhai in Agriculture called on the nation to "raise high the banner of learning from Dazhai, uphold the principle of taking class struggle as the key link, maintain the leadership of Marxists and poor and lower middle-class peasants, widely engage in mass movements, and vigorously implement socialism." At the conference, Chen Yonggui, the leader of Dazhai and then the vice premier for agriculture, called for fully employing the advantages of the people's communes in terms of their large size and public ownership, and strengthening the economy at the commune and production brigade levels to gradually upgrade the basic accounting unit from the production team level to the production brigade level.[18] The Central Committee

---

[16] Lin Yunhui and Gu Xunzhong, *The Rhapsody of the People's Communes,* p. 362.

[17] The leftist-deviation mistakes of the Dazhai Production Brigade in Xiyang county of Shanxi province were not denounced until the debates that emancipated people's minds took place at the end of the 1970s. On November 23, 1980, the Party Central Committee issued a Shanxi Provincial Party Committee document, the Self-Criticism Report on the Lessons Learned from the Movement of Learning from Dazhai in Agriculture. The report identifies the main leftist mistakes of Dazhai brigade and of Xiyang county. They include: (a) persecuting many officials and ordinary people under a man-made class struggle; (b) obstructing the development of the productive forces by advocating "*qiongguo du*" [transition under poverty]; (c) strangling the collective economy's supplemental role and thus blocking the comprehensive development of the socialist economy by endless campaigns to "cut the tails of capitalism" [to eliminate any emerging private business activities]; and (d) undermining the principle of "to each according to his contribution" by endlessly advocating egalitarianism. When issuing the report, the Party Central Committee added a commentary stating that the Shanxi Provincial Party Committee's report summarizes the lessons from the degeneration of Dazhai from an excellent agricultural example to a representative of a typical leftist political line. All regions were to seriously study these lessons to remove any leftist political influences in the agricultural sector and to better implement the rural policies adopted since the Third Plenary Session of the 11th Party Central Committee (Party History Research Center, comp., *Major Historical Events of the Communist Party of China in the New Era (December 1978–March 2008)* (Beijing: History of Chinese Communist Party Publishing House, 2009), pp. 48–49.

[18] In 1975, Chen Yonggui, then a State Council vice premier, wrote to Mao Zedong, suggesting a transition from the "three-tiered ownership structure based on the production team" to a two-tiered structure based on ownership by the production brigade. But Mao did not endorse this proposal.

report to the 11th National Party Congress in August 1977 required that one-third of counties nationwide be upgraded to the "Dazhai model" during the Fifth Five-year Plan period of 1976–80. In November of the same year, the Party Central Committee held a workshop on extending the Dazhai model. At the meeting, Hua Guofeng said, "The basic accounting unit in the rural areas should be moved from the production team level to the production brigade level. This is a necessary precondition for the transition to communism and a benchmark in the extension of the Dazhai model." It was required that between the fall of 1977 and the spring of 1978 10% of the production brigades be selected as pilots for an upgrading of the basic accounting unit. A summary report on the workshop proceedings became the 1977 No. 49 Document of the Party Central Committee.[19]

Although both faced shortages of food and clothing, Anhui and Sichuan provinces took a very opposite approach from that mandated by the central government.

In June 1977, Wan Li was appointed first secretary of the Anhui Provincial Party Committee, Around the time of the Party Central Committee Work Conference in November 1977, the Anhui Provincial Party Committee held a provincial rural work conference. A heated debate took place at the meeting, ending with the Anhui Provincial Party Committee document, Regulations on Several Rural Economic Policy Issues (trial edition). The document placed an emphasis on the following: (a) respecting the autonomy of the production teams in terms of production, distribution, and labor allocations; (b) allowing different forms of production responsibility systems based on the type of farm work, such as group work or individual responsibility practices; and (c) supporting farmers to farm household plots and to engage in family sideline businesses, and then to sell the products at free markets. Later, many localities proposed linking production responsibility with output quotas, thus giving birth to the output contracting system. In addition, many places began to divide up the basic accounting unit. For example, farmers in Shannan commune of Feixi county implemented a household output contracting system, and the provincial Party committee decided not to intervene. Quietly, many other localities adopted similar practices.

In 1978, Anhui province was hit by its most severe drought in one hundred years. The provincial Party committee adopted an extraordinary policy, called "lending fields to survive the famine," to cope with the disaster. This policy, "whoever plants it, harvests it, and owns it," allowed members to borrow the land that the collectives could not cultivate. Each person could borrow three-tenths of a hectare of land to grow wheat and rapeseed. The state did not levy grain taxes or assign mandatory purchase quotas.

After the downfall of the Gang of Four, Chen, supported by the national leaders who followed the "Two Whatever" principle, again proposed that a "transition under poverty" begin.

[19] Wang Weiqun, "Wan Li's Courage," *China Youth Daily*, December 18, 2008. The "Decision-Making Events in China's Rural Reform," compiled by nine agricultural-sector leaders, vividly describes the campaign to extend the Dazhai model in 1977–78. See Zhang Gensheng, comp., *Decision-Making Events in China's Rural Reform* (Zhuhai: Zhuhai Publishing House, 2001), pp. 18–27.

This decision directly triggered movement to a "household responsibility system" (or 包产到户) among farmers across Anhui province. Wan Li, the provincial Party secretary, designated Shannan commune in Shannan district, Feixi county, as a pilot for the system. Shannan's approach quickly spread throughout Anhui, drawing skepticism and even accusations from some. Nevertheless, the household responsibility system gained unstoppable momentum within Anhui province. By 1978, the number of production teams that had adopted the production responsibility system reached 1200; in 1979, the number increased to 38,000, accounting for 10% of the production team total in the province. By the end of 1980, 70% of the production teams in Anhui had implemented the "production responsibility system."[20]

In addition, impoverished production teams in Guizhou, Sichuan, Gansu, Inner Mongolia, and Henan adopted this practice as well, and a number of researchers published articles in support of the policy based on theoretical analyses.[21]

Although the practice won the support of the people and endorsement by the provincial-level leaders, there was still strong resistance, and the opposition had the upper hand politically, even at the central government level. Although the Third Plenary Session of the 11th Party Central Committee in December 1978 had abandoned the "two whatevers" policy, the two documents under review on rural development, the Central Committee Decision on Several Issues Related to Accelerating Rural Development (Draft) and the Regulations on People's Communes in the Rural Areas (Trial Draft), still followed leftist thinking, prohibiting "dividing agricultural fields for family farming" (household production contracting) as well as prohibiting household output contracting. But in September 1979, the Fourth Plenary Session of the 11th Party Central Committee passed the above-mentioned decision, allowing "work group labor-input contracts, output-linked labor remuneration, and above-quota output bonuses, provided that the production teams remained responsible for accounting and distribution." The final decision modified the wording in the draft from prohibiting both practices to "banning dividing the agricultural fields for family farming" but "discouraging household output contracting." In other words, household production contracting (family farming) remained forbidden.[22]

In February 1980, the Fifth Plenary Session of the 11th Party Central Committee decided to reestablish the Secretariat of the Central Committee, and it elected Hu Yaobang as general secretary of the Party. This meant the reform school had taken

[20] Zhang Guangyou and Han Gang, "Wan Li on How the Rural Reforms Began," *The One Hundred Year Tide*, no. 3 (1998); Wang Weiqun, "Wan Li's Courage"; Zheng Yougui, "The Emergence and Development of the Rural Reforms," *Special Subjects in the History of the People's Republic of China (IV)* (Chengdu: Sichuan People's Publishing House, 2009), p. 238.

[21] The following are representative articles: Lu Xueyi, Jia Xinde, and Li Nan, "The Household Output Contracting System Should be Studied Again," *Drafts To Be Finalized (Supplement)*, November 1, 1979; Yang Xun, "The Household Output Contracting System: An Important Theoretical Policy Issue," *China Rural Survey*, no. 5 (1980).

[22] The decision allowed work group labor-input contracts, output-linked labor remunerations, and above-quota output bonuses, provided that the production teams remained responsible for accounting and distribution. However, it banned "dividing agricultural fields for family farming." Furthermore, household output contracting was to be discouraged except in cases of special needs for specific sideline production and in isolated households in remote mountainous areas.

over the top leadership positions (at least in name). However, some people in Party and government organizations still insisted on the "two whatevers" principle. They denounced the household output contracting system for abandoning the socialist road. But at about the same time, Wan Li was appointed to be a vice premier of the State Council and chairman of the State Agricultural Commission. Upon his arrival in Beijing, the *Rural Work Newsletter*, an official publication of the State Agricultural Commission, welcomed him with two articles criticizing the household output contracting system. The first was entitled "Dividing Agricultural Fields for Family Farming Must be Corrected," and the other was entitled "Does Household Output Contracting Uphold Public Ownership and the Principle of Each According to His Contribution?".[23]

The central leadership's indecision regarding the household contracting system further deepened the divisions among the provincial secretaries.

After watching these developments from the sidelines, Deng Xiaoping spoke out in support of household contracting.[24] On April 2, 1980, Yao Yilin, a vice premier of the State Council and chairman of the State Planning Commission, reported to Deng Xiaoping about the discussions that had taken place at a long-term planning conference. He mentioned that the State Agricultural Commission had recommended implementing household output contracting in Gansu, Guizhou, Inner Mongolia, and Yunnan, places where the population density was low, the economy was lagging, and people were living in a state of poverty. Deng supported the recommendation: "The policy should be flexible in these areas. In some areas, contracts can be established with work groups, while in others, they can be made with individual farmers. There is no need for people to be apprehensive about implementing these approaches."[25]

On May 31, 1980, when meeting with some central-level senior officials, Deng Xiaoping highly praised the "household-based production responsibility system" (包产到户) and the "big-contracting" (大包干) experiments that were being carried out in Feixi and Fengyang in Anhui.[26]

In September 1980, the Party Central Committee held a provincial-level first Party secretaries workshop on improving the agricultural production responsibility system. Wan Li appointed Du Runsheng, then secretary general of the Department of Agriculture and Forestry of the Party Central Committee and a vice chairman of the

---

[23] Wang Weiqun, "Wan Li's Courage."

[24] Deng later recalled that it would not have worked if the change had taken place too rapidly; the most compelling evidence for the reform was the tangible, on-the-ground results it delivered. Many people with a different view questioned whether household contracting could still be considered socialism. They might not have voiced their disagreement, but they delayed implementation or remained idle. For two years, some resisted adopting such practices and we awaited their change in stance. See *Chronicle of the Life of Deng Xiaoping (1975–97)* (Beijing: Central Party Literature Press, 2004), vol. 1, p. 1327.

[25] *Du Runsheng's Autobiography: The Major Events in Decision-making during the Rural Reforms* (Beijing: People's Publishing House, 2005), p. 115; Also see *Chronicle of the Life of Deng Xiaoping (1975–97),* vol. 1, pp. 615–616.

[26] Deng Xiaoping, "On Questions of Rural Policy," 1980, in *Selected Works of Deng Xiaoping* (Beijing: People's Publishing House, 1991), vol. 2, pp. 315–316.

State Agricultural Commission, to take the lead in drafting the workshop document. It was hoped that the document would give permission or at least provide support for the household output contracting system. However, no consensus could be reached, even within the State Agricultural Commission, to say nothing of in the workshop itself. The debates grew so heated that they nearly led to the shutdown of the workshop. After consulting with Hu Yaobang and Wan Li, Du Runsheng twice revised the draft document before the conclusion of the workshop. The final document toned down support for household output contracting, proposing instead that the management forms in the rural collective economy should be "diverse," allowing for flexibility and different options across the various regions.

On September 27, 1980, the Party Central Committee issued the workshop document, "On Several Issues Related to Further Improving the Agricultural Production Responsibility System—Minutes of the Provincial-level First Party Secretaries' Workshop held September 14–22, 1980" (Document No. 75 of 1980). According to Du Runsheng, the content of this document reflected a compromise. On the one hand, the document stressed that "the collective economy is the unshakable foundation for agricultural modernization. … In the areas where the collective economy is stable and the existing production responsibility practices can satisfy, or can be improved to satisfy, the needs of the masses, the household output contracting system need not be implemented." On the other hand, the document stipulates: "Various management forms, labor organizations, and remuneration methods should be allowed to coexist. … Any responsibility system that motivates farmers to take an active interest in the collective economy and promotes increased production, income, and goods is a good practice and should be encouraged. However, no one should be bound to only one model. … In the remote mountainous regions and impoverished areas where the production teams for many years 'relied on state re-selling for food, bank loans for production, and government relief for livelihood' and where the masses have lost confidence in the collective economy and were asking for output contracting, the masses' requests are to be supported, and household output or production contracting are to be allowed and maintained for a long time."[27]

As in other instances during China's reforms, this Party Central Committee document, albeit consisting of both compromises and concessions, opened the floodgates for farmers to choose their own modes of farming. With the support of the Central Committee, both household output and production contracting developed rapidly, with the latter recording the fastest growth.[28]

Household contracting practices were able to quickly overcome any resistance due to the following reasons. First, they represented the institutional arrangement that farmers were most willing to accept when the agricultural collectives still owned the land. Under the planned economy, farmers were treated differently from workers

---

[27] *Du Runsheng's Autobiography,* pp. 116–120. Also see Party Literature Research Center, comp., *Selected Important Documents since the Third Plenary Session* (Beijing: People's Publishing House, 1982), p. 507.

[28] Zhang Guangyou and Han Gang, "Wan Li on How Rural Reforms Began"; *Du Runsheng's Autobiography;* Wang Weiqun, "Wan Li's Courage.".

in the urban areas. The former only had a "clay rice bowl" [a job without safeguards], and they had to shoulder any risks on their own, whereas the latter enjoyed "eating from the same big pot" [i.e., receiving the same reward regardless of their work performance] as well as welfare safeguards. Therefore, the transition from a collective economy to household output contracting did not result in any losses for farmers. Second, the ideological hurdles were lowered when family farms could be established on contracted (leased) farmland under collective ownership. Third, the shift to household contracting was accepted by the society because farmers benefited, and the interests of other social groups were also maintained. As far as rural cadres were concerned, those who were practical realized that the economy was on the verge of collapse due to the damage of the Cultural Revolution, and they felt they should support any institutional innovations introduced by farmers. The household output contracting did not weaken their powers or affect their interests. Furthermore, the new system increased family incomes. This was another reason many rural officials supported household contracting.

In January 1982, the Party Central Committee and the State Council issued the first annual "Document No. 1" regarding rural economic policy.[29] The document pointed out that "in general, production responsibility requires contracting. … Among the three main forms, i.e., labor-input contracts, output-linked labor remunerations, and above-quota output bonuses, the latter is the most popular because it eliminates work points and is simple to implement." The document clearly stated, "In general, linking output to contracting is required." It formally sanctioned the practice of "contracting by work, output, or management," and the simplified "contracting by management" was officially endorsed. By the end of 1982, production teams practicing a "dual contract" system constituted 93 percent of all production teams, with most adopting "contracting by management,"[30] which became the primary household responsibility system. This signaled a transition in China's agricultural sector from people's communes, i.e., the collective economy, to family farming on leased farmland.

The spread of contracting practices, particularly production contracting, contributed to agricultural development. As a result, total agricultural output (at constant prices) grew by 6.6% per annum in 1981–86, far exceeding the average annual growth rate of 2.5% in 1953–78 (see Fig. 3.1).

The contracting system, an institutional reform, led to unprecedented changes in China's agricultural production. According to estimates by Justin Lin, the various rural reforms contributed 48.64% of rural output growth in 1978–84; the contribution of the contracting systems was 46.89%.[31] The year 1984 saw the following records:

---

[29] This document consists of the minutes of the National Rural Work Conference held in Beijing in December 1981. From 1981 through 1985 there were four consecutive Central Committee "Number 1" documents related to rural reform. These documents are called the "Five No. 1 Documents."

[30] Rural Development Institute, Chinese Academy of Social Sciences, *The Rural Economic Reforms in China* (Beijing: Economy and Management Publishing House, 1988); State Commission on Reform of the Economic System, comp., *Ten Years of China's Economic Reforms* (Beijing: China Reform Publishing House, 1988).

[31] Justin Lin, *Institution, Technology, and China's Agricultural Development* (Shanghai: SDX Joint Publishing Co., 1994), p. 95.

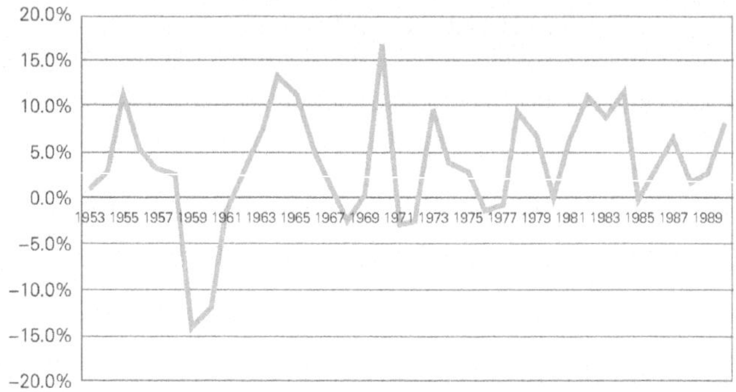

Fig. 3.1 Growth of total agricultural output (1953–90) (constant RMB 100 million). *Source* National Bureau of Statistics

- Grain output reached a historical high of 407.31 million tons, an increase of 33.6% over 1978, or an average annual growth rate of 4.95%.
- Cotton output reached 6.258 million tons, a 1.89 times increase over 1978, or an average annual growth rate of 19.3%.
- Output of oil crops reached 11.91 million tons, a 1.28 times increase over 1978, or an average annual growth rate of 14.7%.
- Sugar output reached 47.8 million tons, a 1.01 times increase over 1978, or an average annual growth rate of 12.3%.[32]

In addition to crop farming, i.e., narrowly defined as agriculture, the reforms were also a driving force behind the rapid development of animal husbandry and aquaculture.

In parallel with the dramatic increase in agricultural growth, farmers' income grew significantly, with per capita net income in the rural areas shooting up from RMB 133.6 in 1978 to RMB 355.3 in 1984.[33]

The impact of the household responsibility system on farmers' income was profound, allowing a shift from the farmers having no property rights to owning their own property.

Prior to the rural reforms, commune members had almost no personal property except for their family dwellings, which did not include the land on which their barely furnished houses were built. In 1978, property values per household in the rural areas were estimated to be less than RMB 500. The collectives also did not own much property. Nationwide, total fixed assets of the agricultural collectives were RMB 72 billion in 1978, or RMB 240 per rural worker.[34]

After the reforms, farmers gained three types of property rights. The first was private property, consisting of deposits, family homes, and household means of

[32] National Bureau of Statistics, *China Statistical Yearbook, 1995* (Beijing: China Statistics Press, 1995), pp. 347–348.

[33] Author's estimates based on the *China Statistical Yearbooks* (multiple years).

[34] Research Office of the State Council, *Investigation and Research*, no. 12 (1978).

production and livelihood. The second was land-use rights. Although the land still belonged to the collectives, farmers had operating rights under long-term contracts, and for the first time they had the right to retain their earnings. Third, farmers gained control over their labor, which led to changes in their attitudes, awareness, and quality. Although these changes in the social structure would take time to become noticeable, it is unquestionable that they had wide-ranging impacts on China's rural society.

During the Communist movement, the dominant view regarding the form of agricultural management has always been that large-scale production is superior to small-scale production. Under capitalist conditions, family farms would be replaced by large farms employing hired labor. Under socialist conditions, they would be replaced by large, publicly-owned farms. Therefore, even after widespread implementation of the household contract responsibility system in rural China, many still believed that this system was necessary only when agricultural productivity was low. Once agricultural productivity improved, it was anticipated that there would be a return to collectivization..

The first person to question this traditional view was Du Runsheng, a prominent advocate of the household responsibility system who was in charge of rural affairs. In a 1982 article arguing in support of household contracting, Du points out that agriculture is organic production and reproduction of materials, characterized by the following features: (a) It is constrained by various changing factors in nature: It requires someone to carefully and flexibly manage it as a master with a high sense of responsibility; (b) Agricultural profits are concentrated in the final product: This necessitates linking the interests of the producers to the final economic outcomes; and (c) The primary means of production in agriculture—land—is a special kind of production resource. Efforts must be made to properly cultivate the land so that it becomes more fertile over time. This requires establishing a stable and direct relationship between the producers and the land, making the producers highly attentive to the land. These three factors endowed the household contract management system with strong vitality.[35] Agricultural economist Chen Xiwen provides a systematic argument on behalf of Du Runsheng's view.[36] According to Chen, the most prominent characteristics of agricultural production are: first, the production processes are integrated with the life processes of plants and animals; second, it is decisively influenced by natural processes, such as temperature, sunlight, precipitation, and airflow, which are variable and beyond human control. This imposes special requirements on the owners, namely that they must oversee daily operations to accurately capture the growth status of plants and animals and the changes in natural conditions, and they must respond accordingly. This means that an effective agricultural system integrates ownership with daily operational management.

While it is feasible for owners to handle daily management and have laborers perform the production activities, Chen Xiwen notes that the challenge in motivating

[35] Du Runsheng, "The Household Output Contracting Responsibility System Has Further Developed the Rural Cooperative Economy," 1982, *Selected Works of Du Runsheng* (Taiyuan: Shanxi People's Publishing House, 2008), pp. 84–102.

[36] Chen Xiwen, *China's Rural Reforms*, pp. 57–60.

agricultural labor lies in the continuous nature of plant and animal life activities. Unlike in industrial settings, where labor contributions can be measured by the quantity and quality of labor in each production phase, in agriculture, labor contributions are linked to final output. Furthermore, the variety of agricultural labor types, the scattered operations, and the seasonal variations add complexity. Addressing this issue within the household simplifies the situation. Because a household is a tightly-knit community of economic interests with minimal differences in goals and interests among its members, transaction costs are reduced significantly.

In summary, households are better suited than collectives or individuals to serve as both owners and daily managers. As economists Lin Yifu, Cai Fang, and Li Zhou note: "Agriculture, with its limited internal economies of scale and with the extreme difficulties in supervising and measuring labor, is more suitable for family management."[37]

Later, Party and government leaders accepted this view. The 1998 Third Plenary Session of the 15th Party Central Committee adopted the Decision on Several Important Issues Concerning Agriculture and Rural Work. The decision confirms that family farming is "in line with the characteristics of agricultural production. It enables households to make decisions based on market conditions, temperatures, the environment, and the conditions to grow crops so as to ensure smooth production. It also enables farmers to use their surplus labor and surplus time to increase their incomes. This operating mode is suitable for manual-labor–based traditional agriculture. It also suits modern agriculture with its advanced science, technology, and production techniques. It has broad applicability and strong vitality and therefore it should be upheld for a long time."[38]

3.3 The Emergence of the Private Sector Through Incremental Reforms

The rural household responsibility reform provided China with a reform strategy that was different from the SOE-centric reforms of the Soviet Union and Eastern Europe. Instead of making major changes in the state sector, China's strategy focused on

[37] Justin Lin, Cai Fang, and Li Zhou, *The China Miracle: Development Strategy and Economic Reform* (Shanghai: SDX Joint Publishing Company, 1994), p. 123. Some researchers did not agree with this view. They insisted that the Marxist conclusion is irrefutable, i.e., either capitalist or socialist large farms will replace family farms. They felt that the idea that family farms had great vitality was untenable in theory and destructive in practice (Zhang Xinguang, "A Historical Review of the Smallholder Economy," *Guizhou Social Sciences*, no. 1 (2008).

[38] The Party Central Committee Decision on Several Major Issues Concerning Agriculture and Rural Work, adopted by the Third Plenary Session of the Central Committee of the 15th Party Congress on October 14, 1998.

creating room for developing non-state enterprises, i.e., the private sector.[39] Hence, it was called a strategy to begin the reforms "outside the system," or an incremental reform strategy.[40]

Before the reform and opening, the various political movements had eliminated all private businesses, including those owned by individual workers, based on Mao Zedong's principle of "eradicating capitalism and small-scale production."[41] In the rural areas, even the tiny household plots and limited sideline production of commune members were banned for being "the tail of capitalism." But as early as the end of the 1970s, some scholars and government officials began seeking a departure from the Mao-era theories and policies to give privately run businesses room to develop. Nevertheless, throughout the 1970s, there were very few results.

Due to the enormous influence of the above-mentioned principle in Mao Zedong Thought, development of the private sector was a highly sensitive political issue. Moreover, Mao-era doctrines still dominated people's minds, even during the "*boluan fanzheng*" (setting things right) period after 1976. This meant that initially private-sector development could only be promoted in a roundabout way when opportunities emerged.

The first breakthrough came from the entrepreneurial efforts of individual laborers.

During the Cultural Revolution, more than 10 million so-called "educated youth" from the urban areas were sent to the countryside.[42] After the end of the Cultural Revolution, they were allowed to return to their homes, but the government faced an urgent need to find jobs for them. At the time, state-owned industrial and commercial enterprises were in a slump, private businesses were banned, and any trafficking of goods for resale was considered to be a crime of profiteering.[43] At the March 1979

[39] In China, the private-sector economy generally refers to all enterprises other than SOEs and quasi-SOEs, such as the rural production cooperatives. This definition is broader than that of merely privately-run enterprises. For instance, the private-sector economy includes township and village enterprises that have ambiguous ownership structures.

[40] In foreign literature, the reform strategy at the initial stage of China's reform is often referred to as "gradualism." However, many Chinese scholars consider this term not to be very precise. They believe that the early reform strategy was a reform "outside the system" or an incremental reform.

[41] When Mao Zedong launched the agricultural collectivization movement, he once said that "in the matter of eliminating capitalism, we are quite lacking in conscience! Marxism is so fierce that there is little conscience involved; it aims to eradicate imperialism, feudalism, capitalism, and small-scale production." Mao Zedong, "On the Co-operative Transformation of Agriculture and the Contemporary Class Struggle," 1955, *Selected Works of Mao Zedong* (Beijing: People's Publishing House, 1977), vol. 5, p. 196.

[42] During the Cultural Revolution, urban youths did not attend classes because their schools were closed down so they could "focus on the revolution," and in December 1968, Mao Zedong called on the young people to go down to the countryside. Hence, during the next nine-plus years, more than 16 million youths moved to and settled in villages and mountainous areas. In 1977, after the overthrow of the Gang of Four, an increasing number of these young people began asking for permission to return to the cities. By the end of 1978, many had already returned home.

[43] The 1977 Criminal Law, promulgated by the National People's Congress, listed profiteering as a criminal offense. This prohibition was maintained until 1997 when an amendment to the Criminal Law removed profiteering from the list of crimes.

National Workshop on Wage System Reform hosted by the Ministry of Labor, Xue Muqiao, a veteran economist and long-time senior Party official, pointed out that "trafficking in goods by small peddlers should no longer be treated as a criminal offense. People waiting for jobs should be allowed to engage in commercial sole proprietorships, which may open up more job opportunities."[44]

In April 1979, the State Council issued a report by the State Administration for Industry and Commerce that accepted Xue's recommendations and indicated that local administrations could, with the consent of the relevant authorities, approve that some formally registered idle laborers could engage in individual labor in repairs, services, and handicrafts, but these businesses were not to employ workers."[45] In August 1980, the CCP Central Committee issued a notice forwarding documents from a National Labor Employment Conference, which confirmed the policy of combining "employment introduced by labor departments, voluntary employment organizations, and self-employment" (commonly known as the "three-door" employment policy). This policy aimed to "encourage and support the development of individual economies in cities and towns."

In June 1981, the Resolution on Certain Questions in the History of Our Party since the Founding of the People's Republic of China, adopted by the Sixth Plenary Session of the 11th Party Central Committee, recognized that "individual businesses [sole proprietorships], operating within a specific limit, are a necessary supplement to public ownership." This was the first official confirmation of the legality of sole proprietorships.

At the end of 1979, because of the prohibition on hiring, all the sole proprietorships were small-scale. However, by the early 1980s, various types of larger private firms with more workers began to appear. These included:

The first type of firm was the township and village enterprise (TVE) that arose unexpectedly.

During a 1987 meeting with foreign visitors, Deng Xiaoping said: "It is totally unexpected to us that the greatest achievement in the rural reform has been the development of the TVEs—a new force suddenly coming to the fore."[46]

The TVEs performed remarkably well during the reform and opening era. Their predecessors were the commune and brigade enterprises that emerged during the establishment of the people's communes in 1958. Due to the Leninist tradition that maintained petty producers had spontaneous capitalist tendencies,[47] the Amended

[44] Xue Muqiao, "On Labor and Wages," and "Several Recommendations Regarding Urban Employment," in *Selected Economics Papers of Xue Muqiao* (Beijing: People's Publishing House, 1984), pp. 216–235.

[45] State Administration for Industry and Commerce, "Report on the Conference of Director-Generals of the Industry and Commerce Bureaus," State Council Document No. 102 (1979).

[46] Deng Xiaoping, "We Shall Speed Up Reform," 1987, in *Selected Works of Deng Xiaoping,* (Beijing: People's Publishing House, 1993), vol. 3, pp. 238–239.

[47] Before the reform and opening, the policy regarding farmers participating in industrial and commercial enterprises was shaped by the goal of preventing the "spontaneous development of capitalism in the rural areas." According to Lenin, "small production engenders capitalism and the

Regulations on the Rural People's Communes, adopted by the Tenth Plenary Session of the 8th Party Central Committee in 1962, stipulated that the commune and brigade enterprises had to serve agricultural production and the farmers' livelihood; they could only procure, process, and sell locally (this policy lasted until the overthrow of the Gang of Four), and they were not allowed to engage in the transportation and trading of commodities. Private businesses were banned. Consequently, the commune and brigade enterprises grew very slowly. In 1978, their number totaled 1.52 million, or one enterprise per every 1924 rural residents. The total output value of these enterprises was RMB 49.1 billion, accounting for 24.1% of total rural output, or 7.17% of the total national output.

As early as the beginning of the reform and opening period, the government realized that the commune and brigade enterprises played a critical role in economic development. In December 1978, the Third Plenary Session of the 11th Party Central Committee cleared the draft Decision on Several Issues Related to Accelerating Agricultural Development, and the next plenary session, in September 1979, adopted it. The decision states, "Commune and brigade enterprises should develop on a large scale, and by 1985 their total output should account for more than one-half, from the current 20%, of the total economic income of the communes, brigades, and production teams." The July 1979 State Council Regulations on Several Issues in Commune and Brigade Enterprise Development specifies that commune and brigade enterprises, as economic entities, should decide on the means of production and what products should be produced. Except for raw materials and products subject to appropriations by the state plan, these enterprises are allowed to procure and sell goods at prices negotiated between the buyers and the sellers. However, many restrictions remained regarding their operational decision-making, merchandise pricing, hiring, and profit distribution.

The "large-scale development" of the commune and brigade enterprises occurred after 1982 when the household contracting practices were adopted nationwide. First, the contracting system significantly raised the efficiency of agricultural production. As a result, there was a huge quantity of surplus labor that became a rich source of labor for the TVEs. Second, the procurement prices of agricultural products were raised on several occasions, leading to higher incomes for farmers and allowing them to have extra income to make investments. These were the forces behind the development of the TVEs.

A further change came in 1984.

In March 1984, the Party Central Committee and the State Council issued the Ministry of Agriculture, Animal Husbandry, and Fishery's Report on Breaking New Ground in the Development of Commune and Brigade Enterprises. In the notice on the issuance of the report, the Party Central Committee and the State Council announced that from then on, the commune (township-level) and brigade (village-level) enterprises would be called township and village enterprises (TVEs), and

bourgeoisie continuously, daily, hourly, spontaneously, and on a mass scale." Vladimir Lenin, "Left-Wing Communism: An Infantile Disorder," 1940, in *Selected Works of Lenin* (Chinese translation. Beijing: People's Publishing House, 1995), vol. 4, p. 135.

they acknowledged the competitive advantages of the TVEs as well as the strategic importance of their development. Furthermore, the notice pointed out that TVEs included not only commune- and brigade-run enterprises but also cooperatives jointly run by commune members and sole proprietorships. It called for "supporting and treating these enterprises equally with the state-owned enterprises. … To facilitate their sound development, [the government] should enthusiastically support, foster, and manage cooperative enterprises, family workshops with separate production but joint procurement and marketing, and sole proprietor businesses."

Township and village enterprises in the different regions had varying characteristics and ownership structures, with the following operational modes. (1) Southern Jiangsu model: These TVEs originated from the commune and brigade enterprises that had expanded during the Cultural Revolution. They were established and run by grassroots governments on behalf of the local communities. Although called the Southern Jiangsu model, these were the country's most prevalent operational mode in the 1980s–90s. (2) Wenzhou–Taizhou model: These TVEs were active in Wenzhou and Taizhou of Zhejiang province. They were established by farmers or handicraft workers who became sole proprietors. Although often affiliated with state-owned or collective-owned enterprises for protection (the so-called "wearing a red hat" phenomenon), they were actually privately owned enterprises. (3) Pearl River delta model: These TVEs, mainly externally oriented, were owned by investors from Hong Kong, Macao, and Taiwan (as well as "fake foreigner" firms owned by investors in the mainland).

After 1984, the TVE sector saw rapid growth in the number of firms and the number of hired workers as well as in terms of total output. By the end of 1985, their number reached 12.225 million, a ninefold increase from the 1.346 million in 1983.

The second type of firm consisted of the rapidly growing foreign investment enterprises.

In 1978, the Third Plenary Session of the 11th Party Central Committee that established the reform and opening policy decided to adjust the approach to the external economy. Publicly owned enterprises were required to develop equitable and mutually beneficial relations with other countries based on self-reliance. An essential aspect of this new approach was to introduce foreign investment in the form of joint ventures. In 1979, China promulgated the Law of the People's Republic of China on Chinese and Foreign Joint Ventures, signaling a dramatic change from prohibiting to actively encouraging foreign direct investments (FDI).

Chinese partners in foreign joint ventures required a good market environment to survive and develop, but the country's overall business climate could not yet meet their needs. Therefore, China's external opening began by fostering favorable local environments for doing business and by developing externally oriented bases, such as the special economic zones (SEZs).

Beginning in 1980, the Chinese government established bases for external opening in several coastal cities. In April 1980, it granted specific policies and flexible measures to Guangdong and Fujian provinces for "opening to the outside world." As a result, four economic zones were established, in Shenzhen, Zhuhai, Shantou,

Table 3.1 Foreign direct investment in China (USD billion)

Years	Committed FDI	Actually utilized FDI
1979–1982	4.958	1.769
1983	1.917	0.916
1984	2.875	1.419
1985	6.333	1.956
1986	3.332	2.244
1987	3.709	2.314
1988	5.297	3.194
1989	5.600	3.393
1990	6.596	3.487

Source National Bureau of Statistics

and Xiamen. Overseas Chinese, Hong Kong and Macao businesspeople, and foreign companies were allowed to invest in these zones where they were granted special tax treatment. In 1984, the government decided to open up fourteen port cities for foreign investors, who were given preferential treatment similar to that enjoyed by the foreign investors in the special economic zones. The port cities were Dalian, Qinhuangdao, Yantai, Qingdao, Lianyungang, Nantong, Shanghai, Ningbo, Wenzhou, Fuzhou, Guangzhou, Zhanjiang, and Beihai (including Fangcheng port). In 1985, this status was also conferred upon the Changjiang delta, the Zhujiang delta, southern Fujian's Xiamen–Zhangzhou–Quanzhou triangle, the East Shandong peninsula, and the East Liaoning peninsula. In April 1988, Hainan Island also became a special economic zone.

The open areas attracted a large amount of foreign investment to establish enterprises.[48] As a result, by 1990 more than 20,000 foreign-invested enterprises had been approved nationwide, with contracted foreign investment amounting to USD 40.615 billion (see Table 3.1).

These foreign-invested enterprises introduced advanced production technologies and management techniques, invigorated the domestic economy, and facilitated improvements in the business environment. In addition, they were the mainstay of exports. In 1990, the twelve coastal provinces exported nearly USD 40 billion in goods, accounting for two-thirds of the country's total exports.

The third category of firm was the emerging private sector.

After the above-mentioned reforms, to a certain extent China's economy was open to both foreign investments and sole proprietorships. However, private sector industrial and commercial enterprises were still banned due to their "exploitation of workers." Finally, the December 1982 Constitution of the People's Republic of China stipulated: "The foundation of China's socioeconomic system is socialist public ownership of the means of production, i.e., whole-people ownership and collective ownership by the masses. … The rural and urban sole proprietorships operating

[48] FDI took three forms: joint ventures, cooperatives, and wholly foreign-owned enterprise.

within the scope specified by law supplement the socialist public economy." But the Constitution still remained silent regarding privately run enterprises.

The main obstacle to permitting private enterprises was the Marxist doctrine held by many that exploitation of surplus value from wage labor is the core and essence of capitalist exploitation, so private businesses' hiring of wage labor should be strictly prohibited. As a result, policy debates at the time centered on whether to allow sole proprietorships to hire workers.

In early 1981, when drafting a Party document, Lin Zili, an economist with the Research Office of the Secretariat of the Party Central Committee,[49] cited a calculation by Marx in Volume I of *Capital*[50] to argue that businesspeople should be allowed to hire workers: if the number of people hired by a sole proprietorship did not exceed seven people, the primary source of livelihood was still the labor of the sole proprietor, and thus the sole proprietors were still workers. The head of the Research Office was convinced by this argument and submitted a draft document for endorsement by Party and government leaders, and in July 1981, the State Council issued the Policy on Non-Agricultural Sole Proprietorships in Urban Areas. The policy allowed such businesses to hire one or two assistants when needed, and those businesses with a high-tech content or requiring people with special skills could have two or three apprentices but no more than five. In an October 16, 1981, document, Several Decisions of the Party Central Committee and the State Council on Seeking New Ways, Invigorating the Economy, and Solving Urban Employment Problems, the policy was formalized as "industrial and commercial sole proprietorships are allowed to hire two assistants and those with special skills are allowed to have five apprentices." Thus, it became legal for sole proprietorships to hire a maximum of seven employees. After privately owned firms gained legal status in 1988, this restriction on the maximum number of employees became the demarcation line between sole proprietorships and private enterprises.

Once the door was opened to permit hiring by private businesspeople, private enterprises began to employ more than seven workers. In early 1983, some politicians and theoreticians who still upheld the former political line and the former system voiced disagreement with "the rise of capitalism everywhere," and they demanded restrictions and a crackdown. But the Party Central Committee's annual Document No. 1, Several Issues Regarding Current Rural Economic Policy, released on January 2, 1983, established a neutral approach toward sole proprietorships that hired more than seven people—they (i.e., the sole proprietorships that hired more than seven people) were "not to be promoted or publicly advocated, but they should not be

[49] Lin Zili (1925–2005) began to study the Chinese economy and Marxist economics in the early 1950s. After the beginning of the reform and opening, he was a member of the management team and theoretical group leader of the Research Office of the Secretariat of the Party Central Committee. In addition, he participated in drafting a series of Party Central Committee documents on reform, including the Decision on Restructuring the Economic System, adopted by the Third Plenary Session of the 12th Party Central Committee.

[50] Karl Marx, "The Rate of Surplus Value," 1867, *Capital*, vol. I, chap. 3, sec. 9 (Chinese translation. Beijing: People's Publishing House, 2012), vol. 1, p. 186.

hastily outlawed." However, some people in central Party organizations insisted on expelling those businesspeople from the Communist Party.[51]

Thereafter, the question of whether employing more than seven people was illegal was brought to the attention of Party and government leaders. Deng Xiaoping's response was, "No arguments," and "Let it be for two years, and then see."[52] Due to this wait-to-see approach, people gradually came to realize that allowing hiring was inevitable and that developing private enterprises was beneficial both to the society and to the working class. On January 22, 1987, the Politburo passed a decision on deepening the rural reforms. For the first time, the decision admitted that it was inevitable for a small number of private enterprises to exist. In October of the same year, the Thirteenth Party Congress was even more explicit by stating that enterprises outside of state ownership had not developed sufficiently. There thus was a need to encourage the development of cooperatives, sole proprietorships, and privately run enterprises in both the urban and rural areas.[53] In April 1988, the First Plenary Session of the 7th National People's Congress passed an amendment to the Constitution of the People's Republic of China, stipulating in Article 11 that "the private economy is allowed to exist and develop within the scope of the law; the private economy is a supplement of the socialist public economy, and; the state protects the lawful rights and interests of the private sector of the economy and exercises guidance, supervision, and control over the private sector of the economy." Private enterprises thus received legal recognition.

Driven by the incremental reform strategy, the privately run economy began to grow from scratch, and by the second half of the 1980s, the privately run economy was pivotal to industrial production and the national economy. In industry, the privately

[51] Li Chang, a member of the Secretariat of CCP Central Committee for Discipline Inspection in the early 1980s, recalled that at a meeting of the Standing Committee of the Discipline Inspection Commission in February 1984, most members believed that if a Party member were to engage in a sole proprietorship and were to hire more than seven workers, he would be engaging in exploitation and therefore he should be expelled from the Party. Due to his objections, Li Chang was isolated from his colleagues. After holding six Standing Committee meetings, the Commission still could not reach a consensus. The Secretariat of the Party Central Committee stepped in, and the Discipline Inspection Commission agreed to adopt a policy proposed by Deng Xiaoping, which was "do not promote, prevent, and publicize the hiring of more than seven people" and wait two years before making any final decision. When drafting the 1984 Number One Document, Notice on Rural Work in 1984, Du Runsheng, director of the Rural Policy Research Office of the Secretariat of the Party Central Committee, faced a similar challenge. See Zhou Shiyuan, *Biography of Li Chang* (Harbin: Harbin Institute of Technology Publishing House, 2009), pp. 338–342, 351.

[52] In 1984, Deng Xiaoping recalled: "Earlier, the hiring workers phenomenon shocked people. Many were very concerned. My opinion was to shelve it for two years." See Deng Xiaoping, "Speech at the Third Plenary Session of the Central Advisory Commission of the Communist Party of China," 1984, *Selected Works of Deng Xiaoping*, vol. 3, p. 91. Deng also recalled: "It was my idea to discourage contention, so as to have more time for action. Once disputes begin, they complicate matters and waste a lot of time. As a result, nothing is accomplished. Don't argue; try bold experiments and blaze new trails." See Deng Xiaoping, "Excerpts of Talks Given in Wuchang, Shenzhen, Zhuhai, and Shanghai," 1992, *Selected Works of Deng Xiaoping*, vol. 3, p. 374.

[53] Zhao Ziyang, "Advance Along the Road of Socialism With Chinese Characteristics: Report at the 13th CCP National Congress," October 25, 1987.

Table 3.2 Shares of different types of ownerships in total industrial output (1978–90)

	1978	1980	1985	1990
State-owned enterprises	77.6	76.0	64.9	54.6
Collective-owned enterprises	22.4	23.5	32.1	35.6
Other*	0.0	0.5	3.0	9.8

Sources China Statistical Yearbooks (multiple years)
* Including private and foreign-invested enterprises

Table 3.3 Share of different types of ownerships in retail sales (1978–90)

	1978	1980	1985	1990
State-owned enterprises	54.6	51.4	40.4	39.6
Collective-owned enterprises	43.3	44.6	37.2	31.7
Other*	2.1	4.0	22.4	28.7

Sources China Statistical Yearbooks (multiple years)
* Including private and foreign-invested enterprises

Table 3.4 Registered private/sole proprietorships in the urban areas (1978–90)[54]

Years	Total employment (million)	No. of private enterprises (millions)	No. of sole proprietorships (million)	Share of private and sole proprietorships in total employment (%)
1978	95.14	–	0.15	0.2
1979	99.99	–	0.32	0.3
1980	105.25	–	0.81	0.8
1985	128.08	–	4.50	3.5
1990	170.41	0.57	6.14	3.9

Sources China Statistical Yearbooks (multiple years)

run economy accounted for about one-third of total output; in the retail sector, growth was even more rapid. The sector, in its strict sense (including foreign-invested enterprises) rose to prominence (Tables 3.2, 3.3 and 3.4).

3.4 Successes and Limitations of the Incremental Reforms

China's economy achieved unprecedented results due to its market-oriented reforms. During the twelve years from 1978 to 1990, GDP grew by 14.6% per annum, per capita disposable income of urban households grew by 5.86% per annum, and per

[54] Nicholas R. Lardy, *Markets Over Mao: The Rise of Private Business in China* (Washington, DC: Peterson Institute for International Economics, 2014) (Chinese translation by Zheng Xiaoxi. Beijing: China Development Press, 2015), p. 90.

capita net income of rural households grew by 9.92% per annum (see Table 3.5 and Fig. 3.2).

In the early 1990s, there were heated debates in academic circles about why the reforms in China achieved such good results in contrast to the failures of the transition in the Soviet Union and Eastern Europe. Most economists saw two different approaches to reform: "shock therapy" (or the big bang) vs. gradualism. They observed that the Soviet Union, and later Russia, suffered severe economic disruptions and a prolonged depression due to its shock therapy approach. In contrast, due to its gradualist approach, China recorded outstanding achievements.

But the above method of analysis which is based on the pace of reform does not adequately explain China's economic reform. By carefully studying China's experience in various fields it becomes clear that China's most successful reforms,

Table 3.5 China's economic growth (1978–90)

	1978	1980	1985	1990
GDP (RMB billion)	362.41	451.7.8	896.44	1854.79
Total industrial output (RMB billion)	423.70	515.40	971.60	2392.40
Total imports and exports (RMB billion)	35.50	57.00	206.67	556.01
Total exports (RMB billion)	16.76	27.12	80.89	298.58
Per capita disposable income of urban households (RMB)	343.40	477.60	739.10	1510.20
Per capita net income (RMB) of rural households (RMB)	133.60	191.30	397.60	686.30

Sources China Statistical Yearbooks (multiple years)

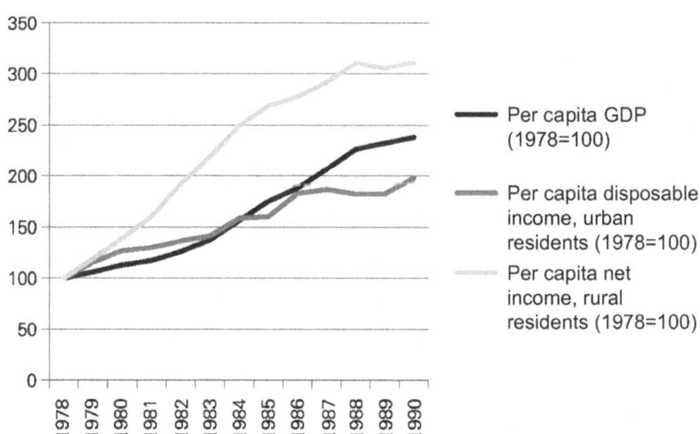

Fig. 3.2 Growth of per capita household income (1978–90). *Sources* National Bureau of Statistics, CEIC

Table 3.6 Kornai on the main features of the two transition strategies

Strategy A: Organic development of the private sector	Strategy B: Accelerated privatization of the state sector
• The most crucial task is to create favorable conditions for market entry and protection of private property so as to enable the private sector to grow from the bottom up • Sales are to be the primary instrument to privatize most state-owned companies • Allocation of state property without any form of compensation should be opposed • The plan to sell SOEs must give priority to enterprises that attract core owners • Budgetary constraints on enterprises must be hardened to maintain financial order and to ensure an efficient market economy	• The most crucial task is to eliminate state ownership as soon as possible • The main privatization instrument is voucher schemes allowing for the free allocation of state property • Preference is to be given to a dispersed ownership structure to enable the development of "people's capitalism." • The development of private enterprises and giving the private economy a more critical role is to be supported, but without highlighting the private sector • Hard budgetary constraints are automatically generated with privatization

Source János Kornai, "Ten Years After 'The Road to a Free Economy': The Author's Self-Evaluation," *Economic Systems* 24, no. 4 (2000), 353–359 (Chinese translation by Ban Yingjie and Wang Shanshan, in *Comparison of Economic and Social Systems*, no. 5 [2000])

e.g., the household contract responsibility system in the rural areas, was implemented very rapidly. In contrast, the most gradual reforms, i.e., the SOE reforms, were rather lackluster.

In 2000, when summarizing the transition strategy in the Central and Eastern European countries, Hungarian economist János Kornai used an analytical framework different from the above dichotomy.[55] According to Kornai, the shock therapy/gradualism dichotomy implies utilizing the pace of change to distinguish the two approaches. However, he argues that whether the change is fast or slow should not be used to judge success. Instead, he envisions two overall strategies for transitioning to a market economy. Strategy A can be called a strategy of organic development, the main task of which is to create a favorable environment for the private sector to develop from the bottom up. Strategy B is a strategy of accelerated state-sector privatization, the main task of which is to privatize the SOEs as soon as possible (Table 3.6).

Kornai points out that the Eastern European countries' post-socialist transition showed that organic development (Strategy A) was the correct choice. The changes in Hungary and Poland demonstrated the advantages of Strategy A: the sound development of the private sector and hard budgetary constraints subjected enterprises to a natural process of survival of the fittest, the debt chains between companies were cut, financial discipline was strengthened, implementation of contracts and the status of credit were improved, and the banking sector began to consolidate. All

[55] János Kornai, "Ten Years After 'The Road to a Free Economy': The Author's Self-Evaluation," *Economic Systems* 24, no. 4 (2000), 353–359. For the Chinese translation, see János Kornai, *Thoughts on the Post-Socialist Transition* (Changchun: Jilin People's Publishing House, 2003), p. 8.

these led to increased productivity and to an easing of unemployment pressures. In contrast, Russia provided the most painful evidence of the failure of Strategy B. Russia's transition embodied all the features of such a strategy. Many state properties were transferred to managerial personnel and privileged bureaucrats. In addition, the oligarchs robbed natural resources, particularly oil and natural gas. Compared to 1989, by 1998 labor productivity in Hungary had risen by 36%, that in Poland had increased by 29%, and that in the Czech Republic had increased by 6%, while, in contrast, labor productivity in Russia had dropped by 33%.

The achievements of China's 1980s' incremental reform strategy are another example of the strength of Strategy A. First, the process opened the door to private entrepreneurship, enabling the private sector to grow rapidly and to gradually replace the state sector as the central pillar of the national economy. The growing private sector brought material benefits to ordinary people. It helped the country avoid economic and social shocks when unexpected events hit the state sector (which had formerly been the central economic pillar). Second, because they grew through intense competition, private enterprises fostered many entrepreneurs and professional management personnel. These people then became part of a new social stratum supporting a modern market economy. It should be noted that under the previous economic and political structure, some officials and SOE managers would inevitably use illegal means to grab public property if the SOEs were privatized too quickly. These people would then become a new parasitic social class, and they would obstruct further reforms. Having experienced powerlessness in the past, entrepreneurs understood the dangers from a lack of social fairness and justice. Many thus became enthusiastic supporters of constitutionalism and the rule of law.

However, the incremental reform strategy still had significant limitations. These limitations were mainly reflected in two aspects: the positive effect of this strategy is in providing survival space for the emerging private economy, but it has only an indirect impact on state-owned enterprises, which still hold most of the social resources. On the one hand, due to the unchanged state-owned system, it was difficult for efficiency to improve significantly, thus obstructing the development of the national economy. On the other hand, the strategy resulted in a dual economic system, whereby the command economy was still dominant.

The dual-track system for resource allocations was most prominently reflected in the dual-track pricing system. Under a strict command economy, all industries and commerce are monopolized by the state, administrative directives dominate resource allocations, money is a passive "shadow" following the distribution of physical goods, and prices are merely tools for enterprise accounting. Raw materials and consumer goods are uniformly allocated, operated, and priced by various planning departments. In such a system, private enterprises without plans for raw material supplies, working capital loans, or sales channels for products cannot survive.

At the beginning of the reform and opening, the government began allowing institutions and organizations to establish their own subsidiary enterprises. Their production and operations were not determined by plans; instead, the prices of their products and services were set according to market supply and demand. At this time, township enterprises were partially allowed to "self-procure" and to "self-sell." Also, as part of the reform to "expand enterprise autonomy," state-owned enterprises and commune and brigade enterprises under the rural people's communes were granted some production and operational autonomy, allowing them to sell products produced beyond their plans at market prices. This created a "second track" of material circulation and pricing outside the planned track—the market track.

In July 1979, the State Council issued the Regulations on Expanding the Operational Autonomy of State-owned Industrial Enterprises, allowing enterprises to sell products beyond their plans. The State Council also issued the Regulations on Several Issues in Developing Commune and Brigade Enterprises, permitting commune and brigade enterprises to "self-procure" and "self-sell" production materials and products not included in the plan, with prices negotiated between the buyers and the sellers. In April 1984, the State Council issued the Interim Provisions on Further Expanding the Autonomy of State-owned Industrial Enterprises, stipulating that apart from products retained by enterprises, products produced beyond the plan, newly developed products, products not purchased by sales departments, and overstocked products, a portion of state-allocated products could be sold independently, with the self-sell price of production materials limited to within 20% above or below the state-set price. In January 1985, to curb price gouging and profiteering by intermediaries, the State Price Bureau and the State Materials Bureau issued the Notice on Lifting Price Restrictions on Overproduction and Self-sell Industrial Products, abolishing the 20% price limit on enterprise self-sell production materials.

Apart from the "dual-track system" for production material allocations and pricing, other areas also developed various "dual-track systems," such as the dual-track system for state bank loan interest rates and market interest rates and the dual-track system for official and market exchange rates.

Initially, the market track was small in scale and impact. However, as private enterprises developed and state-owned enterprises gained more autonomy, the situation changed. By the mid-1980s, the market track began to hold a significant position in total national economic activity, and arbitrage activities between the dual tracks became increasingly prominent.

In the past, there had been similar practices during the mass campaign for iron and steel production in the late 1950s and during the "three years of hardship" in the early 1960s.[56] These practices had generated debates in political and academic circles. For instance, economist Sun Yefang pointed out that if the planning part and the market part, or the lower price part and the higher price part, were separated, there would be no concerns about arbitrage between the different prices. However, when such price spreads continued to exist, the preferential price beneficiaries would sell lower-priced goods on the market to earn from the price spread. In contrast, those

[56] Wu Jinglian and Zhao Renwei, "Problems of the Dual-Track Pricing System in China's Industrial Sector," 1986, in *Works of Wu Jinglian* (Beijing: Central Compilation and Translation Press, 2013), vol. 1, pp. 326–327.

enterprises without preferential treatment would be squeezed. Sun pointed out that such a phenomenon would crop up everywhere and would be difficult to prevent.[57]

When transactions through the market reached a significant level in the mid-1980s, many profiteers engaged in arbitrage between the two tracks. This was the most severe social and economic consequence of the dual-track system. Within a short time, these profiteers could be worth several hundred thousand yuan, or they could even become millionaires. Their profits did not come from the trading of goods (buying controlled materials at a lower price and selling them at a higher price in the market) but rather from buying and selling official approvals for lower-priced resources. They would buy and sell official permissions for allocated materials, import quotas at the official exchange rate, and credit quotas for low-rate state bank loans. Their secret to success was their government backgrounds, thus they were often called government profiteers *(guandao)*.

When the adverse effects of the dual-track system became increasingly apparent, people began to see the limitations of the incremental reform strategy. Thus, in the mid-1980s the need for a comprehensive reform to establish a uniform market-economy system came to the forefront.

[57] Sun Yefang, "Comments on a Draft Report," 1962, *Selected Works of Sun Yefang* (Taiyuan: Shanxi People's Publishing House, 1984); Sun Yefang, "Outline of Speeches on Price Reform Presented at the Seminar on Issues of Socialist Reproduction,"1964, in Ibid., pp. 384–389; Sun Yefang, "Several Prerequisites for Improving the Overall Economic Balance," 1981, in Ibid., pp. 731–732.

Chapter 4
Exploring the Comprehensive Reforms of the 1980s

The incremental reforms in the 1980s led to growth of the private sector in the urban and rural areas and expanded markets. Coupled with the vitality stimulated by opening up to the outside world, there was increasing prosperity in the Chinese economy. However, the limitations of the reforms were becoming more apparent. First, the SOEs were struggling to survive under the mandatory plan even though they had ample economic resources. Second, the rising non-state sector, which was constrained by limited operating space, called for a change in the government's allocation of resources to establish a competitive market system. Third, the dual-track system led to an enormous squandering of resources and widespread corruption, resulting in resentment among the general public leading to calls to eliminate the sources of the corruption. Last, the second upsurge, beginning in early 1984, in opening to the outside world required further changes in the domestic economy.[1] These factors pointed to the need for comprehensive economic reforms to overcome the limitations of the "dominant state economy with supplemental market adjustments" and to establish pro-market reforms.

[1] From March 26 to April 6, 1984, the Party Central Committee and the State Council held a workshop on opening selected coastal cities. Based on a proposal by Deng Xiaoping, it was suggested that fourteen coastal port cities be opened. These included: Dalian, Qinhuangdao, Tianjin, Yantai, Qingdao, Lianyungang, Nantong, Shanghai, Ningbo, Wenzhou, Fuzhou, Guangzhou, Zhanjiang, and Beihai.

W. Jinglian, *China's Economic Reform*, Understanding China,
https://doi.org/10.1007/978-981-96-9607-9_4

4.1 A "Socialist Planned Commodity Economy" as the Reform Objective

Early on Chinese economists began to discuss the objectives of the reform. For example, in Chapter 3 we have introduced the late 1970s'and early 1980s' proposals by Chinese economists to introduce a commodity economy. Today, such a so-called "commodity economy" actually refers to a market economy.[2]

In May 1984, the State Council issued the Regulations on Expanding the Operational Autonomy of State-owned Industrial Enterprises (the so-called "ten regulations") that adopted a "decentralization and profit-sharing" approach rooted in market socialism to redress the poor performance of the SOEs. The ten regulations granted the SOEs limited autonomy in terms of operational planning, marketing, product pricing, purchases of inputs, use of funds, disposal of assets, organizational setup, labor management, wages and bonuses, and business cooperation. However, it was generally recognized that it would be difficult to implement these regulations unless the economic system were changed as well. Chinese economists argued that even if the regulations were to be implemented, SOE performance would not be improved without an overhaul of the entire economic system.

At the time, the Party Central Committee had already decided to hold the Third Plenary Session of the 12th Party Central Committee in December 1984 to launch the reforms of the economic system. On October 4, when meeting Chinese and foreign participants at a seminar on external economic cooperation, Deng Xiaoping announced that the upcoming Central Committee plenary session would launch a comprehensive reform. He said, "The first Third Plenary Session focused on rural reform, whereas this Third Plenary Session will focus on urban reform, including the reform of industry, commerce, and other sectors. We can say this will be a comprehensive reform. Although urban reform will be more complex than rural reform, since we have succeeded in the one, we are confident that we can succeed in the other."[3] The plenary session was to clarify the objectives and the main content of this comprehensive reform.

---

[2] The term "market economy" first became popular in the early 1900s. Prior to that time, Marx had called the economic system a "monetary economy," whereas Lenin, in his Russian way, called it a "commodity economy." In the twentieth century, neoclassical economics, with its target of effectively allocating resources, became more mainstream, and this led to the beginnings of a market economy. However, the Marxist and Leninist traditions still equated a market economy with capitalism. During China's early reform stage, the ideological constraints remained strong and pro-market economists had to use the term "commodity economy" instead of "market economy."

[3] Deng Xiaoping, "Our Magnificent Goal and Basic Policies," in *Selected Works of Deng Xiaoping* (Beijing: People's Publishing House, 1993), vol. 3, p. 78. On October 10, 1984, when meeting Chancellor Helmut Kohl of the Federal Republic of Germany, Deng Xiaoping again stated: "We will hold the Third Plenary Session of the 12th Party Central Committee in a few days. The last Central Committee's Third Plenary Session focused on rural reform. This time, the plenary session will focus on urban reform, including industry, commerce, and other sectors. Therefore, it can be called an overall reform. … After the decision by the upcoming plenary session is published, people will see that our ambition is comprehensive reform." See Deng Xiaoping, "We Regard Reform as a Revolution," 1984, *Selected Works of Deng Xiaoping,* vol. 3, p. 81.

In June 1984, the Central Committee had set up a group to draft the decision to be presented at the forthcoming plenary session. Within about a month, the group came up with an outline. However, given it had been decided to maintain the dominant role of the planned economy, with market adjustments playing only a supplemental role, the outline failed to satisfy the reformist leaders. When meeting the drafting group at the end of July in Beidaihe, Hu Yaobang expressed dissatisfaction with the draft. He thereupon reorganized the group and appointed Lin Jianqing as group leader and Zheng Lijian and Gong Yuzhi as new team members.[4]

Meanwhile, in accordance with a request by Premier Zhao Ziyang, Ma Hong, at the time president of the Chinese Academy of Social Sciences, organized a group to write a paper repudiating any criticisms of a commodity economy. The paper, penned by Zhou Shulian, Zhang Zhuoyuan, and Wu Jinglian, was sent to several veteran leaders to test the waters.[5] To the surprise of Zhao Ziyang and the paper's authors who had expected there would be objections, the veteran leaders actually praised the paper. Upon receiving the positive feedback, Zhao Ziyang wrote to Politburo Standing Committee members Hu Yaobang, Deng Xiaoping, Chen Yun, and Li Xiannian, seeking their advice on three issues regarding reform of the economic system.[6] In his letter, Zhao first reaffirmed a statement in the Resolution on Certain Questions in the History of Our Party since the Founding of the People's Republic of China (adopted at the Sixth Plenary Session of the 11th Party Central Committee in 1981), i.e., China must implement a planned economy based on public ownership but, at the same time, bringing into play the supplemental role of market adjustments. Zhao reiterated that China was characterized by a planned economy, not a market economy. After a series of complex arguments, he concluded: "The socialist economy is a planned commodity economy based on public ownership. The plan must be realized through the law of value, and the law of value is to serve the plan. Therefore, the slogan 'the plan is primary, and the law of value is secondary' is imprecise and should no longer be used." On September 11 and 12, Deng Xiaoping and Chen Yun provided written clearance for Zhao's letter. Even though in the letter Zhao had used the "plan" as a restrictive clause to accompany expression of the reform objective, the letter remained focused on a commodity economy. From this point on, preparation for the decision to be adopted at the Third Plenary Session of the 12th Party Central Committee was based on this new reform objective.[7]

---

[4] Wu Jinglian and Xie Chuntao, "The Debate on a Planned Economy vs. a Market Economy," 1998, in *Works of Wu Jinglian* (Beijing: Central Compilation and Translation Press, 1993), vol. 1, p. 199.

[5] The paper was later published under the title, "A Further Exploration into a Commodity Economy in Our Socialist Country," *Economic Research*, no. 12 (1984).

[6] Party Literature Research Center, *Selected Works Since the 12th Party Congress* (Beijing: People's Publishing House, 1985), vol. 2, pp. 533–538. In this collection, Zhao's letter is entitled "Comments on Three Issues in the Reform of the Economic System."

[7] Wu Jinglian and Xie Chuntao, "The Debate on a Planned Economy vs. a Market Economy," p. 199. Also see Ma Ya, "The Collaboration and Split Between Ma Hong and Zhao Ziyang during the Reform Process," *Ming Pao*, October 13, 2008.

In October 1984, the Third Plenary Session of the 12th Party Central Committee adopted the Decision on Reform of the Economic System, which officially set the goals of the reform and launched the comprehensive reform efforts.

The most important part of this decision was the goal of establishing a "socialist market economy": "In the reform of the planning system, it is necessary, first of all, to discard the traditional idea of pitting the planned economy *against* the commodity economy. We should clearly understand that the socialist planned economy is a planned commodity economy based on public ownership, in which the law of value must be consciously followed and applied. The full development of a commodity economy is an indispensable stage in the economic growth of society and a prerequisite for our economic modernization. It is the only way to invigorate our economy and prompt enterprises to raise their efficiency, carry out flexible operations, and promptly adapt themselves to the complex and changing social demands."

The decision further emphasized the need to implement the following three principles to advance the development of the commodity economy. First, "the key to restructuring the national economy, with the focus on the urban economy, is invigoration of enterprises, particularly the large and medium-sized enterprises owned by the whole people." Second, "as the decision-making power of enterprises grows, pricing will be increasingly important in regulating their production and operation. It is therefore all the more urgent to establish a rational system of pricing. ... The reform of the price system is the key to the reform of the entire economic structure." Third, "shared development of various economic types and operational modes is our long-term principle and an imperative for advancing socialism ... reforming, on the premise of adherence to the socialist system, a series of interrelated links and aspects of the relations of production and the superstructure that are not suited to the development of the forces of production. As a form of self-improvement and development of the socialist system, this reform is to be carried out under Party and government leadership in a planned, systematic, and methodical way."

Although ambiguous about certain concepts due to the ideological constraints, this decision was essential in establishing the reform objective, that is, a "socialist planned commodity economy" and in expanding the space for market-oriented reforms. Deng Xiaoping spoke highly of this important Party document, saying, "the forthcoming Third Plenary Session of the Twelfth Central Committee will go down in Chinese history as a very important event,"[8] adding: "What is socialism and what is Marxism? We were not quite clear about this in the past. Marxism attaches the utmost importance to developing the productive forces. ...The document on reform of the economic structure is a good one, because it explains what socialism is in terms never used by the founders of Marxism-Leninism. There are some new theories. I think it has clarified things."[9] He praised the decision for establishing a "political economy

[8] Deng Xiaoping, "Our Magnificent Goal and Basic Policies," p. 78.

[9] Deng Xiaoping, "Building a Socialism with a Specifically Chinese Characteristic," 1984, in *Selected Works of Deng Xiaoping*, vol. 3, p. 63.

that integrates the fundamental tenets of Marxism with the practice of socialism in China."[10]

The decision played an essential role in emancipating the minds of cadres. As a result, leaders at various levels of government became more willing to overcome the constraints of the rigid institutions in favor of reform. Backed by this policy document, local markets became more vibrant, the economy grew further, and people's livelihoods registered noticeable improvements. The following statistics demonstrate the achievements.

- In the five years from 1979 to 1983, GDP at constant prices grew by 8.05 percent per annum.
- In the next five years, from 1984 to 1988, GDP at constant prices expanded by 12.07 percent per annum.
- In 1979–83, inflation-adjusted per capita disposable income in the urban areas increased by 7.18 percent per annum, and inflation-adjusted per capita net income of rural households shot up by 17.03 percent per annum.
- In 1984–88, inflation-adjusted per capita income maintained relatively high growth rates. It grew by 5.02 percent per annum in the urban areas and by 7.19 percent per annum in the rural areas[11]

4.2 Deepening the Understanding of a Market Economy and Experimenting with a Master Plan for Reform

Although the Third Plenary Session of the 12th Party Central Committee established a socialist commodity economy as the reform objective and pointed out that the reform should aim to increase enterprise profits and allow prices to reflect market demand and supply, the session did not elaborate on the mechanisms of a market economy. Nor did this Party meeting offer a specific route to achieve the reform objective. In addition, it would be impossible to carry out a comprehensive reform without answering questions about the mechanisms of the reform and how to achieve its aims. Therefore, in 1985, many government agencies and research institutes put more resources into further studying the Chinese economy and designing a systematic reform program. The following are the four most important events that took place in that year.

The first event was a joint study project on the Chinese economy organized by the Chinese government and the World Bank, which resulted in the influential World Bank report "China, Long-Term Development Issues and Options."

In 1984, in response to a request from Deng Xiaoping, the World Bank sent a large team of international experts to China, led by Dr. Edwin Lim, chief economist

[10] Deng Xiaoping, "Speech at the Third Plenary Session of the Central Advisory Commission of the Communist Party of China," 1984, in ibid., pp. 83, 91.

[11] *China Statistical Yearbook* (multiple years), at http://data.stats.gov.cn.

for the China Program, and senior economist Dr. Adrian Wood.[12] Supported by a Chinese counterpart team, the group conducted a comprehensive study of the Chinese economy, addressing the main development issues that China would face during the next twenty years. In 1985 the team issued its main report, "China, Long-Term Development Issues and Options" (with six annex volumes, on education, agriculture, the energy sector, the economic model and projections, the economic structure in international perspective, and the transportation sector). The report, in comparing the experiences of various other countries, analyzes the main issues that China would face in the future. Based on these studies, the team proposed options for China to achieve its development goal of quadrupling GNP by the end of the twentieth century. China's leaders attached great importance to this report. In addition to reading the report themselves, they also required that the relevant officials study it. This cooperation between China and the World Bank helped expand the horizons of Chinese economists and improve the government's decision-making capabilities.

The second event was preparation of a master plan, drafted by experts, for the economic reforms—the first such blueprint in China.

Prior to 1985, the proposals for economic reforms described a new system in broad-line sketches. They used the language commonly found in Party and government documents and were imprecise about both the involved technical and economic policy issues. In May 1985, Guo Shuqing, Liu Jirui, and Qiu Shufang, three graduate students trained in modern economics at the Chinese Academy of Social Sciences, wrote to the State Council leaders, arguing that "comprehensive reform is a huge endeavor to engineering a social system. Without clearly set objectives and coordinated reform measures, it will be impossible for our country to move forward." They proposed "preparing and implementing a scientifically prepared overarching program."[13] Thereupon, with Premier Zhao Ziyang's support, the State Commission for Restructuring the Economic System appointed a group of nine young economists, including Guo Shuqing, Lou Jiwei, and Liu Jirui, to prepare the Outline of a Master Plan for Reform of the Economic System (first draft)."[14] The draft report proposed a two-phase approach. The first phase would focus on commodity-market price reform, accompanied by enterprise, fiscal and tax, and financial system reforms. It also

---

[12] On May 26, 1983, when meeting with World Bank President Tom Clausen, Deng Xiaoping told him that China had decided to launch a development program to quadruple total industrial and agricultural outputs from 1980 to 2000. He also said that he had found the World Bank's first China report interesting and useful. Accordingly, he proposed that the World Bank undertake another study to address some key development issues that China would face during the next twenty years, with the goal primarily to provide alternative options based on international experience. See Edwin Lim, "Preface: Fifty Economists Look at Thirty Years of Reform and Opening," in *Fifty Economists Look at Thirty Years of Reform and Opening*, comp. Wu Jinglian et al. (Beijing: Economic Press, 2008), p. 35.

[13] Guo Shuqing, Liu Jirui, and Qiu Shufang, "Comprehensive Reform Urgently Needs Overall Planning: A Critical Issue for Our Reform," *Comparative Economic and Social Studies*, no. 1 (1985).

[14] Guo Shuqing, Lou Jiwei, and Liu Jirui, "Study on Overall Planning for Systemic Reforms," in *Overall Design of China's Economic Reform*, ed. Wu Jinglian et al. (Beijing: China Prospect Publishing House, 1988), pp. 25–47.

included a proposal to adopt a central banking system. The second phase would establish well-functioning factors markets and eliminate the mandatory plan in order to complete the transition from a planned economy to a commodity economy. This was the first such systematic economic design in the history of China's economic reforms.

The third event was the International Symposium on Macroeconomic Management and Reform (the Bashanlun Conference), held in September 1985 and jointly sponsored by the State Commission for Restructuring the Economic System and the Chinese Academy of Social Sciences, with assistance from the World Bank. Several well-known international and Chinese experts participated in the symposium and put forward recommendations regarding major reform issues.[15] The symposium is considered a significant milestone in the process of reform in China.

During the symposium, there were heated discussions on the various options for the reform objective. Hungarian economist Janós Kornai's classification of different economic systems became a central topic in the discussions.[16] The international experts expanded upon Kornai's analysis of the advantages of "market adjustments with macroeconomic management." The Chinese economists who had been trained in modern economics also agreed with Kornai, and in the discussions they determined that "market adjustments with macroeconomic management" should be the primary reform objective.

Another topic eliciting lively discussions was the identification of optimal macroeconomic policies for the transition. In the early Chinese debates, the mainstream view considered that inflation is beneficial to economic development. But the participants at the symposium studied the economic situation at the time, and together with the international experts, who represented various different economic schools, determined that China should undertake contractionary fiscal, financial, and distribution

[15] The international participants included James Tobin, mastermind of Keynesian monetary economics; Sir Alexander K. Cairncross, Oxford University professor and former UK minister for economic affairs; Janós Kornai, Hungarian economist; Włodzimierz Bus, Polish economist; and Otmar Emminger, former president of the Deutsche Bundesbank. The main participants from Chinese government agencies were Xue Muqiao, An Zhiwen, Ma Hong, Liao Jili, Xiang Huaicheng, and Yang Qixin, and the participating economists included Liu Guogang, Dai Yuanchen, Zhou Shulian, Wu Jinglian, Zhang Zhuoyuan, Zhao Renwei, Chen Jiyuan, Lou Jiwei, Guo Shuqing, and Tian Yuan.

[16] Kornai identified two main types of economic systems: Type I, Bureaucratic coordination, and Type II, Market coordination. According to Kornai, Type I is further divided into Type IA, Direct bureaucratic coordination, and Type IB, Indirect bureaucratic coordination. Type II is also divided into two subgroups: Type IIA, Free market coordination, and Type IIB, Market coordination with macroeconomic management. Kornai pointed out that the economic reforms in the socialist countries opted for either Type IB or Type IIB. But the Hungarian reform did not achieve the expected results because for a long time it had become bogged down in indirect bureaucratic coordination (Type IB), during which time enterprises continued to benefit from soft budgetary constraints and state protection. See Guo Shuqing and Zhao Renwei, "International Symposium on Macroeconomic Management, Subject Report (1): Target Model and Transition Steps," in *Selected Speeches Presented at the International Symposium on Macroeconomic Management and Reform*, comp. China Society of Economic Reform (Beijing: Economic Daily Press, 1986), pp. 16–23.

reform policies to cope with the economic overheating and the inflation during the transition. Most of the Chinese scholars agreed with this.

In 1985, as a consensus was reached among the academics and the government officials, the national leadership adopted prudent macroeconomic policies to create a more enabling environment during the initial phase of the economic reforms under the Seventh Five-year Plan (1986–90).[17]

The fourth event was adoption of specific goals for China's economic reforms by the National Party Congress.

The National Party Conference, held at the end of September 1985, passed the Proposal on the Seventh Five-year Socioeconomic Development Plan (1986–90).[18] The document, incorporating the comments from the economists during their review of the draft proposal,[19] points out that the new socialist-economy system would have three mutually related goals. The first goal was to turn "enterprises, especially those under whole-people ownership, into socialist commodity producers with relative independence and operational autonomy, and responsible for their profits and losses." The second goal was to further develop the commodity market, "opening and developing funding and technology markets and gradually improving the market system." The third goal was to "gradually transition from direct state control of enterprises to indirect state control of enterprises, mainly using economic and legal means with necessary administrative measures to control and adjust the economy." The proposal states that to achieve these goals "coordinated reforms should be carried out regarding the planning, price, fiscal, financial, and labor and wage systems. … to

[17] In its section on the principles of social development, the CCP Proposal on the Seventh Five-year Socioeconomic Development Plan (1986–90), identifies two areas to be upheld: the first is "to uphold reform as the top priority and make reform and economic construction mutually adaptative and facilitating. Fundamentally, reform serves economic construction. But at present, arrangements for economic construction should be conducive to the implementation of reform. … To ensure successful reform, the economic growth rate should be set rationally. Reckless races for faster output and production increases should be avoided to prevent economic stress and chaos and to create a favorable economic environment for reform." The second is to "to uphold balanced aggregate demand and supply so that accumulation and consumption are proportional to each other. … Government finance, banking credit, materials supply, and foreign exchange should be balanced, and an equilibrium among the sectors should be maintained. This is a prerogative for coordinated economic relationships, economic stability, and smooth reform implementation" ("The Proposal on the Seventh Five-year Economic and Social Development Plan," in Central Party Literature Research Center, comp., *Selected Important Documents since the 12th Party Congress* (Beijing: People's Publishing House, 1986), p. 798.

[18] Article 12 of the Constitution of the Communist Party of China stipulates that central and local Party committees may convene Party representative conferences to discuss and timely decide on major issues. Accordingly, on October 20, 1984, the Third Plenary Session of the 12th Party Central Committee decided to hold a National Party Conference in September 1985.

[19] Wu Jinglian, "Separated Sectoral Reforms or Coordinated Comprehensive Reforms," in *Works of Wu Jinglian* (Taiyuan: Shanxi People's Publishing House, 1989), pp. 435–436. This article first appeared in the Secretariat of the Workshops, comp., *Bulletin of the Party Central Committee and State Council Workshops on the Seventh Five-year Plan (Fifth Draft)*, no. 1, group 7.

lay a foundation for a vibrant socialist economy with Chinese characteristics" within the period of the Seventh Five-year Plan (1986–90) or a more extended period.[20]

This 12th Party Congress decision indicates that the national leadership had basically agreed to establish a "market economy with macroeconomic management," i.e., Kornai's Type IIB, as the reform objective.

4.3 The Aborted 1986 Plan for Coordinated Reforms

In line with the Decision on the Reform of the Economic System of the Third Plenary Session of the 12th Party Central Committee and the Proposal on the Seventh Five-year Socioeconomic Development Plan (1986–90) of the National Party Conference, in early 1986 Premier Zhao Ziyang, who was concurrently head of the Party Central Committee's Finance and Economy Leading Group, announced that work in 1986 should aim to improve macroeconomic management while also strengthening macroeconomic control and to improve supply while also curbing demand. Meanwhile, preparatory work was to be carried out so that the reforms would be able to take a decisive step forward in 1987.[21]

The State Council undertook a series of steps to prepare for the comprehensive reforms in 1986.

At the beginning of 1986, the State Council held extensive briefings on the economic situation and ideas for further reforms. Economists from different advisory institutions participated in these discussions and proposed various proposals. Wang Xiaoqiang and Song Guoqing presented a proposal for enterprise contracting and leasing reform; Xu Jingan presented a proposal for comprehensive price reform; Wu Jinglian, Lou Jiwei, Zhou Xiaochuan, and Li Jiange presented a proposal for interlinked reforms of enterprise, market, and macroeconomic regulation; and Hua Sheng presented a proposal to reform management responsibility for enterprise assets. However, after carefully listening to the briefings, Premier Zhao pointed out that, to varying degrees, the proposals all lacked feasibility. As a result, it was not expected that any significant reforms would take place in the near future.[22]

Two months later, at a State Council executive meeting on March 13 and then at a meeting of the Party Central Committee's Finance and Economy Leading Group

---

[20] Central Party Literature Research Center, comp., *Selected Important Documents since the 12th Party Congress*, vol. 2, p. 821.

[21] Zhao Ziyang, "The Current Economic Situation and This Year's Economic Tasks: Speech at the National Economic Work Conference," January 13, 1986.

[22] Institute of Economic System Reform, "Analysis of the Current Economic Situation and Reform Strategies for the First Two Years of the Seventh Five-year Plan Period: Summary of the Ninth Workshop on the National Economy," *Economic Development and System Reform*, no. 3 (1986); *China: Development and Reform, 1986* (Chengdu: Sichuan People's Publishing House, 1987); Institute of Economic System Reform and Beijing Youth Economic Society Explorers' Voice, *Selected Reports of the Joint Workshops on Economic Reform and Social Development* (Chengdu: Sichuan People's Publishing House, 1988).

on March 15, Zhao Ziyang unexpectedly announced a plan to introduce interlinking reforms of the price, taxation, and fiscal systems in 1987. According to Zhao, the various economic challenges were "mainly due to the stalemate between the old and the new systems, leading to frequent tensions and conflicts. … [We] should not let this situation drag on, and major steps should be undertaken in 1987 and 1988. Regarding the market system and indirect adjustments of the macroeconomy, the measures should be bolder so as to create favorable conditions for enterprises to become truly responsible for profits and losses and to compete on an even playing field. … Specifically, when preparing for next year's reforms, three areas are to be considered: the price, taxation, and fiscal systems. Reforms in these three areas are interrelated. …. Price system reform is the key, and the other reforms should revolve around this reform."[23]

Based on the decision of the State Council and the Party Central Committee's Finance and Economy Leading Group, a review group led by Vice Premier Tian Jiyun was set up to study the plans to reform the economic system. In addition, a "reform planning office" (a task team) was set up under the review group.[24] Based on a request from Zhao Ziyang, the task team, composed of officials in various State Council agencies as well as economists, was assigned to design an interlinked reform plan for the initial phase of the Seventh Five-year Plan period.

Despite differing views within government and academic circles regarding the interlinked price, taxation, and fiscal systems reforms,[25] the program design proceeded based on the schedule set by the State Council. In August, the review group submitted an interlinked reform program to the State Council and the Party Central Committee Finance and Economy Leading Group, drafted by the reform

---

[23] Zhao Ziyang, "Speech at the State Council Executive Meeting, March 13, 1986" (printout) and "Speech at the Party Central Committee Finance and Economy Leading Group Meeting, March 15, 1986" (printout).

[24] The office director was Gao Shangquan, vice chairman of the State Commission for Restructuring the Economic System, and the deputy directors included Yang Qixian and Fu Fengxiang, two commissioners on the State Commission for Restructuring the Economic System, Wu Jinglian, executive director of the State Council Development Research Center, and Jiang Xi, vice minister of Commerce.

[25] For instance, in an address to a April 25, 1986, Peking University seminar to celebrate the anniversary of the May Fourth movement, Professor Li Yining of Peking University famously stated: "If China's reform fails, it will likely be due to the failure of the price reform; if the reform succeeds, it will be the result of a successful ownership reform" (Li Yining, "A Basic Line of Thought about Economic Reform, Presented to the Peking University Seminar on the Ma -Fourth Movement on April 25, 1986," in *Thoughts on China's Economic Reform* [Beijing: China Prospect Publishing House, 1989], p. 3); Chen Yizi, director of the System Reform Institute of the State Commission for Restructuring the Economic System, recalls in his memoirs that "the program of interlinked price, taxation, and fiscal reforms, put forward by Wu Jinglian and Zhou Xiaochuan, was not practical." He voiced his opposition in a report on his May 1986 study tour to Hungary and Yugoslavia and when meeting Zhao Ziyang in June. According to Chen, Zhao Ziyang "highly praised his view, which cooled down enthusiasm for the interlinked reforms." See China Economic System Reform Institute, comp., *Challenging Explorations: Observations on the Reforms in Hungary and Yugoslavia* (Beijing: Economy and Management Publishing House, 1987), pp. 1–30; *Chen Yizi's Memoirs* (Hong Kong: New Century Media & Consulting Co. Ltd., 2013), pp. 347, 351–352.

planning office. The program placed a priority on price, taxation, fiscal, financial, and trade system reforms. The proposed price reform, similar to that in Czechoslovakia in 1967–68, would adjust prices based on specific calculations, and then prices would be liberalized within one to two years. The dual tracks for pricing the main means of production would be consolidated into one single track by the middle of the Five-year Plan period. Regarding the fiscal and tax reforms, the plan proposed ending the "eating from different pots" approach (the fiscal contracting system) and adopting a tax-sharing system and a value-added tax.[26]

The State Council executive meeting and the Party Central Committee Finance and Economy Leading Group accepted the interlinked reform program. Then, on September 13, 1986, the Leading Group briefed Deng Xiaoping, whereupon Deng spoke highly of the program and pushed for its implementation.[27]

At the briefing, Deng Xiaoping also raised the need for political system reform. He said: "Whenever we move a step forward in economic reform, we are made keenly aware of the need to change the political structure. If we fail to do that, we shall be unable to preserve the gains we have made in the economic reform and to build on them, the growth of the productive forces will be stunted, and our drive for modernization will be impeded."[28] At Deng's request, a central leading group on political system reform headed by Zhao Ziyang was set up.

Although the idea of a "price, tax, and fiscal reform package" sparked interest both inside and outside the Party, the head of the State Council pushed for interlinked reforms to enable enterprises to compete under similar conditions and to "allow the new economic system to become the driving force." But for reasons still unknown, Zhao changed his mind in the fall of 1986 and instructed replacing the interlinked reform program with enterprise contracting.[29] The completed program for interlinked reforms was shelved, and instead a SOE contracting system was implemented nationwide. Macroeconomic policy became expansionary to order to achieve high GDP growth.

---

[26] Lou Jiwei, Xia Jie, and Liu Liqun, "Thoughts on Economic Models and Fiscal and Tax Reforms," 1986, and Lou Jiwei and Liu Liqun, "Suggestions on Fiscal Reforms to Deal with Deficits," 1986, in *Overall Design of China's Economic Reform*, ed. Wu Jinglian et al., pp. 111–151.

[27] Wu Jinglian, *Contemporary Chinese Economic Reform,* 1999 (Beijing: CITIC Publishing House, 2017), p. 90.

[28] Deng Xiaoping, "Remarks on the Domestic Economic Situation," 1986; "Help the People Understand the Importance of Rule of Law," 1986; and "On Reform of the Political Structure," 1986—all in *Selected Works of Deng Xiaoping* vol. 3, pp. 160, 163–164, 176–180.

[29] Zhao Ziyang, "Giving Up the Linked-Reform Program of Price, Tax, and Fiscal Systems and Carrying Out an Operational Contracting System: Comments Made after Yang Peixin's Briefing on Schneider's Opinion" (printout).

4.4 The Late 1980s: A Significant Debate, Economic Turbulence, and the Waning of Reform

As the interlinked price, tax, and fiscal reforms were being shelved, a heated debate erupted among reformers on the future reform strategy and tactics and on the relationship among economic growth, macroeconomic stability, and reform. Two different strategies emerged from this debate. The first strategy prioritized SOE contracting, which was to be accompanied by an expansionary macroeconomic policy to create a favorable business environment for high-speed growth. The second strategy prioritized price liberalization and a competitive market to create an environment for fair competition in the emerging non-state sector (including rural family farms and urban private businesses). This strategy advocated an appropriately tightened monetary policy to create an enabling macroeconomic environment for the price reform, even though, in the short run, such a strategy would slow down economic growth.

The main arguments favoring each strategy are as follows:

The first strategy. The economists believed that price reforms would only create an enabling environment for developing a commodity economy. Only enterprise reform could address interest, responsibility, and motivation problems.

Peking University professor Li Yining pointed out, "Price reform serves mainly to provide the economic reforms with a favorable environment for developing the commodity economy. In contrast, an ownership or enterprise ownership reform can truly deal with the problems of interest, responsibility, incentives, and motivation."[30] Li maintained that the economy was facing a disequilibrium and, "under these circumstances, price readjustments can only have limited effects. It is impractical to expect price reforms to achieve the desired economic relationships. Therefore, the only option for China is to put aside the price reforms and to first carry out an ownership reform."[31] He looked forward to price reform after fifteen years, when the ownership reform will have been completed.[32] Nevertheless, Professor Li stressed that his idea of ownership reform did not imply changing the public ownership of the SOEs. Rather, it would combine the practice of contracting with a joint-stock model. Enterprises could first implement a contracting system and then become joint-stock companies, or vice versa. Alternatively, enterprises could adopt both forms simultaneously or become joint-stock companies without implementing contracting practices. Professor Li hoped that these steps would turn the SOEs into "publicly owned firms truly responsible for their own profits and losses."[33]

Professor Li believed that prices should not be liberalized in an environment of disequilibrium where enterprises could not operate independently and were not responsible for profits and losses. He pointed out: "In such a situation, price reform

[30] Li Yining, "A Basic Line of Thought about Economic Reform," p. 3.

[31] "Accelerating Reform of Public Ownership," *Financial News*, January 18, 1988.

[32] "Li Yining Predicts China Inevitably Will Go for a Joint-stock System," *Theoretical News*, November 3, 1986.

[33] "Deepening Reform Should Focus on Changing the Forms of Public Ownership: A Talk with the Renowned Economist Li Yining," *Financial News*, December 3, 1987.

will merely be 'price ratio reversion,' i.e., shortly after prices are readjusted, they will return to their previous relationships, but the overall price levels will go up. This will not be helpful to improve resource allocations."[34]

The second strategy. The dual-track model of reforming economic institutions and prices would play a positive role both economically and politically and, therefore, should not be changed too hastily.

Hua Sheng, He Jiacheng, and several other young economists argued that the dual-track system was a great innovation in China's economic reform. It provided a way to reform prices with Chinese characteristics and even to achieve a complete reform.[35] In their opinion, the dual-track system was altering the dynamics of the Chinese economy, which was becoming increasingly constrained by market forces. Because the system was already contributing to increased supplies and market activities, it was unnecessary to change it prematurely. The problem was with the microeconomic base (or the microeconomic organizations). In other words, enterprise restructuring was needed. The young economists believed that there were many defects in an approach that changed state-sector–dominated property relationships by developing multiple ownership types. They instead recommended contracting out management of SOE assets to managers (called an "enterprise assets management contracting system").[36]

A study by the influential Institute of Economic System Reform under the State Commission for Restructuring the Economic System argued, based on a socioeconomic perspective, in favor of the role of the dual-track system. The study report stated: "The dual-track system has a mechanism for allocating resources by administrative powers. Under certain conditions, monetizing the vouchers can lead to monetizing administrative powers, i.e., power to allocate vouchers becomes power to allocate money. In other words, these powers can be measured by money. … This corrosive behavior is economically rational. As long as voucher monetization plays its role and the powers derived from the planning system are somewhat contained, it is natural to use resource-allocation powers as a type of capital."[37]

The third argument: Contractionary fiscal and monetary policies would not be conducive to enterprise and economic growth.

The government had implemented inflation control measures in 1985–86. In 1986, as the overheated economy was cooling, for assorted reasons there were calls for expansionary macroeconomic policies. Starting from the second quarter of 1986, the

[34] Li Yining, *The Disequilibrium in the Chinese Economy* (Beijing: China Economic Times Publishing, 1990), p. 8.

[35] Hua Sheng, He Jiacheng, Jiang Yue, Gao Liang, and Zhang Shaojie, "The Road to Price Reform with Chinese Characteristics," *Economic Research*, no. 2 (1985).

[36] Hua Sheng, He Jiacheng, Zhang Xuejun, Luo Xiaopeng, Bian Yongzhuang et al., "Changes in the Functions of the Economy: Preliminary Thinking on Further Reform," and "Restructuring the Microeconomic Base: Updated Thinking on Further Reform," *Economic Research*, nos. 2 and 3 (1986).

[37] "Research Report of the China Institute for Economic System Reform," 1986, in *Prices: The Role of the Dual-Track System and the Direction of Further Reforms*. PUBLICATION INFO???

government significantly relaxed credit controls. In 1987, a proposition was introduced arguing that "inflation is conducive to economic growth," i.e., price increases are unavoidable and proper and mild inflation is conducive, rather than harmful. Therefore, tightening policies to stabilize the economy were unnecessary, and the primary task of monetary policy was to support higher economic growth.[38]

Influenced by the "harmless and helpful inflation" view, government decision-makers followed up on this proposition.[39] From the end of 1984 to the beginning of 1985 as the economy was overheating, the head of the State Council favored tightening macroeconomic policies to control the rampant expansion of aggregate demand. However, after GDP registered zero growth in February 1986, he decided to relax controls on bank lending to support economic growth. As a result, money supply grew rapidly beginning in the second quarter of 1986. In the four years from 1984 to 1987, GNP grew by 11.6 percent per annum, fixed-asset investments rose by 26.3 percent per annum, the monetary income of urban and rural residents increased by 27.5 percent per annum, and money supply (M0) expanded by 28.7 percent per annum. By the fourth quarter of 1987, inflation was again rearing its head.

This situation aroused concern among academics. Within the decision-making bodies, differing views were raised. For instance, at a January 1988 Politburo meeting, Tian Jiyun, a Politburo member and a vice premier, explicitly expressed concerns about "demand greatly exceeding supply" and "uncontrollable price surges," as well as about promoting a contract responsibility system as the main reform measure.[40] However, the main Party and government leaders, influenced by the "harmless inflation" theory, believed that the partial price increases were not due to overall supply and demand, but rather they were merely due to localized issues in agricultural production. Consequently, the 1988 No. 1 Party Document, unlike the earlier No. 1 documents, did not focus on agriculture. Instead, the document focused on explaining the macroeconomic situation. It stressed that the macroeconomy in 1987 was in good shape, with effective growth and without the threat of inflation.

Although there were various views opposing the former reform strategy, Party and government leaders decided to adopt it and to reject the latter strategies.

After ending the interlinked price, tax, and fiscal reforms, Zhao Ziyang, the primary Party and government leader at the time, gave up on the idea of establishing a competitive market system and instead, he turned to support an economic model that combined the state plan (mainly an indirect plan implemented through a

[38] For related discussions, see Xu Xuehan, Zhao Xiaomin, Chen DongqI, Wang Shaofei, Yang Peixin, and Li Chengrui, "Monetary and Price Stabilization: A Discussion on our Country's Inflation," *Finance and Trade Economics*, no. 3 (1988).

[39] Yu Xiu'e and Ren Zhijiang, "Thoughts on the Failure of the 1988 Rushed Price Reform and Its Revelations," *Journal of the Party School of the CCP Central Committee*, no. 3 (2011).

[40] Ding Longjia, "Tian Jiyun on Inflation in 1988," *Yanhuang chunqiu*, no. 2 (2012). According to this article, "Among the economists, quite a few were deeply concerned and put forward proposals to control inflation. Others maintained that mild inflation would not be harmful. This latter view influenced the decision-makers." Wu Jinglian had several times heard Tian Jiyun talk about his views against the inflationary policy and the SOE contracting rollout at formal meetings and in private conversations in 1986–88.

selective industrial policy) with the market. In March–May 1987, the State Planning Commission and the State Commission for Restructuring the Economic System produced several documents related to the design of such an economic system, including the "Minutes of the Seminar on the Relationship between Plan and Market," "Twelve Viewpoints on Reform of the Planning System," and "Basic Thinking about Combining the Plan and the Market."[41] These documents suggested that "For a long time to come, it will be difficult to have a full-fledged means-of-production market, and it will be even more difficult to have well-developed funding and other markets. Under these circumstances, a market adjustment can only be applied within a specific scope and to a certain degree, and it cannot direct all economic activities in the society. In the future, even when the markets are fully developed, necessary adjustments by the plan and state intervention will be indispensable." The documents proposed a slow blending of the plan and the market. This model, first put forward by the research arm of the State Planning Commission at its National Seminar on Macroeconomic Management in 1986, is referred to as "the state adjusts the market; the market guides the enterprises," or "the state controls the market; the market leads the enterprises."[42]

These recommendations, along with suggestions from the State Council Development Research Center modeled on Japan's and South Korea's examples to formulate and implement selective industrial policies, were approved by Zhao Ziyang. He decided that the model of "state regulation of the market, with the market guiding enterprises" would become the target model for China's economic system reform. In October 1987, he announced in his political report to the 13th National Congress of the Communist Party of China that the mechanism for a planned socialist commodity economy should, in general, be "state regulation of the market, with the market guiding enterprises."[43] The state would use economic, legal, and necessary administrative means to adjust market supply and demand, to create a suitable economic and social environment, and thus to guide enterprises in their business decisions."[44] Under this economic mechanism, an indirect state plan, in the form of an industrial policy, will dominate, and the market will be subject to government control.

Hence, the reform objective was reversed from "market coordination with macroeconomic management" (i.e., Kornai's Type IIB) back to a model with strong elements of a state-dominated economy and "indirect bureaucatic coordination" (Type IB, as described by Kornai).

In this context, after the former reform strategy became mainstream, some economists were still arguing in favor of the latter. They advocated slowing down the growth rate, implementing price reforms, and more rapidly forming a competitive

[41] Fang Weizhong, comp., *Marching Through Storms: Chronicles of China's Development and Reform, 1977–89*, vol. 10 (1987), unpublished draft dated 2004, pp. 81–86, 158–184.

[42] Gui Shiyong, comp., *China's Macroeconomic Management* (Beijing: China Economic Publishing House, 1987), pp. 18–26, 68–81, 235–255, 361–368.

[43] See Fang Weizhong, *Marching Through Storms*, vol. 10 (1987), pp. 91–112.

[44] Zhao Ziyang, "Advance Along the Road of Socialism with Chinese Characteristics: Report to the 13th National CCP Congress," October 25, 1987.

market within a relatively relaxed macroeconomic environment. Veteran Chinese economists Xue Muqiao and Qian Jiaju, along with American economist Milton Friedman, supported this view. Xue Muqiao had consistently opposed using expansionary macroeconomic policies to achieve economic growth. In his words, this represented an "excess distribution of national income." Instead, he supported reforming the price system as soon as possible to let market mechanisms play their role. He repeatedly pointed out: "While the hikes in the Consumer Price Index in 1986 and 1987 did not appear to be high, just 6 percent or 7 percent, they were misleading. At the time, prices were semi-controlled and semi-liberalized. Administrative controls were used when the threat of price hikes intensified. Since price increases could not offset most excess money supply, hidden inflation occurred, leading to new price distortions. Energy and raw materials were in shortage, and their plan prices were controlled; meanwhile, negotiated prices skyrocketed. Profiteers, whether with an official identity or in a private capacity, took advantage of the chaotic pricing system and earned windfall profits. Market order was destroyed." Xue proposed "controlling the money supply and liberalizing prices": first, by taking time to contract aggregate demand, and then, by gradually liberalizing most prices so that the market can play its role and "the law of value can adjust the economy spontaneously."

Xue Muqiao was held in high regard, but after 1987, it was thought that his economic thinking was outdated and did not contain any fresh ideas. His judgment that national income had been excessively distributed was criticized several times for being nonscientific, and his proposal to "establish an enabling environment before reform" was considered unrealistic. His critics argued: "Without reform, how can a favorable environment be created?".[45]

At the April 1988 Plenary Session of the Chinese People's Political Consultative Conference, Qian Jiaju, another veteran economist, criticized how prices had been handled. He pointed out that, on the one hand, "price increases exceeded wage increases, causing dissatisfaction among workers. [On the other hand,] prices were irrational, reflecting neither value nor market demand and supply. Under the dual-track means of production prices, the negotiated price was several times higher than the plan-set price (the quoted price). Criminals can take advantage of this opportunity. They bypass the official authorization channels (hence "go through the backdoor"). They throw banquets for government officials and bribe them to gain access to materials at the quoted prices, which they then sell in the market for high markups, and thus they reap massive profits. Sometimes the agencies in charge conspire with the criminals to share the spoils. This is why it is difficult to improve the social atmosphere." Qian Jiaju also pointed out that the overheated investment in infrastructure and the excess money supply were obstacles to price reform and liberalization. He criticized "certain agencies' penchant for grandeur and quick results. It is outdated behavior and a sign of inertia to consider basic construction [infrastructure development] as the symbol and driver of economic development." Qian thus proposed reducing investment in basic construction to eliminate the budget deficits, using the

---

[45] *Xue Muqiao's Memoirs* (Tianjin: Tianjin Publishing House, 1996), pp. 411–418. In his memoirs, Xue provides a detailed description of the anti-inflation debate.

saved funding to support price reforms, "raising wages, and developing education, culture, public health, and science and technology." Because Qian Jiaju was speaking out about what many people were thinking, his 30-min speech received thirty-one rounds of applause from the delegates to the session.[46] However, this well-received and to-the-point speech was rebuked for being demagogic and for smearing the leadership of the Chinese Communist Party.[47]

In August–September 1988, Milton Friedman visited China. At the time, he submitted to Zhao Ziyang a memorandum, and he also met with Zhao in person. On both occasions, Friedman pointed out that because the prices of raw materials were kept artificially low, shortages, quota allocations based on government connections, and bribery were all inevitable. Stating that the dual-track pricing system was an open invitation to corruption and squandering, Friedman proposed controlling the growth of money to contain inflation and accelerating price liberalization but controlling wage increases to change the dual-track pricing system. He believed price and exchange-rate liberalization should be carried out as rapidly as possible.[48]

Friedman enjoyed a high-level reception in Beijing, but his recommendations did not receive the same attention.

The defects of extended short-term Keynesian policies in the West after World War II had led to a realization that using inflation to sustain prosperity was like quenching thirst with poison. Therefore, many countries had turned to money supply controls. The first country to adopt such a policy was the Federal Republic of Germany. In 1948, under the leadership of Ludwig Erhard (1897–1977), who was in charge of economic affairs, West Germany carried out a monetary reform, allowing the country to recover from the ruins of World War II within only a few years and sustaining development for the next twenty years or more. In the West, this was referred to as an "economic miracle." Friedman believed that Erhard's so-called economic miracle involved removing price and wage restrictions and allowing for free-market activities, while strictly controlling monetary aggregates.[49] During the 1955–73 period of rapid economic development, Japan controlled money supply to maintain price stability. The average annual increase in wholesale prices was maintained at 1.5 percent. Yoshio Suzuki, director of the Institute for Monetary and Economic Studies, Bank of Japan, pointed out that the stable general-market prices were an essential condition for Japan's rapid economic development during the period of its economic takeoff. Some

---

[46] Qian Jiaju, "Comments on Prices, Education, and Social Atmosphere," 1988, in *Voices of Overseas Travelers* (Hong Kong: Cosmos Books, 1992).

[47] Qian Jiaju, *From Pursuit to Disillusionment: A Biography of a Chinese Economist* (Taipei: China Times Co., 1993), p. 288.

[48] Milton Friedman, "Memorandum from Milton Friedman to Zhao Ziyang," 1988, in *Milton and Rose D. Friedman, Two Lucky People* (Chicago: University of Chicago Press, 1998), pp. 607–609; Chinese translation published as "Friedman's Recommendations on China's Economic Reform," *Reform*, no. (1988).

[49] Friedman, "Speeches During a Visit to China," in *Friedman on Inflation*, 1980; (Chinese translation by Yang Peixin. Beijing: Chinese Social Sciences Press, 1982), p. 33. Also see Ludwig Erhard, *Prosperity Through Competition* (Chinese translation by Zhu Shikang and Mu Jiaji. Beijing: Commercial Press, 1987).

countries adopted an inflationary policy, and their general price levels increased. If Japan had adopted such a policy, enterprises would not have been able to decide upon optimal resource allocations based on accurate price signals, and the country's economic returns would have decreased and its sustained growth would have become impossible.[50]

Unfortunately, China's national leaders did not accept these recommendations.

In the second half of the 1980s, the socioeconomic contradictions intensified due to the halt of reform and the excess money supply, as manifested by the following:

First, adoption of an expansionary monetary policy and large-scale investments to sustain high-speed growth inevitably led to excess money supply and runaway inflation.

In early May 1988, the Politburo Standing Committee, at General Secretary Zhao Ziyang's suggestion, decided to "storm the fort" of price and wage reforms to establish a market pricing system within the next five years. However, the opinions of some economists differed regarding the timing of such a reform. At a May 27–28 high-level meeting to discuss this decision, economist Liu Guoguang and this author pointed out that it was inappropriate to liberalize prices when expansionary macroeconomic policies were still in place because inflation would be certain to rear its head. We proposed implementing price reforms after the end of monetary expansion and after improvements in the macroeconomic environment. We opposed launching price and wage reforms ("storming the fort") under the existing macroeconomic conditions because (a) price increases in the agricultural sector in the fourth quarter of 1987 were spreading to other sectors, (b) transportation and means of production supply bottlenecks were becoming more severe, (c) sporadic panic buying was taking place, and (d) household savings registered negative growth in April. All these signs pointed to high inflationary pressures. If price reforms were announced without improving the macroeconomic conditions, expectations of widespread inflation would set off severe inflationary and economic fluctuations. Therefore, we recommended taking some time, e.g., three years, to improve the economic climate and control the growth of money supply. After improving the economic climate, most prices could be liberalized to allow market adjustments to play their role. But the leader presiding over the meeting refuted this view. He quoted a report by other economists about a study tour to several Latin American countries, including Brazil, which argued that the Latin American countries had continued to enjoy prosperity, even with inflation as high as a 1000 percent. He called for confidence in "storming the fort" to enact price reforms under high inflation and rapid growth.[51]

---

[50] Yoshio Suzuki, *Japan's Monetary Policy* (Chinese translation by Zhang Yunfang et al. Beijing: China Development Publishing House, 1995).

[51] In his memoirs, Chen Yizi, director of the System Reform Institute of the State Commission for Restructuring the Economic System at the time, confirms what took place at that meeting. See *Chen Yizi's Memoirs*, pp. 505–510.

In an article published in June, veteran economist Xue Muqiao pointed out that it was incorrect to push forward with the price reforms while the hidden inflation was already severe.[52] However, there was no direct response from the top leaders.

Developments during the next three months were completely contrary to the leaders' optimistic expectations. After the Politburo officially announced price/wage reforms, inflation took off, and bank runs and panic buying spread throughout the country. In the second half of 1988, the retail price index increased 26.7 percent from the second half of 1987.[53] Although most goods were still rationed, gross merchandise sales in August increased by 38.6 percent compared to August 1987. Nationwide panic buying was widespread.

Second, the "dual-track" system, with a dominant command economy and a subordinate market economy, and the dual-track pricing system of the means of production, interest rates, and exchange rates provided an institutional basis for widespread rent-seeking.

In the 1970s, in analyses of corruption in certain countries, Western economists had found that the root cause of corruption was intervention and control of enterprises and individual economic activities by the administrative powers, which prevented market competition and created opportunities for excess income to go to a privileged minority. American economists James Buchanan and Anne Krueger described this extra income as rent.[54] Accordingly, activities to gain power over such rent were called "rent-seeking."

Rent-seeking occurs when government control of economic activities increases intervention by official powers. People close to these powers seek rent privileges through either legal or illegal means. This often involves lobbying, bribery, and other methods to receive benefits that lead to higher incomes. The government's administrative powers can foster conditions for rent-seeking, resulting in attempts to "set rents" to generate new opportunities for rent-seeking activities. Consequently, rent-seekers bribe officials to obtain rent, while the officials, in turn, work to maintain or establish new rent-seeking institutions, such as administrative controls. A vicious cycle of corruption then emerges from the causal relationship between rent-seeking and rent-setting.

[52] Xue Muqiao, "The Relationship between Inflation and Price Increases," *Reform*, no. 4 (1988); Xue Muqiao, *China's Economic System Reform* (Tianjin: Tianjin People's Publishing House, 1990), pp. 401–410.

[53] Dai Genyou, "The Causes of the 1988 Inflation and Recommendations Regarding How to Control It," *China Finance*, no. 5 (1989).

[54] Rent originally referred to land rent. However, Alfred Marshall uses the term to refer to rent from all production factors. A price spread occurs when demand for a production factor rises, but supply cannot increase for various reasons. According to Marshall, this is the source of rent. In modern international trade theory and public choice theory, rent continues to refer to income derived from price spreads resulting from the inelasticity of supply. However, the supply inelasticity here is a result of suppressed competition because of government intervention and administrative controls (e.g., import quotas, production permits, price controls, and even limits on the number of employees in some industries). To distinguish between the two different types of rent, some economists call the latter "directly unproductive profit-seeking" (or DUP).

There were three views about corruption in China's market-oriented reforms of the 1980s. These (1) Corruption is commonplace in a market economy. Since the decision had already been made in favor of market-oriented reforms, corruption should be tolerated and there should be no fuss about it, or (2) Corruption is an inevitable product of a market economy. The reform and opening and the market economy were the main sources of corruption. Therefore, administrative controls needed to be enhanced to end the corruption or, even better, to return to a planned economy, or (3) Based on rent-seeking theory and comparative economic studies, corruption is not an inevitable product of a market economy. On the contrary, corruption is caused by the slow pace and lack of thoroughness of the reforms. Therefore, government administrative controls should be limited to those that are necessary. To dismantle the foundation of corruption, there should be oversight and limitations on administrative powers while establishing a new market economy characterized by fair competition.[55]

According to estimates by economist Hu Heli, in 1988 the total price spread of general merchandise was over RMB 150 billion; the total interest spread from state bank loans was over RMB 113.88 billion; and the total foreign exchange spread based on the official exchange rate for imports was RMB 93.04 billion. These three groups of price spreads accounted for 30 percent of national income. Including other forms of rent, the total rent amounted to as much as 40 percent of national income.[56] These huge rents led to a proliferation of corruption by those administrative powers that controlled resources. Grievances among the public reached a boiling point.[57]

Inflation and corruption led to widespread public dissatisfaction, which was followed by the 1989 political turmoil.

The root cause of both the 1988 economic turbulence and the 1989 political turmoil was ineffective implementation of the reforms. However, certain politicians and theoreticians, whom Deng Xiaoping would sharply criticize during his 1992 Southern Tour, took advantage of the opportunity to attack the reforms, claiming

---

[55] Editorial Department of Comparative Economic and Social Studies, comp., *The Exchange of Corruption, Money, and Power* (Beijing: China Prospect Press, 1989).

[56] Hu Heli, "Estimates of China's Rent Value in 1988," *Comparative Economic and Social Studies*, no. 5 (1989).

[57] Deng Xiaoping admitted that this was a problem. When summarizing the causes of the 1989 political turmoil, he said, "One of the causes for the recent turmoil is the growth of corruption, which has made some people lose confidence in the Party and the government. … In this incident there were no slogans against reform and opening to the outside world, but one of the slogans frequently chanted was the demand to combat corruption. Of course, certain persons used this slogan as a pretext for misleading the people. But for our part, if we do not punish corruption, especially among high-level Party leaders, we run the risk of failing to rectify the Party and to achieve our strategic goals. The new leaders should first of all address this problem, which is also an important part of our efforts to rectify the Party. … As for punishing corruption, we should handle at least ten to twenty major cases publicly and without delay. … We should carry out reform and open to the outside world and, at the same time, punish corruption. When people see that these two things are combined, they will have a clearer understanding of our policies and give them greater support." See Deng Xiaoping, "We Must Form a Promising Collective Leadership That Will Carry Out Reform," May 31, 1989, and his comments to several Party Central Committee members on June 18, 1989, in "Urgent Tasks of the Third Generation of Collective leadership," in *Selected Works of Deng Xiaoping*, vol. 3, pp. 300, 313–314.

that from the outset the reforms had been plagued by fundamental errors. They called for a change in the direction of the reforms and a return to the pre-reform system.[58]

The tide of reform had waned.

[58] During his Southern Tour, Deng Xiaoping pointed out, "Some theorists and politicians try to intimidate people by pinning political labels on them. That is not a Right tactic but a "Left" one. "Left" tendencies have a revolutionary connotation, giving the impression that the more "Left" one is, the more revolutionary one is. In the history of the Party, those tendencies have led to dire consequences. Some fine things were destroyed overnight." Deng Xiaoping, "Excerpt of Talks Given in Wuchang, Shenzhen, Zhuhai, and Shanghai," 1992, in *Selected Works of Deng Xiaoping*, vol. 3, p. 375.

Chapter 5
The General Advance of Economic Reform in the 1990s

The 1990s were a decade of tremendous economic change in China. After the 1989 political turmoil, there was a change in public opinion whereby it supported upholding the planned nature of the economy. As a result, the reforms came to an end or even retreated in several essential areas. However, neither the policy suppressing the private sector nor the policy supporting the state sector achieved the expected results. In 1990–91, the SOEs fell victim to the recession despite receiving massive state bank loans. In contrast, the suppressed private sector began to demonstrate more vitality.

Against this backdrop, there were heated debates regarding the direction of the market-oriented reforms. After several rounds of back-and-forth between pro- and anti-reform advocates, Deng Xiaoping's views during his 1992 Southern Tour gained overwhelming support, leading to widespread national demands to restart the reform process. As a result, the 1992 14th National Party Congress established the goal of establishing a "socialist market economy." Thereafter, the Third Plenary Session of the 14th Party Central Committee adopted the Decision on Some Issues Concerning the Establishment of a Socialist Market Economic System.

Implementation of this program advanced comprehensive reform throughout the country.

5.1 Heated Debates on the Reform Objectives in 1989–92

In mid-1989, certain people began criticizing the political line of the 13th Party Congress. They referred to the Central Committee report to the Party Congress as "a program of bourgeois liberalization."

In December 1989, Wang Renzhi, director of the Propaganda Department of the Party Central Committee, gave a lengthy "anti-bourgeois liberalization" speech to a "Party building" theory class at the Central Party School in which he criticized every

W. Jinglian, *China's Economic Reform*, Understanding China,
https://doi.org/10.1007/978-981-96-9607-9_5

aspect of the reforms since the 1970s. Later, the *People's Daily* and *Qiushi* [Seeking Truth], the official journal of the Party Central Committee, published his speech for nationwide study by Party and government officials. According to this speech, the goal of the market-oriented economic reforms was to eliminate the planned economy. The goal of the political reforms was to abandon CCP leadership and to establish a three-branch separation of powers. The reforms would hence replace the socialist system with a capitalist system.[1]

Deng Xiaoping refuted these charges, but the activities opposing the political line of the 13th Party Congress continued. When meeting newly appointed national leaders and receiving foreign visitors, Deng Xiaoping reiterated that the 13th Party Congress had formally adopted the report of the Central Committee and that no single word should be changed.[2] He said that "the principles and policies formulated during the reform and opening to the outside world over the past ten years will not change. The line set at the Party's 13th National Congress will not change. Anyone who changes it will fall."[3] However, the political line suffered significant modifications. For instance, the reform objective adopted at the Third Plenary Session of the 12th Party Congress and at the 13th Party Congress was changed from establishing a "socialist commodity economy" to establishing a "planned economy combined with market regulation."[4] The central newspapers and propaganda departments organized extensive discussions to promote this change in the reform objectives.[5]

In addition to political and theoretical condemnation, a back-peddling economic policy was adopted to enhance control by the state plan and to restrict private-sector development. The policy (a) provided additional support to SOEs and recentralized their administration by creating monopolistic corporate groups; (b) suspended lending to township and village enterprises; (c) imposed heavy penalties for tax

---

[1] Wang Renzhi, "Anti-Bourgeois Liberalization: Speech at the Party Building Theory Class of the Central Party School, December 15, 1989," *People's Daily*, February 22, 1992, and *Qiushi*, no. 4 (1990).

[2] Deng Xiaoping, "We Must Form a Promising Collective Leadership That Will Carry Out Reform," 1989, in *Selected Works of Deng Xiaoping* (Beijing: People's Publishing House,1993), vol. 3, p. 29.

[3] Deng Xiaoping, "We are Confident We Can Handle China's Affairs Well," 1989, in *Selected Works of Deng Xiaoping*, vol. 3, p. 324.

[4] The objective of the 1982 12th Party Congress was to establish "a planned economy as the mainstay." The Third Plenary Session of the 12th Party Central Committee in 1984 modified the objective to establish a "socialist commodity economy," and the 13th Party Congress retained this description. On February 6, 1987, when reviewing preparations for the draft report to be delivered to the 13th Party Congress, Deng Xiaoping pointed out: "In the past, we learned from the Soviet Union and adopted a planned economy. Later, we followed 'a planned economy as the mainstay.' We should no longer follow this line." Deng's opinion became the consensus at the 13th Party Congress. See *Chronicle of Deng Xiaoping's Thought (1975–97)* (Beijing: Central Party Literature Press, 2004), p. 1168. Also see Deng Xiaoping, "The Plan and the Market Are Both Methods for Developing the Productive Forces," 1987, in *Selected Works of Deng Xiaoping,* vol. 3, p. 203.

[5] Wang Mengkui and Wang Zhaodong, comps., *The Objective of the Reform: A Planned Economy Combined with Market Adjustments* (Beijing: Economic Daily Publishing House, 1990).

evasion to suppress private businesses, and (d) carried out a "socialist education movement" in the rural areas and attempted a "second round of cooperative collectivization" in the remote counties of Beijing.

These aggressive tightening measures curtailed the growth of money supply and price increases, leading to sluggish market demand.

The leftist propaganda and policies negatively affected the private sector. In 1989, the *getihu*, or individual businesses (sole proprietorships), and private enterprises were shut down one after another. From end-1988 to end-June 1989, the number of sole proprietorships declined by 15 percent, from 14.549 million to 12.343 million, and employment in this sector declined by 15.7 percent, from 23.049 million to 19.436 million.[6] By the end of 1989, the number of private enterprises was halved.[7] The economic recession and increased unemployment led to intense public discontent.

Fortunately, the leftist policies did not achieve the expected results, as described in the saying, "the fighting spirit aroused by the first round of drums is weakened by the second round, and it is depleted by the third round." While the SOEs did not respond well to the jumpstart measures and continued with their lukewarm growth, the private sector readjusted and reorganized, quickly bouncing back from the massive shutdowns.

In 1991, led by the private sector, the national economy began to recover.

In academic circles, two opposing views clashed regarding whether a socialist economy is a market economy or a planned economy. On July 5, 1990, members of the Standing Committee of the CCP Politburo met with some well-known economists to discuss the economic situation and the likely policy responses.[8] As soon as the meeting began, a heated debate ensued about whether the reform should be "plan-oriented" or "market-oriented." Supporters of a plan-oriented reform stressed that socialism could only work within a planned economy based on public ownership. Therefore, market adjustments should play only a supplemental role in the economy within the limits set by the national plan. They blamed the erroneous market-oriented reform and the so-called upside-down relationship between plan and market for the 1988 inflation and the 1989 political turmoil.

Supporters of the market-oriented reform fought back. They highlighted the need to uphold the political line of the Third Plenary Session of the 11th Party Central Committee regarding market-oriented reform. They also supported reinstating the reform objectives established by the Third Plenary Session of the 12th Party Central Committee and the 13th Party Congress. In their view, the slogan "a planned economy with market adjustments" represented a reversal of these Party decisions. In addition to speaking out at the meeting, Xue Muqiao thereafter wrote a lengthy letter to

---

[6] Lu Baifu, comp., *Overall Restructuring: Major Issues in Restructuring the Ownership Structure in China* (Beijing: China Development Publishing House, 1998), p. 170.

[7] Lin Zhijun, *Ebbs and Flows: Memoirs of an Aide to China's Economic Reforms* (Beijing: Oriental Publishing Center, 1998), p. 449.

[8] About one dozen economists were invited to the meeting, including Xue Muqiao, Liu Guoguang, Su Xing, You Lin, Yuan Mu, Xu Yi, and Wu Jinglian.

the central Party leadership in which he pointed out that the changes in Eastern Europe had been mainly due to a lack of thorough reforms and the recurrence of price volatility, soft budgetary constraints, and easy credit. He argued that China should learn from this situation and grasp the opportunity to continue implementing comprehensive reforms so as to establish an economic system based on a commodity economy. Xue believed that only by doing this could China overcome its hardships and become prosperous.[9]

However, the attacks on the market-oriented reforms and the back-peddling policies crossed Deng Xiaoping's bottom line. By the end of 1990, he fought back.

One day before the Seventh Plenary Session of the 13th Party Central Committee opened on December 24, 1990, Deng made the following comments when meeting top Party and government leaders: The reform and opening should continue. "Do not be afraid of taking a few risks. By now we have developed the ability to take risks. ... As we go further with the reform and open wider to the outside world, we shall be better able to cope with problems if they arise. ... we can't do anything without taking some risks." In particular, Deng mentioned the need to develop a market economy: "We must understand theoretically that the difference between capitalism and socialism is not a market economy as opposed to a planned economy. Socialism has regulation by market forces, and capitalism has controls through planning. Do you think capitalism has absolute freedom without any controls? ... Most-favored-nation status is also a form of control. You must not think that if we have some market economy, we shall be taking the capitalist road. That is simply not true. Both a planned economy and a market economy are necessary. If we did not have a market economy, we would have no access to information from other countries and would have to reconcile ourselves to lagging. ... The greatest superiority of socialism is that it enables all the people to prosper, and common prosperity is the essence of socialism."[10]

Spending the 1991 Spring Festival in Shanghai, Deng made several critical comments when touring the city from January 28 to February 18. First, he called for courage to carry on the reform and opening, saying, "we shall keep to this line and these principles and policies. ...the reform and opening should be upheld. ... It is not enough that only I spoke out. The whole Party should speak out. We should speak for reform and opening for decades." He again referred to a market economy. "A planned economy is not equivalent to socialism, because there is planning under capitalism too; a market economy is not capitalism, because there are markets under socialism too." Finally, he said, "We should be bolder than before in conducting reform and opening to the outside and have the courage to experiment. We must not act like women with bound feet. Once we are sure that something should be done, we should dare to experiment and break a new path."[11]

[9] *Memoirs of Xue Muqiao* (Tianjin: Tianjin People's Publishing House, 2006), pp. 336–338.

[10] Deng Xiaoping, "Seize the Opportunity to Develop the Economy," 1990, *Selected Works of Deng Xiaoping*, vol. 3, p. 364.

[11] Deng Xiaoping, "Excerpts from Talks Given in Wuchang, Shenzhen, Zhuhai and Shanghai, 1991," in *Selected Works of Deng Xiaoping*, vol. 3, p. 367.

After Zhou Ruijin, Party secretary of Shanghai's *Liberation Daily*, and several of his colleagues learned about Deng's remarks, they published four articles in *Liberation Daily* under the byline Huangfu Ping, publicizing Deng's call to seek breakthroughs in establishing a market economy.[12]

The Huangfu Ping articles were like refreshing spring breezes after a dreary winter. Readers eagerly shared them, becoming hopeful that there would be further steps toward reform and opening.

But the four articles infuriated the guardians of the planned economy, and these people launched politically charged criticisms against the reform ideas in the Huangfu Ping articles. *Contemporary Thinking*, the official magazine of the Institute of Contemporary China Studies at the Chinese Academy of Social Sciences (CASS), opened the first shot in a counterattack against the idea that "reform and opening should not indulge in questioning whether a measure is socialist or capitalist"(referring to the above-mentioned remarks by Deng Xiaoping as conveyed in the third Huangfu Ping article, "Be More Conscientious About Further Opening."[13] Other articles followed suit in the counterattack. Almost all the mainstream press joined in the criticism of the Huangfu Ping articles. Deng Liqun, an influential politician and Marxist-Leninist theoretician, published "Upholding the People's Democratic Dictatorship to Prevent Peaceful Evolution" in *People's Daily*, claiming the Chinese people had the dual tasks of class struggle and comprehensive economic construction, a direct attack on the transition from "taking class struggle as the key link" to "taking economic construction as the central task." Such criticisms, denouncing reform and opening for "moving toward the erroneous road of capitalism," "ruining the socialist cause," "advocating vulgar productive-force determinism," and "preaching economic pragmatism," lasted for almost six months. These criticisms aimed to strangle the market-oriented reforms.

The charges against the Huangfu Ping articles aroused deep antipathy because most people in the government and most academics were sympathetic and supportive of the reforms despite the highly charged criticisms. Supporters were mobilized to defend the reform and opening. Many scholars spoke out at a CASS seminar on essential economic theories held on July 4.[14]

Party General Secretary Jiang Zemin took the most significant official step to defend the reforms. From October 17 to December 14, 1991, he presided over eleven seminars at which national leaders met with research directors and economists. Jiang listed three questions for discussion: first, how should the post-World War II capitalist economic development be assessed from a Marxist perspective?; second, what are the crucial lessons to be learned from the dramatic changes in the Soviet Union and

[12] Huangfu Ping, "Be the Bellwether of Reform and Opening," "Reform and Opening Needs New Thinking," "Be More Conscientious About Further Opening," and "Reform and Opening Require a Large Number of Cadres with Both Morals and Talent," *Liberation Daily*, February 15, 1991, March 2, 1991, March 22, 1991, and April 12, 1991.

[13] Liu Bo, "Can Reform and Opening Avoid Asking Whether It Is Socialism or Capitalism," *Contemporary Thinking*, no. 2 (1992).

[14] "Speeches at the Seminar on Several Essential Economic Theories (Excerpts)," *Economic Research*, no. 8 (1991).

Eastern Europe?; and third, how can socialism be developed with Chinese characteristics? Although these questions covered both domestic and international challenges, the focus was on the domestic challenges, which dominated most of the discussions. The economists' dialogue with Party and government leaders emphasized the systems, mechanisms, and effects of the reforms from theoretical and historical perspectives. All the economists favored the market-oriented reforms, with some explaining the market's fundamental role in economic terms, such as the efficient allocation of resources and the incentive compatibility mechanism.[15]

Deng Xiaoping's famous talks on his Southern Tour were most influential in defending the reforms. From January 18 to February 21, 1992, as he toured Wuchang, Shenzhen, Zhuhai, and Shanghai, in front of local officials and public onlookers he called for accelerating the reform and opening. He also pointed out: "Those who cannot take further steps in reform and opening and dare not take risks are afraid that increasing capitalist elements will lead to the capitalist road. [But] whether it is capitalism or socialism is not the issue. A judgment should be based on whether a reform measure is conducive to developing the productive forces in the socialist society, enhancing the comprehensive strength of the socialist country, and improving people's livelihood."[16] He continued: "The fundamental difference between socialism and capitalism is not whether there are a bit more plan or market elements."

At the end of February, the Party Central Committee distributed the minutes of Deng's talks during his Southern Tour as Document No. 2 of 1992 for study by all Party cadres. Thereafter, his comments were also discussed at a Politburo meeting held March 9–10. The Politburo meeting acknowledged the importance of Deng's comments, stating that these remarks would serve as a guide for the ongoing reforms and economic construction. The press release of the Politburo meeting by Xinhua News Agency and *People's Daily* conveyed the following message: grasp the opportunity to accelerate reform and opening and focus on economic construction.[17]

Initially, the media in mainland China did not carry Deng's remarks. Then, in mid-March, overseas reports about the talks began to reach the mainland and were well received, with the general public supporting Deng's criticism of the resurgence of left-leaning trends and demanding continuation of the market-oriented reforms.[18] On the one hand, the economic and political state of affairs made it very clear that without reform and opening China would reach a dead end. On the other, reformers inside and outside the Party and the government were working hard to promote

---

[15] Chen Jun and Hong Nan, comps., *Jiang Zemin and the Formation of the Socialist Market Economic System: An Objective Review of Twenty-Years of a Socialist Market Economy* (Beijing: Central Party Literature Press, 2012).

[16] Deng Xiaoping, "Excerpts from Talks Given in Wuchang, Shenzhen, Zhuhai and Shanghai," p. 372.

[17] CCP Party Literature Research Center, comp., "The Party Politburo Meets to Discuss Several Important Questions about Reform and Opening," in *Selected Important Documents Since the 13th Party Congress* (Beijing: People's Publishing House, 1993), vol. 2, pp. 1970–72.

[18] See "Anti-Leftist Trends and Utilizing Capitalism to Accelerate Reform and Opening: Well-known Chinese Scholars Speak Out," *Economic Herald* (Hong Kong), no. 2261 (March 23, 1992).

reform. As a result, the general atmosphere quickly changed in favor of reform. The above events helped set the stage for further reforms, as encapsulated in the report to the 14th Party Congress in October 1992.

5.2 Establishing the Goal of a Socialist Market Economy

Deng Xiaoping's Talks on his Southern Tour sparked popular demand for reform, and the political situation in the first half of 1992 was clearly favorable for advancing the market-oriented reforms. However, given the ideological inertia, many reformers were unsure whether the 14th Party Congress would declare the goal of the reforms to be the establishment of a market economy.

In a speech to a Central Party School training class for provincial and ministerial officials on June 9, 1992, Jiang Zemin presented several options for the reform objective. After presenting a systematic review of the Party's understanding of the plan and the market since the Third Plenary Session of the 11th Party Central Committee in 1978, he proposed that the report to the upcoming Party congress should "ultimately determine an economic system model that is broadly endorsed by most comrades and that will be used to unify the Party view regarding accelerating the establishment of a new socialist economic system." He pointed out that, in addition to the descriptions in previous official documents, several new expressions of the reform objective had emerged, including "a socialist commodity economy system with a combination of plan and market"; "a socialist planned market economy system"; and "a socialist market economy system." He himself expressed a preference for the term "socialist market economy."[19] Jiang spoke in a consultative tone because some central leaders were worried that directly proposing such a new objective might cause disputes among senior cadres. Contrary to his concerns, however, the term "socialist market economy" won broad support from the participants at the Central Party School training class, thereby establishing a foundation for the reform objectives to be incorporated into the report to the 14th Party Congress.

Ever since the beginning of the reform and opening, China's reformers had sought to expand the role of the market. However, there had been no consensus within the Party leadership regarding what type of economic system should be established, and from time to time there had been indecisiveness and reversals. Therefore, adoption of the "socialist market economy" objective at the 14th Party Congress in October 1992 represented a historical landmark. One year later, the Third Plenary Session of the 14th Party Central Committee highlighted its significance in the Decision on Some Issues Concerning the Establishment of a Socialist Market Economic System (referred to as the "50-Article Decision"). "The 14th Party Congress calls for establishing a socialist market economic system. This is an essential part of the theory of

[19] Jiang Zemin,, "Establishing a Socialist Market Economy System in Our Country," 1992, in *Selected Works of Jiang Zemin* (Beijing: People's Publishing House, 2006), pp. 198–205.

socialism with Chinese characteristics, and it will have far-reaching significance for our modernization cause."

The 14th Party Congress made further advances as well. For example, in 1984, the Third Plenary Session of the 12th Party Central Committee had adopted the objective of establishing a "socialist planned commodity economy" but without defining it in clear economics terms. In contrast, the Party Central Committee report to the 14th Party Congress specified that "the socialist market economy that is to be established aims to let the market play a fundamental role in resource allocations under macro regulation by the socialist state, to ensure economic activities are in line with the law of value and adapted to changes in supply and demand, to allow price leveraging and a competition mechanism to direct resources to areas achieving better results, to put pressures on and to motivate enterprises to achieve the survival of the fittest, [and] to utilize the advantages of market sensitivity to various economic signals to promote timely coordination of production and demand."[20]

5.3 The 50-Article Decision: A Plan for Overall Reform

Establishing the reform objective was a prelude to beginning a "major campaign" to develop market institutions. Efficient market allocations of scarce resources require a complete set of institutions and mechanisms. After the 14th Party Congress adopted the market-economy reform objective, the focus turned to designing a uniform, open, competitive, and orderly market system. In May 1993, the Party Central Committee began preparing an overall plan and, to this end, it set up a 25-member document drafting team. Sixteen working groups with 300 members conducted field studies, and several research institutes provided various proposals. The 50-Article Decision is based on the results of their respective studies and research. It provides an overall design of the institutions and mechanisms for the socialist market economy as well as a holistic action program.[21]

The 50-Article Decision was followed by several sectoral reform programs, such as the State Council's Decision on a Tax-Sharing System of December 15, 1993, the Decision on Financial Sector Reform of December 25, 1993, and the Decision on Deepening Foreign Trade Reform of January 11, 1994.

This overall design of the economic reforms featured the following:

First, the new strategy advocated a "holistic advance with priority breakthroughs." Prior to the 1992 14th Party Congress, China's reform strategy had been characterized by phases of incremental changes outside the system (*tizhiwai*) and no changes to SOE institutions. During that period, one or two specific reforms were given priority

---

[20] Jiang Zemin, "Accelerating the Reform and Opening and the Drive for Modernization to Achieve Greater Successes in Building Socialism with Chinese Characteristics: Report to the 14th CCP Congress (October 12, 1992)," *People's Daily*, October 21, 1992.

[21] Wang Mengkui, "The Drafting Process for the Third Plenary Session of the 14th Party Central Committee Decision: A Memoir," *China Development Observation Journal*, no. 5 (2012).

during each phase, aiming to establish a market economy after many years of change. When preparing the 50-Article Decision, some study groups copied the previous model, recommending "gradual progress with phased-in breakthroughs." However, eventually, the 50-Article Decision modified the wording, and the strategy became a "holistic advance with priority breakthroughs." Although this appears as mere word play with the change of just a few words, the revision represented a significant change in terms of China's reform strategy. The reform would no longer be confined to the periphery of the economy. Instead, it would tackle the formidable challenges in the state sector so as to allow breakthroughs in critical areas to drive the overall reform.

Under the new reform strategy, the 50-Article Decision called for putting in place preliminary socialist market institutions. It proclaimed that Deng Xiaoping's early 1992 talks on his Southern Tour and the results of the 14th Party Congress signaled "a new phase in our country's reform and opening and modernization. … It is the great historical task for the Party and the nation to establish a preliminary new economic system by the end of this century."

The program's second feature was a clearly defined primary task: to foster and develop a market system and to form a uniform, open, competitive, and orderly market. As already noted, the early and mid-1980s government slogans, e.g., "let market adjustments play a role" and "establish a socialist commodity economy," lacked clear economic definitions of either market adjustments or a commodity economy. In the second half of the 1980s, the field of economics in China made considerable progress and the shortcomings of such policy jargon became more apparent. In addition to adopting the reform objective of establishing a "socialist market economy," the 1992 14th Party Congress provided a scientific explanation of the nature and functions of the market. The 50-Article Decision further defined the economic system as one that would efficiently allocate resources.

The decision pointed out, "Letting market mechanisms play a fundamental role in resource allocations requires fostering and developing a market system. The priority is to develop production factor markets, standardize market behavior, break up regional and sectoral fragmentation and remove blockages, prohibit unfair competition, and create an environment for equal competition to form a uniform, open, competitive, and orderly market."

Since the market allocates resources based on price signals that reflect market supply and demand, the most critical task in establishing a market system should be price reform, or, in other words, the development of a market mechanism for determining prices. But this reform was considered too challenging to be the top priority, and the issue of the sequencing of the reforms was hotly debated. Nevertheless, within three years, from 1989 to 1992, the prices of commodities, except petroleum products, were quietly liberalized under the tightened monetary policy adopted at the beginning of 1989 and promoted by reformist-led local governments and line ministries. (In 1994, dual-track pricing for grain was resumed with reinstated fixed-price state procurements.) In addition to requiring continuous liberalization of the remaining means-of-production price controls, the 50-Article Decision assigned top priority to making changes in capital and labor pricing mechanisms to accelerate the development of factor markets. Developing the financial, labor, real estate, technology, and information markets was essential to fostering the growth of a market system.

Given the above considerations, the 50-Article Decision set the following reform priorities.

(1) Reform of the fiscal and tax system

After the People's Republic was established, adapting to the "state syndicate" that eliminated the distinction between the public and the private sectors, the financial and tax system was characterized by the following four features: (A) a unified financial system: Government and enterprise finance were merged into a uniform fiscal system comprised of the government budget, bank credits, and enterprise finance. (B) revenue: The government used its price-setting powers and the monopoly power of the SOEs to organize most budget revenue through means other than taxes. By setting low prices for agricultural products, the surplus created in the rural areas was transferred to the state-owned sector, and almost all the surplus was channeled into the national budget via the profits and taxes of the state-owned enterprises. (C) tax and profits disparities: Enormous profit and tax handover gaps existed among industries, regions, and enterprises. Although SOEs were an economic unit of the state syndicate, SOE profits belonged to the state. The substantial differences in this complex enterprise tax structure led to unfair income distribution among industries and enterprises. (D) a highly centralized system: In 1958, significant steps were taken to decentralize the fiscal system administratively. With the failure of the Great Leap Forward, however, an administrative recentralization took place to deal with the chaotic aftermath of the Leap, and a uniform revenue and expenditure regime was reinstated. This highly centralized fiscal system remained largely intact throughout most of the period prior to the reform and opening. During the early phase of the reform and opening, the government adopted a "delegation of power and revenue-sharing" policy. In 1979, the State Council decided that except for the three municipalities of Beijing, Tianjin, and Shanghai that still followed the nearly unified system, other provinces and autonomous regions could implement a "separate cooking" method, beginning a thirteen-year period of local fiscal contracting. Starting in 1988, this method was solidified into a formal system, known as "fiscal contracting," involving various methods to determine the financial relationship between the local and central governments.

The fiscal contracting system was intended to clarify central-local relations while safeguarding central government budgetary revenue, thus enhancing the motivation of both parties. Under fiscal contracting, local governments had greater interest in developing the local economy and they provided protection and support to local enterprises (including those in the non-state sector). However, fiscal contracting resulted in a series of adverse effects. These included: (a) because of the excessive decline in government revenue, mainly central government revenue, the state was unable to finance its social obligations; (b) because of the unfair revenue-sharing ratios, intergovernmental income distribution varied greatly, what the Chinese called the phenomenon of "unequal shouldering of pain and happiness" and "whipping the fast ox"; (c) because of the entrenched local protectionism and market fragmentation, the so-called "economic fiefdoms" came into being.

Under these circumstances, the fiscal and tax reform was designed to focus on two areas. First, the reform was to "replace the contracting practice with a tax-sharing system whereby expenditure responsibilities were reasonably divided between the central and local governments."[22] Second, the reform was to improve the tax regime by promoting a value-added tax as a primary type of turnover tax, levying a consumption tax on a few goods, streamlining corporate and personal income taxes, standardizing tax rates, and expanding the tax base "in compliance with the principles of a unified tax law, fair tax burdens, a simplified tax regime, and a reasonable separation of authority."

(2) Accelerating reform of the financial system

During the planned economy period, the banking system was characterized by the following: (a) there were no financial assets except for banknotes, (b) money was passive and only used for accounting purposes, (c) cash was strictly controlled through cash management instruments, (d) commercial credits between enterprises were strictly prohibited, (e) central and commercial banking functions were mingled under a mono-banking system, (f) banks had a limited role in the allocation of funds over time, and their loans to enterprises were limited to non-regular working capital, (g) residents could not engage in any financial activities except for opening savings accounts in banks. During the Cultural Revolution, even this limited system was abolished. The People's Bank became an internal unit of the Ministry of Finance.

After the Cultural Revolution, the government began to rebuild the banking system. In the early 1980s, the Bank of China, the Agricultural Bank of China, and the People's Construction Bank of China were separated from the People's Bank of China (PBoC) and the Ministry of Finance. Later, the Industrial and Commercial Bank of China was established. The four banks formed a specialized banking system. In 1983, the State Council assigned central bank functions to the PBoC. Beginning in 1984, local banks and non-bank financial institutions (trust and investment companies and financial leasing companies) were established. In appearance, this commercial banking system resembled those of market-economy countries, while in essence, it differed significantly from them. However, there were still significant differences. China's so-called independent financial institutions remained appendages of administrative agencies, with comingled government and enterprise functions and commercial and policy loans, and the PBoC still treated them as managerial subordinates. Furthermore, the central bank could not effectively play its monetary stabilization role due to functional ambiguities, outdated instruments, and an unreasonable organizational structure.

[22] A tax-sharing system is a budgetary system that divides taxation rights and budgetary revenue between the central and local governments based on a separation of expenditure responsibilities. It considers the characteristics of the various taxes and contains an intergovernmental transfer mechanism. It is similar to the division of tax authority in most large market economies or in fiscal federalism. The core of fiscal federalism is to determine the revenue and expenditure structure for the various government levels based on the nature of their income and outlays.

The 50-Article Decision spelled out three intended changes. First, as the central bank, the PBoC should independently implement monetary policy under the leadership of the State Council. Its primary function should shift from credit controls to using the deposit reserve requirements, central bank lending rates, and open market operations to adjust money supply and stabilize the currency. The PBoC should supervise financial institutions and end doing business with non-financial organizations. Second, the specialized banks should gradually be transformed into commercial banks. Rural and urban cooperative banks should be established step by step wherever needed, and development of non-bank financial institutions should be regulated. Third, policy lending should be clearly defined and separated from commercial lending. Policy loans should be transferred to the new China Development Bank, Exim Bank of China, and Agricultural Development Bank of China.

(3) Reforming the foreign exchange regime

Under the planned economy, the foreign exchange policy overvalued the local currency (RMB) to support import substitution. In August 1979, the State Council issued the Provisions on Developing Foreign Trade and Increasing Foreign Exchange Income, thereby establishing a foreign exchange retention system to motivate export enterprises to earn more foreign exchange. Under this system, export enterprises sold their foreign exchange earnings to the state and the latter allocated retention quotas to the former and to their local governments. Exporters had autonomy to use the foreign exchange within the retention quotas.

However, the foreign exchange retention system was characterized by a mismatch between foreign exchange supply and demand. Some units retained foreign exchange but did not need to use it, while others needed foreign exchange but did not have a retention quota. To resolve this problem, in October 1980 the State Administration of Foreign Exchange granted approval for the Bank of China to engage in foreign exchange adjustment business in twelve major cities, including Beijing and Shanghai. This allowed export enterprises to sell, at market-adjusted prices, their retained foreign exchange to import enterprises that needed it. This created a "dual-track" system whereby both a foreign exchange adjustment market and an official foreign exchange market coexisted.

The dual-exchange rate system had positive effects and institutional shortcomings like those of the dual-track pricing system, and it urgently needed to be reformed. The 1993 50-Article Decision included a brief statement on foreign exchange reform: "Establish a market-based managed floating exchange rate system and a unified and standardized foreign exchange market. Gradually make the RMB a convertible currency." Although brief, the description marked a fundamental change in China's foreign exchange practices.

(4) Establishing a broad-based and multi-tiered social security system

Comprehensive social safeguards are a significant feature of socialism. After its establishment, the People's Republic established a defined benefit,[23] pay-as-you-go (PAYG)[24] social security system, following practices in the Soviet Union and the other socialist countries. The 1952 Labor Insurance Regulations of the People's Republic of China provided labor insurance for workers and their family members that was funded by the state but administered by the enterprises. In the rural areas, people without family support, including widows, widowers, orphans, and elderly without children, received small payments as social safeguards. Other rural residents received almost no social security benefits.

In addition to the drawbacks affecting intergenerational transfers, this system had other defects as well. It depended on government agencies and enterprises for funding and administration. Urban residents without formal employment and rural residents had few social safeguards, and the safeguards offered by state employers could vary greatly. Beneficiaries did not have the right to choose. Because the beneficiaries did not monitor the administrators, the latter became increasingly bureaucratic. As a result, the costs of running the system went up.

The drawbacks of the old safeguards system became more apparent during the reform era. Therefore, it was imperative to establish a new social safety net.

The 50-Article Decision spent considerable space describing a multi-tiered social security system, including social security, social aid, veterans and other unique benefits, mutual assistance, and individual savings accounts.

The primary principles of the new system were the following. First, it should be a broad-based and multi-tiered system. By "broad-based," the system should cover both rural and urban areas and the state and non-state sectors, albeit with different approaches. By "multiple tiers," the system should comprise PAYG minimum livelihood guarantees, a combination of pooled funding and individual savings for retirement and health insurance, and commercial insurance. Second, the different types of social safeguards should have separate funding sources and coverage models. Combined employer and worker contributions should fund urban workers' retirement and health insurance. Farmers' retirement was expected to rely on family support and be supplemented by community assistance. A rural cooperative health system should be developed. Third, a uniform social security agency should be established. The administrative functions and the fund management functions should be separated. The social security agency should be responsible for administrative affairs,

[23] There are mainly two types of social security payments. One is defined benefits, where payments are made according to prior set standards, and the other is defined contributions, where payments are made according to the contribution level.

[24] "Pay-as-you-go" means using current income to cover social security expenses. In other words, the contributions from the currently working generations are used to directly fund the pensions of current retirees. This relies on an immediate disbursement of benefits without the need for prior accumulation. However, transfers between generations may weaken the motivation of the working generations as their contributions are spent on the older generations. Under such a system, the social security system will face significant funding challenges and even deficits as the population ages.

and the social security fund should preserve and increase fund value while ensuring regular payments and the safety and liquidity of the fund.

China's social security design adopted by the Third Plenary Session of the 14th Party Central Committee in 1993 was innovative. It influenced the World Bank's 1994 multi-pillar pension model that included a publicly managed system, a mandatory pension plan, and voluntary individual and enterprise savings.[25] In 2005, the World Bank reviewed the experiences of various countries in providing social safeguards, and it expanded the multi-pillar framework to a five-pillar program.[26]

(5) Establishing a modern enterprise system in the SOEs

A free enterprise system, characterized by free market entry, independent decision-making, operational liberalization, and responsibility for profits and losses, is the microeconomic bedrock of a market economy. It is also a precondition for market competitiveness.[27] In the past, the thrust of SOE reform had been to "revitalize enterprises," i.e., decentralization and profit-sharing, which mainly benefited the SOE management. However, without a checks-and-balances mechanism between the owner and the manager, relaxed constraints and decentralization failed to make enterprises independent and responsible for their own operations, profits, or losses. As a result, the expected higher SOE efficiency was not achieved, and this failure led to widespread insider control.[28] The 50-Article Decision stressed that SOE reform should shift from "revitalizing enterprises" to introducing institutional innovations and establishing a modern enterprise system. As far as the SOEs were concerned, only a modern company structure could suit a market economy. In the language of the decision, this structure should be "a modern enterprise system with clearly defined property rights and demarcated rights and obligations between owners and firms. Under such a system, enterprises do not play administrative roles and they are scientifically managed."

[25] World Bank, *Averting the Old Age Crisis: Policies to Protect the Old and to Promote Growth*, 1994 (Chinese translation. Beijing: China Financial and Economic Publishing House, 1996).

[26] World Bank, *Old-Age Income Support in the 21st Century: An International Perspective on Pension Systems and Reform*, 2005 (Chinese translation. Beijing: China Labor and Social Security Publishing House, 2006).

[27] During the early reform process, some economists discussed this essential issue. For example, see Zhou Xiaochuan, *Thoughts on Reform of the Foreign Trade System* (Beijing: China Prospect Publishing House, 1989), pp. 219, 478.

[28] As early as 1994, at an international seminar on the next steps in China's economic reforms (held at Jinglun Hotel in Beijing), many Chinese and foreign scholars pointed to the need to establish an effective corporate governance mechanism to deal with the problem of insider control. See Wu Jinglian and Zhou Xiaochuan, *Corporate Governance Structure, Debt Restructuring, and Bankruptcy Procedures: Revisiting the 1984 Jinglun Hotel Seminar* (Beijing: Central Compilation and Translation Press, 1999). Unfortunately, these reforms advanced at a crawling pace.

5.4 Progress in Fiscal and Tax, Financial Sector, and Social Security Reforms

(1) Developing a Comprehensive Fiscal and Tax Regime through Further Reform

In December 1993, the State Council issued the Decision on Implementing a Tax-Sharing System, requiring nationwide replacement of fiscal contracting practices with a tax-sharing system beginning from January 1, 1994. The main steps were: (a) to readjust *shiquan,* or the right to do things (expenditure responsibilities) and to readjust fiscal rights between the central and local governments. After the readjustment, the central government would mainly be responsible for national security, foreign affairs, and central government expenditures. It would also be responsible for outlays regarding national structural adjustments of the economy, coordinated regional development, and macroeconomic management. Local governments would be responsible for expenditures related to fulfilling their roles in local socioeconomic development. (b) to readjust the rights of revenue collection between the central and local governments. The reform followed the principle of matching expenditure responsibilities with revenue collection rights, classifying taxes related to safeguarding national interest and implementing macroeconomic management as central government levies, those directly relevant to economic development as shared responsibilities between central and local governments, and responsibilities appropriate for local administration to be collected by local governments. (c) to provide tax revenue rebates to alleviate local resistance to reform. Local governments would receive refunds from local levies transferred to the central government if the revenue exceeded the pre-fixed base amounts.

The 1994 fiscal and tax reform sought to standardize intergovernmental fiscal relationships and to make them more equitable, resulting in interregional interests undergoing significant readjustments. The reform proceeded relatively smoothly and established a tax revenue framework suitable to a market economy. The following were the initial positive results.

First, the tax-sharing system streamlined central-local government relations. It removed the parallel regimes that had existed under the former fiscal contracting system and standardized intergovernmental fiscal allocations. A constraint mechanism was introduced whereby governments at various administrative levels performed their assigned functions, shouldered their own responsibilities, and received their respective revenues. In addition, an attribution mechanism emerged for sharing costs and interests. These mechanisms strengthened the budgetary constraints of local governments and standardized intergovernmental rights and responsibilities. Finally, increased central government transfers made the vertical allocation of fiscal resources more reasonable.

Second, the reform streamlined the tax regime following the principles of a unified tax law, a fair tax burden, a simplified tax structure, and rational decentralization as per the requirements in the 50-Article Decision to set up a tax regime that suited a market economy and that could improve income distribution and facilitate fair competition among enterprises. Specifically, the main tasks were to (a) establish a turnover tax regime with a value-added tax as the primary type, (b) apply a uniform nominal rate of 33 percent to the enterprise income tax, (c) simplify the individual income taxes, (d) levy value-added taxes on specialty crops and land, and consolidate consumption and resource taxes, and (e) establish a central government taxation authority (the State Taxation Administration) and local taxation bureaus to enhance tax administration.

The 1994 reform established a fiscal and tax framework suited to a market economy. Nevertheless, pending further reforms, this system had apparent loopholes and drawbacks. (A) Intergovernmental fiscal imbalances. The 1994 reform did not change the previous division of *shiquan*, or the right to do things (expenditure responsibilities) between the central and local governments. County and township governments were still responsible for many national public services, such as universal nine-year compulsory education and public health. Corresponding revenue sources did not match these heavy expenditure burdens. In areas where fiscal revenue was scarce, public services faced severe shortages and fell behind. Local governments levied various fees to expand their sources of revenue, although such behavior was banned and only reemerged in cycles. The provincial funding platforms borrowed heavily, leading to high implicit debt risks. Local governments increasingly relied on income from land transfers, with related problems becoming more conspicuous, an indirect cause of the rising real estate prices. (B) Lingering "production or economic construction finance." The government continued investing massive fiscal resources in SOEs in competitive fields, and various "city-image-boosting projects" or "political showcase projects," thus disrupting fair market competition. The supply of compulsory education, public healthcare, and other public services was inadequate due to a lack of funding or misappropriations, and thus people became increasingly resentful of the difficulties in obtaining healthcare, schooling, housing, and social security. (C) Government transfer bottlenecks. The biggest obstacle was the ambiguous demarcation of intergovernmental expenditure responsibilities. Since there were no clear rules, case-by-case transfers based on instructions from those in charge exacerbated the inequalities in public services. Local governments became increasingly eager to visit the relevant central authorities to seek funding, reinforcing the institutional basis for rent-seeking.

(2) Financial System Reform and the Development of Financial Markets

The overheating of the economy and the high inflation in 1992–94 exposed the severe problems in the financial sector. The government came to the realization that the financial system urgently needed reform. Beginning in 1994, the following changes were made in accordance with the 50-Article Decision and the State Council's Decision on Financial System Reform.

First, a central banking system was established whereby the PBoC independently implemented monetary policies under the leadership of the central government. The PBoC managed money supply through typical policy instruments, including required reserve ratios, central bank loans, rediscount rates, open market operations, lending limits, and central bank deposit and lending rates. The PBoC also required that commercial banks comply with asset-liability ratios and asset risk classification requirements.

Second, a system of regulation by industry was established. In 1992, the State Council Securities Commission and the China Securities Regulatory Commission were established. In 1997, the Central Financial Sector Work Conference decided that banks, securities firms, and insurance companies should operate and be regulated separately, a principle of "operations and regulation by industry." In April 1998, the State Council Securities Commission was abolished, and the Securities Regulatory Commission took over the PBoC's function to regulate securities firms. In November, the China Insurance Regulatory Commission was established. In 2003, the China Banking Regulatory Commission was established, completing the formation of an industry-specific regulatory framework.

Third, efforts were made to improve the banking industry and to develop non-bank financial institutions. To facilitate the commercial transformation of specialized banks, three policy banks, i.e., the State Development Bank, the China Export–Import Bank, and the China Agricultural Development Bank, were established to take over the policy lending business from the specialized banks. In addition, a cooperative bank sub-sector was established, consisting of urban and rural cooperative banks. These banks served the financial needs of small and medium-sized enterprises, agriculture, and the local economies. In addition, the development of insurance, trust and investment, and securities companies was encouraged (Table 5.1).

Fourth, steps were undertaken to develop a unified, open, orderly, competitive, and strictly regulated market system composed of money and capital markets. (A) The money market consisted of lending, discount, and repurchasing agreement markets. It was expected that these markets would form an equilibrium funds price between the floor and ceiling of deposit and lending rates set by the PBoC. The aim was to gradually liberalize the price regime and establish a market-rate system based on the central bank rates. (B) The capital market comprised the bond and stock markets. Specifically, the interbank bond market, the Shanghai Stock Exchange, and the Shenzhen Stock Exchange, forming the market infrastructure for the issuing and trading of financial products, were self-disciplinary enforcers. (C) A derivatives market came into being. After a standardization and consolidation campaign in 1993, three commodity futures exchanges were established, including the Zhengzhou Commodity Exchange, the Shanghai Futures Exchange, and the Dalian Commodity Exchange. Later, the Shanghai Financial Futures Exchange and the Shanghai Gold Exchange were added to China's commodity and financial derivatives market infrastructure.

An essential component of the financial sector reform was the transformation of the foreign exchange management regime, which will be elaborated upon in Chapter 6.

However, the banking reform in the 1990s had a severe defect: it did not try to turn banks into modern companies. Due to the lack of change in property rights institutions and corporate governance, the commercialization of state banks was deprived of a foundation. As a result, their efficiency remained low and their non-performing loans mounted. Meanwhile, the government moved to tackle the specialized banks' commercial transformation. In the early twenty-first century, the big-four state banks, i.e., China Construction Bank, Bank of China, Industrial and Commercial Bank of

Table 5.1 China's financial system in the Mid-1990s

Financial Institutions	Central bank	People's Bank of China	
	Commercial banks	State-owned commercial banks	Industrial and Commercial Bank of China Agricultural Bank of China China Construction Bank Bank of China
		Joint-stock commercial banks	Bank of Communications CITIC Bank Everbright Bank Huaxia Bank Guangdong Development Bank Shenzhen Development Bank China Merchant Bank Fujian Industrial Bank
	Non-bank financial institutions	Insurance, trust and investment, securities companies Rural and urban credit cooperatives Finance and leasing companies	

Source PBoC, "China Financial Sector Outlook," 1994

China, and Agricultural Bank of China, underwent a financial restructuring, with the divesture of their non-performing assets and injections of government capital. After the restructuring, they were corporatized and opened to overseas strategic investors. With their improved ownership structure, these banks went public on the domestic and overseas stock markets and became listed commercial banks.

(3) Establishing a Broad-based, Multi-tiered Social Security System

First, pension system reform

The development of new social safeguards began in 1995, focusing on basic pensions for urban enterprise employees, as based on decision of the Third Plenary Session of the 14th Party Central Committee.

According to this decision, among the social safeguards, the first to be established was retirement plans funded by "combined social pooling and individual accounts." From the beginning, this reform encountered challenges. The biggest obstacle was the unfunded individual accounts of retirees and middle-aged workers who were close to the age of retirement. During the discussions on implementing social security reforms in 1993–95, some economists had proposed two remedies to fund these individual accounts. The first remedy was to "transfer a portion of SOE assets,"[29] and the second was to have the government issue endorsed bonds.[30] Unfortunately, neither option was adopted due to opposition from the relevant agencies, and the government was forced to use employer contributions (called "social pooling accounts") to pay its pension obligations. The contributions of newer workers were also used for this purpose. But the individual accounts became depleted in some provinces and municipalities, and the central government had to allocate billions of budgetary resources annually to fill the funding gap for basic pensions.

In July 2001, the State Council decided to test-run a pilot program in Liaoning province to improve the urban social security system. The program was based on a Ministry of Labor and Social Security proposal to reduce the share of individual contributions and to allow "social pooling" to be the primary funding source for the basic pension plan. Under the pilot program, individual accounts were separated from social pooling accounts and they were funded by workers' contributions. The contribution rate was reduced from 11 to 8 percent of the contributor's wages. In addition, the enterprise contribution rate was kept at 20 percent of the workers' base wages and was credited entirely to the social pooling funds.

Based on the experience in Liaoning province, the Party Central Committee and the State Council decided to expand the experiment to Jilin and Heilongjiang provinces in 2003, reducing the individual contributions rate to 5 or 6 percent. In December 2005, the State Council issued the Decision on Improving the Basic Retirement Plan for Enterprise Workers, extending the pilot program to eight additional provincial jurisdictions, including Tianjin, Shanghai, Shandong, Shanxi, Hubei, Hunan, Henan, and Xinjiang.

This approach helped improve the financials of the pension system in the pilot regions. The costs led to increased central government transfers because of the small amount of local social security funds and the low investment returns.[31] Even if the government could have afforded the enormous outlays, the system still would have been mainly a PAYG regime without long-term sustainability. Due to the substantial funding shortages, social security funds could not meet the payment obligations in some underdeveloped regions and old industrial bases. Also, because the funds were pooled and used locally by low-level government jurisdictions, surplus and deficit

---

[29] The idea was to transfer some of the SOE assets to the government to fund implicit liabilities, i.e., the pensions of older SOE workers. In 1993, many economists supported this option. See Zhou Xiaochuan and Wang Lin, "Social Security: Economic Analysis and the Proposed System," *Reform*, no. 6 (1994), and Wu Jinglian et al., *Overall Concept and Design for Developing a Market Economy* (Beijing: Central Compilation and Translation Press, 1996), pp. 211–258.

[30] Endorsed bonds refer to the government bonds issued by the Chilean government during the 1981 pension reform. Such bonds were used to repay the government's implicit liabilities to workers who had left the government pension plan and had joined the new pension plan.

[31] According to regulation, social security funds could only be invested in zero-risk bank deposits, hence, the low returns.

funds coexisted between localities. New cities enjoyed an influx of labor, with their social security funds adequately funded with lower contribution requirements.

In addition to enterprise workers, public-sector employees were another main group of pension beneficiaries. Most of the public-sector employees were covered by a PAYG system. They did not need to contribute, but they were entitled to much higher benefits than other residents. This dual-track pension system disillusioned the general public. Beginning in the early 1990s, some localities experimented with various pension reforms for government employees. In 2008, the Pilot Program of Pension Reform for Employees in Quasi-governmental Institutions was issued in parallel with a reclassification of these institutions. In early 2015, the State Council issued the Decision on the Reform of the Pension Plan for Government Employees, merging the pension plans for government employees and for enterprise workers.

Since the beginning of the reform and opening, the rural social security system always lagged behind the urban social security system. However, because urban–rural disparities cannot be fundamentally eliminated in the short term, the rural social security systems are inevitably different from the urban social security systems. In October 1986, the Ministry of Civil Affairs decided to implement community-based rural pension insurance in economically more developed rural areas, and in October 1986, it decided to test-run a community-based rural retirement plan in the better-developed regions; from 1991 to 1993, some counties were selected to experiment with a county-level retirement plan. In July 1999, the State Council pointed out that the rural areas did not have the right conditions to widely adopt the social security system, and it therefore decided to consolidate the experiments and allow the regions with the right conditions to gradually move to commercial retirement plans. In July 2003, the Ministry of Labor and Social Security issued a document requiring "active and steady development of the rural pension system," and thereafter, several regions experimented with a variety of pilots. In 2009, the State Council issued the Guidelines on Piloting the New Rural Social Retirement Plan to experiment with a new model with three funding sources: individual contributions, collectives' supplements, and government subsidies. Together with other safeguards, such as family support, land-use rights, and social aid, the individual-funded and government-administered new retirement plan provided rural retirement security.

In the cities, the social retirement plan covered nonemployees with urban household registrations. In 2011, the State Council issued the Guidelines on Piloting an Urban Resident Social Retirement Plan, with coverage similar to that in the rural retirement plan. Thus, a basic social retirement system covering both rural and urban residents was established. In 2014, the Ministry of Human Resource and Social Security and the Ministry of Finance jointly issued the Provisional Procedures for Integrating the Urban and the Rural Retirement Plans, specifying for the first time that funds and benefits could be transferred between residents' retirement plans and urban workers' retirement plans.

But the pension reform still faced an obstacle that needed to be addressed: the challenge of unfunded individual accounts. Under the previous PAYG system, SOEs paid low wages to workers and funding for retirement was withheld to finance state investments, thus becoming part of the state assets. With the adoption of individual accounts, the state was to return the funds to the workers. Some economists recommended allocating some state assets to the social security funds to fill the funding gap for old workers' pensions.[32]

In 1997, the State Council System Reform Office conducted a study to estimate government liabilities to SOE employee pensions. The World Bank's estimate was 46–69 percent of annual GDP, the Chinese economists' estimate was 71–94 percent,[33] and the Reform Office's estimate was as high as 145 percent. Under the former economic system, workers' wages were low and the state turned the value created by workers into state assets via state investments. Three attempts were made to compensate older workers' pensions with state assets, but the first two rounds were halted midway.[34] The third attempt took place in June 2009, when the Ministry of Finance, the State-owned Assets Supervision and Administration Commission, the China Securities Regulatory Commission, and the National Council for Social Security Fund jointly issued the Measures for Transferring Part of the Domestically Listed Companies' State Shares to Supplement the National Social Security Fund. The measures applied to those joint-stock limited liability companies that had gone public on the domestic securities markets after June 2006, as the "reform of share trading" had established different accounting treatments for those companies' shares before and after that cutoff date. The approach was for the companies to transfer state shares equal to 10 percent of their IPOs to the National Social Security Fund. This was helpful but negligible vis-à-vis the massive government implicit pension liabilities, and it could not solve the problem of the unfunded individual accounts.

Another problem was the narrow social pooling base. Only a few provincial governments realized unified funding within their jurisdictions, to say nothing of

[32] Zhou Xiaochuan and Wang Lin, "Social Security"; Wu Jinglian et al., *Overall Concept,* pp. 211–258; Guo Shuqing et al., "Restructuring Existing State Assets and Compensating Social Security Liabilities," in Guo Shuqing, *Thoughts on Overcoming the Reform Obstacles* (Beijing: Economic Management Publishing House, 1997); Guo Shuqing, "Funding the Pension Funds and Compensating the Implicit Debts," *Comparative Economic and Social Systems*, no. 5 (2000).

[33] Wu Jinglian, "What Are the Main Issues that Need to be Addressed in the Reduction of State-owned Shares?" *Caijing,* no. 1 (2002).

[34] The first attempt was made in 1995. When the Ministry of Finance, the State Economic Restructuring Commission, and the State Economic Commission were ready to work on a list of assets to be allocated, the agency in charge of labor policy convinced Party and government leaders to end the program. The second attempt began in 2000 amid discussions about reducing state holdings of listed SOEs. In 2001, Finance Minister Xiang Huaicheng announced that the government planned to explore new financing channels for the social security system, including monetizing some state-owned assets for social security. In June 2001, the State Council issued the Provisional Measures on Reducing State Holdings to Raise Social Security Funds. Article 5 of these measures stipulated that when issuing new or additional stocks, 10 percent of the amount of financing should be from the sale of state-owned shares. This regulation was halted in October of the same year due to the sharp decline in the stock market. In June 2002, the State Council decided that it would stop enforcing the provisions regarding the reduction of state-owned shares in the domestic market, and it would no longer issue specific implementation measures, except for companies issuing shares abroad. This effort was thus abruptly ended.

nationwide financing as stipulated by the Law on Social Insurance. Moreover, inter-regional transfers were challenging, which severely restricted people's mobility and weakened the effectiveness of human resource allocations.

The Third Plenary Session of the 18th Party Central Committee's Decision on Some Major Issues Concerning Comprehensively Deepening the Reform in 2013 requires a portion of state assets to be transferred to the social security fund, laying out a viable path for addressing the unfunded account problem. The current task is to implement this decision despite the various difficulties.

Second, healthcare system reform

As a result of the 1993 Third Plenary Session of the 14th Party Central Committee, Zhenjiang municipality of Jiangsu province and Jiujiang municipality of Jiangxi province began to experiment with urban employee health insurance reforms, focusing on combining funds from social pooling and individual contributions. Based on the experience of these pilots, the State Economic Restructuring Commission and four other government agencies prepared the Proposal for Expanding the Pilots for Employee Health Insurance Reform, approved by the State Council in April 1996. Under the pilot rollout program, the reform to establish a multi-tiered health insurance system was extended to more than fifty cities. The new system would comprise four tiers: a low-coverage, broad-based basic health insurance plan as the basis and supplemented by enterprise-funded health insurance plans and commercial health insurance; finally, there was also "medical aid" for low-income employees. Based on the expanded experiments, the Party Central Committee and the State Council adopted the Decision on Healthcare Reform and Development in January 1997. The decision requires that the initial phase of a new healthcare system, comprising health services, medical insurance, and enforcement and supervision mechanisms, be established by 2000 to achieve healthcare for everyone and better public health. In December 1998, the State Council issued the Decision on Establishing a Basic Health Insurance System for Urban Employees to guide the nationwide rollover of the reform. The decision outlines that the main task of the reform of medical insurance is to "adapt to the socialist market economy system and, based on financial, enterprise, and individual capacities, establish a social medical insurance system that guarantees the basic medical needs of employees." Accordingly, the decision requires the establishment of a basic medical insurance fund combining social pooling and individual contributions and adherence to the principle of "low level, wide coverage." Basic medical expenses are to be shared between employers and employees, with all urban employers required to participate in the basic medical insurance, managed according to local regulations.

In any country, a healthcare system is comprised of two components: funding medical expenses and providing medical services. With respect to the reform of medical institutions, i.e., the service providers, the 1998 State Council decision mentioned several times that a competitive mechanism should be formed, but the decision stopped short of specifics. Nevertheless, it did provide a detailed design of the basic health insurance funds. From 1999 onward, the State Council-led urban employee health insurance reform centered on establishing a basic insurance system. Medical institution reform was left to experimentation by the local governments.

Introduction of the new healthcare reform coincided with the generational change in the structure of China's leadership. As a result, many people began to question the general direction of the reforms, with debates continuing for several years.

In early 2003, the Social Development Department of the State Council Development Research Center and the World Health Organization launched a study of China's health system reform. In July 2005, *China Youth Daily* reported the study's conclusions with an eye-catching headline: "Current Reform of the Healthcare System Has Not Been Successful." The news report claimed that "the commercialization and market orientation of healthcare were completely incorrect and they violate the basic rules of healthcare."[35] In addition, Xinhua News Agency published a speech by Health Minister Gao Qiang at a seminar titled "Developing the Medical and Health Sector, Contributing to a Harmonious Socialist Society." In his speech, the health system reform was deemed to be problematic and unsuccessful. In particular, Gao criticized the medical institutions' "market-orientation trend," and he stressed the need to uphold the government's leading role and the public goods nature of healthcare.

The opposition to reform of the healthcare system that began in 1999 triggered a debate on the direction of the reform. The focus was on whether the government should provide health services to residents directly through public hospitals or through the market with government subsidies.

In October 2006, the Politburo held a "study session" on healthcare development and invited Professor Li Ling, deputy director of the China Center for Economic Research at Peking University and a long-time advocate of "establishing a government-led healthcare system in China,"[36] to present a lecture. Supporters of Professor Li Ling's views considered the Politburo study session to be "a milestone in formally shifting the basic tone of healthcare reform toward establishing a system of public welfare and strengthened government responsibilities. … [It is] the turning point in China's healthcare system reform."[37]

Supporters of market-based health services were not convinced, however, and they continued to voice their opposition. Furthermore, providing free medical care to the entire population through government-funded public health services was beyond the

[35] "The Latest Study by the State Council Research Agency States that the Current of Reform of the Healthcare System Has Not Been Successful," *China Youth Daily*, July 29, 2005.

[36] Li Ling, "China Should Adopt a Government-led Healthcare System," *China and World Affairs*, no. 5 (2005), 156–162.

[37] Li Ling, "The Healthcare System Reform as Portrayed in the Debate," 2009, in *Healthcare Strengthens the Country: Li Ling on Healthcare System Reform* (Beijing: Peking University Press, 2010); Li Ling and Jiang Nin, "2006: The Turning Point in China's Healthcare System Reform," *China Health Economy Journal*, no. 4 (2007), 5–9.

financial capacity of the state. In June 2006, the State Council directed the National Development and Reform Commission and the Ministry of Health to jointly lead research on this issue. They commissioned parallel studies by nine research teams, including the World Bank, the World Health Organization, the Development Research Center of the State Council, Peking University, Fudan University, McKinsey & Company (China), Beijing Normal University, and Tsinghua University, to design an overall approach and framework for reforming China's medical and health system.

Study workshops were organized by a coordination office. The workshop discussions differed little with respect to how to fund basic healthcare coverage. Everyone agreed that the government should fund basic coverage. However, they did differ with respect to who should provide the health services: free services provided by the government through public hospitals or services through the market. Two options were reviewed: (1) the basic medical insurance fund (the so-called 'third party') would subsidize the demand side, allowing patients to purchase services from medical institutions; (2) state finances compensating the service provider, with public hospitals providing medical services free of charge. According to insiders, most of the research teams supported the first approach, while only one and a half teams supporting the second approach.

As a result, led by the National Development and Reform Commission, the Opinions on Deepening the Reform of the Medical and Health System (Draft for Comments) were developed based on nine proposals, with a focus on "compensation for the demand side" approach, and it was submitted to the State Council for approval.

The reform of the healthcare system during the past thirty years demonstrates that if a healthcare system emphasizes the public goods nature of health services by providing free care for all but lacks the resources to fund public hospitals, it cannot deliver reliable services. More than 10,000 public hospitals currently provide about 85 percent of healthcare services in China, but government direct funding accounts for only 5–10 percent of their operating expenses. The market funds the rest.[38] Without a well-functioning healthcare services market to provide institutional incentives and constraints, issues of "difficulties in accessing healthcare services" (*kanbing nan*) and "expensive healthcare services" (*kanbing gui*) cannot be resolved.

Because the reforms progressed at a slow pace, it took time to establish social security for retirement and healthcare benefits. Therefore, the government instead turned to accelerating the establishment of a minimum livelihood security system.

In 1997, the State Council issued the Circular on Establishing a Minimum Livelihood Security System for Urban Residents, requiring the establishment of the system during the Ninth Five-year Plan period to safeguard urban residents' basic livelihoods. After making considerable progress in establishing minimum safeguards for urban residents in the early twenty-first century, the State Council issued the Circular on Establishing a Minimum Livelihood Security System for Rural Residents in 2007, requiring the establishment of minimum livelihood guarantees for rural residents.

[38] Cai Jiangnan, "How to Carry Out the Healthcare System Reform Through to the End," WeChat Public Account of China–Europe Center for Health Management and Policy, July 27, 2017.

Coverage includes the eligible impoverished rural populations. It has been estimated that in 2008 there were 23.34 million urban beneficiaries and 42.84 million rural beneficiaries of these systems.[39] Thus, the basic minimum livelihood safeguards for urban and rural poor have been established.

In the rural areas, the people's commune cooperative healthcare system (i.e., the barefoot doctors) had collapsed with the expansion of the household contract responsibility system. Although some efforts were made by the central and local governments after 1994, the lack of financial resources and the lack of an effective institutional design remained significant challenges, and only the cooperative healthcare system in the coastal areas survived. In October 2002, the Party Central Committee and the State Council issued the Decision on Further Strengthening Rural Healthcare, announcing that beginning in 2003, a new rural cooperative healthcare model and a medical aid system would gradually be established nationwide. The new cooperative healthcare model would use pooled funding to cover rural residents' healthcare expenses for severe illnesses. In January 2003, the State Council General Office forwarded the Public Health Ministry's Opinions on Establishing a New Rural Cooperative Healthcare System, requiring that the system be established by 2010 to reduce the economic burdens on farmers due to illnesses and to improve their health. According to the requirements of the Eleventh Five-year Plan, by 2010 coverage of the new rural cooperative medical care was to reach over 80 percent of the rural areas. On April 25, 2014, the Ministry of Finance, the National Health and Family Planning Commission, and the Ministry of Human Resource and Social Security jointly issued the Notice on the 2014 Funding Level for the New Rural Cooperative Healthcare System and the Basic Health Insurance for Urban Residents, increasing government subsidies to RMB 320 per capita. In addition, the premium for individual contributions was increased by RMB 20 from the 2013 level, raising the national per capita individual premium to about RMB 90 per annum. By the end of 2014, 736 million people had participated in the new rural cooperative healthcare system, accounting for 98.9 percent of the total rural population.[40] Note that some cities consolidated the urban and rural resident healthcare systems and saw a reduced participation rate. In January 2016, the State Council issued the Opinions on Consolidating the Urban and Rural Resident Basic Healthcare Systems, requiring gradual consolidation of the two systems to establish a national basic healthcare system.

The social security reforms did not progress well, and the unfunded individual accounts remained a massive implicit debt for the government. Meanwhile, social funding pools, with substantial regional differences, were confined to the provincial level. Emerging cities have large surpluses, while old industrial bases are facing severe empty accounts, with pensions even being insufficiently disbursed, raising the

[39] Ministry of Human Resources and Social Security, *China Yearbook on Labor and Social Security, 2008* (Beijing: China Labor and Social Security Publishing House, 2009).

[40] Planning and Information Department of the National Health and Family Planning Commission, "2014 Communiqué on Health and Family Planning Development," November 5, 2015, http://www.nhfpc.gov.cn.

possibility of reverting to a pay-as-you-go system. The burden of pensions and healthcare has become a heavy load on the people, affecting social harmony and justice, hindering consumption growth, and severely troubling socio-economic development in the twenty-first century.

Chapter 6
The External Opening Adds Momentum to Reform and Development

The Third Plenary Session of the 11th Party Central Committee in December 1978 focused on "shifting the emphasis of our Party's work and the attention of the people of the whole country to socialist modernization." Meanwhile, the historic meeting's decision required "a series of significant economic measures to reform the economic management system and its methodology and to develop equal and mutually beneficial economic cooperation with other countries based on self-reliance."[1] Later, this requirement was summarized as "domestic reform and external opening" (reform and opening), which became the cornerstone policy of the Chinese government.

An outstanding feature of China's economic development after the onset of the reforms was the combination of domestic reform and external opening. In other words, China simultaneously carried out domestic market-oriented reforms and engaged in an external opening, which were mutually reinforcing. Reform meant fundamental changes to the command economy, during which the authorities had to give up certain powers. In contrast, opening encountered less resistance than reform because it represented a rapid way to attract investments, market access, and technologies (including those for managerial purposes) by connecting the domestic economy with the mature economies of the developed markets. Therefore, opening tended to make more progress than reform and became an important driving force for the latter. Due to external trade and investment, the domestic economy became more market-oriented, better internationalized, and respectful of the rule of law. Opening facilitated reform, which was a prominent characteristic of China's economic development for nearly forty years. This chapter examines the interactions between opening and reform during this process.

[1] Communiqué of the Third Plenary Session of the 11th Party Central Committee, December 12, 1978.

W. Jinglian, *China's Economic Reform*, Understanding China,
https://doi.org/10.1007/978-981-96-9607-9_6

6.1 The Transition from an Inward-to an Outward-Oriented Economy

The contemporary world is an open world. The great geographical discoveries at the end of the fifteenth century expanded the sphere of activity for the emerging West European countries. Market expansion led to the first industrial revolution in the mid-eighteenth century in England that later spread to Western Europe. One hundred years later, as Marx and Engels put it: "The bourgeoisie has through its exploitation of the world market given a cosmopolitan character to production and consumption in every country. … [new industries] no longer process local raw materials; instead, they utilize resources sourced from the most distant regions. The products of these industries are not only consumed domestically but are distributed and used in all corners of the globe. Instead of the old needs, once fulfilled by local production, we now see new desires that require satisfaction by the products of distant lands and climates. In place of the old local and national seclusion and self-sufficiency, we have intercourse in every direction, and an universal inter-dependence of nations."[2]

Globalization accelerated with the arrival of the twentieth century. Apart from the international trade of goods, capital too began to move across borders. After World War II, the movement of capital was internationalized. In addition to goods and money, production processes were also quickly internationalized.

These circumstances presented a central strategic dilemma to the developing countries: how should external economic relations be handled?

The responses of the developing countries after World War II can be grouped into those of either the inward-looking or outward-looking economies. A closed-door and no-contact-with-the-West policy characterized the initial model. However, during the period of rapid economic globalization, this was impossible. After the end of World War II, the developing countries in succession abandoned the closed-door policy and began to trade with the developed countries. But most countries did not use their comparative advantages to seek out shared development. Instead, they introduced equipment and technologies from abroad to produce domestic substitutes for imports. History tells us that this import-substitution strategy did not achieve the expected goal. In the later part of the century, many developing countries copied the successful approaches of Japan and the "Four Little Dragons," i.e., Singapore, South Korea, Hong Kong (China), and Taiwan (China). They shifted from inward-looking to an outward-looking economies. There is both a higher-level and a lower-level of an outward-looking economy. At the lower level, an economy in which exports increase with moderate protection of the domestic producers is referred to as an "export-oriented economy." At the higher level, there exists an open economy, with fully realized trade and investment and trade facilitation (liberalization) (see Table 6.1).

Import substitution and export orientation are the strategies utilized by the late-comer economies to catch up with the advanced countries. On the surface, these two external economic strategies differed only in terms of priorities. However, they also

[2] Marx and Engels, "Manifesto of the Communist Party," 1848, in *Selected Works of Marx and Engels* (Chinese translation. Beijing: People's Publishing House, 1972), vol. 1, pp. 254–255.

Table 6.1 Types of external economic relations

	Inward-looking	Outward-looking
Higher level	Import substitution	Open economy
Lower level	Closed-door policy	Export-oriented policy (relatively open economy)

had strikingly different trade and foreign exchange policies (see Table 6.2), which led to contrasting outcomes.

The import-substitution approach can be described as follows: first, imports for which there is significant domestic demand based on historical data are identified; then second, local firms are encouraged to produce products with imported technologies, and third, tariff and non-tariff barriers are established, overvaluing the domestic currency, and preferential treatment is provided to domestic producers. These steps are expected to reduce the high startup costs and make investments in targeted industries profitable. Domestically produced products are then substituted for imports.

The export-oriented strategy aimed to provide a certain level of government support for those domestic products enjoying comparative advantages so as to expand their international market shares. The strategic approach is as follows: first, the currency is periodically devalued, and an undervalued exchange rate is maintained for domestic producers to make profits when selling agricultural produce, manufactured goods, and labor in the international market; second, certain exports are subsidized to encourage investments in export capacity building, and certain exporters are subsidized through tax exemptions, tax rebates for exports and imports of parts and components, lending rate reductions, and other measures to help firms overcome international market entry barriers, and third, a trade policy of moderate protection rather than high protection is adopted to prevent producers from abandoning exports in favor of the more profitable domestic market that has been inflated by excessive protectionism.

China is one of the oldest civilizations on earth and in the past it had broad economic and cultural exchanges with other countries. The historic Silk Road is a monument to China's external opening. However, in 1371, Zhu Yuanzhang, the first emperor of the Ming dynasty, promulgated a ban on seagoing. Following this imperial policy, the Ming emperors strictly prohibited both military and civilians from engaging in maritime trade. "No ship was allowed to be on the sea," and violators were to be beheaded. In the sixteenth century, West Europe entered the "Age of Sail,"

Table 6.2 Types of external economic policies

	Import substitution	Export orientation
Trade policy	High-level protection	Moderate protection
Exchange rate policy	Currency overvaluation	Currency undervaluation

but the declining Ming dynasty was still exercising its strict closed-door policy.[3] The successor Qing dynasty continued the seagoing ban, prohibiting all exchanges of ships, people, and goods by sea.

This policy of the Ming and Qing dynasties lasted for nearly 500 years, hindering China's ability to learn from other civilizations. Meanwhile, the feudal system collapsed in West Europe, and the rise of capitalism there led to the emergence of domestic markets and the exploration of international markets. As the productive forces were developing rapidly in the capitalist countries, China was left in a state of stagnation. In 1793, amidst the first industrial revolution in Western Europe, King George III of Great Britain sent a mission led by Lord Macartney (George Macartney) to China with the intention of the two countries establishing trade relations. Emperor Qianlong of China responded, "… our Celestial Empire possesses all things in prolific abundance and lacks no product within its borders. There is, therefore, no need to import the manufactures of outside barbarians in exchange for our produce."[4] The Emperor thus rejected the request of King George III.

But Emperor Qianlong's rejection of exchanges with the West demonstrated his ignorance. He believed that, under his reign, Chinese economic development was at a historical high. From the second half of the seventeenth century to the end of the eighteenth century, China had been ruled by three Qing dynasty emperors: Kangxi, Yongzheng, and Qianlong. This period is known as the "Kangxi Qianlong Age of Prosperity." But the period was merely an afterglow of their authoritarian power. At that time, countries in Western Europe during the Renaissance revival, were experiencing a great emancipation of thinking and a thorough transformation of their socioeconomic systems. Led by Great Britain and driven by institutional changes, the industrial revolution swept throughout the countries of Western Europe, completely changing their respective socioeconomic outlooks. As a result, China was no longer the number one economic power in the world, and it gradually declined to become the "sick man of East Asia."

Deng Xiaoping once summarized this period: "If we count from the mid-Ming dynasty to the Opium Wars, China was in a closed-door state for more than 300 years. If we count from the reign of Emperor Kangxi, the period lasted nearly 200 years. This long period of isolation impoverished China and bred ignorance."[5]

---

[3] In 1405–1431, court eunuch Zheng He commanded seven seafaring voyages at the request of Zhu Di, the third emperor of the Ming dynasty. It has been argued that Zhu Di terminated the seagoing ban to develop external trade during the early Ming dynasty, but the historical record contradicts this claim. Zheng He's expeditions aimed to find the whereabouts of Emperor Jianwen, who was said to be on the run overseas after he was overthrown by Zhu Di. Another likely goal of Zheng He's voyages was to demonstrate the strength of the Celestial Empire. But neither plan had anything to do with the development of trade. During the reign of Zhu Di, the ban on seagoing was more rigid than it had been during the time of the first emperor.

[4] First Historical Archives of China, comp., "Emperor Qianlong: Letter to George III," in *Selected Historical Archives about English Envoy Macartney's Visit to China* (Beijing: China International Cultural Publishing House, 1997). See Emperor Qianlong: Letter to George III, 1793 | US-China Institute (usc.edu) for the English translation of the quote.

[5] Deng Xiaoping, "Speech at the Third Plenary Conference of the Central Advisory Commission," 1984, *Selected Works of Deng Xiaoping* (Beijing: People's Publishing House, 1994), vol. 3, p. 90.

Before the establishment of the People's Republic, the leadership of the Chinese Communist Party had no intention of developing a closed-door economy. In the "On the People's Democratic Dictatorship," published on July 1, 1949, Mao Zedong highlighted that China needed to engage in business and thus sustain trade relations with the West.[6] But in June 1950, the Korean War erupted, and by October of that year, the Chinese People's Volunteer Army had entered Korea, prompting a United Nations resolution that imposed sanctions on China, cutting off almost all economic connections between China and the West.

After 1956, with its centralized planning system in place and following Lenin's trade policy, there was a state monopoly of all trade.[7] Within this highly state-monopolized system there were various sectoral export and import corporations responsible for managing the country's foreign trade.[8] The State Planning Commission issued state plans for procuring exports and allocating imports. The government retained all the profits from foreign trade and absorbed all the losses. Under this system, the role of imports and exports was to exchange needed products and to balance between shortages and surpluses.

After the beginning of the Great Leap Forward in 1958, and particularly after the collapse of China's alliance with the Soviet Union in the early 1960s, Chinese trade with the Soviet Union and the Eastern European countries dropped sharply. National leaders then began to emphasize the importance of "self-sufficiency," and they encouraged Chinese local governments to develop "independent economic systems." The tightened closed-door policy further reduced China's share of global trade to less than 1 percent.

The increased hostility between China and the Soviet Union during the Cultural Revolution culminated in a series of military skirmishes along the border.[9] In this context, Mao Zedong began to revise the strategy that had viewed the United States as China's primary enemy. On the one hand, China accelerated efforts to prepare for any surprise attack from the north; on the other, it sought to improve relations with the West. At the same time, the West had similar needs. In July 1971, U.S. Secretary

---

[6] Mao Zedong, "On the People's Democratic Dictatorship (June 30, 1949)," *Selected Works of Mao Tse-Tung* (Beijing: People's Publishing House, 1991), vol. 4, pp. 1473–1474.

[7] Trade nationalization refers to the nationalization of trade entities and the right to manage and operate trade activities. On April 22, 1918, Lenin signed a decree establishing a foreign trade monopoly that reflected his thinking. See Zhou Guofang, "How to Understand Lenin's Foreign Trade Monopoly," *Social Sciences*, no. 6 (1987).

[8] The monopolistic trade corporations under the Ministry of Foreign Trade included China National Cereals, Oils and Foodstuffs Import and Export Corporation, China National Native Produce and Animal Byproducts Import and Export Corporation, China National Textiles Import and Export Corporation, China National Silk Import and Export Corporation, China National Light Industrial Products Import and Export Corporation, China National Arts & Crafts Import and Export Corporation, China National Chemicals Import and Export Corporation, China National Machinery Import and Export Corporation, and China National Metals and Minerals Import and Export Corporation.

[9] In March 1969, the Soviet army invaded China's Zhenbao Island (Damansky Island) in Heilongjiang province, forcing Chinese border troops to fight back in self-defense. In August of that year, the Soviets ambushed a team of Chinese border troops in Tielieketi (Terekty) in the Xinjiang Autonomous Region, killing all 28 soldiers.

of State Henry Kissinger visited China, and in October of that year, Taiwan was replaced by the People's Republic of China as a permanent member of the UN Security Council. In February 1972, U.S. President Richard Nixon visited China, whereupon the two sides signed the Shanghai Communiqué, laying the foundation for the normalization of relations between the two countries. Thereafter, in 1972 China either established or upgraded diplomatic relations with several Western bloc countries, such as the United Kingdom, as well as with Japan and Australia. (Sino-U.S. diplomatic ties were not officially established until 1979.)

After signing the Shanghai Communiqué, China began to turn away from its former closed-door policy and to develop trade relations with the West. In 1977–78, under the leadership of Hua Guofeng, it imported large quantities of heavy industrial and mining equipment and expanded its foreign trade. However, its goal was not to establish an open economy but rather to establish an "independent and self-sufficient" economy through an import substitution strategy, i.e., replacing imports with domestic products that were manufactured with critical imported equipment and technologies.

China's foreign trade gradually recovered, but it remained at a very low level. The country's share of global trade remained at less than 1 percent.

After returning to the central leadership in 1975, Deng Xiaoping tried to expand the external opening. At a State Council discussion about the State Planning Commission's draft on Several Questions About Accelerating Industrial Development, Deng proposed a major policy to introduce new technologies and equipment and to expand imports and exports. He said, "All in all, we should strive to expand exports … so as to speed up the technical transformation of our industries and to raise the productivity of labor."[10] The Gang of Four, led by Jiang Qing, who at the time was playing a crucial role in policymaking, fiercely rejected Deng's proposal. During the 1976 campaign to counterattack the trend of right-deviationist reversal-of-verdicts, the Gang accused Deng Xiaoping of worshipping all foreign things and denounced him as traitorous. Consequently, China's foreign trade once again began to contract.

In general, between the early 1960s and the late 1970s, China's external economic relations remained stagnant. (See Table 6.3).

The transition from inward-looking to outward-looking external economic policies was not realized until after the overthrow of the Gang of Four.

6.2 The 1980s: A Shift from Import Substitution to Export Orientation

After the end of the Cultural Revolution, Chinese leaders and senior officials began to learn about the economic development taking place in other countries. The Four Little Dragons, Hong Kong Singapore, South Korea, and Taiwan, once at a similar level of

[10] Deng Xiaoping, "Some Comments on Industrial Development," 1975, *Selected Works of Deng Xiaoping* (Beijing: People's Publishing House, 1993), vol. 2, p. 29.

Table 6.3 China's share of global trade

Year	Total foreign trade, China (billion USD)	Share in global trade (%)
1953	2.37	1.5
1957	3.11	1.4
1959	4.38	1.9
1962	2.66	0.9
1970	4.59	0.7
1975	4.75	0.8
1977	14.8	0.6

Sources International Trade, GATT; See Nicholas R. Lardy, *China in the World Economy* (Washington, DC: Institute of International Economics, 1974), p. 2

economic development as China, had emerged as developed industrial economies. Their experiences led to a recognition that China could only reap the benefits of its civilization and modernize by firmly adopting an outward-looking policy and integrating with the global economy. On October 10, 1978, when receiving a delegation of journalists from the Federal Republic of Germany, Deng Xiaoping made the following significant remarks: "For a while in the past, we called learning advanced sciences and technologies 'worshiping all things foreign.' Now everybody knows this is nonsense. In the early 1960s, science and technology in our country did lag behind the rest of the world, but the gap was not wide. The world developed rapidly in the last decade or more, and the gap between us and other countries became enormous. Our economy lagged behind the developed countries for not just 10 years but possibly 20 to 30 years. In certain areas, the gap could even be 50 years. There are 22 years left before the end of this century. By that time, what will the world look like? Our Four Modernizations aim to reach your current level by the end of this century, which is challenging. It will be more difficult to reach your end-century level. We must be good at learning and we will need significant international assistance to modernize. We should introduce advanced technologies and equipment from abroad, which shall be the starting point of China's development.."[11]

Based on this analysis, Deng Xiaoping proposed the open-door policy.

Deng Xiaoping's external economic strategy differed from the import substitution policy of the mid-1970s. It was more similar to the export-oriented approach of Japan and the Four Little Dragons. During the period immediately following the fall of the Gang of Four, China's leaders were attracted to the experiences of the Four Little Dragons in developing an outward-looking economy to achieve high economic growth. Therefore, the leaders decided to adopt an export-oriented strategy

[11] Deng Xiaoping, "Carry Out the Policy of Opening to the Outside World and Learn Advanced Science and Technology from Other Countries," 1978, *Selected Works of Deng Xiaoping*, vol. 2, pp. 132–133.

for economic development, attracting foreign investments in labor-intensive industries and, given China's comparative advantage in labor resources. expanding exports of manufactured goods.

From 1978 to 1993, China's external economic focus gradually shifted from import substitution to an export orientation.

Two milestones mark this transition. The first was the gradual dismantling of the state foreign trade monopoly and the reduction of tariff and non-tariff barriers. The second milestone was the partial opening of the foreign exchange market under a dual-track foreign exchange system.

With respect to its foreign trade, China adopted a gradualist approach to breaking up the state monopoly, including (a) decentralizing approval authority to provincial-level governments, (b) establishing foreign trade corporations under the line ministries, (c) giving foreign trade autonomy to various large and medium-sized SOEs, and (d) providing foreign trade autonomy, such as the right to import raw materials and parts and components for production and to export products to enterprises with foreign investment. Import quotas and licensing were removed step by step. Although in the early 1980s, such controls had been commonplace, by the decade's end, only fifty-three types of goods remained under the quota and licensing regime, and controlled goods accounted for only 46 percent of the country's total exports and imports. Meanwhile, the government progressively reduced tariff protections. In 1982, the average statutory tariff rate was as high as 56 percent, but by 1992 it had gone down to 43.2 percent.

In addition, China reformed its foreign exchange management system and partially opened the foreign exchange market. Under China's traditional inward-looking planned economy, the plan had regulated all export and import activities, and the government allocated foreign currency and set foreign exchange rates. The RMB was usually overvalued to support investments under the import substitution policy. At the onset of reform and opening, the official RMB exchange rate was as high as RMB 1.5: USD 1.0. In October 1980, the State Council allowed SOEs and quasi-governmental institutions to engage in foreign exchange transactions at the internal settlement prices (RMB 2.8: USD 1.0) of the Bank of China, with a floating range of plus or minus 10 percent. After 1985, foreign exchange swap centers were set up, first in Shenzhen and the other special economic zones and then in many other provinces. Foreign- invested enterprises could buy and sell foreign currency through the foreign exchange management authorities. The foreign exchange swap centers also gradually abandoned the floating range, allowing the foreign exchange rates to be determined by supply and demand. A dual-track system of official foreign exchange rates and market rates emerged.

In addition to breaking up the administrative monopoly over foreign trade and reducing the tariff and non-tariff barriers, another strategic move as part of China's external opening was the establishment of the special economic zones (SEZs), following the examples of several other East Asian countries to attract overseas investments and to build large export production bases.

After adopting its export-oriented strategy, the first challenge that China faced was the lack of export production bases to meet demand from the developed markets.

Although endowed with rich human resources, China lacked production enterprises equipped with advanced technologies and management practices. Modern enterprises can only emerge and grow in an enabling environment. Given the country's vast size and long history of implementing a planned economy , however, it was impossible to form a uniform domestic market and to open up the entire country to the outside world within a short time span. Inspired by the success of Singapore and the other East Asian countries, China's leaders decided to use the SEZs as a policy tool.[12] In other words, before an integrated domestic market could come into being, the SEZs, with their enabling local environment, such as an international market, would be established. For this purpose, Shenzhen and other coastal cities were selected because of their proximity to Hong Kong, Macao, and Taiwan and because of their strong connections with overseas Chinese. These coastal areas were accorded strategic priority; from there, the process of external opening would be expanded in phases.

In 1979, the government granted to Guangdong and Fujian "special policies and flexible measures." Specifically, the two provinces enjoyed the following special treatment: (a) fixed quotas for fiscal and foreign exchange revenue. (b) a certain-level of market activities for material supplies and commerce, (c) enlarged local autonomy in terms of planning, pricing, labor and wages, enterprise management, and external economic activities, and (d) special pilot export zones to introduce foreign capital, advanced technologies, and management experience from the Chinese diaspora, and increased exports. In 1980, these pilots became SEZs, after the Standing Committee of the National People Congress decided to establish four SEZs, in Shenzhen, Zhuhai, Shantou, and Xiamen. Within the SEZs, economic activities and operations were driven by market forces rather than being tightly controlled by government regulations. In addition, in 1985 fourteen coastal port cities were designated as "open cities." In 1992, another group of coastal, riverside, and border area cities and several inland provincial capitals were added to the list, thus establishing a broad "belt for external engagement." These places utilized foreign resources effectively, participated in international competition, and spearheaded China's external opening.

The above reform measures led to groundbreaking advances in China's external economic relations.

(1) The rapid growth of foreign trade

The first advance was the change from economic stagnation to rapid growth of foreign trade. The expansion of economic scale that improved international competitiveness was a primary reason behind this rapid growth. However, the more important driver was the expeditious development of processing trade.

[12] In October 1978, Deng Xiaoping visited Japan. In November, he visited Thailand, Malaysia, and Singapore. Singapore's Jurong Industrial Estate, where foreign investment was utilized to build factories for developing an external-oriented economy, left a particularly deep impression on him,. As a result, he became more confident about the opening policy and began to think about establishing SEZs in China's coastal cities adjacent to Hong Kong. See Li Juchuan, "The Sea Apple Tree on the Top of Jurong Hill," *Suzhou Daily*, May 13, 2008.

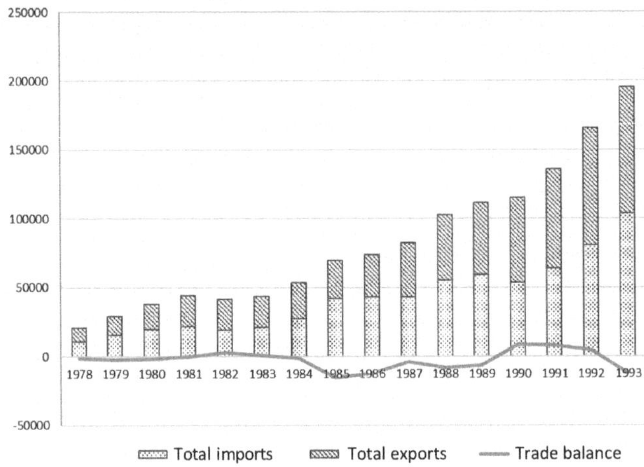

Fig. 6.1 China's foreign trade, 1978–93 (USD million). *Source* National Bureau of Statistics

Beginning from the end of the 1970s, China adopted a processing trade model called "*sanlai yibu*" (three types of processing trade plus compensation trade).[13] Initially, when China's industrial foundation was still weak, a custom manufacturing and compensation trade model utilized overseas equipment, technologies, and funding to develop domestic manufacturing capabilities. The processing industry focused on the domestic market by producing import substitutes. However, as pro-export institutional arrangements and policies became more robust, there was a shift toward export markets and production of import substitutes gradually declined.

The export-oriented strategy led to speedy development of processing trade. China actively participated in the international division of labor and took over the processing of low-value-added goods in the global value chain. Relying on foreign-made equipment and cheap local labor, export enterprises imported intermediate inputs from Japan and South Korea and then turned the inputs into final exports to be shipped to the United States, Japan, and Europe.

Between 1979 and 1993, China's total exports and imports grew from USD 29.33 billion to USD 195.7 billion, an increase of 14.5 percent per annum. As a result, China's share of global trade increased. In 1978, exports and imports of goods totaled only USD 20.64 billion, accounting for 0.79 percent of the world total, and the country ranked 32nd in terms of world trade. By 1993, goods exports and imports reached USD 195.7 billion, representing an increase of 8.5 times and accounting for 2.56 percent of the global total. China's global ranking jumped to no. 11 (Fig. 6.1).

While the amount of exports was increasing rapidly, their composition was undergoing significant improvements. Traditionally, China's main exports had been agricultural products, crude oil, coal, and other low-priced primary goods with marginal profitability. In 1980, the export of primary products totaled USD 9.12 billion,

[13] "*Sanlai yibu*" refers to the custom manufacturing of materials, designs, and parts and components supplied by foreign buyers, and compensation trade.

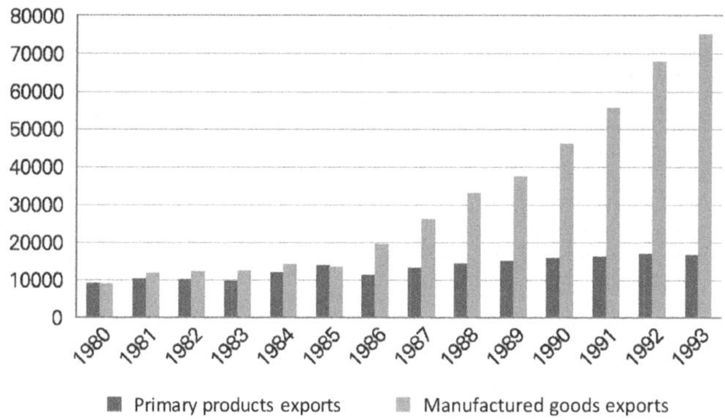

Fig. 6.2 Composition of exports: Primary Products vs. Manufactured Goods, 1980–93 (USD million). *Source* National Bureau of Statistics

accounting for 50.3 percent of total exports. With progress in introducing foreign investments and technologies and building special zones for exports, the share of manufactured products in total exports gradually increased. By 1993, manufactured exports had risen to 81.8 percent of total exports, while the share of primary products had dropped to 18.2 percent. Therefore, by the early 1990s China transitioned from an exporter of mainly primary products to an exporter of manufactured products (Fig. 6.2).

(2) Establishing the SEZs and expanding a belt for external opening

Under the strong leadership of the central government as well as policy support from various departments, the development of export bases made considerable progress. Within the decade from 1980 to 1990, amount of infrastructure investment in Shenzhen and the three other SEZs exceeded RMB 30 billion.

As the most vibrant high-growth areas in the country, these zones were a powerful driving force behind China's rapid economic growth. The large-scale opening led to increased foreign trade, which, in turn, spurred rapid economic development. The best example is Shenzhen, a remote fishing village that was transformed into a modern metropolis almost with the blink of an eye. In 1985, the gross industrial output of the four SEZs was only RMB 5.5 billion, but by 1990 it had reached RMB 49.5 billion, an eightfold increase within five years, or 50 percent per annum.

The core task of the SEZs and the open coastal areas was to introduce foreign capital, advanced technologies, experience in business management, and access to world markets. During the Seventh Five-Year Plan period (1986–1990), the fourteen open coastal cities attracted over USD 10 billion in foreign direct investment. They established more than 2,000 joint ventures, cooperative enterprises, and wholly foreign-owned enterprises. The opening up of these cities significantly boosted the development of an export-oriented economy. In 1990, the twelve coastal provinces, autonomous regions, and municipalities boasted foreign trade exports nearing USD

Table 6.4 Foreign direct investment in China (USD billion)

Year	FDI contracted value	FDI disbursement
1983	1.73	0.92
1984	2.65	1.42
1985	6.33	1.96
1986	3.33	2.24
1987	3.71	2.31
1988	5.30	3.19
1989	5.60	3.39
1990	6.60	3.49
1991	11.98	4.37
1992	58.12	11.01
1993	111.44	27.52

Source National Statistics Bureau

40 billion, representing approximately two-thirds of the country's total foreign trade exports.

The introduction of foreign capital achieved excellent results. This progress accelerated after Deng Xiaoping's talks during his Southern Tour. With the improved investment climate, the economy recorded high growth. Foreign businesspeople were arriving in China in succession with investments. The recipients of these investments extended from the south to the north and from the coastal to the inland areas. More large foreign enterprises and multinational corporations arrived as well, and more sectors were opened to foreign investments. As a result, China's share of large and high-tech projects increased, and the investment types became increasingly diversified. Between 1979 and 1993, foreign capital commitments reached USD314.2 billion, with a total disbursement of USD137.8 billion. Among the total commitments, USD85.8 billion came from external borrowing, of which USD71.8 was disbursed. In total, 17,400 foreign direct investment projects were approved, with USD221.9 billion committed and USD61.8 billion disbursed (Table 6.4). In 1993, the total exports by companies with foreign investment was USD25.24 billion, accounting for 27.5 percent of China's yearly total exports.[14]

(3) The increasingly important role of the external opening: promoting domestic economic reform

A market economy is a complex, highly sophisticated, and massive system. The transformation from a state-dominated economy to a market economy is arduous and complex. China's external opening in the 1980s provided the country with access to mature markets and promoted domestic economic reforms.

[14] Comprehensive Department of National Bureau of Statistics: "Statistical Communique of the National Statistics Bureau of the People's Republic of China on the Economic and Social Development in 1993," February 28, 1994, http://www.stats.gov.cn/tjsj/tjgb/ndtjgb/qgndtjgb/200203/t20020331_30007.html.

First, as a result of foreign trade, domestic prices became more responsive to international market prices and moved closer to market equilibrium. The pricing mechanism is the core of a market system, which is efficient mainly because prices are determined through market competition, reflecting the scarcity of resources and playing a decisive role in resource allocations. Under the controlled economy, prices were severely distorted. Administrative pricing catered to the demands of industrial policies, favoring industry—especially heavy industry—over light industry, which resulted in price distortions. As a result, the prices of primary products were distorted and the prices of processing products were raised. During the initial stage of the reform, China's leaders could not decide whether to launch a reform to liberalize prices so as to correct these distortions. But the external opening forced changes to the pricing mechanism. Foreign trade liberalization, export and import growth, and foreign direct investments helped to correct the price distortions by increasing the prices of primary products and suppressing the prices of manufactured goods. As a result, the price structure in the domestic market moved closer to that in mature markets. The external opening thus played a positive role in the formation of market-based pricing.[15]

Second, the growth of foreign direct investment contributed to the emergence of domestic market institutions. Because the foreign investors came from mature markets, they had a strong demand for a sound business environment. Initially, the government's primary response was to provide them with preferential treatment. However, prolonged preferential treatment for foreign-invested enterprises meant that domestic firms were treated as secondary citizens and were crowded out of the goods and factors markets. Such practices were also out of step with the foreign investors' demands for transparent rules of competition and rule of law.[16] These pressures, from both domestic and foreign-invested enterprises, were thus an important driving force behind China's economic and political reforms.

Third, the special zones and open coastal areas allowed for experimentation with a modern market-economy system. For example, the export bases absorbed the experiences of the advanced market economies and explored new institutional arrangements and government economic management practices, setting good examples for the nationwide economic reforms.

In summary, the most crucial benefit of the external opening was provision of an impetus for reform, hence the repeated "using openness to promote reform" approach for the subsequent successful reforms.

Finally, there would have been no success without China's willingness to reform. If the country had been satisfied with the mere copying of technologies from the advanced countries to obtain direct benefits and had not made any changes to its

---

[15] Zhou Xiaochuan and Yang Zhigang, "Price Reform: Types and Effectiveness Analysis," *Reform*, no. 3 (1992). In this article, the authors compare the various results of proactive and passive price reforms. In addition, they discuss in detail the prominent role of export and import competition to correct domestic price distortions.

[16] Multinational Corporations and Investment Department, UNCTAD, comp., *World Investment Report 1999: Foreign Direct Investment and the Challenge of Development* (Beijing: China Financial and Economic Publishing House, 2000), pp. 11–12.

former institutions, its latecomer advantages would have become a "latecomer curse" and, in the long run, would have hindered socioeconomic development.[17]

6.3 1994: Reforming the Foreign Exchange Regime and Rolling Out an Export-Oriented Strategy

In 1988–93, China's external economic opening was transitioning from its former inward-looking policy to an outward-looking policy and from import substitution to an export orientation. A key feature of this transition was the dual-track exchange rate system, that is, the coexistence of official and market foreign exchange rates. The establishment of a foreign exchange market improved the business environment for foreign-invested enterprises and facilitated foreign trade growth and economic development. However, the dual-track foreign exchange system also led to unfair competition between those enterprises with access to the official rates (mainly the SOEs) and those enterprises having no such access, providing enormous opportunities for rent-seeking.

To alleviate these problems, two steps were taken to merge the two tracks. First, the official RMB exchange rate was allowed to gradually appreciate. By late 1993, the official rate had reached RMB 5.8: USD1.0. Second, by end-1993 the market rate share in total foreign exchange transactions had increased to 80 percent. The Decision on Certain Issues in Establishing a Socialist Market Economy System, adopted at the Third Plenary Session of the 14th Party Central Committee in November 1993, required a two-step consolidation of the foreign exchange tracks into a single regime for both domestic enterprises and foreign-invested firms. The goal was to achieve managed convertibility of the RMB under the current account.

After careful preparations, the People's Bank of China announced replacement of the official exchange rate regime with a "uniformed, managed floating foreign exchange regime based on the market rate," beginning on January 1, 1994. The two foreign exchange tracks were consolidated into a market track. Domestic enterprises and residents bought and sold foreign exchange in banks at the market rate formed on the interbank foreign exchange market, and the central bank conducted market operations to maintain the stability of the RMB exchange rate only when the exchange rate fluctuated beyond a specific floating range. The starting rate, on January 1, 1994, was RMB 8.72: USD 1.0, lower than the lowest market rate before the reforms, or a 51 percent depreciation from the previous official rate of RMB 5.76: USD 1.0. The banks' foreign exchange system of buying and selling was opened to foreign-invested enterprises in 1996, thereby establishing a managed floating rate regime.

[17] The latecomer's curse is a concept first proposed by the late economist Yang Xiaokai in a December 2000 speech, in which he points out that latecomer advantages will become disadvantages (curses) if a country feels satisfied about introducing the advanced countries' technologies, but the government chooses not to follow the developed countries' examples and to improve its economic institutions. See Yang Xiaokai, "Do Not Replace System Reform with Technology Imitation," *Economic Observer*, September 17, 2002.

Before the onset of the Asian financial crisis in October 1997, the RMB exchange rate had appreciated to RMB 8.28: USD 1.0. After the financial crisis erupted, many countries significantly devalued their currencies. But China chose not to devalue to prevent triggering a competitive devaluation. This decision was crucial in containing the spread of the crisis.

In addition to the managed foreign exchange floating rate regime, the 1994 reform established a mandatory foreign exchange settlement and sales system under the current account. Except for certain foreign exchange accounts at banks authorized by the state, enterprises and residents had to sell their foreign exchange income to designated banks, and the latter had to sell on the market any foreign exchange that exceeded the cash limits approved by the State Administration of Foreign Exchange. This arrangement enabled the timely and adequate transfer of foreign exchange income of enterprises and foreign residents to the country's official foreign reserves to ensure import payments. However, this also created a hurdle for RMB exchange rate liberalization, and it had far-reaching consequences for China's money supply and the macroeconomy. In 2008, the revised Regulations on Foreign Exchange Administration ended the mandatory system, allowing enterprises and residents to retain foreign exchange income within permissible limits.

After the 1994 foreign exchange regime reform, the export-oriented strategy was rolled out nationwide, creating a strong impetus for rapid increases in exports and for foreign exchange surpluses in the second half of the 1990s.

Prior to 1994, foreign trade experienced both surpluses and deficits in turn, with deficits occurring in most years. After 1994, however, exports increased rapidly, with consistently large trade surpluses, and after 2004, the trade surpluses grew exponentially, from USD 31.98 billion in 2004 to USD 262.2 billion in 2007 (see Fig. 6.3). As a result, the current and capital accounts in China's international balance of payments (BoP) both registered a surplus. The BoP surpluses continued to rise, except for a drop in 1997 due to the Asian financial crises and the government's commitment not to depreciate the RMB.

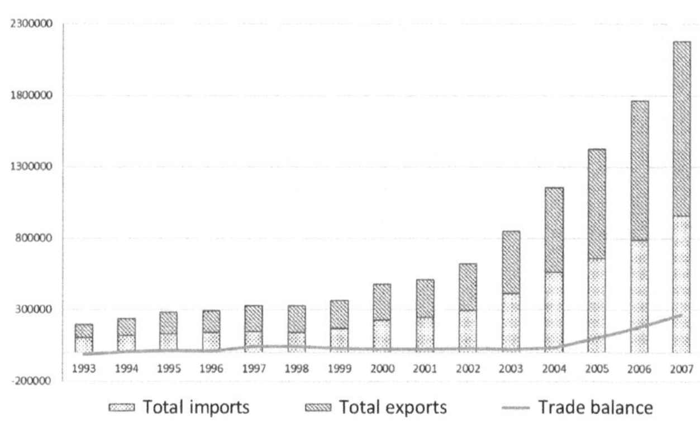

Fig. 6.3 China's exports and imports, 1993–2007 (USD million). *Source* National Bureau of Statistics

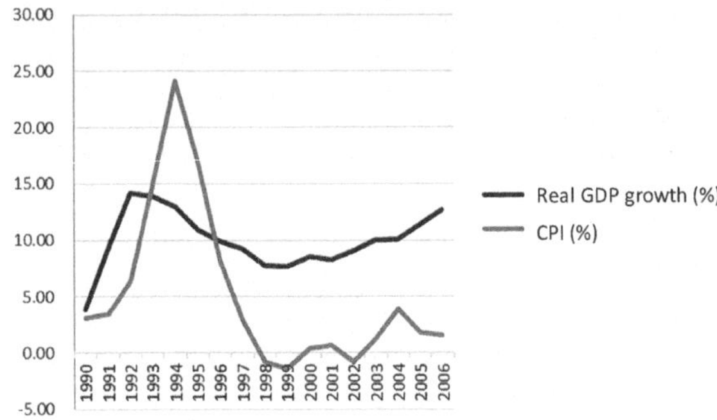

Fig. 6.4 China's economic growth, 1990–2006. *Source* CEIC

Rapid export growth allowed China to fully utilize its comparative advantage: a massive, high-quality, low-cost labor force. This contributed significantly to the transfer of rural surplus labor to the non-agricultural sectors in the urban areas. As a result, with the increasing economic prosperity there was a marked improvement in the people's livelihoods. Because of the fast-paced expansion of exports, China's investment ratio exceeded 40 percent or even close to 50 percent. Despite inadequate domestic consumption, this growth model avoided an economic depression and sustained high economic growth for more than a decade.

Furthermore, the external opening introduced state-of-the-art foreign equipment and technologies. Even before the large-scale investments in human capital began to pay dividends, it had already significantly narrowed the enormous technological gap between China and the advanced countries that had accumulated over the past two hundred years. The technological progress strongly supported high economic growth.

From the second half of the 1990s to 2006, China's economy recorded high growth and low inflation (see Fig. 6.4).

6.4 Toward a Comprehensive Opening

In the 1990s, China made considerable progress in opening up, but it was still at a basic stage of export-oriented economic development. The government continued to promote exports through a certain degree of protection for the domestic market and by undervaluing the currency.

The 1994 reform originally planned to move the RMB exchange rate closer to a market equilibrium by reducing the frequency of PBoC's market interventions and expanding the floating range for foreign exchange. After the foreign exchange reform in 1994, it was expected that the gradual reduction in central bank interventions and the expansion of the range of exchange rate fluctuations would bring the Renminbi closer to an equilibrium point for supply and demand in the foreign exchange market. However, following the outbreak of the Asian financial crisis in 1997, many East Asian countries devalued their currencies in response to the crisis

Table 6.5 Import substitution vs. an export orientation: Strengths and weaknesses

	Import substitution	Export orientation
Strengths	Helps the developing countries acquire specific needed technologies	Demand is not constrained by the level of domestic income Relatively higher-level competition is conducive to efficiency improvements and modernization Competition with foreign producers provides a strong market test for domestic producers
Weaknesses	Trade barriers may protect backwardness and encourage corruption Once raised, trade barriers are difficult to remove Protecting a product increases user costs and reduces product competitiveness	Countries may remain specialized in labor-intensive products, weakening the potential for long-term growth Possible difficulties in developing export markets In sectors other than exports, the level of development will remain stagnant

Source Joseph Stiglitz, *Economics*, 2nd ed. (Chinese Translation. Beijing: People's University Publishing House, 2000)

and hoped that the Renminbi would remain stable to avoid competitive devaluations among currencies. The Chinese government's commitment not to devalue the RMB significantly contributed to the stability in the East Asian economies and to their ability to respond to the crisis. However, as long as the currency depreciations in the neighboring countries continued, China's central bank had no choice but to frequently enter the foreign exchange market to maintain the value of the RMB. The RMB rate was fixed because of its de facto pegging to the U.S. dollar. From the period of the Asian financial crisis until July 2005, the USD to RMB rate was maintained at around USD 1.0: RMB 8.27. Although the rate fluctuated sometimes, the range of the fluctuation was very narrow. But after the end of the Asian financial crisis and after China's export capacity had been strengthened, the undervaluation of the RMB became increasingly conspicuous.

The experiences of other countries show that an export orientation is a trade strategy with both advantages and disadvantages (see Table 6.5). The strategy's adverse effects become more pronounced when exports grow to a certain level. At that point, policy should be adjusted in the direction of a comprehensive economic opening.

Like the East Asian countries under the neo-mercantilist policy of the 1990s, China experienced increasing adverse effects after adoption of the export orientation policy for over a decade.[18] In addition to intensified trade tensions, the following problems occurred:

[18] Based on the experiences of Japan, the Chinese Mainland, and Taiwan (China), this author analyzes the results and the adverse effects of the export-oriented policy in his *Options for China's Growth Model*, 2005 (Beijing: CITIC Publishing House, 2007), pp. 161–172.

First, from a microeconomic perspective, as pointed out by Joseph Stiglitz, while export-oriented strategies remove domestic income constraints on demand, they may "force low-wage developing countries to specialize in labor-intensive products where they have a comparative advantage," thereby weakening long-term growth potential. In other words, the prolonged adoption of export-oriented policies encourages the export of labor-intensive and resource-intensive products, reinforcing an extensive growth model. Such countries consume tremendous resources, but they have low earnings. They are mere laborers working for foreign enterprises.

At the end of the twentieth century, when China had a significant surplus of rural labor, and land available for urban construction was in good supply, the development of labor-intensive processing industries brought about more pluses than minuses. However, the situation changed in the early 2000s: the Lewisian Turning Point had occurred or was about to occur,[19] and domestic technological capabilities had increased. Under these conditions, the export-oriented strategy hindered both innovation and a technological upgrading of domestic enterprises.

After adopting the "*sanlai yibu*" (processing and compensation trade) model in the 1980s, processing trade grew more rapidly than other trade types. In 1996, processing trade exceeded general trade, becoming the largest trade type. Moreover, it accounted for the majority of the trade surplus: the processing trade surplus always exceeded the current year's total trade surplus. In 2005 and 2006, the processing trade surplus was 139.82 percent and 106.43 percent of the total trade surplus, respectively. In 2007, the processing trade's share dropped slightly, but it was still as high as 95.06 percent.[20]

Under the export-oriented policy, processing trade was China's primary trade type for a long period of time. From the perspective of total exports, China appeared to be the factory of the world. But most products were at the low end of the value chain and they were lacking in any technological innovation. Products were thus "Assembled in China" rather than "Made in China,"[21] and Chinese enterprises were Original Equipment Manufacturers (OEMs) for foreign buyers who could buy the products at low prices. Usually, the prices were as low as one-fourth or even one-tenth of the retail prices. OEMs earned only minuscule processing fees.

In January 2004, the *Wall Street Journal* commented on China's role in the global division of labor. The cited example was Logitech International, a Swiss-American joint venture headquartered in California. The company's factory in Suzhou, China, exported 20 million Wanda wireless mouses annually to the U.S. The retail price of

[19] The Lewis Model, developed by Nobel laureate of economics William Arthur Lewis, explains that in a pre-industrialized dual-sector economy, labor supply is unlimited because of the excess labor in the rural areas. A Lewis Turning Point will occur when labor demand and supply change, and labor supply is in shortage. In the early 2000s, Chinese economist Cai Fang concluded that the Lewis Turning Point had already occurred in China, triggering a heated debate on this issue. By the 2010s, the lower-skilled worker shortages and wage increases had become obvious.

[20] Zhang Li, "Analysis of the Structure of China's Trade Surplus and an Evaluation of Its Impact," *China's Foreign Trade*, no. 9 (2008).

[21] Like some other products assembled in China, iPhones and iPads are not labeled as "Made in China."

a Wanda mouse was about USD 40. From its sales, Logitech International took USD 8 (20 percent), wholesalers and retailers took USD 15 (37.5 percent), and parts and components suppliers, such as Motorola and Agilent Technologies, took USD 14 (35 percent). The remaining USD 3 represented the earnings for the Suzhou factory. These earnings were applied to pay the wages of 4,000 workers and to pay energy, transportation, and overhead expenses. The total income of Logitech International's 450 salespeople in California thus exceeded that of the 4,000 workers in the Suzhou factory by a large margin. The commentary concluded that Logitech International's warehouses in Suzhou were "a miniature of today's global economy."[22]

In 2011, several University of California professors decomposed the value chain of iPhones and iPads assembled in China. They found that Apple Inc.'s profits from an iPhone accounted for 58.5 percent of the retail price, and its profits from an iPad accounted for 30.1 percent of the retail price. What remained was only enough for the Chinese enterprises to pay wages.[23] For an iPhone, a Chinese enterprise earned only 1.8 percent of the retail price; for an iPad, it earned 1.6 percent.[24]

Due to the low value-added and the narrow profit margins from exports, Chinese firms had to rely on production volume to make a living. This tactic inevitably led to increased trade tensions and anti-dumping lawsuits, thereby creating more difficulties in expanding exports.

As a result, the following situation emerged: First, China consumed a large amount of non-renewable resources, endured environmental pollution, and carried the stigma of "dumping," yet the major portion of the profits did not accrue to China.[25]

Second, from a macroeconomic perspective, the increasingly apparent adverse effects of the export-oriented policy, together with the investment-driven growth model, led to external economic imbalances. The main symbol of this challenge was the huge trade surpluses, leading to intensified tensions with trade partners and tremendous pressures for an appreciation of the RMB.

At this time, if the foreign exchange regime were to change to a market-based regime (i.e., foreign exchange liberalization), the currency of the trade surplus country would appreciate, rebalancing the country's balance of payments. But this approach would bring enormous pressures on export enterprises to achieve technological innovation and to upgrade their products. But due to interest group inertia, foreign exchange regime reforms are often delayed, and the central bank has to enter the market and buy foreign currency in large quantities. The result is an over-issuance

[22] Andrew Higgins, "As China Surges, It Also Proves a Buttress to American Strength," *Wall Street Journal*, January 30, 2004, Section A1.

[23] At the time, iPhones and iPads were assembled at Foxconn's mainland factories. However, because Foxconn is incorporated in Taiwan, the earnings were not counted as income of mainland enterprises.

[24] Kenneth L. Kraemer, Greg Linden, and Jason Dedrick, "Capturing Value in Global Networks: Apple's iPad and iPhone," February 24, 2012, http://economiadeservicos.com/wp-content/uploads/2017/04/value_ipad_iphone.pdf.

[25] Wu Jinglian, "Meeting the Challenge of the New Growth Model," *Wen Wei Po*, March 9, 2005, Sect. 8.

of currency and excess liquidity. and it may even result in the formation of bubbles that can eventually burst. Chapter 10 will discuss this issue in further detail.

Under this new situation, China's opening strategy required a significant readjustment. The previous strategy of high exports and low imports and boosting demand through trade required a shift toward a more balanced external economic relationship. In terms of trade relations, the goal was not to reduce the total volume of imports and exports but to improve the country's resource allocations and to make better use of global resources through balanced trade, thereby driving China's economic development.

China's decisive action in the direction of a comprehensive opening was its application to accede to the World Trade Organization (WTO), which aims to maintain free trade.

In 1986, China requested that the General Agreement on Tariffs and Trade resume its membership as a contracting party. This move reveals that China had already decided to further open to the outside world and to integrate with the world economy. After fifteen years of complex negotiations, China was finally approved to become a WTO member in November 2001.

During the fifteen years of negotiations, China significantly reduced trade protectionism to meet WTO requirements for trade facilitation, i.e., trade liberalization. It substantially lowered tariff barriers and abolished import quota allocations. Starting from January 1, 2002, China reduced import tariffs on more than 5,300 tariff lines, lowering the average tariff rate from 15.3 percent to 11.3 percent.

As a member country of the WTO, China must comply with nine guiding WTO principles. They are (a) non-discriminatory treatment, (b) most-favored-nation treatment, (c) national treatment, (d) transparency, (e) trade liberalization, (f) market access for goods, (g) reciprocity, (h) preferential treatment to developing and least-developed countries, and (i) equitable dispute settlements. To comply with these principles, China had to further reform its foreign trade policies and practices, e.g., further reducing tariff and non-tariff barriers, repealing import restrictions, ending regular interventions in the foreign exchange market by the central bank, improving the legal framework and the enforcement system, and adopting negative-list entry management for foreign enterprises, etc. More importantly, WTO accession was a channel for China's integration with global economic and trade rules, forcing the country's economic management system to move closer to market practices and rule of law. This was the institutional foundation for China's non-public sector, including foreign enterprises and the private economy, to further develop in the early twenty-first century.

It should be noted that it was not easy to keep all these promises. On the one hand, such reforms would affect the vested interests of certain enterprises and administrative authorities, hence, there was strong resistance from these groups. Conversely, the economy's overall efficiency required improvements to successfully transition from an export-oriented, foreign-capital driven, and external-demand-pulled strategy to a comprehensive opening strategy. After WTO accession, China registered rapid export and import growth. The contribution of market-based demand to economic growth continued to rise, enabling further development of the more efficient non-public sector. All these were conducive to growth with macroeconomic stability. However, the stop-and-go SOE reforms and the regression of these reforms negatively affected economic development. Comprehensive economic efficiency improvements required further market-oriented reforms of the state sector, but such goals could not be achieved overnight.

Chapter 7
The Turn of the Twenty-First Century: Market Forces Driving China's Economic Rise

The advances in the market-oriented reforms of the first half of the 1990s added more market elements to the Chinese economy. The shares of the previously dominant state sector and collective quasi-state industry in the national economy dropped to below 50%.

However, the foundation for market property rights at the time was still unclear. Despite the private sector's significant share in the national economy, private sector property rights were ambiguous. Officially, this growing sector was merely a "supplement to the state economy." To survive, many private businesses had to relinquish partial control to state-owned or collective-owned enterprises, paying the latter firms "management fees" in exchange for being designated as a SOE affiliate (a so-called "red hat" enterprise).

The contradiction between actual economic development and the framework for a Soviet-style socialist economic system elicited very different reactions from people who held varying opinions. The clash between these viewpoints ultimately sparked a major debate at the end of 1996 and the beginning of 1997 about what type of foundational economic system China should adopt.

Although Soviet-style socialism still enjoyed solid political support and had tremendous ideological influence, a return to the fossilized, stagnant, and impoverished past was unimaginable because "circumstances force one's hand." In the end, the 1997 15th Party Congress settled the debate by adopting "public ownership as the mainstay with various other forms of an ownership economy developing together" as the basic economic institution during the primary phase of socialism that was expected to last at least one hundred years. This was considered a major policy breakthrough.

Based on the call of the 15th Party Congress, China adjusted its economic ownership structure at the end of the twentieth century and established a preliminary market economy. As a result, long-suppressed creative forces and an entrepreneurial spirit were released, and underutilized human and physical resources were used more efficiently, thus driving rapid economic growth.

W. Jinglian, *China's Economic Reform*, Understanding China,
https://doi.org/10.1007/978-981-96-9607-9_7

7.1 A Debate on Basic Economic Institutions

Market transactions, in essence, are exchanges of property rights between owners. Observations of the reform process from the end of the 1970s to the early 1990s reveal a unique situation whereby theoretical discussions and policy debates primarily focused on market construction, with little attention to the underlying property rights system. This was because the traditional concepts still dominated the people's minds. Many believed that public ownership, particularly its "higher form," i.e., state ownership, was the economic foundation of a socialist country. Any deviation from this was decried as "discarding the classics and rebelling against orthodoxy" (i.e., deviant and heretical).

Under Stalin's supervision, *Political Economy: A Textbook*, compiled by the USSR's Institute of Economics of the Academy of Sciences under Stalin's supervision, describes the basic socialist economic institution. It states that "public ownership of the means of production is the foundation of socialist relations of production. ... Under socialism, public ownership is dominant in all national economic spheres. ... Socialist public ownership has two forms: (1) whole-people ownership, and (2) collective ownership of cooperative farms. ... In a socialist society, state ownership is the superior and leading mode of ownership." The book further claims that state ownership represents "the most mature and thorough" socialist relations of production. State ownership as "a higher mode of socialist ownership, plays a leading and decisive role in the national economy." Collective ownership is retained as a stopgap arrangement when the agricultural productive forces are underdeveloped. But when the agricultural productive forces advance to a higher level, such collective ownership should gradually transition to "whole-people (state) ownership in all respects."[1]

This Soviet institutional model held decisive influence in the socialist camp. Deeply entrenched and beyond reproach, it was taken as an indisputable given. As early as 1953, the CCP's General Line for the Transition Period: An Outline for Propaganda, reviewed and cleared by Mao Zedong, pointed out that "in essence, the general line is to make socialist ownership of the means of production the only economic foundation for our country and society."[2] After state ownership and quasi-state collective ownership became the sole economic foundation, despite the widespread impoverishment, the CCP adopted a principle to accelerate the transition to state ownership. The Party called for "accomplishing, sooner rather than later, the transition to the whole-people ownership," i.e., state ownership, in all respects.[3]

[1] Institute of Economics, Academy of Sciences (USSR), comp., *Political Economy: A Textbook*, rvsd. 3rd ed. (Chinese translation. Beijing: People's Publishing House, 1959), pp. 114–117, 352–356.

[2] CCP Department of Propaganda, "Mobilize All Forces to Develop China into a Great Socialist Country: An Outline for Study and Propaganda on the Party's General Line for the Transition Period," 1953, in *Reading Materials for Socialist Education Courses* (Beijing: People's Publishing House, 1957), pp. 341–374.

[3] The Decision on the Establishment of the People's Communes in the Rural Areas, adopted by the CCP Politburo in August 1958, required that the collective sector transition to whole-people ownership "within 5–6 years or a longer period," i.e., a transition to sole state ownership. Four

To bypass the insurmountable political barriers caused by this traditional ideology, Deng Xiaoping and other reformist leaders turned to more flexible policies and strategies, including "avoiding disputes," gradually loosening absolute control by state-owned enterprises, and providing a certain degree of space for entrepreneurial activities by the private sector. We have already discussed this process in a previous chapter. In 1979, the government granted foreign investors permission to set up joint ventures in China and allowed individuals to start proprietary businesses within certain limits. Later, such businesses were allowed to hire up to seven workers. In the rural areas, household contracting was permitted, leading to the spread of family farms and followed by the emergence of township and village enterprises.

However, private enterprises were banned until the early 1980s. The Constitution of the People's Republic of China, dated December 1982, stipulates that "the foundation of the People's Republic of China's socioeconomic system is socialist public ownership, i.e., whole-people ownership and collective ownership by the working people. ... The state-run sector is the economic mainstay owned by the whole people. The state protects the strengthening and development of the state-run sector. ...The *getihu* (sole proprietor) sector owned by urban and rural working people within legal limits supplements the socialist public ownership sector." The 1982 Constitution does not mention the private sector.

After the restrictions on employing no more than seven employees were lifted in 1981, the number of workers in private businesses quickly increased, and a private sector based on hired labor began to develop. Deng Xiaoping took a wait-and-see approach and he did not hurry to prohibit such businesses. Some local governments tacitly either acknowledged or quietly encouraged the growth of a private sector because of its positive role in revitalizing the local economy and providing jobs. However, for a long time these businesses were considered illegal or quasi-legal. To survive, many of these firms had to "wear a red hat," that is, maintain an affiliation with the public-owned enterprises.

In October 1987, the 13th Party Congress declared, "The development of the private economy to some extent is beneficial for promoting production, invigorating the market, expanding employment, and better meeting the diverse needs of the people, and it is a necessary and useful supplement to the public ownership economy. To a certain extent, development of the private sector can contribute to higher production, increased market activities, and more jobs. All these will help satisfy people's demand for a better life in various respects."[4] This declaration represents formal recognition of the legality of the private sector. In 1988, the Constitution of the People's Republic of China was amended by the National People's Congress, declaring that "the state allows the existence and development of the private sector

---

months later, in the Decision on Several Questions Related to the People's Communes, the Sixth Plenary Session of the 8th Party Central Committee extended the deadline to "15–20 years or longer." Nevertheless, the need to "accelerate the transition to whole-people ownership in all areas" was repeatedly stressed.

[4] Zhao Ziyang, "Marching on the Road of Socialism with Chinese Characteristics: Report to the 13th National Party Congress (October 25, 1987)," *People's Daily*, November 4, 1987.

within the legal limits," thereby legitimating the private sector's role as a supplement to the public sector. However, the private sector remained a supplement and its development was restricted to ensure dominance of "public ownership led by the state sector."

Nevertheless, despite the various constraints, the private sector gradually expanded vis-à-vis the state-run enterprises by becoming more adaptable and competitive. As a result, the SOE contribution to gross industrial output declined from 78% in 1978 to around 55% in the early 1990s.[5]

At this juncture, Party and government leaders realized that the policy statement "the public-owned economy is the mainstay led by the state-owned sector" required a new explanation to provide more room for the non-public sector to grow. In 1993, the Decision on Several Questions Related to the Establishment of a Socialist Market Economy, adopted by the Third Plenary Session of the 14th PartyCentral Committee, slightly revised this policy statement. The decision states: "Public ownership is the mainstay of the national economy, but the policy can vary for some localities and industries. ... Public ownership's mainstay status is primarily reflected by the dominance of the state and collective sectors in society's total assets and it is embodied in the state sector's control of the economic lifelines and its leading role in economic development. ... The state should create conditions for fair competition between economic entities under different ownership forms. All enterprises should be treated equally."

Although this new explanation [of the basic economic institution] was conservative, some politicians and theoreticians remained disgruntled. These people still insisted on state-sector dominance and they raised doubts about the development of the private sector. Between 1995 and 1997, they successively wrote four lengthy articles, commonly known as the "ten-thousand-character letters."[6] In early 1997, before the opening of the Party congress, they made public their third letter, entitled "Several Issues Related to Upholding the Dominance of Public Ownership," criticizing the development of an economy with diverse ownership forms.[7] This "ten-thousand-character letter" argued that the new interpretation of "public ownership as the mainstay" and "state ownership as the leading form" by the Third Plenary Session of the 14th Central Committee was "quite widely accepted," but they considered it to be "an unfortunate fact." At the same time, they argued that the fundamental economic system of socialism advocates that "socialism takes the ownership by the entire people (i.e., state ownership) as the advanced form of public ownership and as a goal that must be pursued."

---

[5] *China Statistical Yearbook, 1992* (Beijing: China Statistics Publishing House, 1992), p. 26.

[6] Ma Licheng and Lin Zhijun, *Cross Swords: The Third Emancipation Wave in Contemporary China* (Beijing: China Today Publishing House, 1997). This book includes a detailed introduction to the debate triggered by the "ten-thousand-character letters."

[7] "Several Issues Related to Upholding the Mainstay Status of Public Ownership," final draft revised December 21, 1996–January 20, 1997, printout version. Its central arguments can be found in a commentary by a special contributor, entitled "The Main Symbol of Public Ownership's Mainstay Status and How to Uphold It," *Contemporary Thinking*, no. 4 (1996).

The letter claimed that to uphold socialism, China would need to do the following: first, "the state sector, mainly the hundreds of thousands of large, medium, and small industrial enterprises with independent-accounting status and those crucial to the national economy must be maintained as a uniform and complete system"; second, "the state sector must lead the collective sector"; third, "the public sector should treat the non-public sector as a supplement."

The letter sharply criticized the government's hands-off approach toward the trend whereby non-state industrial enterprises were growing more robust than state-sector enterprises, leading to the significant decline of the public sector in the national economy. The authors claimed that if a socialist state with control over political power and ownership rights cannot protect the SOEs, this would be tantamount to implementing a "wrong political line akin to that of Gorbachev."

Advocates of the market-oriented reforms fight back.

Li Youwei, former Party secretary of Shenzhen, was the first to respond. In a speech to a class at the Central Party School, he pointed out that state ownership should be distinguished from whole-people ownership. During the primary stage of socialism, whole-people ownership, i.e., whereby the whole society possesses the means of production, is an idealistic and unrealistic form of possession. Except for SOE employees, people do not have the right to dispose of property or to distribute income. State ownership is the ruling class's form of possession. State ownership can co-exist with other forms of public or private ownership. Such forms of ownership should be mutually conditioned and interdependent, and they should compete with one another on an equal basis. State ownership by the proletariat is suitable for social welfare and public-interest entities, but it is inappropriate to allow state ownership to monopolize or dominate the competitive industries.

In Li's mind, public ownership during the primary stage of socialism is a form of possession under which the majority owns most means of production. This is different from whole-people ownership, the ownership type projected by Marx and Engels whereby the whole society possesses all the means of production. Li further explained that there were various forms of public ownership: (a) state ownership, with the government at various administrative levels as the owner, (b) community ownership, with individual communities forming and owning communal assets, (c) collective ownership, with assets created by pooling the investments of individual workers, (d) civic organization ownership, with association-invested assets, (e) a society-possession system, with workers' investments in corporate equities forming indivisible collective capital, and (f) technological capital, with technology inputs and managerial capital formed by inputting managerial capabilities. In addition to these forms of public ownership, private capital, proprietary businesses, and privately-owned enterprises should be permitted to exist and to develop during the primary stage of socialism. "A mixed ownership structure is where all these forms of ownership intermingle. When productive forces become more advanced and production is socialized, mixed ownership will be increasingly widespread in additional forms."[8]

[8] Li Youwei, "Thoughts on the Ownership Issue," 1996, *Economics Trends*, no. 11 (1997).

The "state sector strategic restructuring" task team of the State Council Development Research Center (DRC) provided a more in-depth and comprehensive response to the third "ten-thousand-character letter."[9]

Responding from a theoretical perspective, the task team cited on-the-ground findings.

The team pointed out that as an ideal, socialism, by default, seeks social justice and shared prosperity. "Whether a country is socialist is not determined by the size of its state sector. … As long as the Communist Party adopts effective policies to prevent the polarization of the distribution of wealth, the socialist character of our country will be maintained." The third letter's statement that "socialism should take state ownership as a higher form of public ownership and as the ultimate objective" repeats the Soviet Union's description of the essential characteristics of a socialist economy, as cited in *Political Economy: A Textbook*. This view was a significant obstacle to further reform and opening. Therefore, it was imperative that China "abandon the Soviet model and the constraints imposed by *the Political Economy: A Textbook*, and provide a clearer definition of socialism."

The task team found that the state sector was overstretched due to its inappropriate status and role. Such a situation was comparable to trying to grasp water with one's hands. The state sector should withdraw from the regular competitive industries and concentrate on the strategic sectors.[10]

The reform advocates also proposed "exploring other forms of public-ownership (e.g., various funds and foundations, cooperative organizations, community ownership). … To accommodate the multi-tiered modern productive forces and the important role of individual creativity, [the government] should support and encourage development of the non-state sector, including cooperatives, private businesses, and foreign-invested enterprises in addition to the public sector, … The state should treat all economic entities of different ownership forms equally. … The focus should be on creating an environment for fair competition to realize 'everyone is equal before market rules.' … [The ownership forms] should not be limited to state or Soviet-style collective ownership." Furthermore, state ownership should not be treated as "a higher form of public ownership and the ultimate objective of socialism."[11]

In parallel with these ideological debates, new economic developments occurred. As the saying goes, "circumstances force one's hand," the economic reality was more convincing than any theoretical arguments.

In the mid-1990s, China encountered a grave problem: the dominant SOEs that accounted for one-half of the economy were facing serious troubles.

Due to the comprehensive reform and the development of the private sector in the early 1990s, the previous seller's market, in which supply could not keep up

---

[9] Wu Jinglian et al., *The Strategic Restructuring of the State Sector* (Beijing: China Development Publishing House, 1998), and Wu Jinglian, "Redefining Socialism," 1997, and Wu Jinglian et al., "Accomplishing the State Sector's Strategic Restructuring," 1997, in *Works of Wu Jinglian* (Beijing: Central Compilation and Translation Press, 2013), vol. 1, pp. 183–191, 596–611.

[10] Wu Jinglian, *Reform: We Are Experiencing an Enormous Challenge* (Beijing: SDX Joint Publishing, 2001), pp. 89–92.

[11] Wu Jinglian, "Redefining Socialism," pp. 183–191.

with demand, became a buyer's market with supply exceeding demand. The former supplemental private sector had developed into a crucial economic force. These changes led to increasingly intense market competition, making it difficult for the SOEs to adapt. By the mid-1990s, SOE losses shot up while their efficiency and profitability dropped.

In 1988, 10.7% of all state-owned industrial enterprises registered losses; in 1995, this figure increased to 33.3%, and in 1998, it increased further to 47.4% of total state-owned industrial enterprises.[12] Many workers were facing the prospect of becoming idle (*xiagang*),[13] with the number of "idle" workers reaching 13.5 million in 1998.[14] Net profits of the SOE sector peaked at RMB 166.73 billion in 1993, but profits then declined in the following years to RMB 53.98 billion in 1997, and net losses of RMB 7.8 billion in 1998.[15] The old industrial bases, in Liaoning, Jilin, and Heilongjiang provinces of the Northeast, were hit the hardest. The blow to the industrial heartland in Liaoning province was particularly damaging. By 1997, SOEs in the province had suffered net losses for three consecutive years. Its 926 large and medium-sized SOEs, 491 were loss-makers, accounting for 53% of all SOEs. Many enterprises were shut down or their production was halved. The widespread SOE losses in the province garnered considerable attention both within and outside of China, with the situation becoming known as the "Liaoning phenomenon."[16]

In sharp contrast, the private sector (non-state-owned enterprises) was snowballing despite the various restrictions (see Tables 7.1 and 7.2). Private firms became a critical force driving Chinese economic development.

Faced with the grave consequences of increased SOE losses, during a July 1997 SOE tour Executive Vice Premier Zhu Rongji called for the SOEs to overcome their difficulties within three years.[17] The 15th Party Congress in September of that year reconfirmed this requirement. In 1998, a three-year program to help the SOEs reduce their losses was launched.

In July 1997, the Asian financial crisis that had first erupted in Thailand was rapidly spreading to the neighboring countries. As Thailand's neighbor and with close trade and financial relations, China was inevitably affected by the crisis. Due to the contraction of the economy and the sizable depreciation of the currency in

---

[12] *China Financial Yearbook, 1999* (Beijing: China Finance Journal Publishing House, 1999), p. 486.

[13] "*Xiagang*," or idled workers, refers to SOE employees who were told not to come to work but who continued to receive their basic wages under valid employment contracts.

[14] Yang Yiyong, "Further Improve the Reemployment Efforts for Laid-off Workers from State-owned Enterprises," *Review of Economic Research*, no. 36 (2000), 2–7.

[15] *China Financial Yearbook, 1990*, pp. 482, 486.

[16] Shao Ning, comp., *Record of the SOE Reforms (1998–2008)* (Beijing: Economy Science Publishing House, 2015), p. 49.

[17] The Three-Year Plan for Turning Around State-Owned Enterprises, proposed by then-premier Zhu Rongji in July 1997 during his inspection tour of state-owned enterprises in Liaoning, called for "about three years to help most large- and medium-sized SOEs emerge from their difficulties through reform, restructuring, transformation, and the strengthening of management. The goal was to turn most of these SOEs into primary-phase modern enterprises by the end of this century."

Table 7.1 Growth of individual (self-employed) industrial and commercial enterprises

Year	No. of enterprises (million)	No. of employees (million)	Capital (RMB billion)	Gross output (RMB billion)
1990	13.283	20.928	39.74	64.24
1991	14.168	22.580	48.82	78.22
1992	15.339	24.677	60.10	92.62
1993	17.669	29.393	85.48	138.69
1994	21.866	37.759	131.86	163.75
1995	25.285	46.136	181.31	279.12
1996	27.037	50.171	216.54	353.86
1997	28.509	54.419	257.40	455.27

Source Cheng Siwei, comp., *China Non-Public-Owned Sector Yearbook, 2007* (Beijing: China Democracy & Construction Press, 2007), p. 754

Table 7.2 Private-sector development (1990–1997)

Year	No. of employees (million)	Growth (%)	Registered capital (RMB billion)	Growth (%)	Gross output (RMB billion)	Growth (%)
1990	1.478	3.7	9.5	13.10	12.18	
1991	1.598	8.1	12.3	29.50	14.66	20.4
1992	2.015	26.1	22.1	79.70	20.51	39.9
1993	3.213	59.5	68.1	208.10	42.17	105.6
1994	5.594	74.0	144.8	112.60	115.40	173.7
1995	8.220	46.9	262.2	81.10	229.52	98.9
1996	10.007	21.7	375.2	43.10	322.66	40.6
1997	11.450	14.4	514.0	37.00	392.25	21.6

Source General Office of the State Administration for Industry and Commerce, comp.,*Compilation of Statistics on Industry and Commerce Administration*

the countries affected by the crisis, China's exports dropped substantially, and there were signs of a slowdown in GDP growth. These challenges exacerbated the problems already facing the SOEs.

In light of the economic contradictions and difficulties, the 15th Party Congress passed a significant policy to adjust and improve the ownership structure in the economy.

7.2 A Major Party Congress Decision: Adjusting and Improving the Ownership Structure

The 15th Party Congress in September 1997 culminated in a historic decision. It announced that the "basic economic institution" for the primary stage of socialism would be maintained for at least one hundred years, i.e., "keeping public ownership as the mainstay and seeking joint development of diverse ownership forms."[18]

As noted earlier, the policy statements about the backbone status of public ownership, the leading role of the state sector, and the joint development of diverse ownership forms actually existed prior to the 15th Party Congress. But the political report to this Party congress expanded on the previous policy statements and produced a new interpretation of the institutional foundation of the economy.

First, the report highlighted "we must have a comprehensive understanding of the meaning of a public ownership economy." The report to the 15th National Congress pointed out that "the public ownership economy not only includes the state-owned economy and the collective economy," but also "we must strive to find forms of public ownership that can greatly promote the development of the productive forces," and "all management methods and organizational forms that reflect the laws of socialized production can be boldly utilized." This provided significant room to broaden the scope of public ownership and made "public ownership as the mainstay" more inclusive.

Second, the report stressed there should be "a strategic restructuring of the national economy." Repeating the statement from the Third Plenary Session of the 14th Party Central Committee, the document explained that "although keeping public ownership as the mainstay and seeking joint development of diverse ownership forms" were applicable at the national level, implementation could vary by locality or industry. It further pointed out that "the state sector must be dominant in the key industries and areas critical to the national economy." In other areas, efforts should be made to "improve the overall quality of state assets and make them more concentrated through restructuring and structural adjustments." The report announced that as long as these principles were upheld, "a reduction in the state sector's share of the national economy will not affect the socialist nature of our country."

The stakes were high in defining the lifeline industries and key areas in the national economy, and opinions varied widely. The Decision on Several Major Issues Concerning SOE Reform and Development, adopted at the Fourth Plenary Session of the 15th Party Central Committee in 1999, identified three such industries and one key area. They were: (a) industries concerning national security, (b) natural monopoly industries, and (c) industries providing essential public goods and services. The so-called key area consisted of backbone enterprises in the pillar and high-tech industries.

[18] Jiang Zemin, "Hold High the Great Banner of Deng Xiaoping Theory for an All-round Advancement of the Cause of Building Socialism with Chinese Characteristics to the 21st Century: Report to the 15th National Congress of the Communist Party of China (September 12, 1997)," *People's Daily*, September 22, 1997.

In addition, the political report made a significant breakthrough: it replaced the former statement, "the private sector is a beneficial supplement to the public sector," with a new declaration stating that "the non-public sector is an important part of our socialist market economy." In 1998, the above principles were incorporated into an amendment to the Constitution of the People's Republic of China, stipulating that "in the primary stage of socialism, the state upholds a basic economic institution where public ownership is the mainstay and various sectors under different ownership forms share economic development. ... The non-public sector, such as proprietary and private enterprises, is an important part of the country's socialist market economy within the legal limits. ... The state protects the legal rights and interests of the proprietary and private enterprises."

Thus, a blueprint had been drawn up for a market economy based on shared economic development by diverse ownership forms.

The 15th Party Congress also identified the most critical economic task: to adjust and improve the economy's ownership structure based on the above blueprint. This was based on the principle: "All ownership forms should be utilized to serve the goals of socialism as long as they satisfy the '*sange youli*' criterion."[19]

Specifically, the following three adjustments were to take place. (A) advancing the state sector in some areas and contracting it elsewhere, i.e., withdrawing from the general competitive industries and shifting the focus to the lifeline and critical industries. (B) seeking more public ownership forms that promote the productive forces and developing a multi-public-ownership sector. (C) encouraging development of the non-public sector and enabling proprietary and private-sector businesses to become a genuine "significant part of the socialist market economy."

The economic ownership structure was adjusted in parallel with the three-year SOE reform and relief program.

Originally, the goal of the three-year program was to support large- and medium-sized SOEs in reducing their workforce and in increasing their efficiency. Later, it became obvious that without SOE transformation and non-state-sector development, the state sector would not improve its efficiency and the idled workers would not be able to find new jobs. During the following three years, substantial progress was made in SOE reform and the financial performance of the SOEs improved. At the same time, development of a multi-ownership structure accelerated. These results formed the institutional foundation for China's rapid economic rise at the turn of the twenty-first century.

---

[19] During his Southern Tour in 1992, Deng Xiaoping coined the criterion "*sange youli*" (three "whether it helps."). He said, "The reason some people are still reluctant to press ahead with reform and opening and with bold experimentation is that they are haunted by fear: fear that so-called capitalist elements may emerge and that they may be taking the capitalist road. In essence, this boils down to the question of whether something is socialism or capitalism. The standard to judge this should mainly be whether it helps develop the productive forces in a socialist society, whether it helps increase the overall strength of the socialist state, and whether it helps raise the living standards of the people." Deng Xiaoping, "Excerpts from Talks Given in Wuchang, Shenzhen, Zhuhai and Shanghai," 1992, *Selected Works of Deng Xiaoping* (Beijing: People's Publishing House, 1993), p. 372.

This round of SOE reform adopted different approaches for large and small firms.

Based on the Decision on Several Major Issues Concerning SOE Reform and Development, the reform advocated the corporatization of large and medium-sized SOEs in three steps: (a) separating the companies' administrative role from their business functions and handing over the administrative functions to the relevant government authorities; (b) adopting a method for splitting and reorganizing, the goal of which was to end the situation whereby a single monopolistic enterprise dominated an industry or sub-industry, thus creating a competitive environment, and (c) restructuring state-owned wholly-owned enterprises into mixed-ownership publicly listed companies with multiple shareholders.

Take the telecommunications sector as an example. Before the reform and opening, the Ministry of Posts and Telecommunications monopolized postal and telecommunications operations. In 1994, to break up the monopoly and promote competition, the government consolidated the state telecommunications entities not affiliated with the ministry into a new telecom operator, China United Network Communications Group Co., Ltd. (China Unicom). In 2000, China Unicom (Hong Kong) was incorporated as a limited liability company in Hong Kong, and it subsequently listed its shares on the Hong Kong Stock Exchange and the New York Stock Exchange. In 1997, mobile communications were separated from the Ministry of Posts and Telecommunications to establish China Telecom Corporation Limited (later renamed China Mobile Communications Corporation), which also went public and was listed in Hong Kong.

The SOE reforms in the natural monopolistic sectors copied the recent successes in other countries. The reforms spun off competitive operations from the SOEs, keeping the monopolistic operations within a must-have limit and subjecting these operations to public monitoring. In 1999, China Telecommunications Corporation (the successor of the Directorate General of Telecommunications, Ministry of Posts and Telecommunications) spun off its pager services and satellite and mobile communications operations and became the monopoly fixed-line network operator. In 2001, China Telecommunications Corporation was split into China Netcom Corporation in the north and China Telecom in the south. Altogether, there were six telecommunications companies, including China Tietong Telecommunications Corporation (China Railcom), a spinoff from the Ministry of Railways. In 2008, the telecom sector underwent a comprehensive restructuring: mobile telecommunications companies received licenses for fixed-line operations, leading to three full-service (fixed-line and mobile) telecom corporations. Other sectors used a similar approach to strengthen competition.

This corporatization approach is called *boli shangshi* (the listing of spinoff companies),[20] that is, the spinning off of the SOEs' core assets, the setting up of limited-liability joint-stock companies to take over these assets,[21] and taking the new companies public through an initial public offering (IPO) and trading on the stock exchanges at home and abroad.

The reform of small SOEs took a different approach. In the mid-1990s, the national leadership's SOE policy was "*zhuada, fangxiao*" (keeping the large enterprises and letting go of the small enterprises), although priority was given to "keeping the big." However, reformist economists favored focusing on "letting go of the small," i.e., letting go of or revitalizing the medium-to-small-sized SOEs. Except for a few small-scale pilots in Shunde, Guangdong province, and in Zhucheng, Shandong province, this type of small SOE reform was not rolled out nationwide due to ideological constraints and criticism against "capitalist privatization." But the 15th Party Congress provided a political basis for "letting go" of the small SOEs by clarifying the basic economic institutions and enhancing the status of the non-public sector (as an essential part of a socialist market economy). Thereafter, transformation of small SOEs (including township and village enterprises based on the Southern Jiangsu model) was carried out throughout the country, leading to an expansion of the sector.

During the "three-year rescue" process for state-owned enterprises, growth of private small enterprises became an important support for the recovery of the state-owned enterprises.

A key component in the three-year program involved "encouraging mergers, standardizing bankruptcies, cutting the workforce, and furloughing workers and reassigning them elsewhere."[22] The reassignment of idled workers followed the example of Shanghai municipality: establishing industry- or local government-run re-employment centers to gather for reassignment the idled workers scattered among the various SOEs.

---

[20] The SOEs suffered from an inflated organizational structure, an excessive workforce, and poor-quality assets. Two methods were adopted to address these problems. Under the first method, a company's non-core assets and redundant workers were spun off through organizational splitting, early retirement, and the introduction of other jobs. After the core assets were restructured, the company went public and was listed on a stock exchange. Such a method is called a "public listing of an entire company" (*zhengti shangshi*). The second method spun off the core assets, restructured them under a new subsidiary, and then took the new subsidiary public. The non-core assets and redundant workers remained in the original company. This is called a "public listing of a spun-off company" (*boli shangshi*).

[21] The Decision of the Fourth Plenary Session of the 15th Party Central Committee states that "To develop diverse forms of ownership, large- and medium-sized state-owned enterprises (SOEs) should be transformed into joint-stock companies through standardized public listings, Chinese-foreign joint ventures, and cross-holding among enterprises. Except for a small number of enterprises that must remain under the state monopoly, efforts should be made to actively develop companies with multiple forms of ownership."

[22] Given the high redundancy (i.e., tens of millions of redundant workers) in the SOE workforce, the government did not simply fire these workers. Instead, workers whose jobs were cut or replaced remained within the SOEs and received pay for their basic living expenses. These people are called "*xiagang*" (idled) workers.

Table 7.3 New jobs by ownership form (million), 1992–1996

Year	State-owned	Collective-owned	Foreign- & HK/Macau/ Taiwan–owned	Private-sector–owned
1992	2.25	−0.07	0.57	0.78
1993	0.31	−2.28	0.66	2.78
1994	2.94	−1.08	1.18	4.42
1995	0.47	−1.38	1.07	4.48
1996	−0.07	−1.31	0.27	2.84

Source Niu Renliang, "The Causes of the Forced Idling in SOEs and a Recommended Response," *People's Daily*, May 28, 1998

Starting in 1995, the Shanghai Municipal Government established reemployment centers for laid-off workers from state-owned enterprises, offering them new job opportunities generated by the industrial revitalization driven by the Pudong development, which created a wealth of new job opportunities. In 1995, 860,000 laid-off workers were absorbed, with 660,000 of them finding new employment within the year. Also in 1996, the inflow and outflow amounted to 200,000 people. However, when this approach was applied to other regions and reemployment centers were widely established across the country, many places soon experienced overcrowding in the reemployment centers due to a lack of new employment opportunities.

Given this problem, in June 1988 the State Council held a national work conference to discuss the redistribution of workers who had been laid-off from state-owned enterprises. Before this conference, in April 1988, the State Council and the Standing Committee of the Chinese People's Political Consultative Conference had co-sponsored a seminar on the subject. Participants at the work conference, hailing from enterprises, government agencies, and academia, reviewed the creation of jobs based on the different ownership forms (see Table 7.3). They unanimously supported using private-sector small- and medium-sized enterprises (SMEs) as the main channel for reemploying the idled SOE workforce, i.e., relying on private-sector enterprises to create new jobs. Accepting this proposal, the State Council came out in support of the development of private-sector SMEs.[23] In May, the Party Central Committee and the State Council held a National Work Conference on the Living Subsistence and Re-employment of Idled SOE Workers, and in June, the authorities issued the Circular on Providing a Living Subsistence and Re-employment for Idled SOE Workers. On both occasions, the development of private-sector SMEs was highlighted as a primary means to reemploy the idled SOE workers.

The government took the following steps to promote the development of private-sector SMEs. (A) ideological obstacles were tackled through a public awareness campaign about the private sector's new status (an essential part of the socialist market economy), as set forth by the 15th Party Congress, to rectify the discrimination against the private sector. (B) a SME department in the State Economic and

[23] Wu Jinglian, "Suggestions for the Re-employment of Idled SOE Workers," 1998, in *Works of Wu Jinglian*, vol. 2, pp. 612–617.

Table 7.4 Urban employment in registered private and individual businesses (million), 1978–2008

Year	Total urban employment (a)	Urban private enterprises (b)	Urban proprietary businesses (c)	Share of (b) + (c) in (a) (%)
1978	95.14	–	0.15	0.2
1980	105.25	–	0.81	0.8
1985	128.08	–	4.50	3.5
1990	170.41	0.57	6.14	3.9
2000	231.51	12.68	21.36	14.7
2001	241.23	15.27	21.31	15.2
2002	251.59	19.99	22.69	17.0
2003	262.30	25.45	23.77	18.8
2004	272.93	29.94	25.21	20.2
2005	283.89	34.58	27.78	22.0
2006	296.30	39.54	30.12	23.5
2007	309.53	45.81	33.10	25.5
2008	321.03	51.24	36.09	27.2
2009	333.22	55.44	42.45	29.4
2010	346.87	60.71	44.67	30.4

Source China Statistical Yearbook, 2013

Trade Commission was established to help SMEs overcome development difficulties. Local governments also added such departments. (C) commercial banks were required to set up SME credit departments so as to improve lending services and to expand the floating range of the lending rate for these enterprises. (D) policy-based financial institutions were set up to provide credit guarantees for the SMEs. (E) tax cuts and exemptions were implemented for the SMEs. For instance, the SME value-added tax rate was reduced from 6 to 4%. (F) government services for the private sector were improved, providing information on management, technologies, industrial development, and global supply and demand.

These steps removed the obstacles to private-sector development, and as a result, the sector began to grow rapidly.

The private sector generated many new jobs, contributing to the success of the re-employment program. From 1997 to 2003, out of 27.8 million idled SOE workers, 18.5 million were reassigned to new jobs, a re-employment rate of 67%.[24]

After the end of the Cultural Revolution in 1978, proprietary businesses and private enterprises employed only 150,000 workers nationwide. But after the urban individual sector began to grow, its total number of employees increased to 4.5 million in 1985 and to 44.67 million in 2010. Furthermore, in the private-enterprise sector, the number of employees began to increase after 1990. In 2010, private businesses employed 60.71 million workers (see Table 7.4).

[24] Shao Ning, comp., *Record of the SOE Reforms (1998–2008)*.

7.3 Joint Development Under Diverse Ownership Forms

Toward the end of the twentieth century, the market-oriented reforms were making progress. Large areas of Southeast China were developing a pattern of coexistence among various forms of ownership, creating two major "growth poles" in the Yangtze River delta and the Pearl River delta regions. Thereafter joint development under diverse forms of ownership also emerged in Southeast China's coastal regions. The two delta areas of Changjiang and Zhujiang were the most robust growth poles.

The first province to experience this development was Zhejiang.

Before the reform and opening, Zhejiang had been a moderately developed province, with the level of economic development at about the national median. In 1980, the province's total industrial output was only RMB 20.1 billion. Notably, the contribution by private industrial and commercial enterprises was minuscule. Total industrial output of private-sector SMEs was RMB 7 million, accounting for 0.035% of the provincial total. But between 1981 and 1985, the private sector in Zhejiang took off. Most private enterprises in the province had begun as family workshops or small businesses with "front shops and back factories," but thereafter they evolved into clusters of enterprises based on specialized markets and unique products that were sold in national and even global markets. In 1985, the province had 2.64 million rural independent businesses and joint-household enterprises.

In this context, Zhejiang's urban per capita household disposable income increased from RMB 429.72 in 1980 to RMB 839.56 in 1985, growing 14.33% per annum within five years. During the same period, the province's rural per capita household net income increased from RMB 219.21 to RMB 548.6.[25]

SMEs in Zhejiang's private sector developed rapidly after 1985. In 2000, the industrial value-added of rural and urban private enterprises accounted for 49% of the provincial total. The rural labor force declined from 67.7% of the total in 1980 to 37.2% in 2000, a reduction of 30.5% within twenty years. The urbanization rate went up from 14.9% in 1980 to 48.7% in 2000, an increase of 33.8% and 12.5% points higher than the national average.[26]

By the end of the twentieth century, Zhejiang's per capita GDP and average annual income topped the other provinces, coming close to those in Shanghai and Beijing.

Guangdong province had been a former reform pilot, with strengths in the outward-looking township and village enterprises. Economic entities of different ownership forms had already co-existed there for a long time. However, by the end of the twentieth century Guangdong lagged behind the Changjiang delta region in terms of state-sector reform and an improved legal environment. More recently, some areas in the province have begun to catch up by improving the investment climate and accelerating the SOE reforms. If it is able to become mutually complementary with the Hong Kong Special Administrative Region, Guangdong's future prospects will be unlimited.

---

[25] *Zhejiang Statistical Yearbook.*

[26] *China Statistical Yearbook* (multiple years).

Jiangsu's economic development has experienced some ups and downs. In the 1980s, the township enterprises under the Southern Jiangsu model outpaced the then-dominant state-owned enterprises, showing significant competitive advantages. However, by the early 1990s, these community-owned enterprises, controlled by local governments, had expanded in scale but were increasingly exhibiting the same shortcomings as the state-owned enterprises, including declining efficiency and sluggish growth. In the past, whenever China's national economy encountered a downturn, Jiangsu was always the first to recover, with growth rates far ahead of those of other provinces. However, at the turn of the twenty-first century, when the Chinese economy rebounded, Jiangsu's performance remained weaker than that in many other regions, and it was even surpassed by Zhejiang. As a result, there was widespread consensus that the township enterprises under the Southern Jiangsu model required institutional reforms.

Two problems had emerged during the small- to medium-sized SOE "letting-go" process. One problem was that people holding power were selling the enterprises to their relatives and friends at 50% discounted prices, or they were even giving them away for free. Another problem was that when transforming the firms into "joint-stock cooperatives," instead of compensating the workers for past-due social security payments, the authorities were pressuring them to buy stocks in the firm, and if the workers refused, they would be fired. These problems caused strong resentment among workers, leading the State Economic and Trade Commission to issue a notice ending such practices. As economic conditions deteriorated when the "letting go" process was terminated, local governments turned to the Wenzhou and Taizhou models in Zhejiang province for survival, introducing new institutional arrangements and restructuring firm ownership. Most township and village enterprises were therefore transformed into independent proprietorships or they were incorporated as company-style enterprises.[27] After this transformation, Southern Jiangsu's economy experienced dramatic changes: GDP growth resumed and industrial production recovered with vigorous investment activities. The regional economy, in particular the outward-looking sector, demonstrated strong vitality.

In the past, Southern Jiangsu's outward-looking economy had not been as strong as that in Guangdong. But in 1994, Suzhou Industrial Park, jointly built by China and Singapore, introduced management rules and regulations of the Singapore government and extended these practices to the development zones in the province. Overseas investments surged due to the significantly improved investment climate and Southern Jiangsu's geographic location next to Shanghai—China's largest commercial and financial center.

By the turn of the twenty-first century, with the rapid private-sector expansion and improved performance, the coastal regions in China's southeast region became an important driving force behind the economic growth in other regions (see Table 7.5).

---

[27] For further details on Jiangsu province's township and village enterprises at the end of the twentieth century, see Xin Wang, "The End of the Southern Jiangsu Model," *China Economic Times*, December 30, 2000. This article discusses the various debates arising from the reform and restructuring of the collective enterprises in the Southern Jiangsu region.

Table 7.5 Economic growth in Zhejiang, Jiangsu, and Guangdong (yearly, %), 1997–2002

Year	GDP				Total exports			
	Zhejiang	Jiangsu	Guangdong	National	Zhejiang	Jiangsu	Guangdong	National
1997	11.1	12.0	10.6	9.2	25.7	21.4	25.6	20.5
1998	10.1	11.0	10.2	7.8	7.5	11.1	1.4	0.4
1999	10.0	10.1	9.5	7.7	18.5	16.9	2.7	6.1
2000	11.0	10.6	10.8	8.5	51.1	40.8	18.3	27.7
2001	10.5	10.2	9.6	8.3	18.2	12.6	3.8	6.7
2002	12.5	11.6	11.7	9.1	28.0	33.3	24.1	22.4

Source Provincial Statistical Yearbooks (multiple years); *China External Economic Statistical Yearbooks* (multiple years); World Bank Database

Table 7.6 Share of the private sector (%), 1990–2000

	Ownership type	1990	1995	1997	1998	1999	2000
GDP	State	47.7	42.1	38.4	38.9	37.4	37.3
	Collective	18.5	20.2	22.1	19.3	18.4	16.5
	Private	33.8	37.7	39.5	41.9	44.2	46.2
Fixed investment	State	66.1	54.4	52.5	54.1	53.4	50.1
	Collective	11.7	16.4	15.4	14.8	14.5	14.6
	Private	22.2	29.1	32.1	31.1	32.0	35.3
Urban employment	State	60.7	59.1	53.1	41.9	38.2	35.0
	Collective	20.8	16.5	13.9	9.1	7.6	6.5
	Private	18.5	24.3	33.0	49.0	54.1	58.5

Source China Statistical Yearbook (multiple years); Xu Xiaonian and Xiao Qian, "Another Type of New Economy," report by the Research Department of China International Capital Corporation, 2003

Energized by the coastal areas' robust economic activities, joint development under diverse ownership forms gradually emerged in the central, western, and other regions. By the end of the twentieth century, private enterprises had become the most significant economic sector, living up to their role as an essential part of the socialist market economy (see Table 7.6).

7.4 Spectacular Achievements and an Unfinished Task

The building of a preliminary market economy and the enhanced links between the domestic and international markets greatly reinforced China's growth momentum. In general, the main forces driving economic growth were the following: (a) new labor inputs, (b) new capital formation, and (c) increased efficiency (total factor productivity [TFP]). After the onset of the reform and opening, China continued to witness high population growth and a high investment rate. However, unlike in the past, these reforms increased the ratio of resource inputs to new productivity, such as improved capital formation ratios and more efficient use of new production capacities.

The reform and opening strengthened the growth momentum through the following channels.

The first and most important channel was the establishment of market institutions, which broadened the space for entrepreneurship and liberated the society's long-suppressed enthusiasm and innovative potential. Under the totalitarian dictatorship prior to the reform and opening, private industrial and commercial businesses were ruthlessly repressed because they were accused of restoring capitalism. But after the mid-1980s, the government gradually relaxed entry controls for private-sector startups. In 1997, the 15th Party Congress recognized the non-public sector as an essential part of a socialist market economy, therefore expanding the space for private-sector development. Society's long-suppressed entrepreneurship and innovation grew exponentially, which led to more than 30 million private enterprises by the end of the twentieth century. The private sector became the fundamental driving force behind China's incredible growth.

Private enterprises grew not only in quantity but also in quality. The private sector was the basis for and the most dynamic part of a market economy, the primary support for economic and social stability, and the leading source of technological innovation. The sector also demonstrated its ability to assist in the economic recovery from the recession after the 1997 Asian financial crisis. It not only was the principal employer for idled urban workers but it also provided new opportunities to alleviate rural poverty and to increase farmers' income, thereby further expanding the market economy in China.

The correlation between the share of the private sector in the regional economy and regional GDP growth at the turn of the twenty-first century reveals that regions with a larger private sector experienced faster GDP growth (Fig. 7.1).

The second channel was the significant acceleration of what developmental economists call the "Kuznets Process."[28] Under the command economy, when the rural and urban areas were isolated from each other, industrialization was carried out through resource mobilization and state-mandated investments. Members of the people's communes were required to receive permission before they could migrate to the cities. Such restrictions seriously slowed down the industrialization and urbanization processes as well as improvements in overall economic efficiency. When the market- economy system was established and private entrepreneurial activities became more vibrant, production factors could flow more smoothly from the less efficient industries to the more efficient industries. In the years following the reform and opening, up to 200 million surplus rural laborers were transferred to the cities

[28] The so-called Kuznets process refers to the shift of labor from the low-efficient agricultural sector to the high-efficient urban industrial sector. In China, this process includes shifting land resources from low-efficient rural areas to high-efficient urban areas.

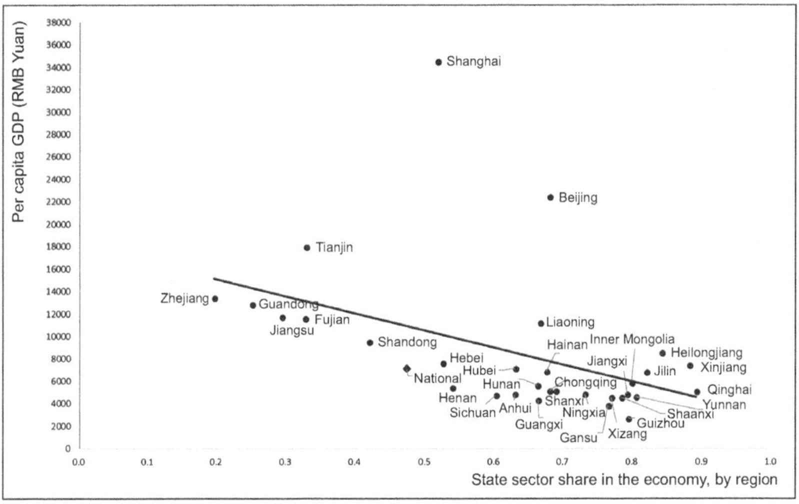

Fig. 7.1 The private sector promoted economic growth (the year 2000 as an example).[29] *Source* China Statistical Yearbook (2001)

to engage in industrial work. Nearly 70,000 sq. km of farmland, almost as much as the entire country of Ireland, was converted for urban uses.

The third channel was the strong support for technological upgrading and efficiency improvements. Because an enormous technological gap existed between China and other countries, the external opening and the introduction of foreign equipment and technologies enabled China to quickly upgrade its manufacturing technologies.

Economist Angus Maddison has analyzed the sources of China's economic growth, revealing the main contributors to the GDP growth. After estimating the changes in China in factor inputs and total factor productivity (TFP) from 1952 to 2003, he found that during the Mao era, labor productivity had increased. Still, capital productivity had declined significantly, and the annual growth rate of TFP was negative 3% (Table 7.7).[30]

Table 7.7 presents the sharp contrast in economic development between the twenty-six years prior to the reform and opening and the thirty years after adoption of the reform and opening policy: During the latter period, the growth of labor inputs was lower, development of human capital slowed down, and expansion of capital inputs remained the same, whereas GDP growth accelerated, labor productivity was much higher, and growth of capital productivity became positive. As a

[29] Due to inconsistencies in the statistical standards for private enterprises across different provincial yearbooks, this figure uses data related to state-owned enterprises for comparative reference.

[30] Angus Maddison, *Chinese Economic Performance in the Long Run, 960–2030 AD*, 2nd ed., rvsd. and updated (Chinese translation by Wu Xiaoying and Ma Debing. Shanghai: Shanghai People's Publishing House, 2011), p. 71. In his calculations, Maddison considers improvements in labor quality as an increase in inputs rather than an enhancement of total factor productivity.

Table 7.7 National basic economic growth accounting (1952–2003)[31]

	China's compound annual growth rate	
	1952–1978	1978–2003
Population	2.02	1.20
GDP	4.39	7.85
Per capita GDP	2.33	6.57
Labor input	2.57	1.89
Education	4.49	2.63
Quality adjusted labor input	4.87	3.23
Non-resident capital (stock)	7.72	7.73
Labor productivity	1.78	5.85
Capital productivity	−3.09	0.11
Capital (stock) per person engaged	5.02	5.73
Total factor productivity	−1.37	2.95
Export volume	2.6	14.42

Source Angus Maddison, *Chinese Economic Performance in the Long Run, 960–2030 AD*, 2nd ed., rvsd. and updated (Chinese translation by Wu Xiaoying and Ma Debing. Shanghai: Shanghai People's Publishing House, 2011), p. 71

result, total factor productivity (TFP) shifted from the previous an annual decline to a growth rate of 2.95% per year. This dramatically illustrates the improvements in efficiency during the reform period.

Perkins and Rawski have produced similar findings. They point out that in 1952–1978 before the reform and opening period, the average annual TFP growth rate was merely 0.5%. In particular, TFP declined from 1965 to 1978. But it rose to 3.8% after the onset of reform and opening from 1978 to 2005, contributing 40% to GDP growth.[32]

Chinese economists Bai Chongen and Zhang Qiong have studied the country's productivity changes in terms of technological efficiency, effective factor utilization, and resource allocation efficiency.[33] Their conclusions align with those of the previous studies, showing an average annual improvement in production efficiency of about 3.78% from 1979 to 2007.

Driven by growth forces, China registered remarkable socioeconomic achievements. During the transition from a low-income to a middle-income country, China

[31] Maddison notes that in calculating total factor productivity, labor input is given a weight of 0.65 (simple labor input 0.325, education as human capital 0.325), and capital is given a weight of 0.35.

[32] Dwight H. Perkins and Thomas G. Rawski, "Forecasting China's Growth to 2025," in Loren Brandt and Thomas G. Rawski, eds., *China's Great Economic Transformation* (NY: Cambridge University Press, 2008).

[33] Bai Chongen and Zhang Qiong, "A Productivity Explanation for China's Slowdown in Economic Growth," *Comparative Studies*, no. 9 (2014).

Table 7.8 Per capita GDP growth in fourteen countries/regions (1913–2003, %)

	1913–1952	1952–1978	1978–2003
China	–0.1	2.3	6.6
Hong Kong, China	1.6	5.4	3.9
India	–0.2	1.7	3.3
Indonesia	0.02	2.5	2.9
Japan	1.30	6.7	2.1
Singapore	1.50	4.8	4.2
South Korea	–0.1	6.3	5.6
Taiwan, China	0.9	6.6	4.7
Australia	0.9	2.4	2.1
France	1.3	3.7	1.6
Germany	0.6	4.3	1.4
Russia	1.8	3.1	–0.6
UK	0.9	2.3	2.1
U.S	1.7	2.2	1.8

Source Maddison, *Chinese Economic Performance in the Long Run, 960–2030 AD*, p. 63

realized nationwide compulsory education, provided increased secondary and higher education opportunities, and expanded its coverage of healthcare for the population. Labor mobility rose, and an increasing number of farmers found jobs in the cities. The system of state-sector–based safeguards was transformed into an expanding and improving social security system.[34]

According to Maddison's calculations, China's per capita GDP grew by 2.33% per annum in 1952–1978, but it accelerated to 6.57% per annum during the reform and opening period.[35] This growth rate is much higher than that in either the United States or Western Europe. It also surpasses the historical highs of almost all other Asian countries, and it is four times higher than the world average (Table 7.8).

China's share in the world economy rose from less than 5% in 1978 to 15% in 2003 (Table 7.9), after which it continued to rise. In 2010, when China's GDP surpassed that of Japan, it became the world's second-largest economy.

From 1978 to 2003, China's GDP per capita as a percentage of the world's average rose from 22.1% to 73.7%. By 2012, China's per capita GDP surpassed $6,000 (in current US dollars), thereby leading the World Bank to classify it as an upper-middle-income country.[36]

---

[34] World Bank and the DRC Joint Task Team, *China 2030: Building a Modern, Harmonious, and Creative Society* (Chinese translation. Beijing: China Financial and Economic Publishing House, 2013), p. 52.

[35] Maddison, *Chinese Economic Performance in the Long Run, 960–2030 AD*, p. 71.

[36] www.worldbank.org.

Table 7.9 China's geopolitical standing in the world (1820–2003)

	1820	1890	1913	1952	1978	2003
Share of world GDP (%)	32.9	13.2	8.8	4.6	4.9	15.1
Share of world population (%)	36.8	26.2	24.4	22.5	22.3	20.5
Per capita GDP (World Average = 100)	90.0	50.3	41.7	23.8	22.1	73.7
GDP ranking	1	2	3	3	4	2
Share of world exports (%)	n.a	1.7	1.6	1.0	0.8	5.9

Source Maddison, *Chinese Economic Performance in the Long Run, 960–2030 AD*, p. 61

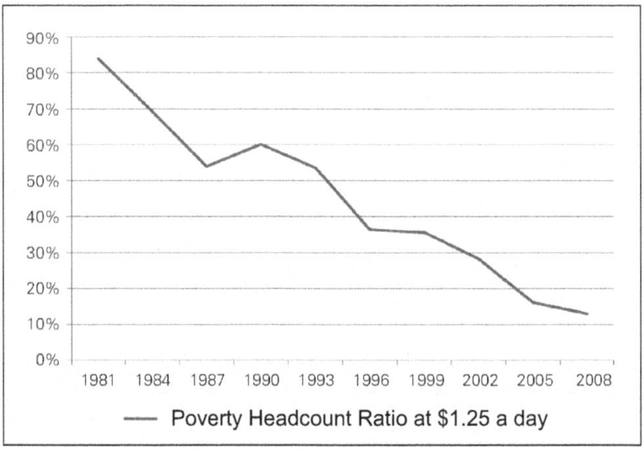

Fig. 7.2 China's poverty rate (1981–2008). *Note* The USD 1.25 per day poverty line is in 2005 PPP terms. *Source* https://data.worldbank.org/

Because the thirty years of rapid economic growth benefited most people, China also recorded excellent results in improving people's livelihoods and in poverty reduction. The achievements in poverty reduction were historic, pulling more than 500 million people out of poverty and cutting the poverty rate by a large margin.[37] Using the poverty line of USD 1.25 (PPP) per day, the proportion of people living in poverty accounted for 84% of the total population in 1981, but it dropped to 16% by 2005[38] (see Fig. 7.2).

Chinese life expectancy rose from 67.2 in 1982 to 72.6 in 2001[39] (see Fig. 7.3).

The country's literacy rate also went up. In 1949, only about one-third of all children were registered in primary schools, and literacy among adults was 20%. By 1982, the literacy rate was 65.5%, and by 2000, it had reached 90.9%. During

[37] World Bank and the DRC Joint Task Team, *China 2030.*

[38] Ibid., https://data.worldbank.org/.

[39] https://data.worldbank.org/.

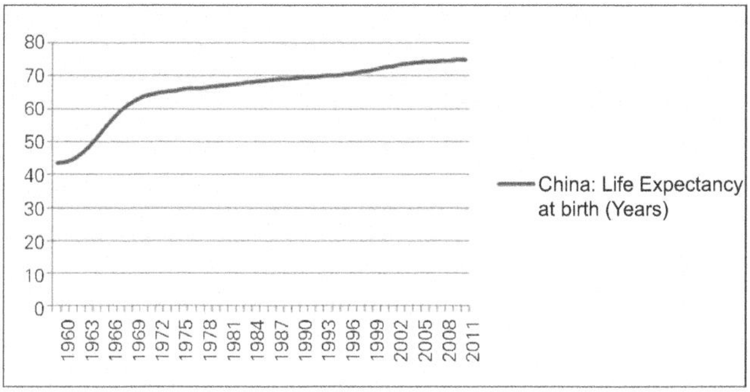

Fig. 7.3 China's life expectancy at birth (Years, 1960–2010). *Source* https://data.worldbank.org/

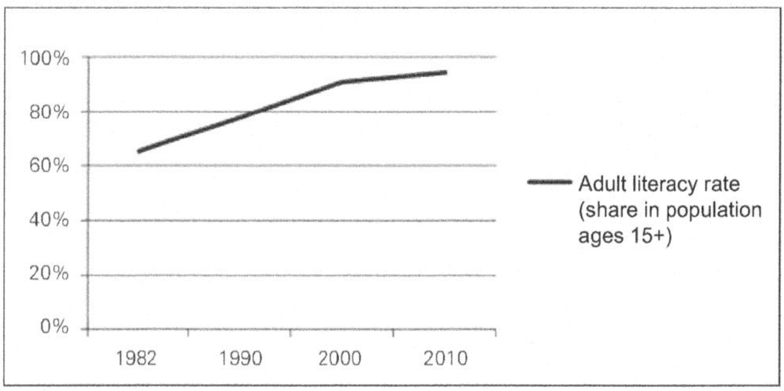

Fig. 7.4 China's literacy rate (1982–2010). *Source* https://data.worldbank.org/

the 1952–2003 period, the average years of schooling per person aged 15 and older increased from 1.7 to 10.2[40] (see Fig. 7.4, Table 7.10).

Higher education suffered a severe setback from the 1960s to the 1970s. Student enrollment in institutions of higher education dropped from 960,000 in 1960 to 48,000 in 1970. Although university enrollment returned to a rising trend after 1970, in 1978 it was still below that in 1960. During the economic reform era, student enrollment in institutions of higher education multiplied, from less than one million in 1978 to 16 million in 2005. Students studying overseas surged from almost no Chinese students in the Western countries during the Mao era to 118,500 in 2005 alone. (Counting from beginning in the 1970s, the total number of overseas students exceeded one million.)[41]

The preliminary framework for a socialist market economy established in China by the turn of the century propelled rapid economic development. This high growth momentum continued into the early twenty-first century. However, the reform still had not yet achieved a complete success, and the legacy of the old system persisted stubbornly in many areas. This legacy was concentrated in the SOE sector, where

[40] Maddison, *Chinese Economic Performance in the Long Run, 960–2030 AD*, p. 67.

[41] Ibid., p. 67.

Table 7.10 Average years of education per person, ages 15–64, ten countries and regions (1950–1992) (equivalent years of primary education)[42]

	1950	1973	1992		1950	1973	1992
France	9.58	11.69	15.96	China	1.60	4.09	8.50
Germany	10.40	11.55	12.17	India	1.35	2.60	5.55
UK	10.84	11.66	14.09	Japan	9.11	12.09	14.86
U.S	11.27	14.58	18.04	South Korea	3.36	6.82	13.55
Spain	5.13	6.29	11.51	Taiwan, China	3.62	7.35	13.83

Source Maddison, *Chinese Economic Performance in the Long Run, 960–2030 AD*, p. 61

the corporatization process had come to an end. As discussed earlier, the reform had made significant progress at the subsidiary level of large companies by the turn of the twenty-first century, and most second-tier companies were listed on the domestic and foreign stock exchanges. The next step in the original plan was to reform the listed companies' holding corporations, i.e., the administrative corporations at the top of the company groups and their surviving enterprises. Typically, these corporations were controlled by insiders. But it proved to be difficult to transform their ownership to a mixed structure according to the decisions of the 15th Party Congress in 1997 and the Fourth Plenary Session of the 15th Party Central Committee in 1999. The corporatization of holding companies, considered the foundation of the state-sector reform, suffered from a phenomenon called "middle-level obstruction."

The legacy of the old system could also be found in the numerous government interventions and the discriminatory policies regarding entry of the non-public sector into industries and factor markets, which prevented the non-public enterprises from fully utilizing their competitive advantages. Many private-sector enterprises adopted opportunistic business strategies, seeking short-term benefits at the expense of technological inputs, spending their time establishing government connections and engaging in rent-seeking activities. As a result, the economy existed in a semi-market and semi-command state, and development continued to suffer from the earlier drawbacks, such as the extensive growth mode and the spread of corruption. To a large extent, this indicates that whether China can maintain a trend of sustained and stable development will largely depend on whether it can continue to advance and thoroughly implement market-oriented and rule-of-law reforms.

[42] Maddison's note: Primary education is given a weight of 1, secondary education a weight of 1.4, and higher a weight of 2, in line with international evidence on relative earnings associated with the different levels of education.

Chapter 8
State-Owned Enterprise Reform and Adjustments to the State Sector in the Economy

The state-owned enterprise (SOE) reform in the early 1980s focused on enlarging enterprise autonomy. After this reform waned, priority was shifted to changes in the non-public sector, called the *tizhiwai* (outside of the system) economy, where considerable progress was made. However, the SOEs, marked by their low efficiency, still controlled the essential industries and possessed enormous resources. Therefore, SOE reform remained a severe problem to be tackled on China's economic reform agenda.

Given the widespread consensus that expanding enterprise autonomy within the framework of market socialism could achieve the desired results, the idea of applying the successful experience of the rural contracting system to state-owned industrial and commercial enterprises became very attractive. Thus, with the advocacy of the state-owned enterprise supervisory bodies and the support of the enterprise managers, a comprehensive reform strategy was developed. This strategy aimed to achieve autonomous management, self-responsibility for profits and losses, self-development, and self-restraint through a contracting system for the state-owned enterprises. By the mid-1980s, most state-owned enterprises had adopted this contracting system.

However, the institutional arrangement for enterprise contracting had a fundamental defect. Instead of clarifying enterprise property rights, the practice made it easier for the two de facto owners, i.e., the contractee and the contractor, to encroach on each other's rights. Enterprise behavior became increasingly short-term, and the contractors pursued their own self-interests at the expense of the enterprise owners. Moreover, the managers made arbitrary decisions, with some even embezzling enterprise funds.

When enterprise contracting failed to deliver the desired results, there were calls for a reorganization of the large SOEs into standard modern companies. In November 1993, the Third Plenary Session of the 14th Party Central Committee decided to transform large- and medium-sized SOEs into modern corporations. In December of that year, the Company Law of the People's Republic of China was promulgated,

W. Jinglian, *China's Economic Reform*, Understanding China,
https://doi.org/10.1007/978-981-96-9607-9_8

which sought to align company processes with international practices. Under the Company Law, the authorities would gradually reorganize the large SOEs into joint-stock companies with limited liability.

However, the property rights system of corporate enterprises was not addressed until the 1997 15th Party Congress that sought to adjust and improve the ownership structure. Two years later, the Fourth Plenary Session of the 15th Party Central Committee specified that most corporatized SOEs should be transformed into mixed-ownership enterprises with diversified shareholders, further clarifying the institutional property rights arrangement.

But changing the SOEs' institutional arrangements was a complex process because any such change challenged the old ideology and impacted the interests of the involved parties. Hence, the reform experienced many ups and downs.

This chapter explains, in chronological order, the theory and practice of the SOE reforms at their various stages.

8.1 The Enterprise Contracting System: SOE Reform with Chinese Characteristics

After the reform to expand enterprise autonomy came to a halt (but with the flawed SOE incentive mechanism continuing), China urgently needed "a management system for production and operations characterized by close connections among responsibilities, rights, and interests, i.e., a system unifying the interests of the state, the enterprise, and the employees, and linking worker remuneration with worker output." In October 1981, the State Council issued the *Opinions* on *Issues Regarding Implementation Contract Management in Industrial Enterprises*, jointly prepared by the State Economic Commission and the State Council System Reform Office. The document proposed three possible operational responsibility approaches for the SOEs: "profit retention," "profit and loss contracting," and "replacing profits [handover] with taxes, and with full responsibility for profits and losses."

Given the success of the rural reforms with production contracting, the members of the Secretariat of the Party Central Committee favored a contracting approach for the state-sector reform. Hence, in January 1983 Party leaders, using slogans such as "when contracting comes to town, problems will be solved" and "contracting at all levels," began to require that industrial and commercial SOEs copy the rural household contracting practices, thus marking the beginning of an enterprise contracting system. Under this system, the enterprise owner, i.e., the contractee, allows the contractor (usually the enterprise manager) to manage enterprise property, with the latter handing over a previously agreed-upon amount of the profits to the former and either retaining the excess or sharing it with the contractee per an agreed-upon sharing ratio. The contractee shall not interfere with the contractor's business activities during the period of the contract.

With promotion by Party leaders, nationwide SOEs adopted this practice within two to three months. But because there were widespread shortages of goods at the time, the SOEs took advantage of their monopoly status to raise prices, thus earning higher profits and providing employee bonuses but also leading to economic disorder and price hikes. This caused discontent among the general public, and it triggered heated debates among national leaders.

In March 1983, the Party Central Committee and the State Council decided to put an end to the contract management responsibility system, and instead they launched a tax-for-profit reform, aiming to align the fiscal and tax regime with the enterprises' "independent management and self-financing" operations.[1] From the end of 1970 to early 1980, there had already been pilots, at several hundred SOEs in eighteen provinces and municipalities, that experimented with this reform.

In the past, SOEs would hand over the majority of their profits to the government. The reform sought to change this practice and instead to tax a portion of their profits at a statutory income tax rate, with the after-tax profits remaining with the SOEs. Based on the March 1983 decision of the Party Central Committee and the State Council, the reform was to be implemented in two phases. During the first phase, beginning in June 1983, state-owned enterprises were required to hand over 55% of their gross income as income tax payments, in addition to handing over a portion of their after-tax profits. The remainder could be retained by the enterprises. Beginning in October 1984, the second phase permitted SOEs to keep all of the after-tax profits. The thinking behind this two-phase reform was that when paying taxes at a uniform rate, there would be equal competition among enterprises, and enterprises would enjoy operational autonomy and full responsibility for their profits and losses.

However, it soon became evident that without price liberalization and given the substantial variation in tax rates, the profits-for-tax reform alone could not ensure that enterprise profit levels accurately reflected the quality of their operations. Initially, the State Council had intended to launch combined price and tax-fiscal reforms to create an environment for fair competition, but in the fall of 1986, the main leadership of the State Council decided to terminate this reform plan. Enterprises, facing differing external conditions and widely varying profitability levels, became subject to a "regulatory tax" with a unique tax rate for each enterprise. The subjective nature of determining these adjusted regulatory tax rates meant that the "profit-for-tax" reform did not achieve its original goal of accurately reflecting the quality of operations.

Yuan Baohua, vice chairman of the State Economic Commission who had strongly supported the SOE contracting practice, commented that "the two-phase tax-for-profit reform was implemented without other complementary reforms, particularly a price reform. Therefore, the results fell far short of the original goal of creating a fair competitive environment whereby the state collects taxes and enterprises, as independent accounting entities, pay the funding costs and take responsibility for profits and losses." He pointed out that because the starting places of the various enterprises differed, economic adjustments through nonregular means (e.g., enterprise-specific

[1] See Tian Jiyun, "Accelerating the Tax-for-Profit Reform," *Economic Management*, no. 1 (1983).

adjusted tax rates) would only exacerbate the inequalities among enterprises, with some firms receiving more benefits at the expense of others.[2] After the tax-for-profit reform was implemented, SOE profits steadily declined over the next twenty-two months.[3]

The tax-for-profit reform thus met with widespread criticism, and price reforms remained postponed without any fixed timetable. In this context, there were new calls to enlarge the power of the enterprises. In October–November 1986, after halting the interlinked tax-price fiscal reforms, the main leadership of the State Council proposed giving managers more autonomy to invigorate the enterprises.[4] For this purpose, it prepared several regulations. During the process, relevant theoretical propositions and institutional arrangements were formed. These would have a far-reaching influence on the later SOE reforms in China.

(1) The most compelling proposition was a new interpretation of "the separation of ownership and management rights and management powers" to highlight the powers of the SOEs and their managers.

In their 1932 book *The Modern Corporation and Private Property*, American jurists Adolf Berle and Gardiner Means were the first to discuss a separation of the ownership rights of owners and the control of corporate executives.[5] They pointed out that given the huge size and complex organizational structure of large enterprises, owners, lacking managerial skills, would hire corporate executives to manage day-to-day operations, hence instituting a separation between ownership and control. Subsequent developments showed that senior executives, in assuming total control of large corporations, became autocratic at the expense of the interests of the shareholders. Beginning in the early 1990s, a "corporate governance movement," aiming to strengthen the owners' ultimate corporate control, emerged in developed countries to address this problem. In a corporation with effective corporate governance, the owner does not transfer all control powers. Instead, she shares specific controls with the executives based on the trade practices and the managers' employment contracts with the executives. Meanwhile, the owners maintained the control of the activities beyond the scope of designated control power through corporate governance institutions, e.g., a general meeting of the shareholders and meetings of the board of directors, or the ultimate control, of the corporation.[6]

[2] Yuan Baohua, "On Socialist Enterprise Management," 1988, *Works of Yuan Baohua* (Beijing: People's University Publishing House, 2013), vol. 7, pp. 108–109.

[3] Shao Ning, comp., *Record of the SOE Reforms (1998–2008)* (Beijing: Economic Science Publishing House, 2015), p. 20.

[4] Fang Weizhong, comp., *Marching through Storms: Chronicle of China's Development and Reform (1977–89)*, vol. 9 (1986), unpublished draft, dated 2004, pp. 136–141.

[5] A. Berle and G. Means, *The Modern Corporation and Private Property*, 1932 (Chinese translation by Gan Huaming et al. Beijing: Commercial Press, 2007).

[6] The theory of the firm, which emerged after the 1970s, provides an in-depth analysis of the firm as an institutional arrangement for team production. The firm has to enter into contracts and exchanges with many production factor owners to gather the resources for team production purposes. To prevent opportunistic behavior, e.g., loafing on the job, by factor-input owners, the production team must

In the 1940s, a different interpretation of the owner-control separation issue appeared in the Soviet Union.[7]

In its early days, the Soviet Union, based on Lenin's state syndicate proposition, aimed to turn the national economy into a grand corporation that would extend to the entire country and be monopolistically managed by the government. In this context, the country only recognized unitary state ownership and denied the legitimacy of any non-state ownership forms. As late as 1922, when the New Economic Policy was put in place to officially adopt market economy operations, Lenin, in his "top-confidential instruction" on the preparation of the civil code, still insisted that "We do not recognize anything 'private,' and [we] regard everything in the economic sphere as falling under public and not private law."[8]

Apparently, this institutional arrangement did not suit the New Economic Policy. In the mid-1920s. Evgeny Bronislavovich Pashukani, the leader of the then mainstream school of the Commodity Exchange Theory of Law, proposed the idea of "ownership sharing between the SOEs and the state" in order to align the Soviet legal system with the trends in general economic recovery and the requirement that all enterprises should conduct commercial accounting. At the end of the 1920s, Stalin won a struggle inside the All-Union Communist Party and launched an opposition to the so-called "Right tendency." Pashukanis' proposition was then labeled anti-revolutionary for the "subversive crime against the uniformity of state ownership." Subsequently, he and his followers were persecuted during the Great Purge of 1936–37. Ensuring the consistency and exclusivity of state ownership became an unwavering principle in the Soviet legal system.[9]

However, this arrangement contradicted the principle of limited enterprise autonomy. In the 1940s, a group of legalists, led by Anatoly Vasilyevich Venediktov, introduced the new concept of "operational rights." The separated owners' main rights to possess, use, and dispose of properties were separated from the ownership rights, these functions were then named operational rights, and assigned SOEs'

---

have a primary contract signee, i.e., the owner of the main assets, to monitor the other contract signees. The residual claims on the firm's total earnings, net of interest, rent, and wages, owed to other factor-input owners per their contracts, are assigned to the primary contract signee to prevent her from loafing on the job. In other words, the owner of the assets has residual claims to the firm. Harvard professor Oliver Hart has further analyzed ownership arrangements of corporate firms. He has pointed out that the owner's residual control rights, or the ultimate control rights, are more important than the residual claim rights. In 2016 Hart won the Nobel Prize in Economics for his theoretical contributions to this issue.

[7] See "Discussions by the Soviet Union's Legal Circles on State (Whole-People) Ownership during the Reform Era (Part 1)—Minutes of the Roundtable Meeting in January 1988," in "The Soviet State and the Law," translated by Chen Hanzhang, in *Jurisprudence Papers*, no. 5 (1988).

[8] Lenin, "On the Tasks of the People's Commissariat for Justice Under the New Economic Policy," 1922, in *The Complete Works of Lenin,* 2nd ed. (Beijing: People's Publishing House, 1990), vol. 47, pp. 424–429. (English translation for *Lenin Collected Works* (Moscow: Progress Publishers, 1971), vol. 36, pp. 560–565.

[9] See: "Soviet Legalists on the State (the Whole People) Ownership during the Reform Era (I)," Minutes of the January 1988 Roundtable Meeting, The Soviet State and the Law, translated by Chen Hanzhang, Translated Jurisprudence Papers, 1988, Issue 5.

general directors and managers under the so-called "appropriate separation of ownership and operational rights." This redefined separation of ownership and operational rights allowed the SOEs to have a certain degree of independence and it gave the management teams significant powers, while, at the same time, maintaining the nominal uniformity of state ownership without risking political condemnations. Therefore, this new concept of operational rights was quickly accepted by the senior leadership. In the 1960s, the Soviet Union's "Civil Legislation Framework" and Civil Code both provided the SOEs with operational rights to possess, use, and dispose of properties.[10] When many large corporations granted senior executives the total control, power abuses by these people became widespread, at the expense of owners' rights.

In 1961, Chinese economist Sun Yefang used the Soviet scholars' proposition when describing his idea of an economic system. He interpreted the "separation of the two types of rights" as the separation of ownership and operational rights. He wrote, "Ownership should be vested in one entity, but the rights to possess, use, and dispose of properties should be granted to another body." This was the institutional arrangement of Sun's "economic management system under whole-people ownership."[11] Influenced by the idea, the Party Central Committee Decision on the Reform of the Economic Structure pointed out that the whole-people ownership should not be mixed up with direct operation of enterprises by state agencies: "Based on Marxist theories and socialist practices, to a certain degree ownership can be separated from operational rights."

In November 1987, the then main Party and government leader offered a new definition of "the separation of the two types of rights" when talking to the State Economic Restructuring Commission, the State Economic Commission, and the Office of the Research Group for Political Reform. According to him, the operational rights had both broad and narrow definitions. "The narrow or incomplete and partial" understanding interpretated these rights as only for day-to-day operations, while, according broader definition and the Marxist's interpretation saw "these rights" fell under the same concept of the rights to possess, use, and dispose of the properties.... How to manage, operate, and develop and expand the businesses should be left to the managers." He requested the three-member group for the finalization of the revised draft "Law of the People's Republic of China on Industrial Enterprises Owned by the Whole People" (the Enterprise Law) to incorporate these views in the law. He said, "the law would be soleless if it fails to specify this point."[12]

---

[10] Yan Yimei, "An Analysis of the Definition of Enterprise in the New Civil Code of the Russian Federation," *Chinese and Foreign Jurisprudence*, no. 4 (1998).

[11] Sun Yefang, "Internal Finance and Economic System Issues in the Whole-People-Owned Economy," 1961, in *Selected Works of Sun Yefang* (Taiyuan: Shanxi Publishing House, 1984), p. 241.

[12] Zhao, Ziyang (1987): "About Enterprise Management Reform." See: Fang Weizhong, comp., "Marching through Storms: Chronicles of China's Development and Reform (1977–89)" (unpublished draft dated 2004), vol. 10 (1987), pp. 335–338.

(2) Another essential proposition of institutional arrangement was to grant the general directors (managers) residual control of properties by appointing them the companies' statutory or legal representatives.

The SOE reform turned enterprises into legal entities with civil capacities and obligations. The problem was that a legal entity is an organization formed by the initial investors; no individual should automatically become its legal representative. Several regulations after 1983 repeatedly stressed that "an enterprise is a legal entity with the general manager as the legal representative. The enterprise has the rights to possess, use, and dispose of the state properties it operates based on government regulations. …"[13] "The enterprise's statutory representative is the general manager, who is responsible for executing the legal entity's rights and obligations, …"[14] and "the general manager of a whole-people-owned industrial enterprise is the head and legal representative of the enterprise, holding all-round responsibility for and playing a central role in the enterprise."[15]

(3) The third significant proposition was the emphasis on enterprise contracting, believed to be the most feasible form to separate leadership and management rights in China. "The State Council Regulations on Deepening Enterprise Reform and Increasing Enterprise Vitality" (December 1986) called for the SOE reform to pivot to "multi-form contract responsibility systems to give managers full operational autonomy." By early 1987 the main Party and government leader had become more in favor of nationwide implementation of the enterprise contracting system.

In April 1987, based on a request from the State Council, the State Economic Commission held a national seminar on the enterprise contracting system, requiring that the provinces and the line ministries further promote contracting practices. In November, in a talk with the State Commission for Restructuring the Economic System (the State Economic System Reform Commission) and the Office of the Research Group for Political Reform, the national leader reiterated that "once the contracting system is implemented, enterprise operational rights will become a reality, and only then can economic return will be improved. … The remarks about the contracting system not being standardized and having created short-term behavior are incorrect. … People working in the theoretical field or engaged in practical work should all focus on improving and developing the enterprise contracting system."[16] By the end of 1987, 78% of the on-budget SOEs had adopted such an approach. Among the large- and medium-sized SOEs, the rate was 80%.[17]

---

[13] State Council, Provisional Regulations on State-Owned Industrial Enterprises, April 1, 1983.

[14] Central Committee and State Council, Regulations on the Duties of the General Manager in Whole-People-Owned Industrial Enterprises, September 15, 1986.

[15] Central Committee and State Council, Supplemental Circular on Implementing the Three Regulations on Whole-People-Owned Industrial Enterprises, November 11, 1986.

[16] Fang Weizhong, comp., "Marching through Storms: Chronicles of China's Development and Reform (1977–89)" (unpublished draft dated 2004), vol. 10 (1987), pp. 338–342.

[17] Yuan Baohua, "On Socialist Enterprise Management," p. 112.

In February 1988, the State Council issued the "Provisional Regulation on Operational Contracting System in Whole-People Owned Industrial Enterprises." The regulation stated that "in accordance with the principle of separation between ownership and operational rights, the operational responsibility contracts should establish the responsibility, rights, and interest of the state and the enterprises, so that enterprises will become autonomous in operation and accountable for their profits and losses. … The contract between an enterprise and its administrative agency, entered through one-on-one negotiations, should specify a reasonable handover baseline. Thereafter, the enterprise earnings would be distributed based on the principle of "ensuring handovers, increasing retentions when earnings exceed the baseline, and letting the enterprise make up shortfalls when the baseline is not met."

In April 1988, the National People's Congress promulgated the Law of the People's Republic of China on Industrial Enterprises Owned by the Whole People, codifying the above ideas on SOE reform. In elaborating on the law, Yuan Baohua, head of the State Economic Commission, pointed out that the provisions "have two implications. First, it means that whole-people ownership of enterprise property cannot be altered. But, because whole-people-owned property cannot be operated by the whole people, operational rights must be assigned to the enterprise managers. The second implication is that when separating ownership from management authority, the former should be weakened while the latter should be strengthened. Provided that state ownership of enterprise property remains intact, enterprise operational rights are, in a broad sense, the rights to possess, utilize, and dispose of enterprise properties. … The separation between ownership and management authority is the essence of the law and the basic theory and practice in China's economic system reform."[18]

Party and government officials spoke highly of these SOE institutional arrangements with Chinese characteristics, calling them "a great innovation by the Chinese people."[19] However, these institutional arrangements suffered from considerable theoretical and practical problems.

First, the practice of contracting did not change the enterprises' subordinate relationship within the government hierarchy, i.e., "vertical subordination." On the surface, the responsibility contracts separated the interests and the obligations of the government and the enterprise, and the latter no longer had to unconditionally follow the superior administrative agency's instructions (as formerly required under the mandatory plan). However, the superior-subordinate relationship between the contractee and the contractor did not change, and the latter was still a junior entity in the administrative hierarchy. To a large extent, the contractor's operational conditions were still determined by the contractee. Hence, the enterprise fell into what Hungarian economist Kornai calls "dual dependency." On the one hand, the enterprise was subordinate to its administrative superior in the hierarchy; on the other, it was subordinate to the market.[20] The amount of profits retained for the enterprise was

[18] Ibid., pp. 130–135.

[19] Ibid., p. 136.

[20] János Kornai, "Dual Dependency of State-Owned Enterprises: The Hungarian Experience" (Chinese translation. *Economic Research*, no. 10 [1985]).

determined by the amount negotiated between the contractee and the contractor. It was also determined by the contractor's relations with various government agencies as well as by the preferential treatment it received in terms of taxation, lending, and material allocations.

Second, the transaction costs of the contract negotiations were high. The essential item in the negotiations was the baseline amount to be handed over to the government. According to the original concept, the baseline was expected to reflect the influence of factors unrelated to enterprise revenue operations. The level of retained profits would then reflect enterprise performance. But fixing a fair baseline was challenging due to the sharp differences in business environments, technologies, and material and product prices. The contracting process often used historical data that did not reflect the current state of enterprise operations because of the ever-changing business conditions. Enterprises with higher profits could see their handover baseline increased for the next contract term, resulting in a ratchet effect of "whipping a fast moving ox."[21] Contractors often hid their current profits to lower their future handover baseline and to gain better contract terms and conditions.

In summary, the contracts negotiated on a one-to-one basis between the contractors and their superior agencies were highly arbitrary and could not avoid situations of "unequal rewards and hardships." Clearly, such a system did not establish a fair and competitive market order.

Third, the contract implementation costs were also high. According to the proponents of this system, after the "contract baseline" was established, the ideal of "independent management and self-financing" was achieved because the SOE could retain excess income but had to cover any shortfalls on its own. In reality, however, because the contractor was simply the SOE manager without much personal property, he was unable to truly "bear the losses" when failing to meet the contracting targets. Some enterprises tried to harden the constraints on the contractors by demanding "contract risk deposits," under which the contractor was required to deposit some money upfront. But compared with the size of the enterprise, an individual's risk deposit was just a drop in the bucket, far from adequate to make up for any losses. Among the 898 large- and medium-sized SOEs in six provinces surveyed by the State System Reform Commission, 160 were loss-makers. The following is how they made up for the payment losses: 7.1% received government subsidies, 5.1% had their baselines adjusted lower, and 35.5% opted for self-funding. None of the enterprises chose to resort to bankruptcy, closure, or mergers. Among those that opted for self-financing, only one enterprise covered all the losses with its own funds, while the others covered only part or a small portion of the losses. Overall, the amount of losses that they bore was relatively low.[22]

[21] Whipping a fast-moving ox—due to the fact that immediate good performance increases future financial burdens—creates a ratchet effect, whereby progress can only move forward and not backward. This inevitably leads enterprises to "take the gains and run" rather than working to further improve profitability.

[22] Zhou Shulian, *From a Planned Economy to a Market Economy* (Beijing: Economic Management Publishing House, 1994), pp. 22–24, 108–109.

The most severe problem of the enterprise contracting system was that it undermined the foundation of enterprise property. The contractor excessively consumed existing assets and did not try to recover the original value of the fixed assets, thus falsely increasing the residual income. Nor did the contractor invest or innovate to increase the capital interests of the owner (the state). Instead of investing in long-term development, the contractor with residual control tended to underreport depreciation and to engage in predatory expansion in order to increase current profits at the expense of capital investments. This is why enterprise short-term behavior was widespread under the contracting system.

When residual control was assigned to the contractor, the enterprise contracting system created two masters for a SOE: the on-the-scenes contractor and the off-the-scenes state, and the former's control of the enterprise became justified. After reviewing the Enterprise Law, an American scholar concluded that the law exceeded any Western company law in terms of the power delegated to enterprise general directors/managers, giving them the highest power.[23] When managers had excessive power without the constraints of the must-have corporate governance structure of a modern enterprise, "insider control" became incontrollable, and the phenomenon spread out.[24]

When contracting was introduced in 1987, the profit retention incentive increased the enterprises' eagerness to produce more and to earn more. The drawbacks began to surface in 1988, when actual profits and tax revenue began to drop. In 1987, total output of whole-people-owned industrial enterprises with independent accounting grew by 11.3%, realized profits and taxes increased by 12.9%, and profit handovers and tax payments increased by 12.2%. In 1988, the first indicator rose by 12.6%, and the second indicator was 17.2% higher. However, the price hike was 7.3% in 1987 and 17.5% in 1988. Discounting for the price hike, realized profits and taxes only grew by 5.2% in 1987 and they declined by 1.1% in 1988. The amount of profits and submitted taxes decreased even further. The third indicator dropped the most.[25]

The contractor gained control of the enterprise, including residual control, during the term of the contract; meanwhile, he had the right to claim earnings above the handover baseline. Under this property rights arrangement, the owner could not exercise residual control, while the contractor expanded his interest by encroaching on the rights of the owners. It was commonplace for contractors to use this power for their own personal interests. The phenomenon of "three types of people engaging in contracting, with expenses for drinking, gambling, and other vices fully covered" even found its way into a popular folk song from the 1980s, titled "Ten Types of

---

[23] W.H. Simon (1996): "The Legal Structure of the Chinese 'Socialist Market' Enterprises," The Journal of Corporation Law, 21(2), pp. 267–306.

[24] Legalist Fang Liufang pointed out that frequent occurrence of serious cases of corruption, bribery, and encroachment of company property in SOEs was, to a large extent, related to the legal requirements of "legal representatives" or "legal persons." (See Fang, Liufang: "The Legal Status, Power, and the Conflict of Interest of SOE Legal Persons," Comparative Jurisprudence, Issue 21, 1999.)

[25] Ibid., pp. 160–161.

People."[26] It is not surprising that major corruption cases frequently occurred in well-known "contract-based" enterprises like Capital Iron and Steel Company.

In the 1990s, the national leaders no longer considered the enterprise contracting system feasible for the SOE reform. However, the mainstream thinking embodies in the system lingered on. The 1992 State Council Regulations on Transforming the Operational Mechanism of Industrial Enterprises Owned by the Whole-People represented a continuation of that thought in the form of State Council directives. The regulations required "turning the enterprises into commodity producers and the operators who have operational and business expansion autonomy, are responsible for profits and losses, and are self-constained. They should be independent legal persons with civil rights and obligations. … Enterprises have the right to possess, utilize, and lawfully dispose of the properties entrusted by the state." The regulation specified 14 enterprise operational rights, such as the decision-making right for production and operation. Meanwhile, "they would bear civil liabilities for operational activities conducted by enterprises' legal representatives and other employees under the name of the legal person."

In November 1993, the Third Plenary Session of the Fourteenth Party Central Committee adopted the Decision on Certain Issues in Establishing a Socialist Market Economy System, a milestone decision in the reform process. However, while stating that the direction of state-owned enterprise reform is toward institutional innovation to establish a modern enterprise system, this decision required "continuous implementation of the Law of Whole-People-Owned Industrial Enterprises and the Regulation on Transforming the Operational Mechanism of Whole-People-Owned Industrial Enterprises to allow enterprises to have rights and obligations without any compromise. To sum up, there was no consensus on the direction of the SOE reform, and the impact of the idea of separating ownership and control rights persisted for a long time.

---

[26] In his well-known novel, *Ruined City,* about life in a 1980s' city, author Jia Pingwa recalls this ballad: "The first class consists of the people's servants, who enjoy happiness from the high without making any effort. The second class consists of the racketeers with government connections and protection. The third class consists of the contractors, whose expenses on good meals, prostitutes, and gambling are all reimbursed. The fourth class includes the lessors, who profit from sitting at home. The fifth class includes those in police uniforms who collect money from the plaintiffs and the defendants. Those in the sixth class hold a scalpel and pocket cash in red envelopes. The seventh class consists of the actors who make money by wriggling their bottoms. The eighth class consists of those engaged in propaganda and who are invited to banquets from time to time. The ninth class includes the teachers who do not know the names of all the expensive dishes. The tenth class includes the masters who must follow the example of the selfless hero Lei Feng." Jia Pingwa, *Ruined City*, 1993 (Beijing: Writers Publishing House, 2009).

8.2 A Modern Company System: Proposal and Implementation

During the fundraising-for-expansion boom in the early 1980s, some people tried their hands at stock issuances because they had heard it was a convenient funding channel. In November 1984, Shanghai Feilo Acoustics Co. entrusted the Securities Office of the Shanghai Branch of the Industrial and Commercial Bank of China to issue its shares to the public. This was the first stock issuance after the onset of the reform and opening. The first stock issuers treated the stocks as bonds to borrow money, and some enterprise shares even paid interest with guaranteed principal repayments.

In the 1985 report "China: Long-Term Development Issues and Options," the World Bank task team reviewed the Chinese economy and proposed transforming the SOEs into modern companies.[27] It found that the core issue for the SOE reform was to establish an appropriate relationship between the state and the enterprise. One option to transform the SOEs into companies was to divide SOE property into shares and to give them to several public agencies as the principal shareholders.

Among Chinese researchers, Jin Lizuo and Wu Jiaxiang, two young economists trained in modern economics, were the first to propose reorganizing the large- and medium-sized SOEs into modern firms. In a 1985 paper, "Joint Stock Organization: Thoughts on Further Reforms,"[28] they suggested enterprises be transformed in three phases. In the first phase, administrative agencies would continue exercising ownership rights as the representatives of the state. Through an assets-for-shares program, several relevant agencies and the local government would jointly hold the SOE as a preliminary form of a joint-stock company. In the second phase, state-run holding companies, or investment and trust companies, would replace the government agencies as the representatives of state ownership. In the last stage, state-owned joint-stock companies with limited liabilities would be listed on the stock exchange and become public companies.

These discussions on corporatization were an eye-opener. Some people felt that such corporatization was an option worth exploring to strengthen government-business relations and to deepen the SOE reform. However, the discussions did not lead to any concrete steps being taken because the vast majority of the public had never seen a modern company and did not understand what a modern company is.

In September 1986, Peking University Professor Li Yining published "Envisioning Ownership Reform in China," breaking new ground for SOE joint-stock company reform. Professor Li elaborated on the necessity and specific steps required

[27] Chinese translation. Beijing: China Financial and Economic Publishing House, 1987.

[28] Jin Lizuo and Wu Jiaxiang, "Joint Stock Organization: Thoughts on Further Reforms," *Economic Development and System Reform*, no. 1 (1985).

to establish joint-stock organizations as the core SOE ownership reform. He advocated reorganizing state-owned and state-run enterprises into public-owned joint-stock firms.[29] In December, the State Council issued Several Regulations on Deepening Enterprise Reform and Enhancing Enterprise Vitality, allowing local governments to permit several large- and medium-sized SOEs that had the right conditions to be pilots for testing the joint-stock organizations. Thereafter, the pilot projects for joint-stock systems in Chinese large and medium-sized enterprises were comprehensively launched.

At the time, most people in academic circles and government agencies did not thoroughly understand modern company mechanisms, and this resulted in many problems in the design of the pilot program. The state, the enterprise, the general public, and the employees jointly held shares in the pilot company. The enterprise shares consisted of the previous "self-accumulated funds" or the "enterprise funds" under the contracting system. For this part of the shares, it was unclear who represented the owner. In addition, the pilot companies followed the principle of "strengthening operational rights while weakening ownership rights." They paid little attention to establishing a corporate governance mechanism or providing any checks and balances between the owner and the manager. Similar to the enterprise contracting system, the pilots continued to designate the chairman of the board of directors as the "statutory representative" of the company, or even as the "representative of the legal entity" or the "legal entity" itself. This practice violated the civil law principle that maintains that the body representing a legal entity should be a board of directors that is entrusted by the shareholders, not the employed managers.[30] These practices made it difficult to establish an effective corporate governance mechanism, and it opened the door to insider control.

After reviewing the SOE reforms in various countries and studying modern firm systems, some theoreticians proposed a reform approach for state-owned enterprises aimed at establishing standardized modern corporations.

On August 24, 1993, *Economics Daily* carried "About Corporatization," an article by Wu Jinglian and Qian Yingyi. The article proposed reorganizing existing non-corporate enterprises (particularly former large and medium-sized state-owned enterprises) into corporate legal entities. These corporate entities, formed by shareholders' contributions, would independently assume civil responsibilities and bear their own profits and losses. The article emphasized that establishing a corporate governance structure is the core of corporatization. Corporate governance creates a system of checks and balances among the owners, the board of directors, and the executive management. The shareholders' meeting is the highest authority within the company, and the shareholders elect the directors based on trust. The directors function as the trustees of the shareholders and they bear fiduciary duties. The board of directors, composed of these directors, is entrusted by the shareholders with management

---

[29] Li Yining, "Ownership Reform and Management of Joint-Stock Enterprises," *China Economic System Reform*, no. 12 (1986).

[30] Fang Liufang, "The Legal Status, Power, and Conflicts of Interest of SOEs' Statutory Representatives."

of the company's assets. The board sets major business strategies and supervises their execution by the management team. The relationship between the board of directors and the company's managers is one of agency; managers are employed by the board and have management rights within the scope of their authorization, and they handle the company's daily operations. The company employs managers under a paid appointment system, whereby managers are responsible for operating the company's affairs according to the law. The board has the right to supervise the performance of the management personnel. Additionally, the board must establish an incentive mechanism to ensure that the managers remain motivated despite the multiple constraints they face from market competition, capital market competition, and competition among managers. The corporate system enables the managers, with positions, authority, responsibilities, constraints, and incentives, to operate independently, thus maximizing their unique role in enterprise operations.

The article also suggested that during the corporatization process, equity diversification can be achieved through methods such as "debt-to-equity swaps" and holdings by social security funds.

Leaders in the business community who were familiar with the organization of modern enterprise and operational rules fully realized the necessity of standardized corporatization reforms. Chen Qingtai, vice chairman of the State Economic and Trade Commission, led the enterprise reform research team in drafting the documents for the Third Plenary Session of the 14th Central Committee. Based on in-depth research into state-owned enterprise reform, he concluded that modernization of large and medium-sized state-owned enterprises should be achieved through modern corporate systems. In August 1993, Jiang Zemin assumed the position of CCP general secretary. During an inspection of large and medium-sized state-owned enterprises in Northeast China, he convened a seminar in Dalian with the heads of state-owned enterprises in North China and Northeast China. At the seminar, General Secretary Jiang pointed out that "a modern enterprise system is a result of socialized mass production and development of a commodity economy. It is an inherent requirement in developing the productive forces. The key to improving the performance of large- and medium-sized SOEs is to establish a modern company system suitable to developing a socialist market economy in which ownership rights are clearly defined and assignment of responsibilities is explicit."[31]

The Third Plenary Session of the 14th Party Central Committee adopted the Decision on Several Issues Concerning the Establishment of a Socialist Market Economic System, pointing out, for the first time, that "the direction of SOE reform is to establish a modern enterprise system. … To meet the requirements of a socialist market economy, a modern enterprise system must be established that clearly defines property rights, explicitly assigns authority with responsibility, separates the administrative role from the enterprise, and applies the science of management." This reform objective marked a shift to a new phase in China's SOE reform: from the long-existing approach of "decentralization and concessions" while retaining the

[31] "August 22, 1993: Jiang Zemin Tours large- and Medium-sized SOEs in the Northeast," at http://cpc.people.com.cn/GB/64162/64165/68640/68662/4730249.html.

same basic institution, to a focus on clearly defining ownership rights and improving corporate governance.

Unfortunately, this decision did not provide a clear definition of a modern corporate system, failing, in particular, to address the necessity of establishing a company governance mechanism, which is central to a modern corporate framework. Instead, the characteristics of a modern enterprise were generalized as "well-defined property rights, clearly assigned (operational) rights and responsibilities, separate administrative and enterprise roles, and scientific management." The practices of modern companies demonstrate that a corporate governance structure that establishes checks and balances between owners and executives is the core structure of a modern firm because of the separation of ownership and control.[32] In a 1987 report submitted for an international seminar on SOE reform, held in the Diaoyutai State Guesthouse, the World Bank stressed the importance of effective corporate governance in those companies established from the former SOEs. This report attracted significant interest among Chinese researchers. However, the authorities did not accept this idea, arguing that "Party cadres and the masses" could hardly understand it. Therefore, the official SOE reform documents did not mention this idea until the late twentieth century.

At the National Economic Work Conference on implementing the Party Central Committee decision, held during December 1–4, 1993, Premier Li Peng announced that the government would "carefully select 100 large- and medium-sized SOEs to experiment with a modern enterprise system during the next year."[33] In November 1994, after several rounds of studying the draft pilot program prepared by the State System Reform Commission and the State Economic and Trade Commission, the State Council approved the "Program to Select 100 SOEs for a Modern Enterprise Experiment," and the experiment was launched 1995. Among the 100 pilots, 70 were under the State Economic and Trade Commission, and the remainder were under the State System Reform Commission.[34]

---

[32] Corporate governance is a set of "fundamental principles, rules, self-disciplinary mechanisms, proactive commitments, and business practices shaped by a country's unique environment, history, and traditions," that guide, constrain, and control company management, operations, and decision-making (OECD, *OECD Principles of Corporate Governance*, 2004, p. 18). Its primary function is to create checks and balances between company owners and managers. Starting in the 1970s, as research into business issues deepened, economists came to a more profound understanding of the agency problems arising from the separation of ownership and control in modern companies. Additionally, as company ownership became more dispersed, the "free rider" problem for investors became more prominent, and financial scandals and bankruptcies resulting from insider control increased, making the supervision of management an important concern for protecting owners' interests. During the 1980s and 1990s, both companies and securities market regulators worldwide began to place greater emphasis on corporate governance. In 1998, the London Stock Exchange in the UK established the first *Combined Code on Corporate Governance*. The Organisation for Economic Co-operation and Development (OECD) released its *Principles of Corporate Governance* in 1999, beginning a global movement to improve corporate governance.

[33] Li Peng, "Accelerate Socialist Market Economy Reform, Maintain Sustained, Fast, and Sound Economic Development," speech at the National Economic Work Conference, December 1, 1993, at http://cpc.people.com.cn/GB/64184/64186/66685/4494214.html.

[34] Shao Ning, comp., *Record of the SOE Reforms (1998–2008)*, pp. 347–363.

At the time, however, there was a lack of consensus about the nature and characteristics of a modern enterprise system. In particular, the leaders did not understand the importance of corporate governance. Since the ownership structure had not yet been adjusted and there was no effective corporate governance mechanism, most pilot enterprises were still owned solely by the state or had the state as the controlling shareholder. The reorganized firms were simply the old firms with a new name. The parent company, an authorized investor, held administrative control over the reorganized firm and continued to appoint the firm management teams and their leaders.

One year after the launch of the experimental program, the State Economic and Trade Commission and the State System Reform Commission began to review the progress thus far, based on the "Target Requirements for the 100 Modern Enterprise Pilots."[35] By the end of 1997, eleven out of the 100 pilots had become joint-stock, limited-liability companies with a diversified ownership structure; six of the pilots had been transformed into limited liability companies, and sixty-nine pilots remained solely state-owned (ten of which were former government agencies). Clearly, these results fell far short of expectations. Virtually no firm had achieved the standard of a modern company. Although the State Economic and Trade Commission's "Implementation Guidance for the 100 Modern Enterprise Pilots" of November 1995 required that, as an essential task in the experiment, the firms establish a corporate governance structure based on the Company Law, and 84 pilot companies had established a board of directors, they were still run according to the principle that "the enterprise is a legal entity with the general manager (the chairman of the board after the experiment) as the representative of the legal entity." Most board members were insiders. One person often concurrently held the positions of board chairman and general manager and was still the "number one boss," similar to that in the former general manager responsibility system. The board of directors existed either in name only or had almost the same composition as the Party committee or the management team. There was no fiduciary arrangement between the board and management, nor was there any management monitoring or any incentive mechanisms. Insider control became rampant, and the holding company continued to intervene in the day-to-day operations of its subsidiaries.

Shao Ning, a former director-general of the Enterprise Department of the State Economic and Trade Commission and later a vice chairman of the State Council State Assets Commission, summarized the 1995–1997 modern enterprise experiment as follows: "Because the role of the actual investor was missing, the firms had only a skeletal frame of a corporation. Several critical mechanisms for decision-making, execution, and monitoring were missing in the structure. The problem of insider control was not solved. … Most companies were still under the sole ownership of the state, and only a few had diversified ownership. The reorganized enterprises were companies in appearance only, and some were merely old wine in new bottles. The expected fundamental changes in the institutional arrangements and mechanisms did

[35] Ibid., pp. 385–389.

not take place."[36] According to Li Rongrong, former chairman of the State Economic and Trade Commission and later chairman of the State Council State Assets Commission, other problems were even worse: "Before the 16th Party Congress in 2002, there was no board of directors in a true sense. … None of the central-government-owned enterprises had set up a board of directors in full compliance with the Company Law."[37]

8.3 Turn of the Twenty-First Century: An Upsurge in SOE Corporatization

The call to transform the SOEs into standard modern companies was precipitated primarily by the worsening state-sector financials at the end of the century.

The reform focusing on weakening ownership rights and enhancing managerial rights was not conducive to establishing an efficient enterprise system, and it exacerbated problems in the SOEs' financials. Before 1988, loss-making SOEs accounted for less than 20% of the total number of SOEs. But by the early 1990s, only one-third of SOEs were profitable, another one-third were loss-makers, and the last one-third were incurring losses but on paper they were showing profits. In 1995, loss-makers accounted for 40% of the total number of SOEs. A comparison of total profits and losses further demonstrates the severity of the problem. In 1994, the state sector made net profits of more than RMB 90 billion. By 1995, this figure had largely leveled off, but in the first half of 1996 the state sector suffered net losses of more than RMB 13 billion. The situation improved slightly in the second half of 1996, but only after the commercial banks cut the lending rates on two occasions. In the first quarter of 1997, net losses of SOEs totaled more than RMB 2 billion, and in 1998, the sector suffered net losses of RMB 7.8 billion (see Table 8.1).[38]

The problem was even more severe in provinces where there was a large state sector. Take the state sector industrial stronghold of Liaoning province as an example: by 1997, provincial industrial SOEs had suffered net losses for three consecutive years. Among 926 large- and medium-sized SOEs, 491 were loss-makers, and many others had to halt production either entirely or partially. Given the widespread provincial SOE losses, this situation was called the "Liaoning phenomenon."[39]

The Third Plenary Session of the 14th Party Central Committee's "Decision on Several Issues Concerning the Establishment of a Socialist Market Economic System" did not define a modern enterprise system, but it did describe four essential

---

[36] Ibid., p. 383.

[37] "The Board of Directors in Central Government Enterprises: A Ten-Year Review," *Caijing*, June 30, 2014.

[38] Xie Chuntao, "SOE Reform: Twists and Turns and Prospects: An Interview with Yang Qixian, Vice President of the China Society of Economic Reform," *Hundred Year Tide*, no. 6 (1997); *Finance Yearbook of China* (multiple years) (Beijing: China Financial and Economic Publishing House).

[39] Shao Ning, comp., *Record of the SOE Reforms (1998–2008)*, p. 49.

Table 8.1 SOE profits and losses (1990–98)

Year	Share of SOE loss-makers (%)	Losses by SOE loss-makers (RMB billion)	Total SOE realized profits (RMB billion)
1990	30.3	93.26	49.15
1991	28.0	92.59	74.45
1992	22.7	75.68	95.52
1993	29.8	47.94	166.73
1994	32.6	62.45	160.80
1995	33.3	80.21	147.02
1996	37.5	112.70	87.67
1997	43.9	142.09	53.98
1998	47.4	196.02	–7.80

Source Finance Yearbook of China (multiple years) (Beijing: China Financial and Economic Publishing House)

characteristics of such a system: "clearly defined property rights, explicitly assigned authority and responsibility, separation of administrative and enterprise roles, and scientific management."

Facing this grim reality, national leaders called for providing help to the SOEs so they could overcome their difficulties within three years[40] and for accelerating the establishment of a standard modern company system.

In 1999, the Fourth Plenary Session of the 15th Party Central Committee adopted the Decision on Key Issues Related to State-Owned Enterprise Reform and Development. This decision called for standardizing the corporatization restructuring, highlighted "the governance structure of corporate legal person (i.e., the corporate governance) as the core of corporatization," and required SOEs to establish effective corporate governance with diversified equity holdings during the transformation.

The main new requirements of this decision for the corporatization of large and medium SOEs included the following. First, except for a very few enterprises that must be kept under the state monopoly, the reform should "actively develop corporations with diversified investors," ... the large and medium-sized SOEs "should be transformed into joint-stock companies through standardized public listing, China-foreign joint ventures, and cross-holdings between enterprises, so as to develop an economy of mixed ownership types." Second, the decision pointed out that "the corporatization reform should establish a legal person governance structure that enables checks and balances between owners and managers." ... and required "all transformed companies to establish effective corporate governance." This was the first time the concept of corporate governance (then called the legal person government structure) appeared in a document from the CCP Central Committee and the

[40] Premier Zhu Rongji issued this call during his July 1997 tour of SOEs in Liaoning province. The National People's Congress in March 1998 passed a decision to "enable large- and medium-sized SOE loss-makers to overcome their difficulties within about three years through reform, reorganization, transformation, and managerial strengthening."

State Council. It was also the first time that public companies were required to establish effective corporate governance. (start a new paragraph here) Higher requirements were raised for companies established at the turn of the century. The corporatization reform of large and medium-sized SOEs after 1998 consisted of three interlinked steps.

First, achieving the separation of government and enterprise responsibilities. During the planned economy period, the functions of the government as a social manager and as an owner were combined. Economic organizations such as "state-owned companies" and "group companies" were both administrative agencies and so-called "enterprises." To separate the responsibilities of government and enterprise and allow different organizations to perform these roles, the newly appointed government in 1998 took significant measures to restructure the ministry-level agencies that had both governmental and corporate functions into "national bureaus" managed by the State Economic and Trade Commission, solely responsible for administrative management. The administrative management functions for foreign trade and telecommunications were assigned to the Ministry of Foreign Trade and Economic Cooperation (MOFTEC) and the Ministry of Information Industry (MII), respectively. Subsequently, these "national bureaus" were dissolved, and their relevant administrative functions were integrated into various functional departments of the Economic and Trade Commission. Those former "administrative companies" lost their status as administrative entities and became enterprises without administrative functions

Second, breaking industry monopolies and promoting competition. Under the planned economy, the government typically only established a single monopolistic enterprise in a given industry or sub-industry to pursue maximum scale. After 1998, the Chinese government adopted a method of splitting and restructuring to break monopolies and foster competition.

Taking the oil industry as an example, before the reforms, the government established the Ministry of Petroleum and the Ministry of Chemical Industry to manage upstream and downstream activities, respectively. These two ministries were later restructured into China Petroleum & Chemical Corporation (SINOPEC) and China National Petroleum Corporation (CNPC), both of which had administrative and enterprise functions. In June 1998, after the administrative functions of these two companies were transferred to the National Oil Industry Bureau under the State Economic and Trade Commission, the government decided to transform them into integrated oil companies. Specifically, downstream facilities like refining and retail in the northern region were handed over from SINOPEC to CNPC, while CNPC's oil fields in the southern region were transferred to SINOPEC. This restructuring allowed the two companies to invest and operate in each other's territories, resulting in three competing integrated oil companies in China, including China National Offshore Oil Corporation (CNOOC), which engaged in offshore oil extraction. Similar approaches were employed in other industries to foster competition.

For certain industries with natural monopoly characteristics, the successful practices adopted by various countries in reforming monopolistic sectors during the past two decades were applied, including opening competitive segments while limiting monopoly operations to the most necessary areas, ensuring these monopolistic enterprises operate under social oversight. For instance, the fixed-line telephone sector in telecommunications has a natural monopoly, while mobile communications does not. Therefore, China established three mobile communications companies: China Mobile, China Telecom, and China Unicom, while disaggregating the fixed-line telephone business and distributing it among these three companies. The electricity sector adopted the principle of "separation of the grid and the plant, with competitive bidding for grid access," allowing the deregulation of both power generation and sales, while transmission and distribution were organized into monopolistic companies operating under the supervision of the National Energy Administration.

Third, enterprise restructuring and public listings. (start a new paragraph here) Among the two methods of "full listing" and "spinoff listing," the former is more effective but requires a longer time, while the latter shows results more quickly but it is accompanied by several problems. The restructuring of state-owned industrial and commercial enterprises in China generally adopted the latter method. For example, in October 1999, CNPC spun off its core assets in oil extraction, refining, chemicals, and retail, reorganizing into PetroChina Company Limited (referred to as "China Petroleum"), which subsequently went public in Hong Kong and New York. Of CNPC's 1.54 million original employees, 1.06 million were retained by the "existing enterprise," while the remaining 480,000 were employed by PetroChina. The latter introduced some public and strategic investors through its initial public offering (IPO) in March 2000, changing its wholly state-owned nature and going public on the Hong Kong Stock Exchange and the New York Stock Exchange in the forms of H-shares and American Depositary Receipts (ADRs). At the turn of the century, several original state-owned large enterprises gradually went public in domestic and foreign securities markets, including Qingdao Beer (Hong Kong H-shares in 1993, Shanghai A-shares in the same year), China Mobile (Hong Kong red chip in 1997), China Petroleum (Hong Kong H-shares in 2000, Shanghai A-shares in 2007), China Unicom (Hong Kong red chip in 2000, Shanghai A-shares in 2002), China Petrochemical (Hong Kong H-shares in 2000, Shanghai A-shares in 2001), and Baosteel (Shanghai A-shares in 2000), among others.

Adoption of the latter method for state-owned enterprise reform resulted in a "three-tier" structure within the state-owned sector: the first tier was the government level, where the State-owned Assets Supervision and Administration Commission was established to centralize ownership functions. The second tier consisted of the so-called "operating institutions" of state-owned assets, which included entities mentioned in Article 64 of the 1993 Company Law,[41] such as "national investment companies, state-controlled companies, and state-owned asset management companies, as well as qualified enterprise groups." These institutions exercised shareholder rights within the restructured companies of the third tier.

---

[41] Economic Law Office of the Legislative Affairs Commission of the Standing Committee of the National People's Congress, comp., *Statutory Interpretation and Application of the Company Law of the People's Republic of China* (Beijing: China Democracy and Legislation Publishing House, 2000), p. 122.

This state asset management structure had major institutional defects.

First, the majority of "state-authorized investment institutions" had not undergone corporatization, nor had they established effective corporate governance. The members of their "leadership teams" served both as full representatives of the state shareholders and as employed professional managers, violating the fundamental principles of corporate governance. This dual role became the breeding ground for "insider control" and corruption.

Second, publicly listed companies remained subordinate to investment organizations. The latter controlled the former, and their dispatched personnel often interfered with company operations, making it difficult for the publicly listed companies to operate independently as legal entities.

At the end of 2000, 63.4% of the publicly listed company shares, including those held by the state, were non-tradable. These non-tradable shares could not circulate freely, making it difficult for insider control to be constrained by market mechanisms. Under this second restructuring approach (*boli shangshi*), the unspun-off assets remained in the surviving companies, which became authorized investment organizations. Publicly listed companies did not have complete independence from the surviving companies or the controlling shareholders regarding personnel, finances, and assets. Because of the high proportion of non-core assets and redundant personnel, the surviving enterprises relied on resources from the publicly listed companies for survival. As controlling shareholders, the surviving enterprises had plenty of means to extract resources from the publicly listed companies, such as related party transactions. This led to several instances where large state-owned enterprises raised funds from the stock market and extracted benefits from the listed companies.

Third, the most conspicuous problem was the inability to rein in insider control.

Runaway insider control was common during the transition of the socialist economies. After studying enterprises in the socialist countries that were undergoing transition, Japanese economist Masahiko Aoki pointed out the need to restrict insider control during the transition.[42] Such runaway insider control also widely existed in Chinese enterprises that had gained operational autonomy without effective corporate governance during the transition, in enterprises under the contracting system, and in joint-stock companies. During China's SOE reform, a type of thinking that endured for a long time focused on decentralization and concessions to enterprise executives. Because of this influence, various nonstandard practices occurred during the corporatization process. For instance, legal provisions on "statutory representatives" and "representatives of legal entities" facilitated insider control.[43]

---

[42] Masahiko Aoki, "Controlling Insider Control: Issues of Corporate Governance in Transition Economies" (Chinese translation of Masahiko Aoki and Qian Yingyi, comps., *Corporate Governance in Transition Economies: Insider Control and the Role of Banks* (Beijing: China Economic Publishing House, 1995), pp. 15–35.

[43] At a 2005 seminar on the board of directors experiments in wholly-state-owned companies, Li Rongrong, chairman of the State-owned Assets Supervision and Administration Commission, pointed out that a major problem in establishing a modern enterprise system was the incomplete corporate governance. Many large SOEs were incorporated according to the Company Law, but

In 2000, the China Securities Regulatory Commission (CSRC) prepared a Code of Corporate Governance for Listed Companies to address the above problems. Taking into consideration the characteristics of corporate governance in China's listed companies during the transition, the requirements highlighted the following: a controlling shareholder should deal with the listed company and the other shareholders in good faith; a listed company should be independent and free from interference by the controlling shareholder; and the personnel, assets, and finances of a controlling shareholder should be separate from the listed company. In February 2002, the CSRC and the State Economic and Trade Commission jointly issued the corporate governance code. The code specified six principles: equal treatment for all shareholders and protection of the shareholders' legitimate rights and interests, strengthening the duty of the board directors to act in good faith with diligence, setting up a supervisory board to play a monitoring role, adopting sound performance evaluation, incentive, and constraint systems, protecting the stakeholders' legitimate rights, and improving the disclosure and transparency of the listed companies. The code functioned as a guideline for listed companies to establish a modern enterprise system and it also provided an institutional framework for others to strengthen corporate governance.

The Decision on Several Issues in Perfecting the Socialist Market Economy, adopted by the Third Plenary Session of the 16th Party Central Committee in October 2003, stresses the need to "follow the requirements of a modern enterprise to standardize the rights and obligations of a company's general meeting of shareholders, board of directors, supervisory board, and executives, and to improve the executive appointment process. The meeting of the general shareholders should make decisions about the composition of the board of directors and the supervisory board, and the board of directors should select the executives, thus establishing checks and balances among the company's highest authority, the decision-making body, the supervisory body, and the executives. However, due to the defects in the overall structure of the state sector, the problems related to corporate governance and insider control were not resolved.

---

they had not established a board of directors. In those wholly-state-owned enterprises and state-holding companies with a board, the board of directors did not play an adequate role, and there were severe insider control problems. "Board members duplicated the management teams, and it still was a general manager's responsibility system. As the same person simultaneously functioned as chairman of the board of directors, the Party secretary, and the general manager, he had too much power, and his decisions represented the final word." Li Rongrong, "The Board of Directors Pilots Are as Significant as the Launch of Shenzhou 6," 2005, in Li Rongrong, *Managing Enterprises by Law* (Beijing: China Economic Publishing House, 2013), p. 159.

8.4 State-Sector Reform After the Establishment of SASAC

One important issue facing state-owned enterprises in establishing a modern corporate governance system was their long-standing problem of absentee ownership. In 1988, the State Assets Administration, responsible for state assets management, was established. However, as an administrative body, this agency could not function as an asset manager, and multiple agencies continued to have overlapping roles in the SOEs' personnel and planning decisions. There was no fundamental transformation in terms of SOE management.

In 1998, the State Council ministries underwent a comprehensive reorganization to separate the roles of government and enterprise. The line ministries of metallurgy, machinery, chemical industry, and internal trade ceased being the managers of enterprises in their respective sectors. This function was handed over to nine state administrations under the State Economic and Trade Commission. A working committee for large-sized enterprises was established under the Party Central Committee to supervise the management teams of 162 enterprises that previously had been subject to State Council oversight. Thus, control over the SOEs was scattered among five ministerial agencies: the State Economic and Trade Commission was responsible for guiding the SOE reform and control, the Ministry of Finance managed SOE capital, the Ministry of Labor and Social Security oversaw income distribution policies, the State Planning Commission was in charge of enterprise development and project reviews, and the Party's Organization Department made personnel decisions based on the principle that cadres should be managed by the Party.

To address this fragmentation problem, the 16th Party Congress in 2002 called for a reform to the state assets management system by establishing state assets management bodies as representatives of the investors at various levels of government. In March 2003, the National People's Congress decided to establish the State-owned Assets Supervision and Administration Commission (SASAC), which represented the state in performing the duties for investors central-government-owned SOEs in the non-financial sectors. Provincial and municipal governments also established state assets management agencies in charge of local-government-owned SOEs.

As soon as SASAC was established, some economists pointed out that the Company Law was the fundamental law for corporatized enterprises, and that SASAC should comply with this law when exercising owners' rights. When performing its duties on behalf of the state shareholder, SASAC was to follow the corporate governance framework stipulated in the Company Law.[44] However, most state-authorized investment organizations that SASAC directly managed, or in other words, the parent companies of central-government-owned SOEs, were wholly-state-owned

---

[44] Wu Jinglian, "Several Recommendations on State-sector Reform After the Establishment of SASAC: Speech on Behalf of the Task Team for SOE Reform and State Assets Management Reform under the Economic Committee of the Chinese People's Political Consultative Conference for the National Standing Committee Meeting of the Chinese People's Political Consultative Conference, July 10, 2003," in *Works of Wu Jinglian* (Beijing: Central Compilation and Translation Press, 2013), vol. 2, pp. 648–655.

enterprises governed by the Law of the People's Republic of China on Industrial Enterprises Owned by the Whole People. While a few wholly-state-owned companies established boards of directors after the Company Law was promulgated in 1993, they later revoked the board and returned to the factory-director (manager) responsibility system under the Law on Industrial Enterprises Owned by the Whole People.[45]

Without establishing standardized corporate governance mechanisms, the State-owned Assets Supervision and Administration Commission (SASAC) could only directly manage these enterprises in terms of "personnel, operations, and assets." In May 2003, the State Council issued the Interim Regulations on the Supervision and Administration of State-Owned Assets of Enterprises, which specified SASAC's primary duties as follows: (a) performing the duties of the investor and guiding and promoting SOE reform and reorganization; (b) on behalf of the state, dispatching a supervisory board to certain large SOEs; (c) appointing and dismissing enterprise executives and evaluating their performance and deciding on their performance-based remuneration; (d) supervising the preservation and appreciation of state-owned assets managed by enterprises; and (e) drafting laws and administrative regulations on state assets management, preparing related rules and procedures, and guiding local governments in local state assets management by law. These requirements exceeded the investor's duties stated in the Company Law.[46]

In 2008, the Law on State-owned Assets was promulgated and entered into effect. This law stipulated that "in a state-invested enterprise, the investor's representative has the rights to receive the returns on assets, participate in major decision-making, and select managers," thereby further enhancing SASAC's role in managing the SOEs' personnel matters, business affairs, and assets.

Despite SASAC's enhanced direct supervision and the assessment of state-owned company leaders following its establishment, effective corporate governance mechanisms were still not in place and insider control continued to cause severe governance problems. The massive losses in futures trading by CAO (China Aviation Oil [Singapore] Corp. Ltd.), a subsidiary of China National Aviation Fuel Group (CNAF) under

[45] Shao Ning, comp., *Record of the SOE Reforms (1998–2008)*, p. 50, reports that at the end of 2008, among 143 central-government-owned enterprises directly managed by SASAC, 109 were incorporated under the Law of the People's Republic of China on Industrial Enterprises Owned by the Whole People.

[46] Wu Jinglian, "Several Recommendations on State-sector Reform After the Establishment of SASAC," pp. 652–653.

then CEO Chen Jiulin in 2004,[47] and the corruption scandal involving Chen Tonghai, SINOPEC's former president,[48] are indicative of the severity of the problem.

Given these grave problems in state-owned sole proprietorships and state-controlled companies, the leadership of SASAC realized that "the core issue in SOE reform must be to perfect the corporate governance structure and to establish standardized boards of directors."[49]

In June 2004, SASAC issued the Circular on Establishing and Improving Board of Directors Pilots in Solely State-Owned Companies among Central-Government-Owned Enterprises.[50] The experiment included introducing external directors, enhancing the rules and procedures for the board, reassigning board chairpersons if they were insiders, and improving coordination between SASAC and the pilots' board of directors, management team, and the externally appointed supervisory board.[51]

In October 2008, SASAC'S Party Committee and the Organization Department of the Party Central Committee jointly issued the Guidance on Selecting and Appointing Senior Executives by the Board of Directors in the Board-of-Directors Pilots of Central-Government-Owned Enterprises. This was the first time Party organization authorities delegated power to select and appoint senior executives to the board of directors of central-government-owned enterprises, establishing a tiered SOE human

[47] CNAF's massive losses in futures trading: In 2004, CNAF suffered an enormous loss of USD 550 million in its overseas oil futures market trading. On the surface, the loss was caused by mistakes in oil derivatives trading, but in reality, it was due to a corporate governance scandal. First, the transactions violated a government ban. The Chinese government had specifically banned oil options speculation, but a CNAF subsidiary in Singapore had disregarded the ban. In August 1998, the State Council issued the Circular on Rectifying and Standardizing the Futures Market, stating that "enterprises with licenses for overseas futures trading are only allowed to engage in hedging transactions, and all speculative activities are banned." Second, the company breached the law by making over-the-counter deals exceeding its spot market transaction volume. Article 4 of the Provisional Regulations on Futures Transactions, issued by the State Council in June 1999, states that "futures transactions must be conducted on futures exchanges. Over-the-counter futures transactions outside the futures exchanges are prohibited." Article 48 states that "SOEs' futures transactions should be limited to hedging, and the total transaction volume should be appropriate to the total spot market transaction volume during the same period." This case marked a loss of control by all relevant authorities: Neither Singapore Exchange Limited nor CNAF's internal control system detected the problem.

[48] From 1999 to 2007, former SINOPEC president Chen Tonghai accepted bribes related to company operations, land deals, and project contracts in an amount equivalent to more than RMB 195.73 million. In July 2009, Chen was sentenced to death with a two-year reprieve and deprived of his political rights for life. All his personal property was expropriated. Among all the corruption cases of SOE executives, Chen's case was number one in terms of his seniority, the size of the enterprise, and the amount of the involved bribery.

[49] Li Rongrong, "The Board of Directors' Pilots in Central-Government-Owned Enterprises Represent a Corporate Governance Revolution," 2007, in *Managing Enterprises by Law* (Beijing: China Economic Publishing House, 2013), p. 163.

[50] The circular lists the first pilots, including the Shenhua Group, Shanghai Baosteel, Tietong, Chengtong Holdings Group, and National Pharmaceutical Group.

[51] Li Rongrong, "The Board of Directors' Pilots in Central-Government-Owned Enterprises Represent a Corporate Governance Revolution," pp. 163–165, 173–174.

resource system whereby the investor would choose and appoint the board directors, and the board would appoint and supervise the management team.[52]

However, the reform did not make much progress. In 2010, among the 140 central-government-owned enterprises, only 24 were participating in the experiment. Many obstacles still blocked implementation of the reform.

Another approach to overcome insider control was more familiar in China: strengthening the leading role of the SOE Party committees in business decision-making and personnel appointments.

From 1949 to the mid-1950s, China's SOEs had copied the former Soviet Union's "factory-director responsibility system." In 1956, the 8th Party Congress changed this system to a "factory-director responsibility system under the leadership of the Party committee." From the launch of the Cultural Revolution in 1966 to the end of the 1970s, SOEs were under the direct leadership of "revolutionary committees," or Party committees.

After the end of the Cultural Revolution, there were efforts to rectify the situation. Many supported restoration of the pre–Cultural Revolution enterprise leadership system, which involved factory directors (managers) under the leadership of the Party committee. However, given the lessons learned from the Cultural Revolution, when Party organizations become entangled in daily business affairs and there was the problem of "the Party not managing the Party," Deng Xiaoping proposed a different approach to strengthen Party leadership over enterprises. In his speech, "Reforming the Party and the State Leadership System" at the Politburo meeting on August 18, 1980, he suggested: "To enable Party committees to focus on ideological and political work and organizational supervision, it is necessary to gradually and systematically change the factory director (manager) responsibility system under the leadership of Party committees, implementing pilot projects and gradually expanding the practice. This will involve factory management committees, company boards of directors, and joint committees of economic entities taking on leadership and supervisory roles under the factory director (manager) responsibility system." Although Deng Xiaoping's proposal was approved by the Politburo, the reform of enterprise leadership proceeded slowly, the system proposed by Deng did not begin trial implementation until after the 13th CCP Party Congress in 1987. The Party committees of state-owned enterprises, which originally performed leadership functions, were reassigned to be managed by the Party committees of the regions where the enterprises were located, according to the principle of territorial management of grassroots Party organizations. Their functions included supervising Party members and ensuring implementation of Party policies and guidelines.

After the political turbulence of 1989, the policy was readjusted. In August, the Party Central Committee issued the Circular on Strengthening Party Building, which pointed out that "grassroots Party organizations hold a core political position in enterprises and should play a core political role. … Enterprise Party committees

[52] Li Rongrong, "Speech at the Concluding Conference on the Campaign to Study and Practice the Scientific Outlook on Development," February 23, 2009, http://www.sasac.gov.cn/n1180/n4175042/n5662428/n5665862/6225846.html.

should participate in discussions about major issues and provide comments and recommendations."

In October 1993, the Third Plenary Session of the 14th Party Central Committee set the goals of "establishing a modern enterprise system" as the target of the SOE reform. The relationship between the Party committee and the board of directors once again was an important issue in the discussions on SOE reform. Issue no.13/1995 of *Internal Manuscripts*, a publication put out by *Hongqi* (Red Flag), carried an article entitled "A Strategic Perspective on the Current Status of Party Building in Large- and Medium-sized SOEs," written by an official in the Central Party Organization Department.[53] The author stated that the working class in China is mainly distributed in large and medium-sized state-owned enterprises. This means that these enterprises must be under Party leadership, as controlling these enterprises is equivalent to controlling the economic strength of the entire country. Party control required standardization of the decision-making process, which should be: "Party committee decisions are made first, then followed by board of directors decisions."

On January 24, 1997, the CCP Central Committee issued the Notice on Further Strengthening and Improving Party Work in State-Owned Enterprises, which emphasized the role of Party leadership in state-owned enterprises, stating that Party work in these enterprises should permeate all production and operation processes.

In August 1999, in Dalian, Party General Secretary Jiang Zemin held a seminar on SOE reform and development with participants from eight provinces and municipalities in Northeast and North China. At the meeting, Jiang pointed out that "at present, most state-holding companies have a general shareholders meeting, a board of directors, a supervisory board on the one hand, and the Party committee, the trade union, and the workers' congress on the other. A mutual-participation approach should be considered to deal with the relationship between these two sets of bodies. In SOEs and state-holding companies, Party committee leaders and workers' representatives can become members of the board of directors or members of the supervisory board in line with the relevant rules and procedures. Meanwhile, the chairman of the board of directors, the head of the supervisory board, and the general manager can become Party committee members according to the Party Charter and the relevant rules. The secretary of the Party committee and the chairman of the board of directors can be the same person. The purpose of these measures is to develop a uniform decision-making mechanism in the companies." He also pointed out, "The Party organizations in the enterprises should seriously implement the Party's basic political line and policy and carry out related activities for production and operations. The Party organization should participate in decision-making on major issues and support the general shareholders' meeting, the board of directors, and the factory director when performing their respective duties as prescribed by law."

[53] Han Xu, "Looking at the Current Status of Party Construction from a Strategic Perspective: A Discussion with Comrade Wu Jinglian," *Internal Manuscript* (now renamed *Red Flag Manuscript*), no. 13 (1995).

In July 2010, the General Office of the Party Central Committee and the General Office of the State Council issued the Opinions on Further Promoting Implementation of the "Three Majors and One Large" Decision-Making System in State-Owned Enterprises. The document stipulated that matters related to major decisions, major personnel appointments and removals, major project arrangements, and large-scale financial operations (referred to *Sanzhong Yida*, meaning three major decisions and one large operation) must be collectively decided upon by the decision-making bodies of the state-owned enterprises, such as the Party committee (or Party leadership group), board of directors, or the managerial team in enterprises without a board of directors. It also required that when the board of directors or managerial team in enterprises without a board of directors considers matters related to the "three major decisions and one large operation," they should first communicate with the Party committee (or the Party leadership group) and seek their opinions. Party committee (or Party leadership group) members on the board of directors or on the managerial team should implement the opinions and decisions of the Party organization. Additionally, important personnel appointments and removals should be preceded by soliciting opinions from the disciplinary inspection and supervision institutions in the state-owned enterprises and the institutions responsible for state-owned asset management.

Another major task of SASAC was to adjust the ownership structure of the national economy according to the decisions on state-owned enterprises made by the 15th National Congress of the Communist Party of China and the 15th Central Committee's Fourth Plenary Session. This involved systematically withdrawing from areas where enterprises do not have a competitive advantage, reallocating resources to improve public services provided by the government, strengthening critical industries and key sectors vital to the national economy, and addressing areas that private enterprises are unwilling to enter.

The situation changed in the mid-2000s.

In May 2002, Party General Secretary Jiang Zemin undertook a research trip in Chongqing to focus on Party building and development of the western region. On May 22, during an inspection of Southwest Aluminum (Group) Co., Ltd., after listening to an introduction by the company's director in front of a 30,000-ton die-forging hydraulic press, Jiang Zemin said: "The comprehensive national strength and international standing of our country largely depend on many state-owned enterprises with strong technical capabilities like this one. We must make significant efforts to run these enterprises well and make them strong."[54] The 16th National Party Congress in November 2002 adopted a significant policy to "steadfastly enhance and develop the public-owned economy" and "unwaveringly encourage, support, and guide the development of the non-public sector."

In February 2003, an internal document revealed that during the process of state-owned assets withdrawing from the general competitive sectors, there were signs of irregularities and asset losses during the transfer process. Some enterprise management teams engaged in opaque operations, with a few managers using acquisitions

[54] "Jiang Zemin Conducts a Field-Study in Chongqing in May 2002," Xinhuanet, May 26, 2002.

as a means to siphon off state assets. In response, Party and government leaders issued directives requiring investigation and study of the issues arising from the restructuring of state-owned enterprises.[55]

In early 2004, a debate emerged about the state-sector reform, questioning and negating the reform and opening. Some people placed blame for the loss of state assets during the transformation of small to medium-sized SOEs on the policy to "let go of small firms," and they criticized the market-oriented reform for fostering corruption and increasing the wealth gap between the rich and the poor. This led to calls to reestablish the dominant position of the state sector.

In the summer of 2004, Larry Hsien Ping Lang, a professor a Chinese University in Hong Kong, published some papers and made some speeches criticizing well-known private enterprises, such as TCL, Haier, and Greencool, for embezzling state assets during the SOE transformation process. Gu Chujun, Greencool chairman who had returned from overseas to create the company, rejected Lang's charges, leading to a heated debate between Lang and Gu. Many leftists strongly supported Hsien Ping Lang's position. In September 2005, Gu Chujun was arrested, and in 2008 he was sentenced to ten years in prison for registering his company with falsified documents and for misappropriation of funds.

As a result of this major debate, the pace of state-owned economic reform and restructuring slowed down. SASAC carried out several SOE reorganizations based on the principle of "combining like terms" to make the firms bigger and stronger. The process began in 2004 when China National Scientific Instruments and Materials Import and Export Corporation was merged with China National Biotech Group, and China National Pharmaceutical Group Co., Ltd. took over China National Group Corporation of Traditional & Herbal Medicine. By 2011, the reorganizations had reduced the number of central-government-owned enterprises to 118. This reduction was achieved by adding 4 through transfers and new establishments, decreasing 2 through divestitures and cancellations, and reducing 76 through restructuring. However, this reduction in the number of state-owned enterprises still fell short of the goal of concentrating state-owned economic resources in key areas and critical industries related to national interest and security. Both the majority of central and local state-owned enterprises were still mainly distributed across the general competitive sectors.

Despite the mergers aimed at creating "enterprise giants" and the expansion of enterprise scale—whereby the number of state-owned enterprises in the "Fortune Global 500" grew from 3 in 1998 to 50 in 2010 (including financial institutions)—the issue of being "large but not strong" persisted. Some enterprises still faced long-term losses, with over one-third of the enterprises reporting losses. In 2010, there were 43,500 loss-making enterprises with a loss ratio of 35.0% and total losses amounting to 435.3 billion yuan.

The multiple rounds of mergers led to the consolidation of subsidiaries and sub-subsidiaries within the original corporate groups, resulting in internal corporate hierarchies, numerous management levels, dispersed business operations, and a

---

[55] Shao Ning, comp., *Record of the SOE Reforms (1998–2008)*, p. 413.

lack of focus on core activities. In 2006, the state issued the Guiding Opinions on Promoting the Adjustment of State-owned Capital and the Restructuring of State-owned Enterprises, placing an emphasis on simplifying the corporate organizational structures and consolidating the overly hierarchical subsidiaries. Measures such as closures, bankruptcies, dissolutions, mergers, and revocations of corporate status were proposed to keep the management layers within three levels. However, the problems persisted in obstructing the establishment and improvement of internal management mechanisms within central enterprises, thereby limiting their operational efficiency and competitiveness.[56]

The industrial structural adjustments in the early twenty-first century expanded the state sector. In 2004, the government adopted the policy of "protecting and supporting some enterprises while suppressing and controlling others" to address the overheating economy. Industrial policy favored large enterprises, leading to a further expansion of the state sector. For instance, the Industrial Policy for the Development of the Cement Industry required that outdated equipment, such as mechanical shaft kilns (less than 2.8m in diameter), various dry hollow kilns, and wet kiln, be retired and that enterprises with less than 200,000-tons in annual production be closed. The May 2004 Industrial Policy for the Automobile Industry required raising the industry's concentration rate to ensure that large-scale automobile enterprises could enter the Global 500 by 2010. According to this document, total investment in a new automaker should not be less than RMB 2 billion, including RMB 800 million of self-funding. There was also a required minimum production level based on automobile type. The Technical Standards for Refined Oil Wholesalers (draft for comments) of June 2005 required that new wholesalers have at least two years of business experience and own or hold controlling shares in over 30 gas stations. The July 2005 Policy for the Development of the Steel Industry required an increase in industry concentration through mergers, reorganizations, and expansions of backbone enterprise groups. By 2020, steel production in the top-ten domestic steelmaker groups was to be more than 70% of the industry total (from over 50% in 2010). The Notice on Several Issues about Coal Industry Infrastructure Projects stressed the need to introduce large-size projects, cut smaller projects, and continue constructing large coal production bases. The document required an accelerated process of consolidating or transforming small coal mines and closing those that had opened without rational planning or that lacked safe production facilities. In early 2006, a National Development and Reform Commission official announced that China would accelerate construction of thirteen large coal production bases. By 2010, their annual standard coal production was projected to reach 1.7 billion tons, accounting for 78% of the national total.[57]

---

[56] Xiao Yanqing, "SASAC to Accelerate Making Central-Government-Owned Enterprises Slimmer and Better," November 1, 2016. "At present, there are 51,573 central-government enterprise subsidiaries. Twelve firms have over 1000 subsidiaries. The structure of the most complex hierarchical legal entity includes seventeen layers, with as many as eight levels of management. This has significantly reduced management efficiency." http://finance.people.com.cn/n1/2016/1101/c1004-28823182.html.

[57] See "Focus on Re-nationalization," *China Newsweek*, no. 11 (March 27, 2006).

These new industrial policy requirements changed the policy on adjusting the ownership structure in the spirit of "what to do and what not to do" adopted at the 15th Party Congress and the Fourth Plenary Session of the 15th Party Central Committee. As a result, the scale of the state-owned economy tended to expand even in sectors not considered crucial to the "lifeline of the national economy and key areas."

On December 5, 2006, the General Office of the State Council issued a SASAC document entitled Guidance on the Readjustment of State Capital and the Reorganization of SOEs, calling for "further concentration of state capital in national security and economic lifeline industries and key areas, and accelerated growth of enterprises with intellectual property rights and enterprises producing well-known brands that are more competitive internationally, … relevant departments should promptly research and determine the specific industries and fields, and issue corresponding industry and enterprise directories."

On December 18, SASAC Chairman Li Rongrong announced specific arrangements to enhance the control of central-government-owned enterprises. He said, in general, these enterprises should be located in three areas according to their business lines: (a) critical areas related to national security and lifeline industries in the national economy, (b) primary and pillar industries, and (c) other industries and areas. According to these arrangements, the degree of control varied by area. The state sector should maintain absolute control in the first area, including the military industry, power grids and power generation, petroleum and petrochemicals, telecommunications, coal, aviation, and shipping. The state sector should control the essential backbone enterprises in the second area, including equipment manufacturing, automobiles, electronic information technology, construction, the steel industry, non-ferrous metals, chemicals, prospecting and technological design, and science and technology, but state capital should hold absolute or relative control in influential backbone enterprises that are industry leaders. The state sector was required to maintain an influence in the third area, mainly in terms of trade and logistics, investment, pharmaceuticals, construction materials, agriculture, and geological surveys in the form of state-owned capital holding controlling stakes in leading enterprises in influential sectors and in selected pharmaceutical, agricultural, and geological survey enterprises.[58]

Under these arrangements, there was an upsurge in mergers in civil aviation, highway construction, steel industry, coal industry, and refined oil wholesalers from 2003 to 2006, with SOEs taking over many of the private-sector enterprises. According to statistics of the Ministry of Finance, the assets of non-financial SOEs increased by 54% during this period.[59] Central-government-owned enterprises gained a powerful monopoly in energy, raw materials, transportation, and telecommunications. In 2007, the total assets of enterprises under SASAC reached RMB 14.6 trillion, a 100% increase from 2002.

[58] "China Specifies Seven Industries To Be Controlled by the State Sector," *People's Daily Online*, December 18, 2016, http://finance.people.com.cn/GB/1037/5184638.html.

[59] *Finance Yearbook of China*, multiple years.

The trend to re-nationalize, or *guojin mintui* ("the state sector advances while the private sector retreats") climaxed in 2008–2009.

The mergers and restructuring of coal mines in Shanxi province and the takeover of Rizhao Steel Co. by Shandong Iron and Steel Group were called landmark events in the media. On September 2, 2008, the Shanxi provincial government issued Implementation Opinions on Accelerating the Merger and Reorganization of Coal Mining Enterprises, requiring the integration and concentration of coal mining enterprises under the leadership of local governments, following the principle that one main entity should develop each mining area, and one entity could develop multiple mining areas. The provincial government designated eight SOE groups as "legal takeover bodies." Any enterprise failing to meet the new scale standards was excluded from the restructuring process or became a target for acquisition. The provincial government determined how to calculate the compensation for private businesspeople's legal mining rights. Most takeover prices for private-owned mines came to less than 50% of the actual value. According to some reports, private businesspeople lost RMB 40–60 billion during the takeovers.[60]

In July 2007, the Shandong provincial government issued the Opinions on Accelerating the Restructuring of the Steel Industry, announcing the merger of two state-owned companies, Ji'nan Iron and Steel Group and Laiwu Iron and Steel Group, to form Shandong Iron and Steel Group Co., Ltd., and consolidating all local steel companies, which would integrate the province's steel enterprises, including the private steelmaker titan Rizhao Steel Co. Rizhao had been profitable while Shandong Steel had incurred losses, thus the former did not want to be merged with the latter. Nevertheless, Rizhao Steel Co., under pressure, signed a merger agreement in November 2008, under which Shandong Steel would hold 67% and Rizhao would hold 33% of the shares in the new company. The merger agreement fell through, however, because Shandong Steel could not provide sufficient funds to acquire Rizhao Steel. Nevertheless, the attempt by a loss-making state enterprise to be merged with a profitable private enterprise had a significant impact nationwide.

In 2008, the global financial crisis broke out. To stabilize economic growth, the National Development and Reform Commission, together with the Ministry of Industry and Information Technology, prepared the Work Plan for a Program to Readjust and Revitalize Priority Industries and consequently issued ten programs to revitalize the steel, automobile, shipbuilding, petrochemical, textile, non-ferrous metal, equipment manufacturing, electronic information technology, and logistics industries. The government introduced a RMB 4 trillion investment program in line with the policy to "expand demand and secure growth." In 2009, most new loans (RMB 10 trillion), various subsidies, and preferential tax treatments went to the SOEs, particularly the central-government-managed SOEs.

---

[60] The provincial regulations required that, in order to continue its business, an enterprise should produce at least 0.9 million tons of coal annually, which was ten times the entry threshold for private mining enterprises set in 2006. See Zhong Ruiqing, "Analysis of the Legitimacy of Shanxi's Coal Mine Merger and Restructuring Plan," *Jurisprudence*, no. 1 (2010).

While maintaining a powerful monopoly in the energy, raw materials, transportation, telecommunications, and financial sectors, well-funded SOEs also entered areas, such as the real estate sector, that they earlier had been discouraged from entering. In 2010, among 123 central enterprises, 78 (excluding 16 primarily engaged in real estate) had established a total of 227 real estate subsidiaries. These enterprises often purchased land at exorbitant prices, causing considerable stir in the industry. Consequently, in March 2010, SASAC issued an order that these enterprises exit the real estate sector within a specified timeframe.[61] However, based on a report in *International Financial News* under the *People's Daily*, by 2012 less than one-fourth of the companies had complied with SASAC's exit requirement, and some were continuing to buy land lots and were taking advantage of funding from central-government-owned enterprises.[62] Some enterprises not only failed to exit but also used the public resources and the financing advantages of central enterprises to expand and to acquire land without paying dividends to the state, their largest shareholder.

Another cause of the *guojin mintui* phenomenon was the SOE performance evaluation mechanism. Immediately after it was established, SASAC began to develop an SOE performance evaluation system, including both annual and end-term evaluations, and a performance-based remuneration system. The leading indicator in the annual evaluations was total profits and economic value-added based on after-tax profits minus the cost of capital. The primary measurement at the end of the three-year-term evaluation was changes in the value of state capital (comparing the end-term value of state capital and equities against the beginning-of-term value) and the total turnover of assets. The SOEs were required to become stronger and bigger and to increase their economic vitality, control, and influence. Because priority was given to becoming bigger and because the evaluation period was short, the system generated distorted incentives in two areas. The first distortion was the incentive for scale expansion. Given the slow progress in SOE reform, the soft budgetary constraints inherited from the planned economy, and the existing "investment hunger," the evaluation system enhanced an "expansion impulse." After 2009, there was a new upsurge in bank-loan-funded investments, and the SOEs' leverage ratio increased. By 2013, the SOEs' debt-to-assets ratio reached 66.7%, with the indicator for the forestry and warehousing industries at over 80%. By 2015, the debt ratio of central-government-owned enterprises exceeded 65%, with the indicator higher than 70% in more than 40 firms. The coal and steel industries had the highest debt ratio and the most severe overcapacity; some firms' debt ratios exceeded 80%. The debt ratio in the construction, power generation, and civil aviation industries was over 70%.

Driven by these factors, the state sector expanded rapidly. From 2002 to 2011, total assets of central government enterprises increased from RMB 7.13 trillion to RMB 28 trillion, and their total sales grew from RMB 3.36 trillion to RMB 201 trillion. In 2012, the value-added of SOEs was about RMB 13.08 trillion, accounting for 25.2% of GDP. The value-added of manufacturing SOEs was RMB 3301.4 billion, accounting for 20.7% of the industry total; that of financial SOEs was RMB 2585

[61] *Daily Economic News*, April 9, 2010.

[62] *International Financial News*, December 12, 2012.

billion, accounting for 90% of the industry total; and that of extractive SOEs was RMB 1725.9 billion, accounting for 95.8% of the industry total. SOEs also accounted for significant shares in the power generation, telecommunications, fuel gas, water, construction, transportation, and warehousing industries.

The government's "visible hand" placed a priority on allocating resources to SOEs, thereby enhancing the state sector's control and influence. Government agencies engaged directly in resource allocations and they used their administrative power to set rents, leading to "dual pricing" for land and lending between the SOEs and the private sector. Tsinghua University professor Bai Chongen has referred to this phenomenon, created by the preferential policies for SOEs, as the "new dual pricing" of factors such as land and credit between state-owned and private enterprises, which resulted in inefficient resource allocations and contributed to the spread of rent-seeking and corruption.

Chapter 9
A Difficult Challenge: Changing the Economic Growth Mode

From the beginning of the First Five-year Plan period in 1953, structural imbalances and low efficiency, due to the extensive growth mode, always interfered with China's socioeconomic development. After the onset of the reform and opening, the government sought to address this problem, but there were no noticeable results until the Ninth Five-year Plan period (1996–2000) when a shift from extensive to intensive growth was put on the agenda, along with the goal of completing the transformation from a planned economy to a market economy. There was some progress in changing the economic growth mode after the 1993 Third Plenary Session of the 14th Party Central Committee. But shortly thereafter, things took a turn for the worst.

As has been said, "disaster lurks behind good fortune." The rapid economic growth and enhanced national strength at the end of the twentieth century reduced the desire to improve economic efficiency. Economic development returned to its former extensive growth mode.

After the beginning of the twenty-first century, the repeated surge in a wave of massive investments to support rapid GDP growth caused socioeconomic contradictions and led to a gradual accumulation of risks. The Eleventh Five-year Plan (2006–10) and the Twelfth Five-year Plan (2011–15) once again placed transformation of the economic growth mode on the agenda to address the accompanying tensions and to prevent systemic risks. With the lack of an imperative for reform and the existing institutional obstacles, the task of improving economic efficiency and achieving a shift in the economic growth mode gained urgency.

9.1 Adoption of a Soviet-Style Economic Growth Mode

In the early days of the People's Republic, China followed the Soviet pattern of planned economic development, with Soviet experts assisting in the preparations for the First Five-year Plan. Although the specific arrangements for sectoral development

W. Jinglian, *China's Economic Reform*, Understanding China,
https://doi.org/10.1007/978-981-96-9607-9_9

reflected China's specific characteristics, the economic development policy and the path to industrialization closely followed the growth mode that had been established in the 1930s by the Soviet Union. An examination of the Soviet economic growth mode provides valuable insights into the flaws in China's economic growth strategy.

After four years of efforts under the market system of the New Economic Policy, the Soviet Union's industrial and agricultural production in 1924, the same year that Lenin died, had largely returned to the pre-1917 Revolution levels. Within the Russian Communist Party (Bolsheviks), triggered by arguments regarding the approach and speed of industrialization, there were debates among the leaders regarding what economic policy should be adopted. The debates boiled down to a question of whether the Soviet Union should continue implementing the New Economic Policy and a market economy or whether it should establish a planned economy with administrative centralization. There were three camps: the Left, led by Lev D. Trotsky,[1] the Right, led by Nikolai I. Bukharin,[2] and the Centralists, led by Stalin.

The Left called for an end to the New Economic Policy. Members of this group proposed using the state's coercive power to extract significant resources from the peasants so as to ensure rapid industrial development. Grigory A. Feldman, a participant in the debate, noted: "The proletariat has become the main force behind production and can arbitrarily allocate its power between production of the means of production and production of consumer goods." In this way, the proportion of the means of production sector can be increased to achieve industrialization at an extremely high speed.[3] The Right favored the balanced development of industry and agriculture under the New Economic Policy. Bukharin pointed out: "The greater the demands by the peasants, the faster our industrial development will be. With more rapid accumulation by the peasants, our industrial accumulation will be accelerated." Maintaining an alliance with the peasants required continuous implementation of the New Economic Policy and its market institutions.

---

[1] Lev D. Trotsky (1879–1940), a leftist in the Russian Communist Party, had been one of the main leaders of the Russian October Revolution and chairman of the revolution's military committee during the Russian Civil War. Opposing Stalin's Theory of Socialism in One Country, Trotsky advocated "world revolution." He was expelled from the Communist Party in 1927 and was killed by a Soviet assassin in 1940.

[2] Nikolai I. Bukharin (1888–1938) was one of the main leaders of the Communist Party of the Soviet Union after Lenin's death. His writings, e.g., "The Economics of the Transition Period" (1920) and "The ABC of Communism" (with Evgenii Preobrazhensky, 1921), influenced the older generation of revolutionaries in the Chinese Communist Party. Executed as a spy and a saboteur in 1938, he had been the head of the right opposition defending the New Economic Policy during the Party debates at the end of the 1920s. In 1988, the Supreme Court of the Soviet Union rehabilitated his political status and reputation as well as that of others who had been persecuted in the same case.

[3] Grigory A. Feldman (1885–1958) worked in the Soviet Union's State Planning Commission from 1923 to 1931. His report on the growth of national income served as the theoretical basis for the country's First Five-year Plan (1928–32). See Zhang Liangqiu, "Debates on Several Socialist Political Economy Issues in the Sixty Years of the Soviet Union," in Economic Research Journal, comp., *Arguments on China's Socialist Economic Theories (1949–85)* (Beijing: China Financial and Economic Publishing House, 1985), vol. 2, pp. 597–599.

But ultimately Stalin defeated first the Left and then the Right in an inner-Party struggle. After purging Bukharin and other "right opportunists" who "worshipped the market's spontaneous order," Stalin adopted a political line that was more radical than even the propositions of Trotsky and the other leftists. In 1929, he launched a coercive collectivization campaign, promoting an industrialization policy that prioritized heavy industry based in large state-owned corporations.

At the time, the two different propositions, i.e., whether to maintain stable economic growth and to consolidate the alliance with the peasants through balanced development, or to prioritize the development of heavy industry to strengthen national defense, were the two options that the Soviet Union was considering. However, Stalin turned the selection of an economic development mode into a political struggle between the two classes and the two political lines to overwhelm his inner-Party rivals. He claimed that the method of prioritizing development of heavy industry was the "socialist industrialization path," as distinct from the "capitalist industrialization path." The alternative option, he asserted, was "right opportunism," and he argued that "industrialization does not mean developing just any industry. The core and the foundation of industrialization is the development of heavy industry (fuel, the metals industries, etc.)."[4] According to Stalin, "The Soviet approach to industrialization is fundamentally different from the capitalist approach. In the capitalist countries, industrialization usually begins with the light industries. … The Communist parties cannot take this path. …Therefore, the Communist Party in our country has rejected this usual path, and instead, it began industrialization with the development of heavy industry development."[5] He also stated that "rapid development of the entire industrial sector, in particular the producers of the means of production, is the foundation of, and the key to, national industrialization and economic transformation based on socialist development. …What does rapid industrial development mean? It means increasing investment in the industrial infrastructure as much as possible."[6]

Under Stalin's "socialist industrialization mode," beginning with the First Five-year Plan period (1928–32), the Soviet Union made enormous investments in the heavy industries centered on the military, carried out coercive collectivization, and forced farmers to make "tribute payments" for industrialization. These measures severely damaged agriculture and placed light industry and commerce in a subordinate position despite their roles in satisfying the people's consumption needs. While the development of heavy industry played a certain role in wartime successes, the slow

[4] Josef Stalin, "The Economic Situation of the Soviet Union and the Policy of the Party," 1926, in *Selected Works of Stalin* (Chinese translation. Beijing: People's Publishing House, 1979), vol. 1, p. 462.

[5] Josef Stalin, "Speech at a Meeting of Voters of the Stalin Electoral District, Moscow," 1946, in *Selected Works of Stalin* (Chinese translation. Beijing: People's Publishing House, 1979), vol. 2, p. 496.

[6] Josef Stalin, "Industrialization of the Country and the Right Deviation in the C.P.S.U.(B.)," 1929, in *Selected Works of Stalin* (Chinese translation in ibid.), p. 17.

development of light industry, the agricultural decline, and the large-scale abnormal peasant deaths imposed a heavy toll on the Soviet people.[7]

In his final work, *Economic Problems of Socialism in the USSR*, Stalin elevates the two pillars of his socialist industrialization mode, namely, that "the growth of the means of production should take precedence under expanded reproduction" and that "accumulation (i.e., investment) is the sole source of expanded reproduction (i.e., growth)," to the status of the "basic principles of Marxist reproduction theory" and as objectively necessary "economic laws."

In reality, investment-driven growth is a periodic phenomenon that only occurred during the specific period after the first industrial revolution rather than a general rule throughout history.

Economists such as Paul A. Samuelson, Simon Kuznets, and Michael E. Porter have divided the economic development of the early industrialized countries into the following stages: (a) the pre-takeoff stage, when growth is mainly driven by developing land and other natural resources, (b) the early economic growth stage, when machines replace labor, (c) the modern economic growth stage, when development is mainly driven by technological progress and improvements in efficiency, and (d) the information technology era when information and communications technologies transform the economies.[8]

The first industrial revolution ushered in the early economic growth stage in the late eighteenth century. At that time, growth was due to the replacement of manual labor by machines, and machine tools, coal, steel, and other heavy industrial products were all in high demand. By default, economic growth during this stage was mainly driven by investments since the heavy industries were all capital-intensive. This growth mode had been the force behind the high growth in Western Europe in the nineteenth century. In 1939, British economist Roy F. Harrod developed a model depicting this early growth mode in the advanced industrialized countries. In 1946, Polish American economist Evsey D. Domar published a similar work. Their work is referred to as the Harrod–Domar growth model:

$$g = i/v$$

where "g" represents the growth rate, "i" represents the investment rate, and "v" represents the capital-output ratio.

The model assumes that the capital-output ratio will remain unchanged for a long time. Under this condition, a country's total output depends on the amount of capital; hence, the output growth rate is determined by the investment rate in the economy. Therefore, Stalin's "fundamental principle of Marxist reproduction theory," i.e., investment as the sole source of growth, has nothing to do with Marxism. It is simply another expression of the Harrod–Domar model.

---

[7] Zuo Fengrong and Shen Zhihua, *The Tortuous Process of Modernization in Russia* (Beijing: Social Sciences Academic Press, 2009), pp. 55–105.

[8] This is a summary by this author based on various reviews. See Wu Jinglian, *Options for China's Growth Mode,* 2006 (Beijing: CITIC Publishing House, 2017), pp. 19–46.

But from his analysis of this growth model, Marx derived the conclusion that capitalism was on the verge of collapse. According to Marx, reliance on investment-driven growth is indicative of the inherent contradictions within capitalism that will eventually lead to its downfall.

In *Capital*, Marx demonstrates that throughout history capital accumulation was a process whereby the investment rate continued to rise and the consumption rate continued to decline. Marx calls this historical trend the "rising organic composition of capital," which he believed would inevitably lead to economic crises caused by overproduction, an impoverished proletariat class, and an intensified class struggle. When these contradictions escalated, he maintains, the "knell of capitalist private property sounds. The expropriators are expropriated."[9]

Marx therefore believed that capitalism would die. This prediction did not pass the test of history not because his theorization had defects but due to the second industrial revolution that began in the late nineteenth century. This revolution led to widespread application of technologies based on science and a new era of modern economic growth in the developed countries. During this new era, economic growth was no longer driven by increases in the size of capital; instead, the impetus for growth was technological progress and improvements in efficiency. The fastest-growing economic sector was not industry, to say nothing of heavy industry; rather, it was services, industrial research and development, industrial design, and other productive services. Meanwhile, a middle-income class (white-collar workers) emerged, representing the advanced productive forces. The social structure in the West was evolving in the direction of an olive shape, and to a certain extent, the social tensions that had intensified at the turn of the twentieth century began to subside.

The revolutionary shift in the economic growth model in the early industrialized countries is also reflected in economic theory. In 1956 and 1957, Nobel economics laureate Robert M. Solow published two classic papers questioning the Harrod–Domar model.[10] He pointed out that when other factors remain constant, increasing capital input alone will lead to diminishing investment returns and a rising incremental capital-output ratio (ICOR). In other words, the investment rate must be raised continuously to maintain a specific growth rate. But this would be impossible for any country. Since the early twentieth century, the investment rate in the West did not increase, but the long-run growth rate was still maintained. Why did this happen? The following is Solow's explanation: In addition to capital, labor, and other resource inputs, the most important factor driving economic growth is technological progress, i.e., improvements in efficiency. Solow's analysis of American economic development during the first half of the twentieth century proves this proposition. From 1909 to 1949, seven-eighths of the per capita income increases in the U.S. could be attributed to technological progress, and only one-eighth was due to investments.

---

[9] Karl Marx, "Capital," 1867 (Chinese translation. Beijing: People's Publishing House, 1975), vol. 1, p. 688.

[10] R.M. Solow, "A Contribution to the Theory of Economic Growth," *Quarterly Journal of Economics* 70 (February 1956), 65–94; R.M. Solow, "Technical Change and Aggregate Production Function," *The Review of Economics and Statistics* 39 (August 1957), 312–320.

Based on this analysis, the production coefficient function (the relationship between total output and various driving factors) should be written as:

$$Y = A \cdot K^{\alpha} \cdot L^{1-\alpha}$$

where Y is total output, K is total capital, and L is labor input. In this model, A represents the residual value beyond the contributions of capital K and labor L. This term, known as the "Solow residual," measures the contribution of "technological progress," or total factor productivity (TFP).[11]

Stalin's "socialist industrialization path" that prioritizes heavy industry is nothing but a replica of the West's early growth mode in the context of the Soviet Union.

Despite the severe theoretical and practical defects in the Soviet Union's development and industrialization mode, other socialist countries, influenced by Stalin and the Soviet Union, regarded the Soviet mode as the standard, and therefore they also adopted an investment-driven, extensive growth mode that prioritized heavy industry.

China was no exception. In his Report on the First Five-year Plan to the National People's Congress, Li Fuchun, a vice premier and chairman of the State Planning Commission, pointed out that "the industrialization to be realized in our country is socialist industrialization, following the example of the Soviet Union and directly assisted by the Soviet Union and the other people's democratic countries. It is not capitalist industrialization." Li also stressed that "the key to socialist industrialization is to prioritize the development of heavy industry. Only by establishing powerful heavy industries, i.e., modern iron and steel, machine tool manufacturing, electricity, fuels, non-ferrous metals, and basic chemical industries, can we produce various types of machine equipment ..., significantly improve production technologies and labor productivity, continuously increase production of agriculture and consumer goods, and ensure continuous improvements in the people's livelihoods. Therefore, prioritizing heavy industrial development is the only correct policy to make our country richer and stronger and to bring happiness to our people. This policy will enable China to establish a powerful physical foundation for socialism."[12]

"An Outline for Study and Propaganda on the Party's General Line for the Transition Period," a policy platform prepared under guidance of Mao Zedong, directly quotes Stalin to underscore the correctness of prioritizing the development of heavy industry and to highlight the essential need for China to adopt this policy. The outline states, "Stalin says, 'industrialization is not about developing any industry. The key to, and the foundation for, industrialization is to develop the heavy industries (e.g., fuels and metallurgy). After all, the goal of industrialization is to develop our country's means of production and machine tool manufacturing' ("The Economic Situation of

[11] For a further introduction to Solow's growth theories, see W. Esterley, "The Elusive Quest for Growth," 2001 (Chinese translation by Jiang Shiming. Beijing: CITIC Publishing House, 2016), pp. 25–64, 135–159.

[12] Li Fuchun, "Report on the First Five-year Economic Development Plan to the Second Session of the 1st National People's Congress on July 5–6, 1955," in *Documents of the Second Session of the 1st National People's Congress of the People's Republic of China* (Beijing: People's Publishing House, 1955), pp. 160–161.

the Soviet Union and the Policy of the Party"). Only when the heavy industries are established can other industries, transportation, and agriculture obtain equipment for development and upgrading. In the past, our basis for heavy industry was fragile, the economy was not independent, and the country could not strengthen its national defense. All the imperialist countries came to bully us. The Chinese people suffered enough pain. ... All these show that the central task of socialist industrialization in our country must be the development of heavy industry. From their development of light industry, it took the capitalist countries 50 to 100 years to industrialize. In contrast, the Soviet Union took only ten-plus years to realize industrialization under the socialist industrialization principle prioritizing the development of heavy industry. The path that the Soviet Union followed in the past serves as our model to emulate today."[13]

When the General Line for the Transition Period was issued in 1953 and when the First Five-year Plan period was introduced, the CCP Central Committee under Mao Zedong envisaged achieving the goal of "socialist transformation and national industrialization to make China a great socialist country" within three five-year-plan periods, or a little longer. The tremendous achievements in economic development during the first half of the 1950s led Mao to believe that the transition process could be significantly accelerated.

In the summer of 1955, Mao criticized the "right-deviationist, conservative thinking" of officials in charge of agriculture. As a result, the "socialist transformation of agriculture, handicrafts, and capitalist industry and commerce" was accelerated.

A January 1, 1956, editorial in *People's Daily* conveyed the new economic directives issued by the CCP Central Committee as based on Mao's instructions. These directives emphasized "doing everything as efficiently, quickly, and as well as possible, completing and exceeding the 'First Five-year Plan' ahead of schedule, and advancing socialist industrialization."[14]

Under these circumstances, an atmosphere conducive to an economic "leap forward" rapidly took shape. But overly high plan targets and capital investments led to fiscal stresses and shortages of steel, cement, and timber. Production aimed to

---

[13] Organization Department of the Party Central Committee, "Mobilize All Forces to Develop China into a Great Socialist Country: An Outline for Study and Propaganda on the Party's General Line for the Transition Period," in *Reading Materials for Socialist Education Courses* (Beijing: People's Publishing House, 1957), bk. 1, pp. 341–344. Stalin believed that industrialization would be realized when industrial output reached 70 percent of total industrial and agricultural output. In his "Concluding Report on the First Five-year Plan" (1933), Stalin states that "the Soviet Union reached the targets of the First Five-year Plan (1928–32) within four years, turning an agricultural country into an industrial country because when comparing between industrial and agricultural output, the share of industrial output rose to 70 percent in the fourth year of the First Five-year Plan period (1932) from 48 percent at the beginning of the period (1928)," *Collected Works of J.V. Stalin* (Chinese translation. Beijing: People's Publishing House, 1956), vol. 13, p. 164.

[14] Editorial, "Endeavor to Comprehensively Achieve and to Exceed the First Five-year Plan Targets Ahead of Schedule," *People's Daily,* January 1, 1956.

increase quantity overlooked quality and workplace safety. The agricultural cooperatives grew too large, and they interfered excessively in the affairs of their members. Farmers were overburdened, and people became resentful.

Faced with this grave economic situation, national leaders like Zhou Enlai and Chen Yun proposed that two trends be addressed simultaneously, that is, countering both conservatism and "rashness" (*mao jin*).

In "On the Ten Major Relationships" of April 1956, Mao proposed the policy of concurrently developing industry and agriculture and expanding the light and heavy industries together, while also prioritizing the growth of heavy industry. He stated, "The emphasis in our country's construction is on heavy industry. The production of the means of production must be given priority. That is settled. But it definitely does not follow that the production of the means of subsistence, especially grain, can be neglected. ... the relationship between heavy industry on the one hand and light industry and agriculture on the other must be properly handled. ... The problem now facing us is that of continuing to adjust properly the ratio between investment in heavy industry on the one hand and in agriculture and light industry on the other in order to bring about greater development of the latter. Does this mean that heavy industry is no longer primary? No. It continues to assert the priority in our investment focus. But the proportion of agriculture and light industry must be somewhat increased."

While recognizing the need to properly adjust the relationship between heavy industry on the one hand and light industry and agriculture on the other, Mao launched a harsh critique of Zhou Enlai and Chen Yun's proposal to simultaneously combat both conservatism and "rashness."[15] When introducing the Great Leap Forward in 1958, Mao proposed taking "steel as the key link," and he called for concentrating human resources, materials, and funding on developing iron and steel and other heavy industries. He described the steel industry as a marshal commanding his troops in battle: once the steel industry expanded, the entire economy would go full steam ahead. In Mao's words, this was like "one horse galloping ahead followed by ten thousand horses."

When the political atmosphere began to favor "anti-rashness" in 1956, long-time finance minister Bo Yibo, at the 8th CCP National Congress, described the rule of thumb for controlling the size of the state budget and accumulation (investment). He pointed out that based on experience gained in previous years, the appropriate proportion of accumulation in the national income should be no less than 20 percent, or somewhat more. This rate "can secure rapid development of our industry, particularly heavy industry, and, at the same time, ensure a gradual rise in consumption, so that the Chinese people's livelihoods will continue to improve year after year."[16] After the Great Leap Forward was launched, these proportional requirements were abandoned, and the lopsidedness in the economic structure was taken to an extreme.

[15] Shi Wei, "Rash Advance, Anti-Rash Advance, Criticism of Anti-Rash Advance," *Party Literature*, no. 2 (1990).

[16] Bo Yibo, "Properly Handle the Proportions of Accumulation and Consumption: Speech at the 8th CCP National Congress," 1956, in *Selected Works of Bo Yibo (1937–92)* (Beijing: People's Publishing House, 1992), p. 255.

Table 9.1 Sectoral distribution of China's capital investments (%)

	1953–57	1958–62	1963–65	1966–70	1971–75	1976–80
Agriculture	7.1	11.3	17.7	10.7	9.8	10.5
Industry	42.5	60.4	49.8	55.5	55.4	52.6
Heavy industry	36.1	54.0	45.9	51.1	49.6	45.9
Geological Exploration	2.4	1.2	0.4	0.5	0.7	1.3
Construction	3.7	1.3	2.1	1.8	1.6	1.8
Transportation, Postal Communications, Telecommunications	15.3	13.5	12.7	15.4	18.0	12.9
Commerce	3.6	2.0	2.5	2.1	2.9	3.7
Science, Education, Public Health	7.6	3.8	5.7	2.8	3.1	5.4
Urban Utilities	2.5	2.3	2.9	1.8	1.9	4.1
Other	15.3	4.2	6.2	9.4	6.6	7.7

Source Nobuo Maruyama, *Industrialization and Technological Development in China,* 1988 (Chinese translation by Gao Zhiqian, Liang Ce, and Wan Zhiqing. Beijing: People's University Publishing House, 1992), p. 59, Table 2–7

In the 1950s–60s, the average investment rate of low-income countries was between 20 and 30 percent. In contrast, China's average annual investment rate was as high as 39.1 percent in 1958–60, with most investment going to heavy industry.

The Great Leap Forward, which attempted to achieve exceptionally high economic growth through massive investments, resulted in a deteriorating economic situation and massive losses of wealth and lives. Nevertheless, the disaster did not lead to a correction in the traditional (Soviet-style) industrialization strategy. In 1964, Mao Zedong put forward the slogan: "Prepare for war and famine to serve the people." He advocated reversing the order of priorities between agriculture, light industry, and heavy industry, suggesting that "we should defy the conventional order." He stated that the levels of food, clothing, and daily necessities should not be lowered, but it would be sufficient if they were to be increased only slightly each year. The focus was to concentrate manpower, material resources, and financial resources on developing heavy industry, particularly military industrial construction, with the aim of "preparing for war."[17]

For decades, from the First Five-year Plan period to the years after 1976 when the Cultural Revolution ended, the concentration of all resources on developing heavy industry was an essential characteristic of China's economic development (see Table 9.1).

[17] *Chronicle of Mao Zedong (1949–1976)* (Beijing: Central Party Literature Press, 2013), vol. 5, pp. 500–501.

9.2 From Adjustment of the Economic Structure to Transformation of the Growth Mode

After the decade of turmoil, the national leadership was eager to make up for the time lost during the Cultural Revolution, but the institutional sources of the existing problems were overlooked.[18] Because the economy had recovered rapidly and the Gang of Four was no longer in control, many leaders believed that the time was ripe for a "new leap forward" in growth.

In February 1978, the National People's Congress passed the Outline of the Ten-Year Economic Development Program (1976–85), requiring completion of 120 new or existing projects so as to establish fourteen large national heavy industrial bases, with capital investments equal to those of the prior twenty-eight years. Informal meetings of the State Council in July–September 1978 emphasized importing advanced technologies and equipment in large quantities to achieve the "new leap forward." In the following months, contracts were signed to introduce nine large-scale chemical projects costing 16 billion yuan, as well as the Baoshan Steel Plant, 100 sets of comprehensive coal mining equipment, and 22 other projects with a total cost of 60 billion yuan. The scale of such massive investments and the simultaneous peak in so many large projects had a significant impact on the national economy. China's economy was already fragile, having survived the turbulence of the decade-long Cultural Revolution, and the fresh surge in investments caused a new round of economic fluctuations.

At the time, level-headed government officials and economists expressed reservations about such an "import-led leap forward." They believed that an economic readjustment was essential before steady development could be realized. In a group discussion of the Northeast Region during the Party Central Committee Work Conference on December 10, 1978, Chen Yun said that projects introducing foreign technology and equipment should be approved and implemented gradually rather than all at once. He stressed that both production and infrastructure construction should avoid material shortages to prevent squeezing resources away from agriculture, light industry, and urban construction.[19] In March 1979, together with Vice Premier Li Xiannian, he wrote to the Party Central Committee, proposing "steady steps rather than rushing back and forth. ... Currently, the national economy is characterized by imbalances and severely disproportionate relationships. ... There is a need to take two or three years to readjust the economy."[20] As advocated by Chen Yun and others,

[18] According to Yuan Baohua, vice chairman of the State Economic Commission and a long-time participant in central government economic affairs, "At the time, Comrade Hua Guofeng was preoccupied with the idea of making up for the time lost during the Cultural Revolution," in "Economic Recovery After the Cultural Revolution: An Interview with Comrade Yuan Baohua," *Hundred Year Tide*, no. 7 (2002).

[19] Chen Yun, "Five Comments on Current Economic Issues," 1978, *Selected Works of Chen Yun* (Beijing: People's Publishing House, 1995), vol. 3, p. 237.

[20] Chen Yun and Li, Xiannian, "A Letter to the Party Central Committee about Economic and Financial Affairs," 1979, in ibid., p. 248.

in April 1979 the Party Central Committee and the State Council decided to take three years to "readjust, reform, rectify, and improve" the economy, with the goals of cutting back on industrial investments and raising the proportion of agricultural and light industry investments. However, implementation was sluggish due to the entrenched influence of the Soviet-style growth mode on those cadres in charge of economic work. When Xue Muqiao, an adviser to the Institute of Economic Research under the State Planning Commission and an older generation leader in economic affairs, in several internal speeches criticized the slow progress in readjusting the economy, the head of the State Planning Commission faulted him for "dampening the enthusiasm [for economic growth]."[21]

As a result, the economy suffered rising fiscal deficits and increasing inflationary pressures. Given this situation, in March 1980 the Politburo Standing Committee decided to readjust the economic policy. It set up a Central Leading Group for Financial and Economic Affairs, headed by Premier Zhao Ziyang, and Yao Yilin was appointed chairman of the State Planning Commission. At a State Council seminar on long-term planning held shortly after this Politburo decision, both Chen Yun and Deng Xiaoping opposed the high-investment and high-growth policy. They proposed: (A) reducing the accumulation rate to around 25 percent, keeping total capital investments at about RMB 50 billion for the next two to three years, and, to a certain extent, increasing the consumption rate. (B) decelerating economic growth, with the growth rate of industry to be reduced to about 7 or 8 percent, or even 5 or 6 percent. (C) readjusting the economic structure to allow for faster development of agriculture and light industry. (D) allowing more flexibility with respect to urban and rural ownership issues. (E) subjecting all undertakings to comparisons of the results, and (F) significantly utilizing foreign trade to promote domestic economic development.[22] Such views suggested the need for a readjustment of the extensive growth mode. After discussing these issues for over a year, at the December 1980 economic work conference the Party Central Committee adopted a new general line for economic affairs to "further readjust the economy."

The two rounds of readjustment in 1979 and 1981 improved the economic structure and raised economic efficiency. Agriculture, which had previously been disrupted, began to show some signs of improvements, and the previously underdeveloped light industry was also strengthened. As a result, the extreme poverty among farmers was alleviated, and the issue of long-standing shortages of agricultural products and consumer goods began to be addressed. The service industries, such as commerce, dining, and hospitality, focusing on consumption, grew rapidly, while the production-oriented service sectors, including foreign trade, transportation, and finance, also began to expand.

In 1980–81, the government and its research institutions undertook a thorough examination of the causes of the economic difficulties and the potential solutions. The result was the so-called Ten Major Principles of Economic Construction, which

[21] *Memoirs of Xue Muqiao,* 1996 (Tianjin: Tianjin People's Publishing House, 2006), pp. 262–267.

[22] China Society for Economic Reform, comp., *Chronicle of Major Events during the Reform and Opening (1978–2008)* (Beijing: China Financial and Economic Publishing House, 2008), p. 33.

became official government policy after the Fourth Plenary Session of the 5th National People's Congress in December 1981.[23]

The Ten Principles point out that in order to achieve sound economic development, "the economy should be stabilized as soon as possible through economic readjustments. ... The old leftist practices should be effectively abandoned. A new path that is realistic about the pace of growth should be developed based on China's actual conditions to bring about better economic returns and more material benefits for the people."

The Ten Principles focused on economic returns. China "should do everything possible to improve the economic returns from production, construction, and the circulation of commodities. ... The industrial structure, products, technology, enterprises, and organization, and the location of industries and economic sectors are not rational. ... There are many drawbacks in our economic management system. ... [These] are the greatest obstacles to enhancing the economic returns."

Specifically, the Ten Principles, seeking to improve the economic structure and increase the economic returns, included the following: (1) Relying on policy and science to accelerate agricultural development. (2) Attaching importance to developing the consumer goods industries and further readjusting the focus of heavy industry services. (3) Improving energy efficiency and strengthening the development of energy, communications, and transportation. (4) Gradually upgrading priority technologies to allow existing enterprises to play a role. (5) Undertaking a phased enterprise rectification and, if necessary, reorganization. (6) Paying attention to wealth generation, accumulation, and utilization to save or to increase funding for economic construction. (7) Upholding the opening policy and enhancing China's capabilities for self-reliance. (8) Actively implementing a prudent economic reform policy to motivate various forces. (9) Improving the scientific and cultural proficiency of the labor force and tackling fundamental research projects. (10) Doing everything from the perspective of serving the people and balancing production and economic development on the one hand and improving the people's livelihoods on the other.

Adoption of the Ten Principles indicated that China intended to free itself from the Soviet-style economic mode and to explore a new economic development path.

The Ten Principles were remedies for the structural distortions caused by past policies. But they did not touch upon the causes, i.e., the investment-driven growth mode biased in favor of speed over efficiency. They also lacked a thorough reflection on the Soviet-style industrialization policy and its institutional foundation.

Proponents of Stalin's industrialization path soon launched a counter-attack, demonstrating that Stalin's approach and the "theory of socialist reproduction" were still critically important in China. This was because any changes in the industrialization path and the economic growth mode would hurt the interests of certain government agencies and large enterprises. Less than one year after the second round of economic readjustments, the Central Committee's *Red Flag* magazine carried, in

[23] Zhao Ziyang, *The Current Economic Situation and Future Economic Construction Principles: Report on the Work of the Government at the Fourth Plenary Session of the 5th National People's Congress (November 30 and December 1, 1981)* (Beijing: People's Publishing House, 1981).

three consecutive issues, a lengthy article entitled "The Fundamental Principles of the Theory of Marxist Reproduction Must Be Upheld," written by Deng Liqun, vice president of the Chinese Academy of Social Sciences and a long-time senior official in charge of Party ideological affairs. The article used Stalin's "Marxist theory of reproduction" (a theory that had already been proven to be wrong academically)[24] to criticize those economists who disagreed with the heavy-industry-biased policy and who instead strongly advocated an economic readjustment, accusing them of rejecting the "basic principles of Marxist reproduction" and calling for a correction of their views.[25] The twin hurdles of ideology and vested interests resulted in a partial resurgence of the old investment-driven economic growth model before the national economic adjustments had even been fully implemented.

Because the root causes of the problems of the extensive growth mode had not been resolved, two rounds of economic overheating and inflation occurred in 1984–85 and 1993–94. In 1995, when studying the lessons learned from the overheating in 1993 and 1994 and preparing for the Ninth Five-Year Plan (1996–2000), the State Planning Commission suggested to the central leadership that the economic growth model be changed.

In 1959, some Soviet economists had already suggested the need to transform from an extensive growth mode to an intensive growth mode. However, by the late 1960s it became evident that while the gap in total economic activity between the USSR and the United States had narrowed, the Soviet growth rate was still declining. If this trend were to continue, the ambitious Soviet plan would fail. More critically, the gap in technological advances and living standards between the two superpowers had widened. Additionally, the technological gap and disparity in living standards between the Soviet Union and the United States had continued to widen rather than narrowing. Soviet economists who tried to find the reasons for this concluded that the main problem lay in the different growth models: the Western economies primarily relied on efficiency improvements, while the Soviet Union pursued high-speed growth without similar efficiency improvements. They thereby derived the terms "extensive growth" and "intensive growth" from Marx's discussion on the different growth

---

[24] According to Stalin, one of the fundamental principles of Marxist reproduction is that "accumulation (investment) is the only source of expanded reproduction (growth)." But it is common knowledge in economics that this argument is untenable because it puts aside the more important driver of growth, i.e., efficiency. Meanwhile, the so-called "principle that the growth of the means of production should have priority in expanded reproduction" was also refuted by some rigorous arguments during the 1970s and 1980s. For the detailed arguments, see He Juhuang, "About Prioritizing Growth of the Means of Production," *Economic Research*, no. 9 (1979); Yu Yongding, "A Discussion on Prioritizing the Growth of the Means of Production," *Reform and Strategy*, no. 4 (1985).

[25] Deng Liqun, "The Fundamental Principles of Marxist Reproduction Theory Must Be Upheld," *Red Flag*, no. 5–7 (1982).

modes in *Capital: Volume Two*[26] to describe the two different economic growth models. Subsequently, a shift from extensive to intensive growth was called for.

From the perspective of modern economics and the production function, the economic implications of these two growth modes are very clear.

Two forces drive economic growth: increases in factor inputs and improvements in factor utilization efficiency, i.e., higher total factor productivity (TFP). Based on the terminology of Soviet and East European economists, extensive growth refers to the first mode, driven by an increase in inputs. In contrast, intensive growth refers to the second mode, driven by higher TFP.[27]

The Soviet Union could not transform its growth mode because it could not overcome the institutional obstacles. Chinese leaders recognized and learned this lesson while preparing for the Ninth Five-Year Plan, and they understood that any change in the growth model could only be accomplished through systemic reforms. The Party Central Committee's Proposal for the Ninth Five-Year.

Plan (1996–2000) for National Economic and Social Development and the Long-range Objectives to the Year 2010 required two fundamental transformations: a shift from the traditional planned economy to a socialist market economy and a shift from extensive growth to intensive growth.

In 1996, the 8th National People's Congress passed the Outline of the Ninth Five-Year Plan (1996–2000) for National Socioeconomic Development and Vision 2010, in which "the main economic work" during the plan period would be the accomplishment of these two fundamental transformations.

During the Ninth Five-Year Plan period, which was precisely the time when a comprehensive reform was being advanced according to the Decision on Several Issues Concerning the Establishment of a Socialist Market Economic System, passed at the Third Plenary Session of the 14th Party Central Committee in November 1993, progress was made in changing the economic growth model. This is why China was able to achieve an average annual GDP growth rate of 8.3 percent despite the impact of the Asian financial crisis.

---

[26] Marx's original passage on this topic is: "In the process of expanded reproduction, if the scale of production is increased, it means an expansion in its extent; if production efficiency is improved, it means an expansion in its content." See Karl Marx, "Capital," 1867 (Chinese translation. Beijing: People's Publishing House, 1992), vol. 2, p. 192.

[27] Kornai explains the extensive and intensive growth modes as follows. One type of growth results from the input of production factors, such as production increases from more capital and labor inputs. The other type of growth results from improved efficiency in the utilization of capital, labor, and other production factors. In the Soviet Union and the East European countries, the first type was called extensive growth, and the second was called intensive growth. See János Kornai, *The Socialist System: The Political Economy of Communism* (Chinese translation by Zhang An. Beijing: Central Compilation and Translation Press, 2007), pp. 171–178. In Chinese media, some people have described the transformation of the growth mode as a shift from investment-driven to consumption-driven growth. This is an apparent misunderstanding.

9.3 The Return of the Extensive Growth Mode During the Tenth Five-Year Plan Period

The Ninth Five-year Plan achieved good results. However, success in economic development had its downsides: "Once the scar is healed, one forgets the pain." During the Tenth Five-year Plan period (2001–5) the extensive growth mode returned.

First, unlike in the previous five-year plan, the Tenth Five-year Plan took readjustment of the economic structure, rather than the transformation of the growth mode, as the "main line of economic work."[28]

It should be noted that "economic structure" is a broad concept. Any misallocation of resources can be called a "structural problem." The key questions are: Who will adjust the structure? How should this be done? And what is the goal of the restructuring? An economic adjustment is a reallocation of economic resources. In a modern economy, there are two basic approaches to resource allocations and re-allocations. One approach is to allow the market to allocate resources: allocations and reallocations are made by the pricing system, formed through market competition, that can flexibly reflect the relative scarcity of resources. Under the other approach, the government, as the primary allocator, distributes and redistributes resources by administrative directives and financial, fiscal, and price tools. The former approach allows scarce resources to flow to higher efficiency areas through free exchanges, whereas the latter reflects the will and needs of government officials. Because errors are an inherent part of human decision-making, the economic structure deteriorates when government officials make mistakes.

In China, the term "structural adjustment" usually refers to actions by the government. However, because the government cannot predict the optimal economic structure, an "industrial policy" based on the perception of the government cannot achieve the expected structural improvements or better efficiency in resource allocations. It might even lead to the opposite. Beginning from the later years of the Cultural Revolution, an increasing number enlightened people began to realize that the root cause of the distortions in the Chinese economy was the excessive government role in resource allocations. They therefore believed China should implement market-oriented reforms, and it should shift from a selective to a functional industrial policy.[29] This change in mainstream thinking led to the following policy adjustments: the 1992 14th Party Congress stated that the market should play "a basic role" in resource

---

[28] The Fourth Plenary Session of the 9th National People's Congress approved the Outline of the Tenth Five-year Plan (2001–2005) for National Socioeconomic Development on March 15, 2001. This five-year plan mentions a growth mode transformation only on one occasion, in Chap. 4, Part 2, "Accelerating Industrial Reorganization and Upgrading" in the phrase "accelerating the industrial growth mode transformation."

[29] Liu He, "The Basis for and Characteristics of China's Industrial Policy When Advancing Toward a Large Open Economy," 1995, in Liu He, *A Study of Structural Changes* (Beijing: China Financial and Economic Publishing House, 2002), pp. 182–192: Wu Jinglian, "A Challenge to Industrial Policy: Transformation Rather Than Pondering Continuation or Discontinuation," 2017, in*: China's New Economic Era: Building a New Economic System* (Economists 50 Forum Series) (Beijing: CITIC Publishing House, 2018), pp. 349–370.

allocations, and the Ninth Five-year Plan adopted in 1995 required a fundamental transformation of the economic system and the growth mode.

In the early twenty-first century, the following developments occurred because China's market-oriented reform had still not been accomplished and the government at various administrative levels still retained significant power in terms of resource allocations: government intervention in economic activities was reinforced, and transformation of the growth mode was reversed.

One important reason for this setback was the acceleration of government-led urbanization.

Prior to the reform and opening, China's urbanization process had been slow. In 1979, the urbanization rate (urban residents as a percentage of the total population) was only 17.92 percent. After the reform and opening, urbanization was somewhat accelerated but it was still slower than that in countries with similar levels of economic development. According to the National Bureau of Statistics, in the eighteen years from 1978 to 1996, urbanization grew by 0.74 percent per annum. But at the turn of the twenty-first century, urbanization began to accelerate. After 1997, the average annual growth rate of urbanization rose to around 1.5 percent. This trend continued into the early twenty-first century.

Under Chinese conditions, rapid urbanization required enormous investments, mainly funded by a government financing approach that relied on land finance (*tudi caizheng*). The land property rights system allowed the government to obtain enormous resources by requisitioning land from the rural collectives. The law stipulated that rural land belonged to the collectives and that the state owned urban land.[30] The government took over the land from the rural collectives at a low price based on the value of agricultural output and then leased the land lots at urban land prices. Revenue from the price differentials exceeded RMB 10 trillion.[31] Furthermore, the government could use the land as collateral to borrow from the banks.[32] It can be said that governments at various administrative levels had resources to pad their political records.

The government mainly took two approaches to urbanization. The first was a "city-building movement," or "boosting city-image projects," and the second was

[30] During the 1950s' agricultural collectivization the farmers' land plots became collectively owned. Article 10 of the 1982 Constitution stipulates that "the state owns urban land. Except where the law specifies state ownership, land in the rural areas and the suburbs of cities belongs to the collectives. The collectives also own homesteads, household plots, and mountainous lots retained for household use. The state can legally requisition land if it is in the interest of the general public. No organization or individual may embezzle, trade, lease, or use other illegal means to transfer land."

[31] In the "Communiqu é on Chinese Land and Resources," the Ministry of Land and Resources reported that in 2003–12 RMB 14.49 trillion from land transfers went to governments at various administrative levels. See Lu Qian, "Land-Transfer-Supported Government Finance: Is This China's Great Systemic Innovation?" Caixin.com, October 9, 2017.

[32] In the early twenty-first century, as the costs of land development increased, loans collateralized by land became a common source of government funding. Such loans exceeded RMB 1 trillion in 2007 and reached RMB 11.33 trillion in 2015. See Liu Shouying, "The Formation and Dilemma of a Land-Dependent Development Mode," Aisixiang.com, January 24, 2017.

a "movement to develop heavy and chemical industries," or "political showcase projects."

Urbanization, in essence, refers to the urbanization of the population. When people are concentrated in the cities and they interact in the cities, an economy of scale emerges for the generation of new ideas, technologies, and institutions.[33] Land urbanization provides the physical conditions for a concentration of the population. However, in China's recent government-led urbanization, land urbanization emerged as the primary focus. Many local governments rushed to expand the size of the cities or to build new cities. In 2004, the Ministry of Land and Resources reported that in and around 2000, governments at various administrative levels established 6,866 development zones, occupying 38,600 square kilometers (579,000 *mu*) of land.[34] Grand buildings, huge public squares, and large development zones popped up everywhere. The pace of land urbanization far exceeded the pace of population urbanization. "Factories in gardens," with only one-story buildings occupying more than six square kilometers (10,000 *mu*) of land were commonplace. From 1990 to 2011, China's urban population, including non-permanent residents, increased by 1.28 times, while developed urban areas increased by 3.39 times.[35] There were many unoccupied buildings and ghost towns, with an astonishing amount of waste in investments and land resources. Per capita land occupation by urban residents and land occupation per RMB 10,000 industrial and commercial output were several times higher than that in the developed countries. Although China was far from realizing urbanization, many places already faced land shortages for development.[36]

Due to the one-sided pursuit of scale while ignoring specialization, the creative effects of urbanization were suppressed. Meanwhile, the city-building movement not only resulted in a significant waste of investments and land resources but also reduced the operational efficiency of the built cities, with prominent negative effects including traffic congestion, environmental degradation, a lower quality of life, and increased living costs.

These problems are indicative of the imbalances caused by government-led urbanization. Historically, cities evolved from either capital towns, i.e., political centers, or marketplaces, i.e., commodity transfer centers. In the modern era, urbanization in most countries was led by the market. In contrast, China's urbanization was driven by the government. In a market-led urbanization process, the development of cities spontaneously balances the positive and negative effects of urbanization. For instance, when car manufacturing began to grow in the early twentieth century, it was based in large cities like Detroit to obtain a sufficient number of skilled workers and other means of support. By the mid-twentieth century, automotive manufacturing had

---

[33] Wu Jinglian, "All-Round Deepening of Reform and a New Type of Urbanization," 2013, in *Facing the Era of Great Transformation* (Beijing: SDX Joint Publishing, 2014), pp. 140–148.

[34] Ministry of Land and Resources, "China's Farmland Suffers Net Losses of Nearly 40 million *mu* in 2003," *Land and Resources*, no. 3 (2004), 47.

[35] See "Population Urbanization Lags Behind Land Urbanization," *China Economic Weekly*, December 31, 2013.

[36] Wu Jinglian, "Efficiency Problems and Policy Options from China's Urbanization," 2012, in *Works of Wu Jinglian* (Beijing: Central Compilation and Translation Press, 2013), vol. 2, p. 864.

become a conventional technology. But remaining in the large cities was no longer economical due to the high living costs and high wages. Factories, one after another, moved out of the large cities and dispersed into the medium and small towns. In contrast, in a government-led urbanization process, since larger urbanization scales correspond to higher administrative levels, and higher administrative levels have greater power to allocate resources, each level of government mobilizes and invests resources to expand the scale of their respective cities. This is a unidirectional force.

Supporting this urban expansion was the concept of "land finance." Governments acquired land ownership at very low acquisition costs and then converted it to urban construction land through bidding, auctioning, and listing processes, collecting substantial land transfer fees and reaping significant profits. Land revenue became the primary source of fiscal income for local governments, incentivizing them to compete in "land grabbing" and to support large-scale city-building movements with land transfer fees and land mortgage loans. Since the amount of disposable income available to local governments was closely tied to land prices, the continuous rise in housing prices became essential for local governments to secure high land transfer fees and to repay the loans used for extensive urban construction. Consequently, this fiscal model effectively tied local government finances to rising housing prices—while soaring housing prices would cause public dissatisfaction, falling prices would lead to fiscal difficulties for local governments.

Aside from the urban construction movement, another manifestation of the reversal in the mode of economic growth at the beginning of the twenty-first century was the wave of "heavy industrialization" in many regions, where there was a rush to invest in capital-intensive heavy industries. In academic circles, some economists referenced the work of German economist Walther G. Hoffmann to support this trend.

In Hoffmann's 1931 work *The Growth of Industrial Economics*, he extrapolates industrial development trends during the "early stage of industrialization" and the "mid-stage of industrialization" to the "late stage of industrialization," predicting that in the late stage, capital goods (i.e., the means of production, as referred to by Marx) would experience preferential growth. This prediction was referred to by some economists as the "Hoffmann Experience Theorem," suggesting that the late stage of industrialization is characterized by a phase of capital-intensive heavy industrialization.[37]

Because automotive manufacturing, petrochemicals, and other heavy and chemical industries generated higher output, paid more taxes, and delivered more profits, many local Party and government leaders prioritized the development of heavy industry. Disregarding local conditions and comparative advantages, these officials used their resource allocation powers to raise the GDP of their respective jurisdictions by "making the local economy heavier," or focusing on heavy and chemical industrialization. At the turn of the twenty-first century, there was an upsurge in large-scale investment as a broad range of heavy industry projects were approved and implemented. According to a February 2005 media report, beginning in 2000 there was a trend in China to shift the growth mode toward heavy industry. An increasing number

[37] Wu Jinglian, *Options for China's Growth Mode*, pp. 127–128..

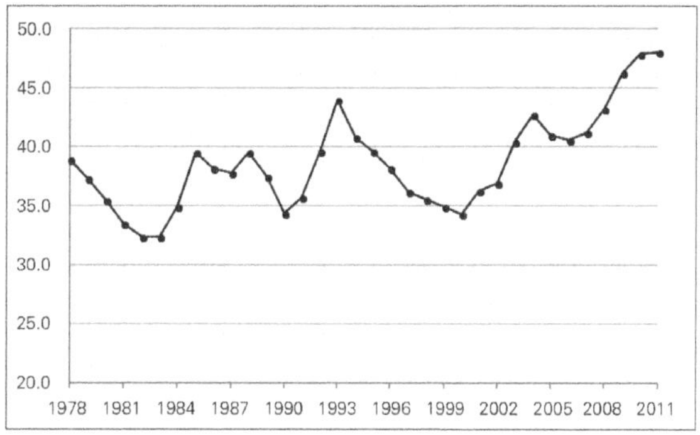

Fig. 9.1 Continuous rise in China's investment rate (%). *Source* CEIC

of provincial and municipal governments sought to move away from light industry and to move into the heavy and chemical industries. Even Shenzhen, the city most successful in IT, and Zhejiang, with its well-developed medium and small enterprise sector, attempted to shift to heavy industry.[38] The development of heavy industry inundated the country as these currents converged by the turn of the twenty-first century.

In analyzing the early growth mode, development economics demonstrates that an overreliance on investment for growth leads to a continuing rise in an economy's investment rate. In China, the share of investment in GDP increased from 25 percent at the beginning of the reform and opening to over 44 percent in 2004, far exceeding the highest historical levels in other countries[39] and also a historical high in China (see Fig. 9.1).

Like the past iterations of economic overheating, the excess investments soon led to tremendous stresses on the supply of coal, electricity, petroleum, and transportation. Once again, the government had to carry out a macroeconomic readjustment to control the overheating.

The reversal of the transformation of the growth mode at the turn of the twenty-first century triggered a debate from 2003 to 2005 about the economic development policy for the Eleventh Five-year Plan (2006–10).

An essential result of this debate was an analysis of the deeper causes of the unsatisfactory results in the transformation of the growth mode during the Tenth Five-year Plan period. Reflecting on the analytical findings, the Decision on Several Issues in Perfecting the Socialist Market Economy, adopted by the Third Plenary Session of the 16th Party Central Committee in 2003, pointed out that "development

[38] Wang Qing, "The Debate on Heavy Industry," *China Industrial and Commercial Times*, February 4, 2005.

[39] The 44 percent investment rate was much higher than the peak during the high growth period in Japan, when the country tended to over-invest. In the case of the United States, the investment rate never exceeded 20 percent, even during the period of high-speed industrialization at the turn of the twentieth century and during the post–World War II recovery period.

of the productive forces still faces various institutional obstacles." The obstacles can be summarized falling into the following four areas.[40]

First, Party and government officials still held power to allocate land, mineral resources, funds (e.g., bank loans), and other vital resources. Second, because GDP and the physical output growth rates were the leading performance indicators, Party and government officials used their powers to mobilize and allocate resources to stimulate rapid, extensive growth. Third, the existing fiscal and tax system meant officials had to pursue GDP growth. On the revenue side, half of the budgetary resources came from taxes on value-added production, which relied on an increase in physical GDP growth. On the expenditure side, many responsibilities that should have been borne by the central government (referred to as the "authority" in China) were delegated to local governments. Local governments had to generate sufficient funds through the expansion of GDP in order to fulfill their expenditure responsibilities. Fourth, the pricing system inherited from the planned economy was distorted, with the prices of the production factors artificially suppressed. This system encouraged the expansion of high-resource-input, low-economic-efficiency projects, leading to resource wastages and environmental destruction.

The waste of resources, damage to the environment, and the internal and external imbalances caused by the extensive growth during the Tenth Five-year Plan period demonstrate that extensive growth is unsustainable. To overcome the aforementioned socioeconomic contradictions, it was necessary to shift from an extensive growth model supported by resource inputs to an intensive growth model driven by technological progress and efficiency improvements. Thus, the Recommendations of the CCP Central Committee on the Formulation of the Eleventh Five-year Plan in 2005 and the Eleventh Five-year Plan, approved by the National People's Congress in 2006, both stipulated that transforming the economic growth model should be the main line of the Eleventh Five-Year Plan.

However, because the reforms did not meet their original requirements, by the last year of the Eleventh Five-year Plan, there was no significant progress in the transformation of the economic growth model. Therefore, the CCP Central Committee announced that "accelerating the transformation of the economic development model is urgent." The Recommendations of the CCP Central Committee on the Formulation of the Twelfth Five-year Plan (2011–15) suggested that "accelerating the transformation of the economic development model should be the main line, running through the entire process and through all fields of economic and social development, to ensure substantial progress in transforming the economic development model."

[40] Wu Jinglian, *Options for China's Growth Mode*, pp. 124–125.

9.4 The Disastrous Consequences of the Failure to Transform the Growth Mode

By depending on high levels of investment, the extensive growth model achieved rapid increases in output for a time, despite resulting in significant resource depletion. But the negative results that began to surface in the early twenty-first century worsened by the 2010s.

The first undesirable result was the exhaustion of land, fresh water, and other scarce resources, leading to an accelerated ecological deterioration.

China's per capita natural resources are limited, and its ecological environment is fragile. The country should have adopted a development mode that utilized resources more efficiently. Unfortunately, this was not the case. A huge amount was spent to sustain the high growth rate, leading to a rapid depletion of resources. Although external trade brought in oil and minerals, the substantial demand for imports drove up prices in global markets, causing costs for domestic enterprises to surge (Table 9.2).

In a report to the National People's Congress, Xu Shaoshi, chairman of the National Development and Reform Commission, noted that while in 2012 China's GDP accounted for 11.2 percent of the world's total, its share of energy consumption share was much higher (see Table 9.3). In some regions, the pollution of air, water, and land had already reached levels that could not even meet the basic requirements for human survival.

According to a Report of the Ministry of Environmental Protection on the State of the Environment, emissions and discharges of primary pollutants in China far exceeded its environmental self-purification capabilities, resulting in a continuous deterioration of China's environment during the first decade of the twenty-first century.

Industrial solid wastes went up from 816 million tons in 2000 to 3,256 million tons in 2008, of which 450 million tons were not processed.

Table 9.2 Comparison of China's per capita resources with world averages (%)

Resources	China's Per Capita Resources)	Share of World Average
Farmland	0.1 hectare	42
Freshwater	2,257 cubic meters	27
Forests	0.12 hectare	20
Potential gross value of mineral reserves	9,300 USD	58
Coal (proved, recoverable reserves)	98.94 tons	53
Oil (remaining reserves)	2.7 tons	11
Natural gas (proved, recoverable reserves)	769 cubic meters	3

Source Shi Dou and Zheng Junwei, "A Study of China's Energy Development Strategy," *Earth Science Updates,* no. 15 (2000)

Table 9.3 China's resource consumption as a share of the world total (%)

Resource type	Percentage of world total consumption
Energy	21.3
Steel	45.0
Cement	54.0

Source Xu Shaoshi, "Report on Energy Conservation and Emissions Reduction Work by the State Council—April 21, 2014," presented to the 12th National People's Congress Standing Committee, China National People's Congress Network, April 21, 2014

Freshwater pollution was widespread. Surface water samples were collected monthly from 968 monitoring sites at 423 main rivers and 62 key lakes. The samples showed that most water sites were polluted to varying degrees. "Category I—Good quality water" accounted for 3.4 percent of all the monitoring sites, "Category II—Lightly polluted but drinkable after regular water treatment" accounted for 30.4 percent, and "Category III—Polluted but drinkable after special water treatment" accounted for 29.3 percent. "Category IV—Poor quality and not drinkable" and "Category V—Poor quality and should not be touched directly" accounted for 36.9 percent. Among the 4,896 groundwater monitoring sites, those with excellent water quality accounted for only 10.8 percent of the total, those with good water quality accounted for 25.9 percent, those with somewhat good water quality were 1.8 percent, and those with poor water quality or worse accounted for 61.5 percent.

Among 470 cities, those suffering from acid rain accounted for 29.8 percent. Nationwide, the area of water and soil erosion reached 2,949,100 sq.km., accounting for 30.6 percent of China's total land area.[41]

Based on this report on the environment, air was also severely polluted. Among 161 cities that had established air-quality monitoring sites in 2012, only 16 cities, including Zhoushan, Fuzhou, Shenzhen, and Zhuhai, met the acceptable standards. The remaining 145 cities, including Beijing, Shanghai, Tianjin, and Guangzhou, failed to meet the air quality standards. In Beijing, China's capital, the annual average concentration of PM2.5 particles was 89.5 μg per cubic meter, exceeding the national standard of 35 μg per cubic meter by 145.43 percent.[42]

In some regions, the state of water resources was particularly worrisome. The North China Plain was suffering from severe water shortages. Still, Beijing, Tianjin, Hebei, and Shanxi spent much money on developing high-water-consumption industries, such as coal, steel, and automobiles. Hebei province alone had a steel production capacity exceeding 250 million tons, including small-scale smelting facilities known

[41] For the figures quoted here, see Ministry of Environmental Protection, "Report on the State of the Environment in China, 2014," June 5, 2015.

[42] In 2012, China issued a new set of Ambient Air Quality Standards, which adopted the Level I Interim Targets of the WHO. The pollution indexes at this level were much higher than the standard air quality guidelines (AQG). According to the WHO, long-time exposure to pollution at this interim target level will increase the risk of death by 15 percent.

for high consumption, high costs, and high pollution of water.[43] Even larger-scale, higher-technology plants consumed 16 tons of water to produce one ton of steel. When surface water was insufficient, groundwater was used. An August 2021 groundwater measurement report by the China Institute of Geo-Environment Monitoring shows that the water table for the North China Plain had dropped more rapidly than had previously been estimated. Over-extraction was depleting the shallow aquifer, and people were digging farther into the deep aquifer. According to this report, Hebei's deep aquifer water table dropped by 2.9 m in 2000. Some municipalities in the province even saw their water table drop by 6 m. Furthermore, the deep aquifer is nonrenewable. As the deep aquifer was being depleted in the North China Plain, the region was losing its last-resort water resource.[44] To cut treatment costs and dodge the environmental regulations, some enterprises were draining industrial wastewater through seepage pits and wells, or they were draining it directly using high-pressure pumps, polluting the water resources and causing life-threatening hazards.[45]

To a certain extent, China's leaders were worried about the adverse effects caused by the slow progress in the transformation of the growth mode. In his speech to the Fourth Plenary Session of the 16th Party Central Committee, General Secretary Hu Jintao pointed out, "If the economic growth mode is not fundamentally changed, our energy resources will be unsustainable and the eco-environment will be overburdened. In such a case, we will fail in our duties toward the people, history, and future generations."[46]

The second undesirable result of the extensive growth model of structural distortions between investment and consumption, causing inadequate final demand and a severe overcapacity in specific industries.

One conspicuous example of the misallocation of resources was the imbalance in investment and consumption. The extensive growth mode had led to repeated overly high investments and meager consumption rates. In 1993–95, the investment rate had again exceeded 40 percent, and the household final consumption rate had declined to below 45 percent.[47] According to the Tenth Five-year Plan (2001–5), the household consumption rate should have reached 50 percent and the fixed investment

---

[43] A 2014 famous quip on the web goes: "China is the world's no. 1 in steel production (excluding Hebei province), Hebei is no. 2 (excluding Tangshan municipality), Tangshan is no. 3 (excluding its unreported output), Japan is no. 4, the U.S. is no. 5, India is no. 6, Russia is no. 7, South Korea is no. 8, Tangshan is no. 9 (excluding its unreported output), and Germany is no. 10." See Xu Jin, "China Must Break the Vicious Cycle of Overcapacity," March 27, 2014, http://www.ftchinese.com/story/001055463.

[44] Lester R. Brown, *Plan B 2.0: Rescuing a Planet Under Stress and a Civilization in Trouble* (Chinese translation. Beijing: Oriental Publishing Co. Ltd., 2003), p. 24.

[45] Gao Yuanzhi et al., "Underground Drainage: A Fatal Threat Is Quietly Approaching," *Banyuetan*, no. 8 (2010), 9–12.

[46] Sheng Huaren, "Improving the Legal Framework to Prevent and Clean Up Water Pollution: Speech at the National People's Congress Seminar on the Environment and Protection of Resources (Summary)," January 10, 2005, http://www.people.com.cn/GB/14576/15097/3108571.html.

[47] Investment (or total capital formation) usually accounts for 20 percent–30 percent of GDP in the developing countries, while in the developed countries, it accounts for 15 percent–20 percent. Continuous excessive high investment suppresses household consumption demand. It often leads to

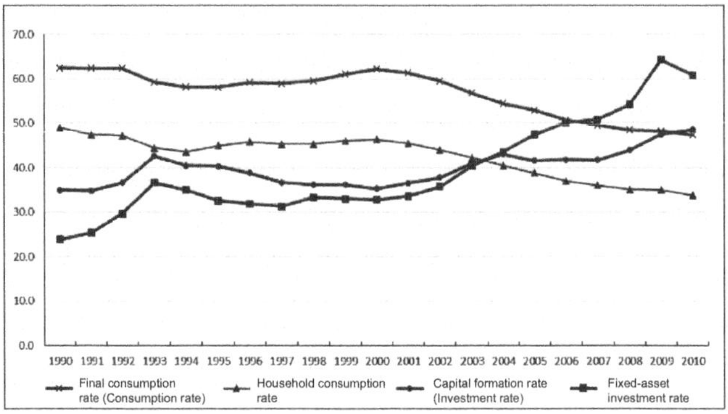

Fig. 9.2 China's consumption and investment rates (%). *Sources China Statistical Yearbooks* (multiple years)

rate should have been reduced to 35 percent. However, the investment rate increased during this period and the consumption rate dropped (see Fig. 9.2).

The rapid increase in the investment rate led to a rapid expansion of production capacity. At the same time, however, final domestic consumption was suppressed, leading to a severe overcapacity.

The upsurge in investments in the heavy and chemical industries began in the steel industry in the early twenty-first century. From that period onward, the industry suffered from successive overcapacities. Against this backdrop, the government undertook a macroeconomic readjustment in 2004, requiring that the relevant agencies protect some industries and suppress others, based on a selective industrial policy that sought to rectify the "excess investments" and "overcapacities." However, such administrative means did not achieve any observable results. In March 2006, the State Council issued the Circular on Accelerating Structural Adjustments in Industries with an Overcapacity, pointing out that "industries such as steel, electrolytic aluminum, calcium carbide, ferroalloy, coke, and automobiles have an apparent overcapacity. Although production and demand for cement, coal, electricity, and textiles are balanced, the number of ongoing projects is huge, giving rise to a potential overcapacity. … Some local governments and enterprises continue to introduce new projects in these industries. The problem of production capacity exceeding demand is worsening. … If this trend is allowed to develop, resource and environmental tensions will become more conspicuous, with worsening structural imbalances, more enterprise bankruptcies, and higher unemployment." In response to these problems, the State Council circular required that "governments at various administrative levels and sectoral authorities shall strengthen projection capabilities, avoid taking actions without a clear vision, be more proactive and conscientious, make the most of the situation, and turn a negative into a positive by accelerating the structural adjustments in industries with an overcapacity."

slow improvements in living standards for low-income people, industrial overcapacities, declining enterprise profits, and an increasing number of bad loans, which may trigger a financial crisis.

The circular also contained general requirements on the approach to the structural adjustments: "On the one hand, governments at various administrative levels should create conditions for the market to play its role by deepening reform and rectifying market order. On the other hand, they should combine economic, legal, and necessary administrative means, improve government guidance, and promote implementation progress." However, the structural adjustments continued to rely on administrative means.

Local governments inherently protect local enterprises, especially the state-owned enterprises they own. This led to the paradox of increased overcapacity despite efforts to curb it. According to figures from the State Council, by the end of 2012 the capacity utilization rates for China's steel, cement, electrolytic aluminum, flat glass, and shipbuilding industries were at low levels of 72 percent, 73.7 percent, 71.9 percent, 73.1 percent, and 75 percent, respectively, due to an ongoing lack of action.[48]

Take the steel industry in Hebei province as an example. Industrial growth began to accelerate at the turn of the twenty-first century. Thereafter, the province's steel output was increasing by over 10 percent per annum: 40.35 million tons in 2003 and 73.86 million tons in 2005, an increase of 33.51 million tons within two years, or an average annual growth rate of 35 percent. Meanwhile, North China was suffering from severe water shortages, and the large-scale development of the high water-consumption steel industry was attracting the attention of the central authorities. The 2005 Policy on the Development of the Steel Industry, issued by the National Development and Reform Commission, pointed out that North China lacked water resources but had a high overcapacity in steel production. Therefore, the region should "strictly control the addition of production facilities and capacity expansion." In 2006, four government agencies, i.e., the National Development and Reform Commission, the Ministry of Land and Resources, the State Environmental Protection Administration, and the China Banking Regulatory Commission, jointly issued the Circular on Cleaning Up Industry in Hebei Province and the Newly Increased Steel Production Capacity to Promote a Structural Adjustment in the Steel Industry," pointing out that since 2003, Hebei province's steel industry had been experiencing "blind capacity expansion and severe construction violations." The circular mandated that construction projects initiated since 2003 should be reviewed, and enterprises, production capacities, and equipment that did not comply with investment approvals, filing procedures, industrial policies, and environmental access conditions should be phased out or rectified. The policy specifically called for the elimination of 11.44 million tons of outdated

[48] The State Council circular included abstract requirements for rectifying market order and creating [favorable] conditions for a market mechanism. However, it also contained specific measures regarding combining economic, legal, and necessary administrative means to strengthen government guidance and implementation efforts. For instance, there were measures to raise the entry threshold, strictly control new projects, continue the rectification and consolidation but treat ongoing and proposed projects differently, retire outdated production capacities in phases, and dismantle or destroy unused facilities. There were also requirements to support major technological upgrading and projects for new products by large steel groups, construction of high-output and high-efficiency coal mines, and reorganization of advanced large steel enterprises, and together with local steel firms, to create iron and steel enterprise groups with an annual capacity of over 30 million tons.

capacity in the Tangshan and Handan areas of Hebei province. Instead of decreasing, however, Hebei's steel production increased for more than ten years. In 2007, the province's steel output reached 107 million tons and in 2013 it shot up to 189 million tons.

Similar situations were reported in other provinces, and the government intensified its response. Eight years after the 2006 circular, in October 2013, the State Council issued another document, Guidance on Solving the Grievous Overcapacity.[49] By this time, the problem had deteriorated from an "apparent" to a "grievous" overcapacity. The guidance document pointed out that "some industries are suffering a severe overcapacity, leading to a sharp decline in profits and widespread business troubles. ... [An even more problematic] overcapacity is tending to worsen as those industries are still engaging in ongoing and proposed projects. ... [If the situation is not addressed, it will lead to] increases in industry-wide losses, unemployment, and non-performing bank loans, as well as aggravated energy bottlenecks and eco-environmental damages, threatening the industries' sound development and even the broad goals of improving the people's livelihoods and maintaining social stability."

The third undesirable result the extensive growth model was suppressed development of the services sector, which is critical to raising overall economic efficiency.

China is endowed with rich human resources. An essential developmental challenge is to implement an industrial structure that is conducive to creating as many jobs and employment opportunities as possible. As is well known, among the three economic sectors, services are the most significant source of providing jobs. Furthermore, among enterprises of varying sizes, small firms are the most capable of creating jobs. Given its resource endowments, China should endeavor to develop the services sector and small enterprises, which had been overlooked under the planned economy. A heavy industrialization strategy is contrary to this correct direction for industrial development. Based on the early stage development mode, China had prioritized development of the industrial sector, particularly large enterprises in the heavy and chemical industries, and it had focused on "material production" rather than on providing resources for research and development, design, marketing, and post-sale services. The massive labor force was underemployed, and this inadequate utilization

[49] In 2013, various ministries issued documents requiring rectification of overcapacity. In January, the Ministry of Industry and Information Technology, the National Development and Reform Commission, and other authorities jointly issued the Guidance on Enterprise Mergers and Reorganizations in Priority Industries, announcing that central government financial incentive funds would support post-merger enterprises and those that had shut down obsolete capacities. In May, the National Development and Reform Commission and the Ministry of Industry and Information Technology jointly issued the Circular on Firmly Suppressing Blind Expansion of Industries with Grievous Overcapacity, place a priority on solving the overcapacity problem in the steel, cement, electrolytic aluminum, plate glass, and shipbuilding industries in 2013. In July–September of that year, the Ministry of Industry and Information Technology issued three lists of enterprises, ranging in over nineteen industries, such as iron and steel smelting and coke production, that should shut down their obsolete capacities.

of human resources meant the potential for higher economic efficiency was underdeveloped. In addition to its role in job creation, the services sector is also essential to improving overall economic efficiency.

The Soviet-style "socialist industrialization" prioritized material production and related theories and policies that denied services as a production sector. Against this backdrop, China's services sector was either ignored or suppressed, and its share of total output was low. Despite several rounds of structural adjustments after the reform and opening, the services sector was still growing slowly. In the early twenty-first century, its share of China's GDP remained lower than the world average, even when compared with the average levels in some low-income countries (Table 9.4).

In the early twenty-first century, China's structural distortions were becoming increasingly obvious. The tertiary industry's share of GDP was declining as investment-driven growth and the disproportionate emphasis on expanding heavy industry dominated the economy (see Table 9.5).

The fourth undesirable result of the extensive growth model was lower investment efficiency and total factor productivity.

Excessive investments and the preferential policy toward large SOEs under the strategy of prioritizing SOE development led to a decline in investment efficiency and TFP.

Table 9.4 A comparison of the share of the Tertiary Sector in China with other middle-income countries in the early twenty-first century (%)

	2000	2002	2002	2003
Argentina	66.88	68.07	56.78	54.06
Brazil	67.73	67.78	67.22	65.83
China	39.82	41.27	42.30	42.09
India	50.98	51.99	53.13	53.25
Mexico	61.61	63.31	63.55	62.70
Russian Federation	55.62	57.71	60.94	61.17
Thailand	54.66	54.95	54.26	52.50
Middle income countries	49.65	50.88	51.41	51.20
World	64.27	65.29	65.87	65.86

Source World Bank Databank

Table 9.5 Changes in the proportion of the Tertiary Sector in China in the early twenty-first century (%)

Year	Tertiary sector's GDP share
2002	41.5
2003	41.2
2004	40.4
2005	40.5
2006	40.9

Source National Statistics Bureau

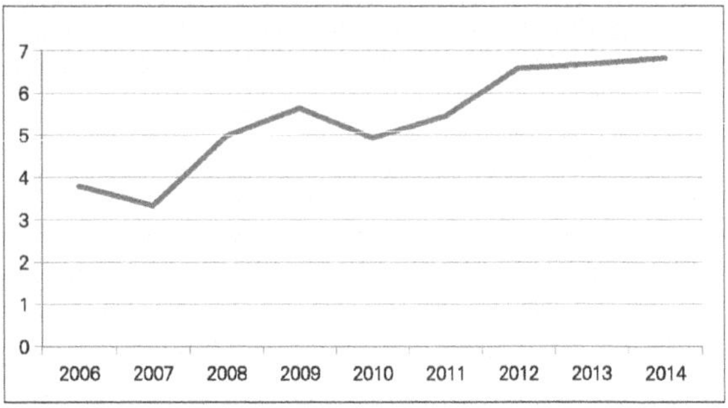

Fig. 9.3 Changes in China's ICOR. *Source* National Bureau of Statistics

First of all, as Solow has pointed out, reliance solely on investment to drive growth will inevitably lead to diminishing investment returns. Starting in the early twenty-first century, when the fever to invest in heavy industry began, China's investment efficiency dropped as its rate of investment rose.

In 2004, National Development and Reform Commission Chairman Ma Kai noted that in the United States, Germany, France, and India, the investment rate was between 10 and 20 percent of GDP, while it was 40 percent–45 percent in China. The former countries needed investments of 100 million to 200 million yuan to generate an additional 100 million yuan of GDP, whereas in recent years China had required approximately 500 million yuan to generate the same additional yuan of GDP. This means China's Incremental Capital-Output Ratio (ICOR) was 2.5–5 times higher than that in the aforementioned countries. Furthermore, China's ICOR saw a further increase after 2007 (see Fig. 9.3).[50]

The fifth undesirable result of the extensive growth model was a negative impact on improvements in living standards or reductions in income inequality. Marx, in his analysis of the early industrialization process in capitalist countries, notes that income distribution based on the factors of production can lead to income disparities, especially during periods of rapid industrialization. This situation will exacerbate the gap between the rich and the poor, making it difficult to raise the overall standard of living. In recent years, China's problems in improving the people's livelihoods and reducing wealth polarization have been directly related to its investment-driven, heavy-industry-focused industrialization.

Furthermore, because the urbanization process had taken an enormous amount of farmland without providing adequate compensation to the farmers, tens of millions had become landless. A strange phenomenon was occurring whereby "the urban areas looked like Europe, but the rural areas looked like Africa." There was also a pseudo-urbanization. Although they worked in cities, hundreds of millions of migrant workers were not urbanized in terms of their social status, incomes, or access to government services, and a substantial portion of the city dwellers were not urban residents. Instead, they remained farmers who were temporarily living in the cities.

---

50 Ma Kai, "Adopt and Apply the Scientific Outlook on Development to Fundamentally Change the Growth Mode: Speech at the China Development Forum, 2004 (full text)," March 21, 2004, www.people.com.cn/GB/jingji/8215/32688/32689/2403665.html.

Under these circumstances, it was challenging to raise the technological level and efficiency of the manufacturing and services industries in the urban areas. The poor-rich divide was another adverse consequence of the pseudo-urbanization. It has often been said that the dual urban–rural economy is a leading cause of the widening wealth polarization. Further observations point to a double dual economic structure: one that is between the urban and the rural areas, and the other that is within the urban areas. The two dual economies are a primary cause of the expanding poor-rich divide and the intensifying social tensions. They are also the source of many of the recent "mass incidents" (public protests involving large groups of people) occurring in the coastal regions.[51]

[51] Wu Jinglian, "Efficiency Problems and Policy Options in China's Urbanization," 2012, *Works of Wu Jinglian*, vol. 2, p. 865.

Chapter 10
Looming Systemic Risks in the Macroeconomy

China's economy began to take off at the end of the twentieth century. After entering the WTO in 2001, external demand expanded rapidly. The trade sector, largely driven by private and foreign-invested enterprises, experienced significant growth while also contributing to a substantial accumulation of savings within the economy. These savings enabled China to overcome the adverse impacts of the 2008 global financial crisis through an enormous government infrastructure investment program, and by 2010 the country had become the world's second-largest economy. However, the high-speed economic development was accompanied by macroeconomic challenges, such as excessive currency expansion and credit inflation due to the extensive growth mode inherited from the first thirty years of reform and opening. By the beginning of the twenty-first century, some of these macroeconomic problems had worsened, and once again the economic growth mode became the focus of attention.

While the source of the problems, i.e., expansionary macroeconomic policies under an extensive growth mode, remained unchanged, there was a sharp difference in the form of the macroeconomic problems between those during the first thirty years of reform and opening and those in the first decade of the twenty-first century. During the early stage of reform, the main macroeconomic challenge was inflation, or a general increase in prices.[1] However, with the growth of a market economy, particularly the stocks and property markets, the macroeconomic challenges included inflated asset prices and over-leveraged balance sheets. Beginning in 2009, these challenges became increasingly obvious (Fig. 10.1).

In essence, this change in the form of the macroeconomy reflected the progress of the reforms. The market-oriented reforms had been fruitful in the goods and general services sectors, and the traditional shortages in a socialist economy had disappeared. However, progress in reforming capital markets was slow, leading to an overaccumulation of financial capital in several areas.

[1] Inflation refers to a general increase in prices for goods and services. However, the Chinese term, *tonghuo pengzhang* (literally, meaning currency inflation) is the source of some misunderstandings.

W. Jinglian, *China's Economic Reform*, Understanding China,
https://doi.org/10.1007/978-981-96-9607-9_10

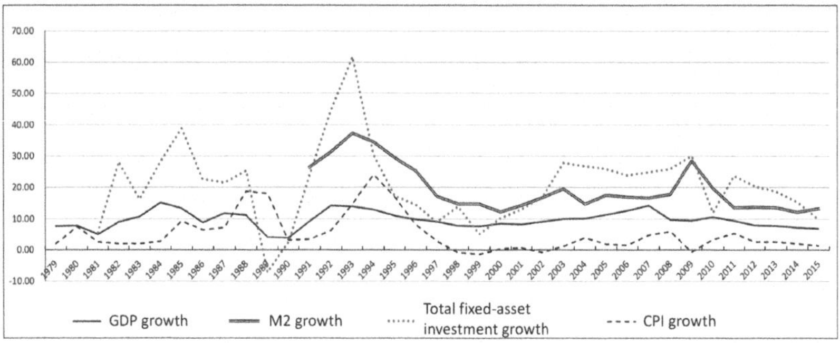

Fig. 10.1 China: Changes in macroeconomic indicators, 1979–2015 (YoY, %). *Source* National Bureau of Statistics

Due to these changes, the macroeconomic consequences differed from those in the past, thereby requiring different responses.

This chapter discusses the macroeconomic challenges after the onset of reform and opening, particularly in the new century.

10.1 Stimulus Policy, Monetary Expansion, and Two Forms of Inflation

In the twenty years from the end of the 1970s when the reform and opening first began to the end of the twentieth century, there was one prominent feature in China's macroeconomy: repeated overheating and inflation—notably in 1980, 1985, 1988, and 1993.

China was not alone in this respect. After beginning their reforms, the socialist countries of Eastern Europe were also troubled by cycles of inflation.

Why did the socialist countries repeatedly experience inflation during their transition processes? Undoubtedly, the root cause was the investment-driven growth mode, as discussed in Chapter 9. In China, the reform and opening had loosened controls over the command economy, and market demand in the areas of goods and general services was relatively thorough, effectively eliminating the shortage characteristics of a traditional socialist economy. However, progress in the reform of capital markets was slow, resulting in an overaccumulation of financial capital in a number of sectors. As national will for high-speed growth remained strong, monetary and credit expansion caused repeated rounds of inflation. In addition, several secondary causes also emerged during this period.

(1) Hidden Inflation Becomes More Noticeable

Hungarian economist János Kornai has demonstrated that a planned economy is a shortage economy,[2] with constant inflationary pressures. Because of the "socialist industrialization path" that prioritizes heavy industrial development, and what Kornai calls "investment hunger" and an "expansion impulse," currency expansion and commodity shortages are commonplace, and inflationary pressures continue to exist.

Aggregate demand far exceeding aggregate supply is a constant under a command economy. However, shortages do not lead to price increases because the prices for most commodities are administratively fixed. Supply shortages are hidden under "administrative repression," and they appear as rationing systems and additional rent-seeking costs. This was also the case in China. Before the reform and opening, the state allocated ("requisitioned, and then allotted") the essential means of production under the plan. Furthermore, minimum daily necessities, from grains, edible oils, and clothing to toilet paper, were provided by ration stamps. Therefore, the shortages did not appear as price hikes.

The situation changed after introduction of the market-oriented reforms. The core institution of a market economy is a free price system. Such an economy can effectively allocate resources because prices determined through market transactions reflect supply and demand or the scarcity of resources. Price liberalization (a market determination of prices) is the underlying premise of an effectively functioning market system. A market-oriented reform inevitably liberalizes the prices of goods and services as well as the factors of production (natural resources, labor, and capital). When shortages exist, price liberalization will reveal the hidden inflation. Rises in the general price levels are unavoidable during the transition from a shortage economy to a market economy.

(2) Rising Expenditures and Declining Revenue in the Government Budget, Particularly at the Early Stage of the Transition

An effective market-economy reform clearly improves economic efficiency and the macroeconomy. However, efficiency improvements take time. In addition, such a reform will significantly alter the previous distribution of economic interests. To reduce resistance and to secure support, the Chinese government increased the benefits for those people who had been hurt under the old system, protecting, as much as possible, the interests of most people and providing some compensation to those who were suffering losses during the reform. As a result, government expenditures increased. These expenditures can be considered the costs of the reform.

With these two forces at work simultaneously, the initial phase of the reform tended to be characterized by increased fiscal deficits and monetary expansion, generating more inflationary pressures.

(3) Shortcomings in Macroeconomic Management and Policy Mistakes During the Reform Process Prevent Inflation From Being Curbed at an Early Stage

---

[2] János Kornai, *Economics of Shortage*, 1978 (Chinese translation by Zhang Xiaoguang et al. Beijing: Economic Science Publishing House, 1986).

First, well-built institutions (a soft infrastructure) are prerequisite for sound macroeconomic management. These include, for example, an independent and efficient central bank, an effective monetary policy transmission mechanism, and strict budgetary constraints on enterprise finances. Unfortunately, these conditions were missing during China's transition period, particularly at the initial stage. Second, maintaining macroeconomic stability through fiscal, monetary, and income policies is a sophisticated art for a government, and it took some time for Chinese government officials to learn how to manage the macroeconomy because they were used to managing the economy by administrative directives under the planned economy and they were unfamiliar with modern economics. In other words, achieving satisfactory results from the outset was not an easy task.

When the first round of inflation occurred in 1980, the command economy was still dominant in China. At the time, macroeconomic tightening was achieved through administrative directives.

When the second round of inflation hit in 1985, the market-oriented reform had already achieved some initial results, and the influence of monetary policy on the macroeconomy was more noticeable. However, economists and policymakers had differing views about whether the economy was overheating and whether tightening policies were needed, thus delaying any decision-making.

As early as the second half of 1984, the increase in money supply was accelerated in parallel with a doubling of GDP earlier than the planned date and an a spending boom under the slogan of "able to make money and spend it." For instance, cash (M0) grew by 49.5 percent in 1983. In the first quarter of 1985, cash (M0) registered a yearly increase of 59 percent, narrow money (M1) rose by an average of 39 percent, and broad money (M2) grew by 44 percent from the same period of 1984. Then, beginning in the second quarter of the year, prices increased rapidly.[3]

In this context, in early 1985, when the signs of economic overheating surfaced, the economic decision-making authorities and academic economists became engaged in heated debates about the macroeconomic situation.

Economists favoring expansionary macroeconomic policies argued that, during the process of external opening and domestic economic invigorating, and when the economy was taking off, it was an inherent demand that the money supply expanded faster than the economic growth. They felt that China, a developing socialist country, would remain in a state of disequilibrium whereby aggregate demand would exceed aggregate supply for the foreseeable period. Artificially suppressing demand and restraining the money supply by macroeconomic control measures would affect high-speed growth and hurt the interests of various parties, thus weakening support for reform.

In contrast, another group of economists believed that international experience has repeatedly shown that inflation is detrimental both to development and to reform. Moreover, considering the society's capacity to bear it, comprehensive economic reforms, including price system reforms, should be based on the premise that total

[3] Wu Jinglian, *Modern China's Economic Reform*, 1999 (Beijing: CITIC Publishing House, 2017), pp. 465–469.

demand and total supply are relatively balanced, the economic environment is relatively relaxed, and the state has a certain degree of fiscal flexibility. The underlying premise is that this will help avoid serious inflation when implementing the preliminary reform measures. They believed that the Party Central Committee and the government should respond decisively to restrain demand and to improve supply. When economic conditions improve, the leadership could then quickly launch a first series of combined reforms to jumpstart a new economic system so that the economy would develop in a virtuous cycle.[4]

In early 1985, State Council leaders realized that the circulation of currency was abnormal. In the first half of the year, they held three provincial governor meetings, asking the officials to take steps to stop the explosion of investment and consumption funds. Due to different views within the central leadership, however, the meetings yielded few results. A consensus on the macroeconomic situation was not reached until mid-year when Deng Xiaoping intervened. The central government then dispatched inspection groups to the provinces to monitor and supervise the reduction in infrastructure projects. Meanwhile, the People's Bank of China tightened monetary policy. In addition to reinforcing controls over credit quotas, the central bank on two occasions raised deposit and lending rates. Because of these administrative and economic measures, money supply declined in the second half of 1985. Furthermore, investment growth slowed down every month in the third quarter of 1985. In the first quarter of 1986, the annual growth rate of M0 decreased to 14 percent, and the annual growth rate of M2 dropped to 13 percent. As a consequence, the Consumer Price Index went down quickly.

During debates about the economic overheating, one event significantly clarified the theoretical issues: the International Conference on Macroeconomic Management (the Bashanlun Conference), jointly sponsored by the State Economic System Reform Commission, the Chinese Academy of Social Sciences, and the World Bank and held September 2–7, 1985.[5]

Speeches at the conference by two foreign experts, Otmar Emminger, former Bundesbank president, and James Tobin, a Nobel laureate in economics, set the tone for the government's macroeconomic policies.[6] Based on information in the China

---

[4] *Memoirs of Xue Muqiao* (Tianjin: Tianjin People's Publishing House, 2006), pp. 314–317; Wu Jinglian, Li Jiange, and Ding Ningning, "The Current State of Currency Circulation and the Policy Responses," 1984, in Wu Jinglian and Hu Ji, comps., *Dynamic Analysis of the Chinese Economy and a Study of the Policy Responses* (Beijing: People's University Publishing House, 1989), pp. 1–11; Wu Jinglian, "A Further Comment on Maintaining a Sound Economic Environment for Reform," *Economic Research*, no. 5 (1985); Liu Guoguang and Zhao Renwei, "Several Current Issues Facing China's Economic Reforms," 1985, in China Society for Economic Reform, comp., *Macroeconomic Management and Reform: Selected Speeches at the International Symposium on Macroeconomic Management* (Beijing: Economic Daily Publishing House, 1986), pp. 193–203.

[5] See China Society for Economic Reform, comp., *Macroeconomic Management and Reform.*

[6] The research results of Yale University professor James Tobin, representing Keynesian and neoclassical economics, are an important component of macroeconomic models explaining relations between financial markets and economic activities. After adding physical assets, including land, buildings, inventories, and raw materials, the Tobin asset allocation model became an essential analytical tool to understand the direct effects of money supply on product prices. In 1981, Tobin

Economic Update of the World Bank, the two experts pointed out that China was in danger of facing serious inflation. They proposed an approach to simultaneously tighten fiscal, monetary, and income policies rather than combining of a loose fiscal policy with a tight monetary policy that is often used in Western countries when facing mild inflation. For a while, Emminger and Tobin's assessments of China's economic situation and their policy proposals quieted the "mainstream economics voices claiming that inflation is beneficial to economic development." Thus, the two experts' opinions had a positive impact on China's macroeconomic policies.

The policy-level conclusions of the debates were presented at the National Conference of the Chinese Communist Party, held later in September 1985. In his speech at the conference, Deng Xiaoping made it clear: "It is projected that … the annual growth rate … will be about 7 per cent. … That growth rate cannot be considered low. If the growth rate were too high, it would create many problems that would have a negative effect on the reform and on social conduct. It is better to be prudent. We must control the scale of investment in fixed assets and see that capital construction is not over-extended."[7]

The Party Central Committee's Proposals on the Formulation of the Seventh Five-year Plan for National Socioeconomic Development, passed at the National Party Conference, contained four guiding principles to be upheld during the Seventh Five-year Plan period (1986–90), two of which concerned macroeconomic management. One proposal emphasized the importance of prioritizing the reforms and ensuring that reforms and construction are mutually adaptive and promote each other. Fundamentally, the reforms are meant to serve construction, and in the current context, construction arrangements should facilitate the progress of the reforms. To ensure the smooth implementation of the reforms, it was crucial to reasonably determine the economic growth rate, avoid blind comparisons and the pursuit of output growth and production speed, and prevent economic tensions and disorder, thereby creating a favorable economic environment for reforms. The other guiding principle required maintaining a balance between aggregate demand and supply so that the accumulation and consumption rates were appropriate. The key was to set a reasonable scale of fixed investments to balance government receipts and outlays, bank credits, material supplies, and foreign exchange and to achieve an overall balance among these sectors.[8]

The above statements at the National Party Conference represented a thoughtful summary of the lessons learned about how to correctly handle the relationship between reform and growth and between reform and the economic environment. Unfortunately, shortly after the Party conference, these costly lessons were forgotten. In February 1986, economic growth slowed down and monetary policy once again

received the Nobel Economics Award for his analysis of financial markets and their relations to expenditure decisions, employment, production, and prices.

[7] Deng Xiaoping, "Speech at the CCP National Congress," 1985, *Selected Works of Deng Xiaoping* (Beijing: People's Publishing House, 1993), vol. 3, p. 143.

[8] "CCP Central Committee's Proposals on the Formulation of the Seventh Five-year Plan for National Economic and Social Development," passed at the National Party Congress on September 23, 1985.

became expansionary. While growth gradually accelerated, inflationary pressures accumulated. In early 1987, there was another debate about macroeconomic policies, during which the proposals to tighten monetary policy were criticized. The prevailing view was to achieve high-speed growth through an expansionary monetary policy, which then led to the third episode of macroeconomic fluctuations, i.e., serious inflation and countrywide panic buying.[9]

Starting in August 1988, with the sharp reduction in fixed-asset investments, control over the purchasing power of social groups (i.e., the non-household purchasing power), and the strengthening of macro-control policies (decided at the September Central Work Conference) to implement a "hard landing," the People's Bank of China adopted a series of tight monetary and credit policies, raising the reserve requirement ratio and deposit and loan interest rates, which quickly brought down the inflation rate. By the third quarter of 1989, the annual growth rate of narrow money (M1) had declined to –1 percent and that of broad money (M2) had decreased to 13 percent. Money supply hit a trough and prices came down swiftly. Meanwhile, market demand was weak, industrial production contracted, factories faced idle capacity, and unemployment pressures increased. The economy was entering an unprecedented "overcooling" state.

But in 1991, the Chinese economy, led by the private sector, gradually reemerged from the economic fluctuations of 1988 and the political turbulence of 1989. In early 1992, Deng Xiaoping took his famous Southern Tour during which he called for a resumption of the reforms. His remarks were well received both within and outside the government, beginning a new wave of economic development.

During the 1992 economic boom, there were two opposing trends. On the one hand, most local governments and enterprises were enthusiastic about reform and they proactively took steps to engage in reform and opening, thus leading to an expanded role for the market. On the other hand, central government agencies were passive in promoting reform. They failed to implement the necessary reforms in fiscal policy, finance, and state-owned enterprises, all of which were necessary at the national level. Instead, the central government adopted an expansionary monetary policy to stimulate growth. In 1992, narrow money (M1) grew by 35.7 percent, and broad money (M2) registered a 31.3 percent increase. In that context, local governments and SOEs focused on expanding capital investments. Once again, there was rapid overheating of the economy.

From mid-1992 to mid-1993, assessments of the macroeconomic situation were quite diverse. There were roughly four different views. (1) The first view found that the pace of the market-oriented reforms was too fast, causing the overheating. The subtext was that the reforms should be slowed down and control by the plan should be enhanced. (2) The second view saw eye to eye with the first view regarding the macroeconomic situation. But this group believed that the overheating was, after all, due to the stagnant reforms in critical areas, which made it challenging to improve economic efficiency. People holding this view called for decisive steps to stabilize

[9] Wu Jinglian, *Contemporary Chinese Economic Reforms*, 1999 (Beijing: CITIC Publishing House, 2017), pp. 469–472.

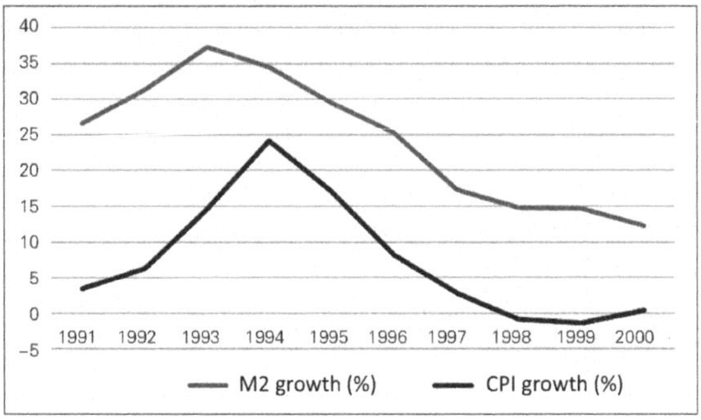

Fig. 10.2 Increases in Money Supply and CPI (1990–2000) *Source* The People's Bank of China and the National Bureau of Statistics

the economy and promote reforms. (3) The third view believed that the economic situation was sound, with high-speed growth and without any danger of inflation. People holding this view were satisfied with the government's economic work and they believed it should be continued. (4) Those holding the fourth view were dissatisfied with the pace of reform, but they felt that economic growth was gratifying. People in this group argued that in other countries inflation had always accompanied high-speed growth; hence, tightening measures should not be adopted so as to avoid any dampening of the momentum for high growth.

The debate lasted for about one year until the spring of 1993. At that time, the threat of serious inflation was evident, as the Consumer Price Index rose by over 10 percent year on year, and the RMB to USD exchange rate was devalued by 45 percent from November 1992 to May 1993. Only by then, views about the state of the economy slowly gradually came into alignment. Finally, in April 1993, Deng Xiaoping intervened, and Zhu Rongji, vice premier in charge of economic affairs, took resolute stabilization measures, eventually achieving macroeconomic stability (Fig. 10.2).[10]

The following section discusses macroeconomic developments and the new challenges after the turn of the twenty-first century.

10.2 Monetary and Credit Expansion Amid an Investment Boom

After the 1997 Asian financial crisis, China's macroeconomic policy shifted from the contractionary policy of the mid-1990s to an expansionary policy. After the eruption of the 2008 global financial crisis, the macroeconomic management authorities implemented stronger stimulus policies. A sharp increase in money supply followed. Broad money (M2) grew from RMB 13.46 trillion in early 2000 to RMB 97.42 trillion in 2012, or by an average annual rate of 18.35 percent.

[10] Ibid., pp. 472–476.

The following factors were responsible for the rapid increase in currency in circulation.

First, the government used expansionary monetary policy to fuel an unprecedented investment boom.

The end of 2002 and early 2003 was a period of generational change for Party and government leaders. In this context, many new local leaders adopted massive investment plans for large industrial development projects ("political showcase projects") and urban development projects ("boosting city-image projects").

Among these plans, urbanization investment, focusing on real estate investment, was particularly prominent due to the significant economic benefits. On the one hand, attracting more foreign capital to invest in the real estate industry could directly stimulate local GDP growth. On the other hand, large-scale infrastructure investments significantly increased urban land value, which enhanced local government finances and alleviated the tight general budget situation.[11] As a result, many cities expanded their spatial plans, elevated their status, rapidly expanded the scale of urban construction, and experienced high-speed growth in urban construction investment. Investments to raise the share of heavy industry in the local industrial structure also increased. From 2003 to 2008, the nationwide annual average growth rate in fixed asset investments exceeded 25 percent, with real estate investment being particularly prominent.

Again, assessments of the situation starting in 2003 differed among industry practitioners and within academic and political circles. The dominant view was that only a few industries were suffering from a "partial overheating." People holding this view believed there would be no overall overheating as long as a "selective support and suppression policy" was implemented to support the cooling industries and to control those in breach of the regulations. However, microeconomic interventions failed to address the macroeconomic problems. On the one hand, administrative controls aimed at expanding the production capacity of industries, such as steel, cement, and electrolytic aluminum, supported by strong demand did not curb their expansion impulses. On the other hand, even for industries identified as "locally overheated," such as the real estate industry, administrative "window guidance" was unclear. In June 2003, the People's Bank of China issued the "Circular on Further Strengthening Management of Real Estate Loans" (Central Bank Directive No. 121), "Further Strengthening Management of Real Estate Loans." The directive required tightening the issuance of loans for land banking purposes, standardizing working capital loans to construction enterprises, and increasing mortgage downpayments and mortgage rates for second houses. These requirements aimed to contain excessive real estate loan and investment growth. Two months later, the State Council issued its "Circular on Promoting Sound Development of the Real Estate Market" (State Council Document No. 81). The State Council circular established the real estate sector as a pillar industry for economic development and pointed to the need for its sustained growth. Consequently, real estate loans by banks increased. In 2003,

[11] Jia Kang, "A Study of China's Local Debts and their Resolution," *ChinaBond*, no. 9 (2013).

commercial real estate loans grew by 49.1 percent and mortgage loans increased by 42.9 percent.

Second, the global financial crisis that began in 2007 reinforced the push to "expand demand and sustain growth" by increasing the issuance of currency and expanding investment.

Amid the consequences of the 1997 Asian financial crisis, China had implemented expansionary macroeconomic policies to alleviate the impact of the crisis, and it had achieved steady growth. However, signs of an economic overheating were appearing both before and after 2007. The December 2007 Central Work Conference reached a consensus on 2008: a prudent fiscal policy and a tight monetary policy would be adopted. However, in July 2007 the global financial crisis began first in the United States and then spread to other countries. Against this backdrop, the Chinese government had to change its policy stance and turn to expansionary macroeconomic policies. In the second half of 2008, China's industrial production and speed of GDP growth began to slow down. In November, the State Council Executive Meeting, presided over by Premier Wen Jiabao, decided to expand domestic demand and promote economic growth by taking strong measures that were to be "swift, hard-hitting, precise, and well-delivered." The key action was to increase investments, i.e., relying on investment demand to regain a GDP growth rate of over 8 percent (and ensuring a minimum growth rate of 8 percent). To stimulate the domestic market, the government required that the banking system expand lending and enhance the financial sector's support for economic growth. This was accompanied by a RMB 4 trillion two-year government investment program (see Fig. 10.3). The RMB 4 trillion in loans, amplified by the money multiplier effect, created tens of trillions of RMB in purchasing power. In 2009, commercial banks added nearly RMB 10 trillion in loans, a yearly increase of 32.8 percent. With the surge in aggregate demand, GDP growth quickly picked up. In that year alone (2009), China's economy grew by 9.1 percent, driven by a massive injection of money. Broad money (M2) increased by 27.7 percent; from this level, it gained another 19.46 percent in 2010, further expanding the currency in circulation.

Third, the rapid increase in foreign exchange reserves led to an unintended loosening of the central bank's monetary policy

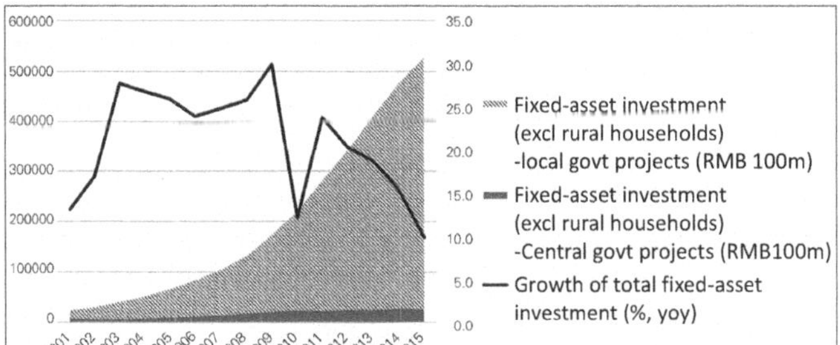

Fig. 10.3 Fixed investments and growth rate (2001–15). *Source* National Bureau of Statistics

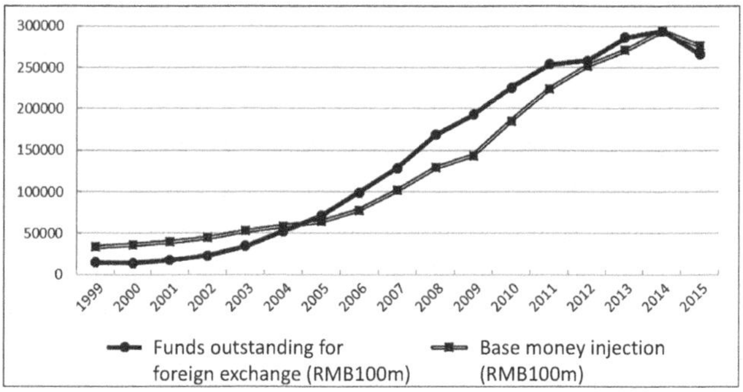

Fig. 10.4 PBoC Balance Sheet: FOFFE and Base Money. *Sources* National Bureau of Statistics, PBoC

In the 1990s, the comprehensive implementation of an export-oriented policy greatly advanced China's economy. However, like the other East Asian countries and regions that had adopted export-oriented strategies, China encountered several problems after a period of successful implementation: a significant rise in foreign exchange reserves, escalating trade tensions, and a narrowing scope for monetary policy. Starting from the mid-1990s, China's international balance of payments began to show a continuous increase in both the current account and the capital account surpluses. In 2001, the growth of national foreign exchange reserves reached 28 percent, and thereafter the rate remained at above 30 percent. The most rapid increase occurred in 2004, when the annual growth of foreign exchange reserves hit a record 51 percent. During this time, the People's Bank of China's balance sheet saw substantial increases in both foreign exchange reserves and the issuance of base money (see Fig. 10.4).

In July 2005, the People's Bank of China announced a return to a managed floating exchange rate regime. Only then did the RMB begin to appreciate. In general, there are two approaches to reform the foreign exchange regime: either to liberalize once and for all or to let the value of currency slowly crawl up. The advantage of the first approach is that it completes the reform in one step, like a sharp knife cutting through a messy knot. But it can also have a substantial impact on the economy. Therefore, China opted for the gradual appreciation approach to avoid any economic shocks. Nevertheless, the market's persistent expectations of a further RMB appreciation, coupled with a significant interest rate gap between China and the U.S., attracted "hot money" from international investors at an accelerated pace. All these factors intensified pressures for a RMB appreciation, forcing the People's Bank of China to continue injecting base money to acquire foreign exchange.[12]

In June 2002, responding to the rapid growth of currency in circulation, the People's Bank of China began open market operations (mainly through treasury repurchasing agreements) to reduce the excess liquidity in the interbank market.

[12] Li Chao and Zhou Chengjun, "Excess Liquidity and Foreign Exchange Reserves in China," *Economic Research,* no. 12 (2008).

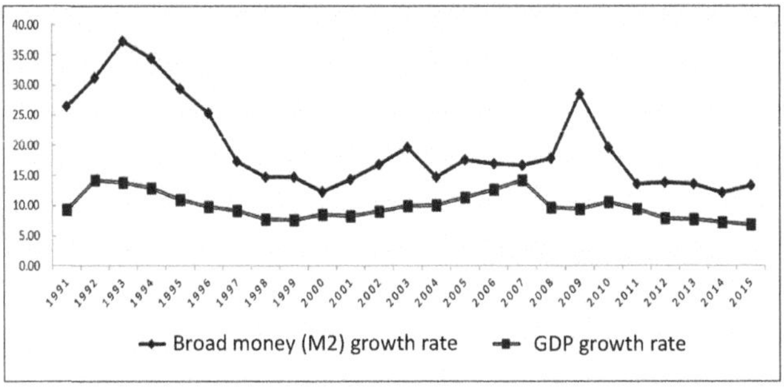

Fig. 10.5 China: Growth rates of broad money (M2) and GDP. *Source* National Bureau of Statistics

However, due to the overwhelming growth in foreign exchange reserves, by the end of September 2002 the central bank had exhausted its position of over 300 billion yuan in government bonds. As a result, starting from September 24, 2002, the People's Bank began issuing central bank bills to absorb interbank market liquidity. Despite these efforts to offset the massive release of base money, it was difficult for these central bank measures to be fully effective. The excessive issuance of money caused by the increase in foreign exchange reserves only began to ease in about 2012, when the exchange rate reform was largely in place.

Fourth, procyclical macroeconomic policies exacerbated the economic fluctuations.

The key task in macroeconomic management is adjusting aggregate demand to ensure economic stability. Given the problem of policy lags, macroeconomic policies should be implemented with foresight and be executed countercyclically. However, people relied on their actual experiences, leading to corresponding measures being taken only after inflation had already occurred.[13] Such procyclical responses worsened the economic fluctuations.

The decade from 2003 to 2012 was characterized by massive currency issuances (see Figs. 10.5 and 10.6).

From 2003 to 2008, the M2 to GDP ratio was kept at 1.5–1.6 times. However, after 2009, this ratio began to rise, reaching a high level of 1.93 times in 2014 (see Fig. 10.7).

[13] In a January 28, 2010, speech, Central Bank Governor Zhou Xiaochuan pointed out that China had lacked foresight in its assessment of the macroeconomic situation and the transmission mechanisms had been ineffective. As a result, monetary policy adjustments that should have been predictive often coincided with the economic cycle, becoming pro-cyclical rather than counter-cyclical.

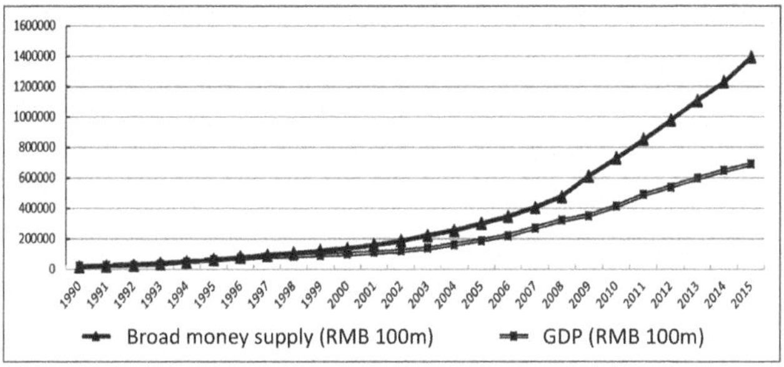

Fig. 10.6 China: broad money (M2) and GDP. *Source* National Bureau of Statistics

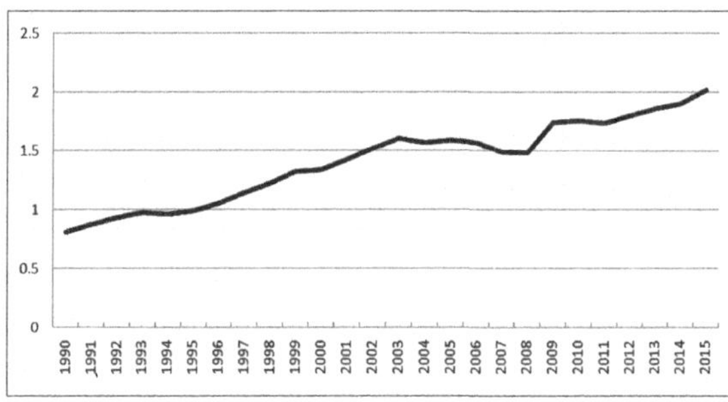

Fig. 10.7 China: The broad money (M2) to GDP Ratio. *Source* National Bureau of Statistics

10.3 The Consequences of Monetary Expansion: Asset Bubbles and Balance Sheet Risks

While the expansionary macroeconomic policies lasted for several decades, their effects on the Consumer Price Index (CPI) were not always the same. Figure 10.8 shows that 2008 was the year of demarcation. Before 2008, the CPI increase was positively correlated with the growth of money supply. After that year, growth in the money supply accelerated, but the CPI did not increase. In that context, some people came to the conclusion that the idea that "inflation is a monetary phenomenon" was no longer valid, although it remained widely accepted among economists.

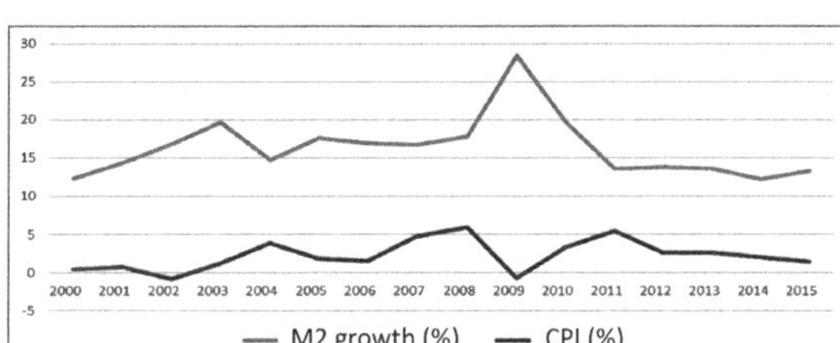

Fig. 10.8 Money supply growth and CPI (2000–15). *Sources* PBoC, National Bureau of Statistics

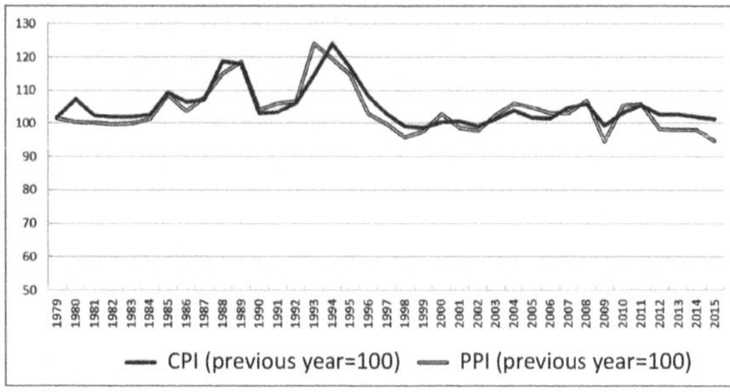

Fig. 10.9 The CPI and PPI (previous year = 100). *Source* National Bureau of Statistics

This author believes that such a conclusion was too rushed. The statement "inflation is a monetary phenomenon," as stated by Milton Friedman, merely highlights the correlation between the overall price level and money supply (money supply × velocity of money). Historically, an excessive issuance of money has often led to a sustained increase in the price level of goods and services, primarily reflected in the Consumer Price Index (CPI). Thus, many people interpret Friedman's statement about inflation as a monetary phenomenon in a narrow sense, viewing it solely as an increase in the prices of goods and services.[14] This interpretation continued when assessing the state of the economy in the twenty-first century. Inflation was more moderate than it had been in the 1980s and the 1990s due to the positive effects of the rapid productivity improvements in the trade sector in parallel with China's increased integration with the global economy.[15] However, domestically, moderate inflation was closely associated with monetary expansion, and relatively slow productivity improvements in the non-trade sectors, and increasing labor costs maintained moderate inflation levels. But from the second half of 2007, inflation surged rapidly. The CPI broke through the moderate inflation baseline of 3 percent in the second quarter of 2007 and climbed to a high of 8 percent by 2008. The global financial crisis changed the situation considerably. Due to weak export demand, the contribution of net exports rapidly declined. Coupled with the continued sharp drop in global commodity and energy prices after the financial crisis, both the Consumer Price Index (CPI) and the Producer Price Index (PPI) remained sluggish, even declining to near-deflation levels (see Fig. 10.9). The persistent decline in commodity and energy prices reflected the financial deleveraging faced by the major developed countries after the financial crisis, which lasted for about a decade before showing signs of stabilization and recovery during the past two years. These developments showed that in addition to money supply, the global economic and financial situations also affected domestic prices for goods and services as China's economy was becoming more integrated with the world economy.

[14] In *Inflation: Causes and Consequences,* Milton Friedman points out, "Inflation is always and everywhere a monetary phenomenon, in the sense that it is and can be produced only by a more rapid increase in the quantity of money than in output" (New York: Asia Publishing House, 1963).

[15] After China joined the WTO, the huge amount of manufactured exports from China were blamed for the global deflationary pressures.

In fact, beyond the commodity markets, the price levels of assets such as securities, real estate, and collectibles are also closely related to changes in the money supply or liquidity. Initially, in early market economies, assets occupied a small market share, so people did not pay much attention to their impact on overall price levels. However, as the market share of these assets has increased—sometimes even exceeding that of consumer goods—excess liquidity resulting from monetary over-expansion often flows into assets like securities, real estate, and collectibles rather than into overproduced consumer goods, leading to asset price inflation.

This situation repeatedly occurred in the developed economies. The most well-known case is Japan at the end of the twentieth century. In 1985, finance ministers and central bank governors of the developed countries met at the Plaza Hotel in New York City and signed the Plaza Accord. The most significant agreement under the accord was the commitment by Japan and the Federal Republic of Germany to abandon administrative interventions in exchange rates, resulting in sharp appreciations of the Japanese yen and the West German mark. However, the Federal Republic of Germany and Japan took different approaches to the serious contraction in export demand. Germany overcame the crisis by strengthening competitiveness and improving efficiency, and its economy remained strong. Japan stabilized the economy with a heavy-handed expansionary monetary policy, quickly raising domestic demand. That policy resulted in booming stock and real estate markets without causing inflation. In this context, the Japanese macroeconomic authorities could not agree on a shift to a more prudent approach. The monetary expansion lasted until a few months before the capital market collapsed and a systemic financial crisis erupted in 1990.

In China, consecutive years of currency over-issuance created asset bubbles and a highly leveraged national balance sheet. As a result, systemic financial risks accumulated.

On the stock market, the Shanghai Stock Exchange Composite Index experienced a decrease from 2214.2 in 2001 to its lowest point of 1005 in July 2005. Then, in January 2006, the index began to go up. On October 16, 2007, the index reached a historical high of 6124.04 (from 1163.88 at the beginning of the year). According to Wind Information data, the average price-to-earnings ratio of A shares on the Shanghai Stock Exchange rose from 17.61 times in January 2006 to 69.64 times in October 2007 (to a certain extent, the price-to-earnings ratio reflects stock price inflation).[16]

[16] The P/E ratio is determined by dividing a company's share price by its annual earnings per share. (It can also be expressed by dividing a company's market value by its profits attributable to shareholders.) The ratio indicates how many years it will take for an investor to recover his investment from a company's profits. The Shiller P/E 10 is a measure to assess share price rationality, computed by dividing the inflation-adjusted S&P Composite Stock Price Index by the prior ten-year moving average of inflation-adjusted earnings. See Robert Shiller, *Irrational Exuberance* (Chinese translation. Beijing: People's University Publishing House, 2000).

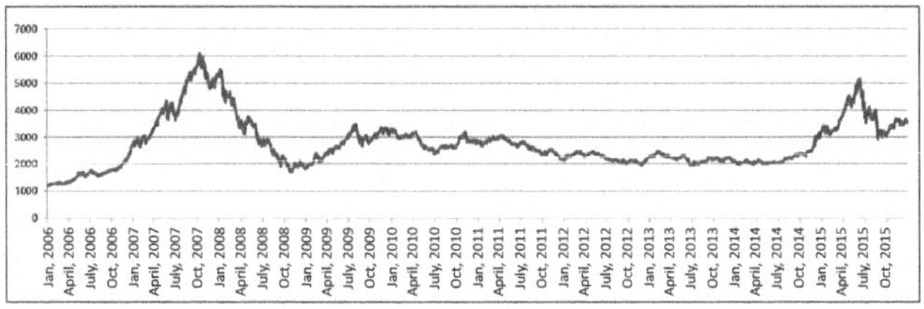

Fig. 10.10 Changes in the SSE Composite Index. *Source* Wind Information Co. Ltd.

But no bubble can last forever. When enough people believe that stock prices will stop rising and they begin to sell their holdings, stock prices can collapse.[17]

Beginning in October 2007, stock prices dropped, with the Shanghai Stock Exchange Composite Index losing more than two-thirds of its value within less than a year. Thereafter, the stock market remained in a slump and the stock index struggled to recover. This pattern of sharp rises and falls was repeated; in October 2014, both the Shanghai and Shenzhen stock markets surged rapidly due to the support of the regulatory authorities and the mainstream media. Over the next eight months, the Shanghai and Shenzhen Composite indices rose by 150 percent. However, on June 15, 2015, the market suddenly turned downward. From June 15 to July 4, the Shanghai Composite Index fell by 29.91 percent, with the value of the stock market evaporating by over 20 trillion yuan and resulting in a stock market crash even more serious than that in 2008 (see Fig. 10.10).

Developments in the real estate market were somewhat different. While the stock market went up and down, the real estate market went up and up. Traditionally, Chinese people have always believed in real estate because it is a physical object. Therefore, housing is their first choice for maintaining and increasing wealth. However, real estate values, like security values, can disappear in a flash when the market crashes. People swarmed into the real estate market because of a lack of other investment opportunities. Particularly in Beijing and other first-tier cities, housing prices continued to increase because people believed the government would buttress the local real estate markets (see Fig. 10.11).

A house is both a residence and an investment at the same time. When housing prices rise too high for residential purposes, complaints surge because ordinary

[17] Wu Jinglian writes, "The capital market is imperfect. It does not have a Pareto efficiency equilibrium, and price changes depend on buyers' and sellers' expectations of future prices. Such expectations have a self-sustaining or self-realizing character. This means that when the price of a commodity (be it a physical or a financial product) rises continuously, more people will snap up the commodity on the market. This will then cause the price to go even higher, thus reinforcing expectations of a price increase: the higher the price, the more people will buy the commodity, and vice versa. As long as enough people buy stocks, there will eventually be a mega bull market. But an economic bubble cannot inflate forever. When prices are too high and begin to turn south, a positive feedback effect will soon occur. The more people sell stock, the further will stock prices drop, and vice versa, leading to a stock market crash (market collapse)." See Wu Jinglian, "How to Assess Excessive Speculation and a Bubble Economy," in *Ten Years of the Stock Market* (Shanghai: Far East Publishing House, 2001), p. 140.

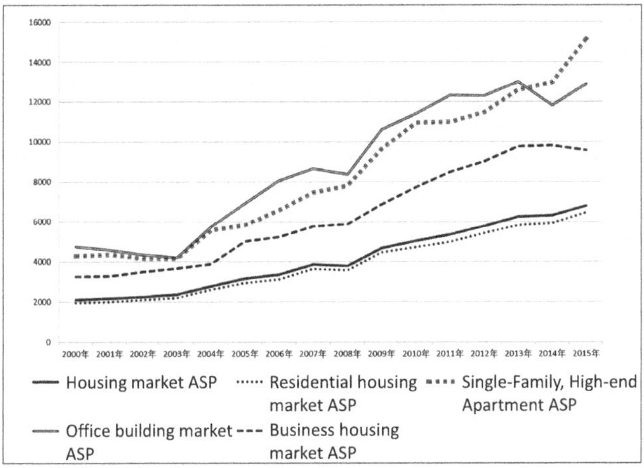

Fig. 10.11 Housing price changes in 35 large- and medium-sized cities (2000–15, RMB/sqm). *Source* National Bureau of Statistics

Table 10.1 Share of incremental housing loans in total incremental loans

Year:	2010	2011	2012	2013	2014	2015	2016
Share:	26.90%	17.50%	17.40%	28.10%	28.10%	30.60%	44.80%

Source People's Bank of China

people, and even those in the middle-income bracket, find themselves unable to afford to buy or rent a home.[18] As investments, houses become valuable and worth hoarding when hot money floods the market. People with surplus cash buy multiple homes as investments, driving up housing prices.

On the one hand, the enormous investment demand kept housing prices high; on the other, ordinary people could not afford adequate living space due to elevated housing and rental costs. The problem hurt urban economic development and exacerbated social tensions.

On the other, the vast funding influx shored up housing prices. The housing industry attracted enormous profit-seeking funds due to higher price expectations, and massive mortgage loans sustained strong demand for housing and high housing prices. Asset bubbles quickly formed (Table 10.1).

Assets bubbles and a higher leverage ratio (debt ratio) on the national balance sheet are two sides of the same coin.

[18] According to Wind Information, in the early twenty-first century the housing price to income ratio in China's first-tier cities was around twenty times, exceeding the international warning threshold by three to six times.

In addition to asset price inflation and bubbles, excessive currency issuances and surplus liquidity inevitably led to a persistently high leverage ratio and growing financial risks on the national balance sheet.[19] As early as the early twenty-first century, some scholars, noting the extensive borrowing by local governments, raised concerns about local government debt. However, during the fever for "heavy industrialization" and the construction of large and new cities, this non-mainstream concern did not attract much attention. It was only addressed with some preliminary work being done by specialized institutions.

A few specialized agencies did engage in basic preparations, however. In 2002, the National Bureau of Statistics issued "China's System of National Accounts (2002)," which revised the methodologies for compiling the national balance sheet. On a trial basis, the bureau prepared the national balance sheets for 1997 to 2004.

At the end of 2008, local governments, responding to the central government's decision to use 4 trillion yuan in fiscal investments and the loose credit policies to "expand demand and ensure growth," increased their investment efforts.

They invested heavily in urban development projects and enterprises through their funding vehicles (local government investment companies).[20] As a result, local government debt risks once again garnered significant attention.

Among the writings on China's local government debts and risks, the most influential and controversial was an article written by Professor Victor Shih, at the time at Northwestern University, entitled "China's 8000 Credit Risks," published in the *Asian Wall Street Journal*, on February 9, 2010.[21] In it, Professor Shih considers the investments made by the 8,000 investment firms, established by local governments in response to the central government's economic stimulus policy, as a threat to China's financial stability. According to Shih's estimates, as of end-2009, China's local government debts amounted to RMB 11.4 trillion (equivalent to USD 1.7 trillion), equal to 34 percent of the country's GDP in that year rather than the official measure of RMB 6 trillion, or 18 percent of GDP. Professor Shih projected that China's total debts would account for 71 percent of GDP in 2009 and would reach 96 percent by the end of 2011. The article triggered heated discussions within and outside China. Many people in China questioned his estimates, finding they were "speculative conclusions based on erroneous projections."[22]

The explosive growth of local government debts after 2008 also attracted the attention of China's financial regulatory authorities. For instance, on June 10, 2010, the

[19] The national balance sheet reflects an economy's overall position. It is an aggregate of four economic sectors' balance sheets, including governments, enterprises (financial and non-financial), households, and the external sectors.

[20] Because the Budget Law forbids direct borrowing by local governments, many local governments suffering from a serious imbalance between budgetary revenue and expenditures established financing vehicles to raise funds to invest in "boost city-image projects" and "political showcase projects" that were managed by legal entity enterprises. The debt payments were funded by the fees collected on public facilities and other government resources.

[21] Victor Shih, "China's 8000 Credit Risks," *Asian Wall Street Journal*, February 9, 2010.

[22] Yisheng Xu, "Where Victor Shih Erred," *China Business News*, March 25, 2010.

Table 10.2 China: Assets and liabilities of the government sector (RMB trillion)

	Assets	Liabilities	Net Assets
Estimates by Ma Jun's team (2010)	61.00	22.00	38.00
Estimates by Cao Yuanzheng's team (2008)	17.21	7.52	9.69
Estimates by Li Yang's team (2010)	142.3	72.7	69.60 (broad definition)
	93.0	72.7	20.3 (narrow definition)

Sources Ma Jun et al., "Resolving Long-term Risks on the National Balance Sheet," *Caijing*, June 12, 2012; Cao Yuanzheng et al., "Reshaping the National Balance Sheet Capacity'; Li Yang et al., "China's Sovereign Balance Sheet and Associated Risks," *Economic Research*, no. 6–7 (2012)

State Council, in the "Circular on Strengthening Management of Local Government Funding Platforms," called for strengthening management of the funding vehicles.

Meanwhile, some scholars and research institutions studied China's national balance sheet. In June–August 2012, three research groups published interim reports on the issue. One research team included a joint team composed of Ma Jun, then chief economist of Deutsche Bank for Greater China, and Fudan University researchers, another research team, the Bank of China team, was headed by Chief Economist Cao Yuanzheng, and the third research team, the Chinese Academy of Social Sciences team, was led by CASS Vice President Li Yang.[23] The three reports differed in terms of their methodologies, focuses, and risk assessments.[24]

First, the team reports differed in terms of their estimates of the asset and liability situations of the government sector (Table 10.2).

Given the substantial level of government net assets, the CASS team report was optimistic about the government's debt risks while also pointing out the risks in real estate loans, enterprise debts, and past-due social security benefits. According to the report, because the country had vast net sovereign assets which were continuing to expand, "the Chinese government has adequate sovereign assets to cover its sovereign liabilities. For a considerable period, the likelihood of a sovereign debt crisis is extremely low in China. A repayment risk, by and large, does not exist in China."[25]

[23] The first two teams' initial reports were published in the June 12, 2012, issue of *Caijing* magazine. The CASS team's report was published in the media on August 9, 2012. *Economic Research,* nos. 6–7 (2012) also carried the CASS report as a two part academic paper under the title "Assessment of China's Sovereign Balance Sheet and the Associated Risks."

[24] Ma Jun's team used a valuation method. Considering the price factor, particularly changes in asset prices, the team estimated each asset's worth and then compiled the national balance sheet. The technique reduced the gap between the annual national balance sheet and what occurred within the year. The drawback was that there could be a vast difference between years. Cao Yuanzheng's team used an extrapolation method, taking past National Bureau of Statistics data as the baseline and estimating the yearly changes.

[25] Li Yang, "Assessment of China's Sovereign Balance Sheet and Associated Risks (Part 2)," *Economic Research*, no. 7 (2012).

Later, however, the debt problem became more pronounced. In a June 2013 speech, Professor Li Yang noted, "In recent years, particularly after 2009, China's national balance sheet has become less healthy and the risks have increased." He said that as of 2010, China's balance sheet was still relatively healthy; while not the best in the world, it was comparatively good. However, in recent years, there had been a trend of deterioration in the balance sheet. The turning point toward deterioration occurred in 2009, with all the data showing adverse changes from that year and the leverage ratio increasing rapidly (see Table 10.3).

The other two teams were less optimistic about the likelihood of a debt crisis. Ma Jun pointed out that although positive net assets might indicate the soundness of the balance sheet, this should not be the primary indicator for gauging debt risks because of uncertainties in asset liquidity and differences in a country's ability to borrow at low rates. Based on a consensus among fiscal economists and international organizations, Ma Jun's team and the Bank of China team used the debt-to-GDP ratio as the essential indicator of government debt sustainability. Ma Jun reported that the Chinese government's leverage ratio (debt to GDP) was 18.1 percent in 2012 and that it would continue to rise. This assessment factored in the following risks: local government debts, railway sector debts, deficiencies in pension funds, rising healthcare costs, and increasing environmental governance costs. It also assumed that there would be no further reforms in the government revenue to GDP ratio, the government's non-interest expenditure to GDP ratio, the retirement age, and the health insurance system, as well as no transfer of state holdings to the Social Security Fund and no cash out-of-state assets to replenish the local governments' funding platforms (see Table 10.4).

Considering that China's economic growth was slowing down and that the implicit debts related to social security payments and other liabilities would increase significantly in the future, Ma Jun's team and Cao Yuanzheng's team came to a similar conclusion: while the government did not have obvious debt risks in 2012, the medium- and long-term risks could not t be overlooked.

Table 10.3 Changes in the Chinese economy's overall leverage ratio, 2005–2012 (%)

Year		2005	2006	2007	2008	2009	2010	2011	2012
Debt to GDP ratio		150	148	147	146	176	184	186	194

Source Li Yang, "Speech at the Seminar Celebrating the Fifth Anniversary of the Boyuan Foundation," at http://business.sohu.com/20130630/n380278916.shtml, June 30, 2013

Table 10.4 Leverage ratios of the Chinese government balance sheet, 2012–2050 (%)

2012	2015	2020	2030	2040	2050
18.7	25.7	33.1	48.7	84.7	161.5

Source Ma Jun, et al., *A Study of China's National Balance Sheet* (Beijing: Social Sciences Academic Press. 2012), p. 184

Table 10.5 Nationwide government debts (RMB trillion)

Year	Administrative Level	Government Debt Liabilities	Government Contingent Debts	
			Debts Guaranteed by Governments	Debts for which Governments Might Have Remedial Responsibility
End-June 2012	Central government	9.81	0.26	2.31
	Local governments	10.89	2.67	4.34
	Total	20.70	2.93	6.65

Source National Audit Office, "Nationwide Audit Results of Government Debts," December 30, 2013

Ma Jun pointed out that if the central government did not provide support, non-performing assets would likely be equal to 30 percent of the total local government and railway sector debts. Assuming the central government would cover the non-performing assets, fiscal pressures, given the debt maturity structures, would mainly occur within the five years from 2013 to 2017. In such a case, the central government would have additional annual expenditures averaging RMB 700 billion, or RMB 3.5 trillion in total.[26]

According to the requirements of the State Council, the National Audit Office organized a nationwide audit from August to September 2013 and published the results in December of that year.[27] The audit revealed that, as of the end of June 2013, the total debt for which governments at all levels were responsible for repayment amounted to 20.70 trillion yuan. Additionally, there were 2.93 trillion yuan in debt for which governments were responsible for guarantees and 6.65 trillion yuan in debt that might require some form of rescue (see Table 10.5 for details). By the end of 2012, the debt for which governments were responsible for repayment was equivalent to 36.74 percent of that year's GDP.

The audits discovered the following problems. (1) The debt liabilities of local governments were increasing rapidly. Outstanding debt owed by provincial, municipal, and county governments totaled RMB 10.58 trillion, an addition of RMB 3.87 trillion, or an average annual growth rate of 19.97 percent from the end of 2010. (2) Some regions and industries suffered heavy debt burdens. As of end-2012, three provincial governments, 99 municipal governments, 195 county governments, and 3,465 township governments had an "outstanding debt to comprehensive finance capacity" ratio exceeding 100 percent. (3) Local governments relied extensively on land transfer income to service their debts. As of end-2012, 11 provincial governments, 316 municipal governments, and 1,396 county governments had RMB 3.49

[26] Ma Jun, et al., *A Study of China's National Balance Sheet* (Beijing: Social Sciences Academic Press. 2012), p. 113.

[27] National Audit Office, "Nationwide Audit Results of Government Debts," December 30, 2013.

trillion in outstanding debt backed by land transfer income, accounting for 37.23 percent of the total outstanding debt at these three government levels.

Therefore, China's macroeconomic policies faced a dilemma: they could be neither loose nor tight.[28] Maintaining the expansionary policies to "expand demand and sustain growth" would further inflate the asset bubble and worsen the leverage problem on the balance sheet, thereby exacerbating the systemic risks. Contractionary policies, however, could stall the economy.[29]

10.4 The Macroeconomy: A Renewed Policy Assessment and a Challenging Task

The weaknesses in the national balance sheet led to a renewed assessment of the expansionary macroeconomic policies because international experience had demonstrated that systemic financial risks often follow an excess leverage ratio.

In the 1970s, American economist Hyman P. Minsky proposed a hypothesis about financial instability in a market economy. He argued that an endogenous stability-instability cycle existed in free market economies. During an economic boom, investors assume higher risks and borrow more, leading to higher leverage ratios on the balance sheet and asset bubbles. When the cash flows cannot cover the loan repayments or the interest payments, loan withdrawals by lenders, widespread disruptions in corporate funding chains, and a collapse in asset values may be triggered, and a financial crisis will erupt. This is called a "Minsky Moment."[30]

In the aftermath of the 2008 global financial crisis, Richard Koo, chief economist at Nomura Research Institute, in *The Great Recession: How to Survive and Thrive in a Financial Crisis*,[31] suggested that the 1929 Great Depression, the Japanese financial crises in the 1990s, and the latest global financial crisis were all "balance sheet recessions" caused by the bursting of asset bubbles backed by high leverage ratios on the balance sheet.

In their well-known book, *This Time Is Different: Eight Centuries of Financial Folly*,"[32] American economists Carmen M. Reinhart and Kenneth S. Rogoff review many financial crises over the last 800 years and they point out that prior to the crisis

---

[28] Wu Jinglian, "Thoughts about Overcoming the Macroeconomic Dilemma," *Economic Observer*, no. 10 (2010). This article also appears in *Works of Wu Jinglian* (Beijing: Central Compilation and Translation Press, 2013), vol. 2, pp. 1005–1014.

[29] In aviation, a stall refers to a condition whereby the lift is smaller than the plane's weight, causing the plane to quickly sink and for the pilot to lose control.

[30] Hyman Minsky, *Stabilizing an Unstable Economy*, 1986 (Chinese revised translation by Wang Shifeng. Beijing: Tsinghua University Press, 2015).

[31] Richard Koo, *The Great Recession: How to Survive and Develop in a Financial Crisis* (Beijing: Oriental Publishing Co. Ltd., 2008); Richard Koo, *The Escape from Balance Sheet Recession and the QE Trap* (New York: Wiley, 2014).

[32] Carmen M. Reinhart and Kenneth S. Rogoff, *This Time Is Different: Eight Centuries of Financial Folly*, 2009 (Chinese translation. Beijing: Mechanical Industry Press, 2012).

that began in 2007, the U.S. economy had "almost all the signs of a financial crisis," including an asset price bubble, a climbing leverage ratio, perennial current account deficits, and slow economic growth.

The presages of a systemic financial crisis, as described by the two American economists, were obvious in the second half of the 2010s.

One group favored expansionary macroeconomic policies to expand demand and sustain growth. Members of this group advocated measures such as massive projects to develop railways, highways, and other infrastructure projects financed by public investments and a monetary easing by the central bank (i.e., increasing the money supply and expanding credit).

This view held the upper hand in the debates of the early twenty-first century. After the 2008 global financial crisis, China launched a strong stimulus program with vast investments to raise the GDP growth rate.

However, the strong stimulus only had short-term effects. The repeated use of expansionary macroeconomic policies led to the following consequences. Diminishing returns from investments soon emerged: the more the investments, the weaker their effect on growth. Conversely, the monetary policy was ineffective when the excess leverage ratio caused a balance sheet recession, as noted by Richard Koo. When cash is king, people are reluctant to borrow for long-term investments. If they have cash to spare, they will be more willing to invest in cashable assets rather than in businesses that are less liquid and difficult to cash out, thus resulting in an ever-rising leverage ratio and worsening asset bubbles.

Figure 10.12 shows that the two-year RMB 4 trillion investment program and the one-year RMB 10 trillion lending program in 2009 quickly increased the GDP growth rate by three to four percentage points. In the short span from Q4 2009 to Q2 2010, the growth rate exceeded 10 percent, before starting to decline. After 2009, there were practically yearly stimulus measures. Although the stimulus measures remained strong, their effects continued to decrease, and the period of economic recovery became increasingly shorter. By 2015, the stimulus policies had almost lost steam, and the GDP growth rate was continuing to decline. The following are the GDP growth rates over the four years from 2011 to 2015: 9.2 percent in 2011, 7.8 percent in 2012, 7.7 percent in 2013, and 7.4 percent in 2014, and 7 percent in the first half of 2015 and 6.9 percent in the third quarter of 2015.

Against this backdrop, another group of scholars pointed out that excessive use of stimulus policies exacerbates the leverage ratio and accelerates the accumulation of risks. By 2015, an increasing number of studies both at home and abroad had found that China's leverage ratio was exceeding the 200 percent debt safety ratio, although there were minor differences in their respective calculations. For instance, the Chinese Academy of Social Sciences report, *China's National Balance Sheet (2015)*[33] pointed out that the economy's leverage ratio increased from 170 percent in 2008 to 235.7 percent in 2014, a rise of 65.7 percent during those six years. In its report, the McKinsey Global Institute estimates that China's total debt increased from USD 7.4 trillion in 2007 to USD 28.2 trillion in 2014, and the debt-to-GDP

[33] Li Yang, *China's National Balance Sheet (2015)* (Beijing: China Social Sciences Press, 2015).

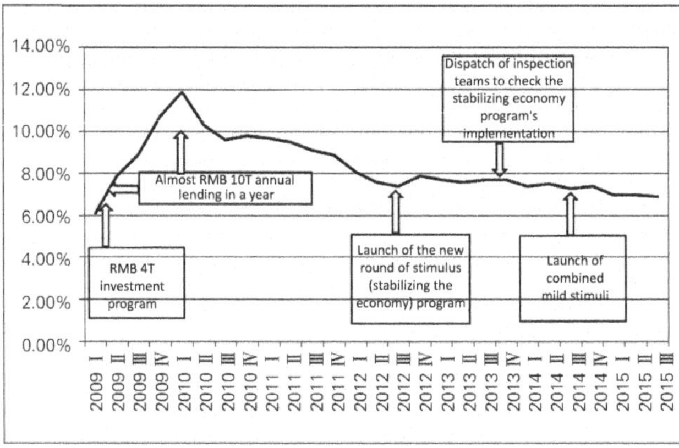

Fig. 10.12 Quarterly GDP growth rates (2009–15). *Sources* National Bureau of Statistics; Xinhuanet.com

ratio went up from 158 to 283 percent.[34] Particularly noteworthy was the leverage ratio of nonfinancial enterprises, which soared from 72 percent of GDP in 2007 to 125 percent of GDP, far exceeding the accepted 90 percent safety value (Fig. 10.13). Figure 10.13 shows that the leverage ratio on China's national balance sheet increased slowly from 2000 to 2007, but then it skyrocketed after 2007, with the total leverage ratio reaching 283 percent. The nonfinancial corporate (mainly SOE) debt-to-GDP ratio far exceeded the accepted safety value.[35]

A see-saw effect (a "whack-a-mole" effect) occurred: when the government implements stimulus measures to stabilize growth, the result is increased leverage. Conversely, when these measures are withdrawn, the economy will face adverse repercussions. In this context, the only solution is to stabilize the overall economy and control and reduce the risks. While ensuring that no systemic crisis occurs, the government should primarily direct efforts to deepening the comprehensive reforms and to relying on reform and opening to improve the supply-side efficiency and to bring about a transformation of the economic growth mode. It is only in this way that China will be able to overcome the above dilemma and achieve sustained and stable economic development.[36]

[34] McKinsey Global Institute, "Debt and (Not Much) Deleveraging," February 2015.

[35] Some analysts believed a systemic crisis was unlikely in China because China's balance sheet leverage ratio was far below the Japanese 400 percent level. However, they probably failed to notice the following differences. First, while Japan's national balance sheet had a high debt ratio, it was mainly concentrated on the government's balance sheet. Second, corporate cash flows remained abundant, and government debt was backed by sovereign credit, making a debt repayment crisis unlikely. In contrast, non-financial corporate debt, which significantly exceeds the recognized warning line, is the dominant component of China's national balance sheet. As a result, in recent years frequent corporate cash flow disruptions and debt defaults have emerged, signaling a serious warning that systemic risks must be closely monitored.

[36] See Wu Jinglian's speech at the Beijing Financial Street Forum, September 15, 2017.

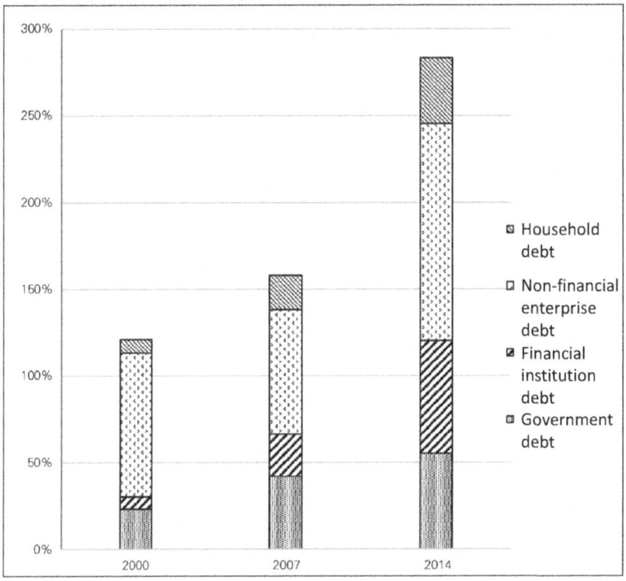

Fig. 10.13 The accelerated rise in the leverage ratio (Debt to GDP ratio). *Source* McKinsey Global Institute, "Debt and (Not Much) Deleveraging," February 2015)

Chapter 11
The Spread of Corruption

The Chinese leadership prioritized "anti-corruption" as its primary mission early in the reform and opening period. When introducing the reforms, the Third Plenary Session of the 11th Party Central Committee reestablished the Central Commission for Discipline Inspection (CCDI). In November 1980, CCDI Secretary Chen Yun, who would hold the position for a decade, famously stated: "The conduct of the Party in power is a matter of life or death."[1] In January 1982, the authorities launched a massive "anti-economic-crime" campaign. According to an April 1983 CCDI report, more than 27,000 people were expelled from the Party or given other disciplinary punishments.[2]

However, the measures failed to contain the spread of corruption due to the unaddressed institutional defects.

As discussed in Chap. 4, rent-seeking under the dual system of "primarily a planned economy with supplemental market adjustments" was widespread in the 1980s, contributing to the 1988 economic turmoil and the 1989 political turbulence. Learning from these lessons, the reforms after 1990 attempted to contain the spread of corruption.

However, the anti-corruption drive could not secure a decisive victory because the measures failed to address the root causes of corruption: the interference of political power in socioeconomic activities.

After administrative controls were enhanced and the institutional foundation for rent-seeking was reinforced in the early twenty-first century, corruption worsened, bringing with it severe social and economic consequences.

Anti-corruption is one of the biggest political challenges facing China in the twenty-first century.

---

[1] Chen Yun, "The Conduct of the Party in Power Is a Life and Death Issue," 1980, in *Selected Works of Chen Yun* (Beijing: People's Publishing House, 1995), vol. 3, p. 273.

[2] Chen Yun, "Speech at the Second Plenary Session of the Twelfth Party Central Committee," 1983, in ibid., p. 331.

W. Jinglian, *China's Economic Reform*, Understanding China,
https://doi.org/10.1007/978-981-96-9607-9_11

11.1 Efforts in the 1990s to Eliminate the Institutional Basis for Rent-Seeking

During the initial stage of reform and opening, the Communist Party sought to redress the so-called "unhealthy Party conduct (*dangfeng*)," hoping to curb the spread of corruption by educating officials and enforcing laws and disciplinary measures. But this approach was like "curing the symptom without addressing the cause." In the late 1980s, after numerous discussions about the phenomenon of official profiteering, people began to focus on how to eliminate the institutional basis for rent-seeking.

Deng Xiaoping realized that public resentment of corruption was a major cause of the 1989 political turbulence. In a talk with several newly promoted Party leaders on June 16, 1989, he said: "... we should do some things to satisfy the people. There are chiefly two things: one is to carry out the reform and opening to the outside world with greater daring, and the other is to move swiftly to punish corruption. ... In this incident [the 1989 turmoil] there were no slogans against reform and opening to the outside world, but one of the slogans frequently chanted was the demand to combat corruption. ... For our part, if we do not punish corruption, especially among high-level Party leaders, we run the risk of failing to rectify the Party and to achieve our strategic goals. The new leaders should first of all address this problem, which is also an important part of our efforts to rectify the Party. ... We should carry out reform and opening to the outside world and, at the same time, punish corruption. When people see that these two things are combined, they will have a clearer understanding of our policies and give them greater support."[3]

Following the resumption of the reforms in the early 1990s, measures were taken to eliminate the institutional basis for rent-seeking, including (a) promoting market-oriented reforms and merging the dual tracks into a single-track market system, (b) limiting the number of administrative permits and reducing the reach of government, and (c) implementing the rule of law and establishing rule-based markets.

Chapter 4 shows that in the mid-1980s, the government had already planned to take the first step, i.e., to consolidate the dual pricing system into a free pricing system in order to eliminate the essential institutional basis for rent-seeking. However, because of opposition, the plan was terminated before implementation. In 1988, the government once again tried to liberalize the pricing system for the means of production within three years, but the government announcement, alongside its expansionary macroeconomic policies, triggered nationwide panic buying and bank runs. Subsequently, Party and government leaders announced that "the dual-track pricing system is a product of certain historical conditions. When the commodity economy is still underdeveloped, and the market is far from mature, it appears to be infeasible to abruptly abolish such a system. The dual-track pricing system for certain important

[3] Deng Xiaoping, "The Urgent Task of the Third-Generation Leadership," 1989, *Selected Works of Deng Xiaoping* (Beijing: People's Publishing House, 1993), vol. 3, pp. 313–314.

primary products and raw materials cannot and should not be abolished in the short term." Thus, the focus of the reform returned to improving the SOE contract system.[4]

The reform in the early 1990s began with a price liberalization for most means of production.

The government implemented strict contractionary macroeconomic policies after the 1988 economic turmoil, particularly after the 1989 political turbulence. As soon as monetary expansion was curtailed, prices began to fall and the dual-track regime gradually moved to market pricing. At about the time of Deng Xiaoping's "Southern Tour Talks" in 1992, prices for most of the means of production— e.g., prices for steel—quietly became market-determined (Table 11.1).

With the free exchange of goods and the merging of the two pricing tracks, profiteers could no longer amass wealth by selling official permits for planned goods allocations. When the market was liberalized and resource allocations were directed by prices reflecting supply and demand on the market, and thus became more efficient, goods were abundant. As a result, the previous rampant official profiteering and other rent-seeking behaviors in allocating goods disappeared. In 1994, the dual-track foreign exchange regime was consolidated into a single-track market regime, eliminating rent-seeking opportunities through the use of import licenses to acquire low-priced foreign exchange.

But price liberalization for most goods eliminated only a small part of the space for rent-seeking. It did not uproot the institutional foundation for such activities. The factors markets were far from liberalized, the allocation of funds and land was still controlled by administrative power, and the market did not determine prices for these resources. The credit and land leasing markets emerged as new hotspots for high-frequency corruption.

During China's urbanization process, farmers only had the right to utilize farmland within the terms of their contracts. When rural land was turned into urban land, the government could obtain the land from the rural collectives at low prices fixed by the buyers, and by the early 1990s, when urbanization accelerated, land transactions had become a paradise for rent-seeking activities (see Sect. 9.3 for details).

As noted earlier in this book, under such conditions people would use their powers to seek rent wherever possible. Such people distorted the reform policies or used other means to establish an institutional foundation for rent-seeking and to create new rent-seeking opportunities. New "dual-track systems" emerged as soon as the old dual-track systems faded, thus exacerbating the corruption.

When participating in a discussion of the Shaanxi provincial delegation to the National People's Congress on March 8, 2004, Premier Wen Jiabao pointed out: "A functional transformation is a major task in reforming our government. The government previously managed many things beyond its capacity and did not do it very well. This is the cause of the overstaffed departments, unwieldy organizations, and 'mountains of paperwork and oceans of meetings' (repetitive and low-efficient bureaucratic processes). Furthermore, this problem obstructed development

[4] Zhao Ziyang, "Report to the Third Plenary Session of the 13th Party Central Committee (September 26, 1988)," *People's Daily*, October 28, 1988.

Table 11.1 Changes in the proportions of various pricing mechanisms, 1978–93 (%)

Years	Retail			Agricultural products			Means of production		
	State-fixed price	State-guidance price	Market price	State-fixed price	State-guidance price	Market price	State-fixed price	State-guidance price	Market price
1978	97.0	0	3.0	92.2	2.2	5.6	100.0	0	0
1985	47.0	19.0	34.0	37.0	23.0	40.0	64.0	23.0	13.0
1986	35.0	25.0	40.0	35.3	21.0	43.7	–	–	–
1987	33.7	28.0	38.3	29.4	16.8	53.8	–	–	–
1988	28.9	21.8	49.3	24.0	19.0	57.0	60.0	0	40.0
1989	31.3	23.2	45.5	35.3	24.3	40.4	–	–	–
1990	29.8	17.2	53.0	25.0	23.4	51.6	44.6	19.0	36.4
1991	20.9	10.3	68.8	22.2	20.0	57.8	36.0	18.3	45.7
1992	5.9	1.1	93.0	12.5	5.7	81.8	18.7	7.5	73.8
1993	4.8	1.4	93.8	10.4	2.1	87.5	13.8	5.1	81.1

Note Values as % of the total under each of the three pricing mechanisms
Source "Table of Changes in the Shares of the Three Pricing Mechanisms since 1978," *China Price Statistical Yearbook 2007*, p. 468

of the productive forces. We should transform government functions and let enterprises, intermediary agencies, and the market handle matters that should be done by them so that the government can concentrate on the essential matters." Starting from the Second Session of the 10th National People's Congress in 2004, each State Council report on the Work of Government highlighted the need to let enterprises, the market, and intermediary organizations handle matters that should not be managed by the government and to increase the role of the market in resource allocations. But efforts to streamline government approvals and enhance the regulatory model yielded little success. No breakthrough was achieved until 2013, when the new government launched a reform to transform government functions.

Against this backdrop, the government undertook the following steps to reform its review and approval regime. First, in the early twenty-first century an administrative review reform was carried out to reduce and improve administrative procedures. In addition, on July 1, 2004, an Administrative Licensing Law went into effect, prohibiting governments at various administrative levels from demanding licenses at will. Lastly, regulation of the securities markets was improved.

Freely engaging in activities not banned by law is a citizen's natural right. The basic principle of behavioral choice in modern countries is that "everything which is not forbidden is allowed." In other words, citizens can do all things that are not explicitly banned by law.[5] But under the Soviet-style "state syndicate," because citizens were subordinates of the state a different principle was applied. Any activity by citizens had to be within the scope defined by the government or have received prior approval. China inherited this Soviet tradition, resulting in pervasive administrative licensing. Entering the market was impossible without undergoing administrative reviews and approvals.

Statistics show that in 2000, there were over 4,000 matters at the ministerial level, and more than 2,000 matters at the provincial and municipal levels, that were subject to administrative approvals.[6] Moreover, some county and township governments also had administrative licensing requirements.

Inspired by a discussion among economists at the end of the twentieth century, Wei Jianxing, the then secretary of the CCDI, during an inspection tour of Guangdong province in April 2000, spoke of the need to "counter corruption at its origins." He pointed out that "inappropriate uses of power represent the origin of corruption. … In recent years, some officials in leading positions have breached the law and Party discipline. Many people have abused the administrative licensing powers, personally approving land transfers, loans, and construction projects in disregard of the relevant regulations, and they have received huge bribes and have become criminals. … Reforming the administrative review regime is important to prevent and combat corruption at its origins. Except for those approval requirements that must be canceled, the remaining requirements should be reformed as follows. Items that the market can manage should be processed through bidding, auctions, and other market

---

[5] This is the "negative list" system for market entry.

[6] Shen Lutao, et al., "News Analysis: Why Excessive Administrative Approvals Exist?" Xinhuanet.com, August 25, 2002.

mechanisms. However, those that cannot be handled by market processes—especially those administrative powers prone to abuse or corruption—should be separated out. After that, mutual monitoring and constraints among the administrative bodies should be enhanced to prevent an excessive concentration of power in a few hands, the lack of internal monitoring, and under-the-table deals."[7]

In November 2000, a plenary session of the 15th CCDI adopted a resolution calling for "further preventing corruption at its roots and intensifying the Party's anti-corruption work." The top priority was to "reform the administrative review regime and to standardize related powers." The CCDI required governments at various administrative levels to take stock of the items subject to administrative review: "Those that can be done away with should be removed, and those that the market mechanisms can replace should be left to the market. For those administrative approval projects that must be retained, mechanisms for supervising and restricting administrative powers must be established and improved. Procedures should be standardized, approval steps reduced, and approval processes and results made public to allow for public oversight."

These CCDI regulations addressed the core issues of corruption and were supported by the public. In October 2001, the State Council issued a notice titled Implementation Opinions on the Reform of the Administrative Approval System (Guo Fa [2001] No. 33), which required that all departments under the State Council thoroughly review their administrative approval requirements. Departments were to propose whether to cancel, retain, delegate, or transfer these requirements to market mechanisms. The Office of the Leading Group for the Reform of the Administrative Approval System then submitted recommendations regarding the handling of these projects, which were then discussed by the leading group and reviewed by the Office of the Premier in the State Council before being finalized and announced as State Council decisions.

Between November 2002 and 2004, a total of 1,795 administrative approval requirements were canceled or adjusted.[8]

Those who had benefited from rent-seeking within the administrative review system tried every means to obstruct the reform efforts. They lay in wait to make a comeback. The European Enlightenment philosopher Montesquieu once said, "... constant experience shows us that every man vested with power is apt to abuse it. ..."[9] As soon as this wave in the "campaign to counter corruption at its origins" passed, many administrative or disguised review requirements resurfaced.

Experience in attempting to streamline the administrative review requirements in 2001–4 revealed that the excessive administrative reviews were due to, among other

[7] "During his Tour of Guangdong Province and Shenzhen Municipality Wei Jianxing Stresses the Need to Prevent and Counter Corruption at its Origins," *People's Daily* (Overseas Edition), April 25, 2000.

[8] State Council Decision on Removing and Decentralizing Several Administrative Reviews, http://www.360doc.com/content/14/0216/09/7499155_352870731.shtml.

[9] Montesquieu, "The Spirit of Law" (Chinese translation by Zhang Yanxing. Beijing: Commercial Press, 1961), vol. 1, p. 154.

reasons, too many administrative agencies having licensing power.[10] The need to standardize the administrative licensing authority became clear. Thus, another reform measure was undertaken to reduce administrative interference and rent-seeking activities: the Administrative Licensing Law of the People's Republic of China was passed by the Standing Committee of the National People's Congress on August 23, 2003 (effective July 1, 2004). Most importantly, this law limits administrative licensing powers, specifying that only the National People's Congress, its Standing Committee, the State Council, and those provincial/municipal people's congresses with legislative power have administrative licensing authority. If the law were to be strictly enforced, excessive administrative licensing would be constrained and there would be a significantly reduced number of administrative reviews. This could be a strong impetus for standardizing government behavior. The State Council held a meeting to promote enforcement of the law, calling on governments at various organizational levels to abide by and implement this law. Before the law was promulgated, the State Council also announced that it would remove all but 500 items that were subject to administrative review requirements.

Unfortunately, the measures were not strictly enforced. For example, some administrative litigation cases challenging administrative licensing were dismissed by the courts, while others did not receive appropriate legal remedies.

A more severe reversal occurred after the economic overheating in the early twenty-first century. The government enhanced its control over the entire economy. Some government agencies used administrative means to readjust the economic structure and rein in the overheated investments by "protecting and supporting some industries, while suppressing and controlling others." The administrative review regime not only was reestablished under various forms but it was even expanded, leading to intensified tensions.

Improving regulation of the securities market was equally challenging.

The securities market in China has a high degree of information mismatch. For instance, knowledge about a listed company is vastly different between ordinary small investors, often referred to as "*gumin*" or individual traders, and company insiders who have access to more detailed and privileged information. Without strict rule of law and regulation, market losses due to the information mismatch will severely hurt the party that lacks good information but will bring vast wealth to the well-informed party, resulting in a failure of, or a loss of, market mechanisms.

Regulation of the securities markets focuses on compliance. Mandatory disclosure requirements aim to alleviate the information mismatch and to prevent the minority who have an information advantage from hurting the interests of the majority. For a long time, however, China employed a different regulatory approach, relying primarily on administrative review as the main tool to remedy the mismatch. In May 1993, the State Council issued the Interim Provisions on Administration

[10] For instance, the Implementation Opinions on the Reform of the Administrative Approval System, issued by the State Council in October 2001, confirmed that departments under the State Council have the authority to establish administrative approvals based on the decisions, orders, and requirements of the State Council.

of the Issuance and Trading of Stocks, establishing lengthy administrative review procedures for stock issuances, public listings and trading, and acquisitions and mergers.

The primary drawback of this regulatory regime was that it created a substantial opportunity for rent-seeking. Every time a new review step was added, it was an opportunity for rent-seeking. First, a company had to obtain a recommendation from the provincial-level Party and government agencies before it could apply for an IPO and a public listing. China's IPO process then involved multi-layered reviews about the size and price of an issue, making the listing application a complex process with significant rent-seeking possibilities. The complex listing process created a (backdoor listing) market for "shell resources," an anomaly in China's securities markets. A bankrupt, listed shell company (a so-called shell resource) could be sold for millions of RMB, or even billions of RMB, because the opportunity cost could be the same if were to go through the regulatory process and have to mete out gratuities to various parties.

In a 1996 paper, Professor Gao Xiqing, who had served as a senior executive at the China Securities Regulatory Commission (CSRC), pointed out that "there is still no evidence that management of China's securities market has made any definitive choice between mandatory information disclosures and substantive review systems. The power of substantive review remains a 'sword' wielded by the securities market regulators. Since the CSRC was established four years ago, the commission has approved 360 companies' IPOs and listings. Year in and year out, crowds of leaders and their associates from thirty-one provincial-level governments, fourteen municipalities separately listed in the state plan, and various government bodies and enterprises visited the CSRC and other state agencies seeking IPO rights for their regions, sectors, or enterprises. To give up this enormous and far-reaching power will require a 'revolution of the soul' of any organization, particularly any agency born out of the traditional, centralized, planned economy."[11]

Starting from the early twenty-first century, the authorities formulated and implemented laws and regulations to rectify the chaotic market and strengthen compliance-based regulation. One of the reforms was the transition, beginning in 2000, from a multi-party "review and approval regime" to a regulatory "check and permit regime" for the issuance of stocks. Compared to earlier practices, the new review regime introduced the following improvements: (a) official removal of the allocation of quotas, (b) abolition of a local government/relevant agency recommendation requirement, (c) determination of the issue price through negotiations between an issuer and its underwriter(s) based on market conditions and inquiries by institutional investors, and (d) prioritization of mandatory disclosure requirements. In addition, the authorities also issued rules to standardize the disclosure requirements for listed companies. However, this regime, albeit with reduced review layers, was far from a registration-based system.

[11] Gao Xiqing, "The Theoretical Basis for Mandatory Information Disclosures in the Securities Market," *Securities Market Herald*, October 1996, pp. 4–17.

In March 2002, the Ministry of Public Security established the Securities Crimes Investigation Bureau, which was tasked to collaborate with the CSRC to crack down on information-mismatch–related criminal activities, such as market manipulation and insider deals.

Regarding internal corporate controls, the CSRC issued rules and procedures to strengthen the corporate governance structure of public companies. For instance, it established requirements for independent directors and made the board of directors responsible for strengthening internal controls.

But all these measures fell short of containing the increases in rent-seeking activities. Instead, the reform became a stop-and-go process, even returning to the starting point when special vested interest groups were adversely affected.

A survey on corruption in China's financial sector, conducted by Xie Ping and Lu Lei of the Research Bureau of the People's Bank of China in 2002–3, reveals that rent-seeking behavior was widespread in domestic financial institutions. Of the 3,561 respondents to the survey, 81.1 percent believed corrupt deals were widespread and commonplace; most respondents felt that the financial regulators themselves had severe corruption problems, and the greater the excess profits of the financial institutions, the more severe the problems. In addition, most respondents believed that the securities regulator had more grievous corruption problems than its peers in the insurance and banking industries. Among all regulated financial institutions, corruption was the most severe in securities firms.[12]

11.2 The Early Twenty-First Century: Tightened Government Control and Its Negative Effects in Containing Corruption

In the early twenty-first century, the market-oriented, rule-of-law–based efforts to eradicate the institutional basis for corruption suffered setbacks. From an economic perspective, the intensified administrative reviews beginning in 2004 significantly reinforced the institutional foundation for rent-seeking.

In the second half of 2003, signs of an economic overheating emerged, leading to varying opinions, both within and outside the government, about the macroeconomic situation and policy responses. There were three groups. Members of the first group who agreed that the macroeconomy was overheating and who favored "appropriately tightening and timely fine-tuning" policies to handle the economic aggregates. Those in the second group believed that the enthusiasm for growth should be well-protected: "Morale should be boosted, not dampened," and the government does not need to and should not apply the brakes. The third group saw only a partial overheating in the economy. The members of this group opposed overall control of the money supply. They advocated a selective policy to "protect and support some

[12] Xie Ping and Lu Lei, *Economic Analysis of Financial Corruption in China: Systems, Behavior, and Design of the Mechanism* (Beijing: CITIC Publishing House, 2005).

industries while suppressing and controlling others," i.e., providing administrative and economic support to sectors that had run out of steam, while enhancing project reviews and investment controls for the overheated sectors. At first, government leaders considered whether to adopt the recommendations of the first or the second groups. Finally, in early 2004, the leaders accepted the third group's macroeconomic assessment and recommended responses.

The primary tool for readjusting the economic structure was project reviews and investment controls by the National Development and Reform Commission (NDRC), in conjunction with fiscal policy and the central bank credit guidance to commercial banks. The State Council's Decision on Establishing Administrative Licenses for the Really Necessary Administrative Examination and Approval Items specified that "current State Council administrative licensing requirements for fixed-investment projects remain valid."[13] As administrative licensing was retained, the authorities in charge of investment matters gained tremendous power. They identified three industries as being overheated: iron and steel, electrolytic aluminum, and cement, but the list grew longer as the economy became increasingly heated under the expansionary macroeconomic policies. The expanding scope of investment controls brought back the administrative licensing regime, and the number of items subject to reviews and approvals exceeded that in the pre-2001 period. According to Professor Wang Liming, a well-known jurist and vice president of People's University, as of end-2010 the number of matters subject to State Council reviews exceeded 3,600, and the number subject to provincial-government reviews was more than 54,200.[14]

After the global financial crisis erupted in 2008, the Chinese government adopted an "expanding demand and sustaining growth" policy, substantially enhancing its administrative measures. On November 5, 2008, the State Council launched a two-year, RMB 4 trillion investment program to stimulate economic growth.[15] Thereafter, throngs of provincial government officials frequented the NDRC with project proposals and funding requests since the commission held immense power in terms of investment project reviews and approvals. A commentator on economic and financial affairs described the phenomenon as follows: "In the Sanlihe area of Beijing, where the NDRC is located, hotels were overbooked. Even a Home Inn hotel, a budget hotel in the middle of a residential community, was crowded with visitors seeking lodging, but the unlucky ones were told that all 100-plus rooms had already been taken. There were also reports that that the basement rentals of nearby residential buildings were fully packed with visitors." The commentator continued, "The Sanlihe story is nothing new: '*paobu qianjin*' (visiting the ministries to seek funding)

---

[13] State Council Document Order no. 412, Decision on Establishing Administrative Licenses for the Really Necessary Administrative Examination and Approval Items, issued on June 29, 2004.

[14] Wang Liming, "Reform and Improvements in the Legal System for Market Entities," *Chinese University Social Sciences*, no. 4 (2014).

[15] "The State Council Lays Out Measures to Expand Domestic Demand to Promote Economic Growth," www.gov.cn, November 9, 2008.

has been a well-known slang term for over a decade. The difference this winter is that fights for projects are taking place by the minute."[16]

In the early twenty-first century, a government-led urbanization movement, through government allocations of resources, led to socioeconomic changes. During this process, land became the primary target of massive rent-seeking activities. In the planned economy, land owned by the state had been allocated to the SOEs for free: there was no pricing nor were there any charges. After the onset of the reforms, however, the state began to lease out land to the users. Under current law, rural land belongs to the rural collectives, while the state owned urban land. In many places, local governments acquired land from the rural collectives at low prices and then leased it to users. The immense price spreads were the primary source of revenue for many local governments, giving birth to "land-transfer–dependent government finance." To a large extent, local government officials could arbitrarily decide whether to lease land lots, how many plots should be leased, and at what prices. Well-connected people received the best-located lots at low prices and then turned them over to other users at inflated prices that were several to dozens of times higher than the original prices. Even parties involved in the second, third, and fourth turnovers could reap substantial profits. Moreover, if these individuals could secure loans from state-owned banks at negative real interest rates, such transactions would be transformed into a zero-capital but highly profitable business.

In the early 1990s, several municipalities experienced a surge in real estate speculation, encouraged or directed by the local governments. Corrupt officials and unscrupulous businesspeople amassed significant wealth. But such good days did not last long for them. Starting with the macroeconomic tightening in 1993, the central government began to strictly enforce regulatory actions in the financial sector, and it intensified efforts to counter corruption in local government land leasing deals. Several medium-sized cities that had attracted attention for their land-leasing deals and real estate speculation saw housing prices plummet. Many Party and government land management officials were found to be corrupt and hence were punished, but it took a full decade for the housing market in these cities to recover.

China saw an urbanization boom at the turn of the twenty-first century. During the countrywide urbanization movement, the dual-track system led to substantial price spreads between land acquisition and land leasing, which became an essential source of local government revenue. Unfortunately, this also provided a convenient way for corrupt officials to embezzle public wealth. End-2002 and early 2003 was a time for a new generation of leaders to take office. Thereafter, many new local leaders devised grandiose plans to build image-boosting and political showcase projects. As a result, an unprecedented upsurge in investment occurred. The so-called "red-hat businessmen" who were well-connected with the powerful made windfall profits from such government projects. This led to numerous land-transaction–related corruption cases, many involving huge sums of money and numerous senior officials.

---

[16] Huang Yikun, "Madness in Sanlihe," *Caijing*, December 22, 2008.

During the heavy and chemical industrialization drive and the "building new and bigger cities" campaign in the early twenty-first century, the spread in land transaction prices generated trillions of RMB in government revenue, providing enormous opportunities for rent-seeking. Many officials in charge of land management and investment embezzled hundreds of millions of RMB in public funding. It was not rare for provincial-level officials, their predecessors, and their successors to be sentenced for corruption. For instance, from 1989 to 2010, four Party secretaries and general directors of the Transportation Bureau of the Henan Provincial Government received heavy sentences for corruption-related crimes. (One official was imprisoned for 15 years, and the other three were sentenced to life imprisonment.)

Another source of corruption in the early twenty-first century was rent-seeking within the capital markets.

When the capital markets were opened in China, two different propositions or policy lines were put forward about regulating the issuance of securities. The first view favored administrative reviews, and the second advocated mandatory disclosures. The reform in the early twenty-first century aimed to gradually transition from a substantive review regime to a registration regime based on information disclosures. But this was a struggling, stop-and-go process. Years later, securities regulatory authorities were still conducting substantive reviews for new issuances. In addition, they were providing "window guidance" on issue prices and frequencies. New issues were often suspended to maintain "market stability," and some companies were "persuaded" to withdraw their applications—all these added listing costs and uncertainties. Stock issuance reviews also had to "coordinate" with the selective industrial policies. The "check and permit regime" in place since 2000 became essentially the same as the previous "review and approval regime." The Shanghai and Shenzhen stock exchanges, as the primary-board markets, remained the venue for siphoning funds and rent-seeking. On the Growth Enterprise Market (GEM), also known as the second-board market, which had been launched in 2009, well-connected individuals rushed to purchase shares of firms before stock issuances had been applied for. They then profited substantially from the high issue prices, elevated price-to-earnings ratios, and large quantities of IPOs, earning hundreds of millions of RMB. Thereafter, the performance of the listed companies deteriorated, with their stocks dropping below the issue prices. Some of the issuers cashed out and even fled abroad.

From a political perspective, as demonstrated in previous chapters, conservative forces supporting the old political line and system would resurface at critical moments during the reform process, attempting to advocate a reversal. At the beginning of the twenty-first century, the general public grew increasingly resentful of the rampant corruption and the widening gap between the rich and the poor, both of which were exacerbated by the insufficient reform progress and the persistent systemic flaws. The conservative forces utilized this public resentment to attack the market-oriented reforms.

In 2003, Ma Bing, who had served as a deputy general director of the State Council Development and Research Center, circulated among his followers a write-up entitled "Miscellaneous Notes." The write-up claimed that Deng Xiaoping's criticism of the policy of "taking class struggle as the key link" had betrayed Marxist doctrine as well as Lenin's theory of continuous revolution under proletarian dictatorship. Hence, Ma called for a pushback.[17] After the opponents of the market-oriented reform consolidated their thoughts, a book entitled *The Path in Deng Xiaoping's Late Years* appeared on several leftist websites, systematically criticizing the reform and opening policy[18] and claiming that "the reform has completed and institutionalized privatization, Westernization, corruption, and a polarization of wealth."[19]

The opponents of the market-oriented reform blamed the reform for a so-called erroneous "revisionist line." They argued that reform in the economic arena had "accelerated privatization … [with] the central leadership actively calling for greater efforts to develop the non-public economy. … In recent years, the '*zhuada fangxiao*' policy to hold on to large firms and to let go of small firms has caused grievous problems." In the political arena, the reform was criticized for "continuous implementation of [bourgeois] liberalization … having abandoned the Marxist theories of class struggle and betraying the proletarian dictatorship. … In the last two years, the central leadership has come up with several perplexing slogans and propositions that lack a class identity and revolutionary characteristics, such as '*yiren weiben*' [taking people's interests as the starting point], 'peaceful rise,' 'harmonious society,' and 'well-off society.'" In foreign affairs, the opponents believed that "a policy of capitulation and compromise has been implemented. … Regarding the national democratic revolutions and the struggle against world imperialism …, instead of supporting them, we have smeared these revolutionary movements as 'terrorist organizations,' following in the footprints of imperialism."[20]

These individuals advocated a complete overhaul of the reform and opening policy, calling for re-nationalization and re-collectivization. "In the urban areas, all public properties privatized during the reform should be taken back and become whole-people-owned. In the rural areas, policy should be to nationalize land ownership, collectivize labor, and socialize lifestyles." Politically, these people called for raising the banner of class struggle and continuing the revolution under the dictatorship of the proletariat, and rehabilitating Jiang Qing, Zhang Chunqiao, Yao Wenyuan, and Wang Hongwen [the Gang of Four]. They favored launching a "Great Proletarian Cultural Revolution" once every seven or eight years. They believed in "an all-round dictatorship over the bourgeoise both within and outside the Party."[21]

The reform and opening supporters came down firmly against these anti-reform agitators. Top Party and government leaders made their attitudes public in early 2006. In discussions of the Shanghai delegation to the National People's Congress

---

[17] Ma Bing, "Only Mao Tse-Tung Thought Can Save China," *In Memory of Mao Tse Tung (White Paper)*, p. 59.

[18] Shui Luzhou, *The Path in Deng Xiaoping's Late Years*, in *China and the World*, 2006, www.zgysj.com.

[19] Ma Bing, "The Situation and the Task: We Should Seriously Consider Them and Pay Attention to the Big Picture," *In Memory of Mao Tse Tung (White Paper)*, p. 180.

[20] Ma Bing, "The Current Situation and Recommendations," 2005, in *On the Current Situation and Tasks (White Paper)*, pp. 59–64.

[21] Ma Bing, "Continuous Revolution," *In Memory of Mao Tse Tung (White Paper)*, pp. 1–2.

in March 2006 and in the Report to the 17th Party Congress on behalf of the 16th Party Central Committee in October 2007, Hu Jintao reiterated that China "should unswervingly uphold the direction of the reform, continuously improve the socialist market-economy system, and bring into full play the market's fundamental role in resource allocations. The reform responds to the wishes of the Party and the people and aligns with the times. The direction and path are correct, and the effects and achievements of the reforms should not be negated. Halting or backtracking the reform is a dead-end."

After the 17th Party Congress, the reform opponents changed their tactics. Instead of attacking the Party and government leadership, they assaulted private businessmen, the so-called "neo-liberal economists," and "public intellectuals" who supported the reforms. Meanwhile, they also continued smearing the reforms by taking advantage of their ideological influence.

In various speeches and reports in 2004, Professor Lang Xianping (Larry Hsien Ping Lang) alleged that several famous private-sector enterprises had stolen state assets during the transformation of the small- and medium-sized SOES.[22] He also negated the entire ongoing SOE reform, arguing that "SOE profits are not lower than those in the private sector. … China should immediately end the SOE property rights reform. … The future path should be big government, centralization, government as the driving force, and industrial consolidation."[23]

Many economists who had studied China's reforms refuted Professor Lang's allegations. They pointed out that the problems in the SOE reforms had been due to institutional defects and to a lack of constraints on the power of government officials. Denying the necessity of reform because of the existing problems was akin to "stopping eating for fear of choking," which would ultimately lead to adverse outcomes.[24]

People against the SOE property rights reform in particular, and the market-oriented reforms in general, launched a vigorous campaign defending Professor Lang. First, ten economics professors jointly issued an "academic statement" expressing solidarity with Lang.[25] Several research institutes and websites then criticized the

---

[22] Lang Xianping, "Questions About TCL's Property Rights Reform Plan," "Haier Zhongjian Is an Indirect Path to an MBO," "Exuberant Greencool Holdings in the '*Guojin Mintui*' Carnival," "A Critique of the Dominant Neoliberal School in China's Property Rights Reform," https://business.sohu.com, June 17, August 2, 16, and 29, 2004.

[23] Lang Xianping, "China Should Immediately End the SOE Property Rights Reform," www.ifeng.com, August 27, 2004.

[24] Han Chaohua, "Has Lang Xianping Hit the Nail on the Head?" https://business.sohu.com, September 6, 2004; Zhang Wenkui, "My Fundamental Differences with Lang Xianping," *International Financial News*, September 3, 2004.

[25] Cheng Enfu, Ding Bing, et al., "An Academic Statement on Professor Lang Xianping's Questions on the Trendy Property Rights Theories and the Embezzlement of State Assets," https://finance.sina.com.cn, September 15, 2004.

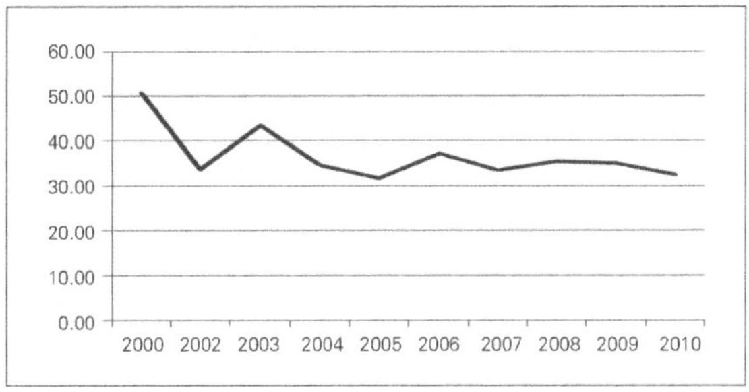

Fig. 11.1 China: changes in the control of corruption (%). *Source* The World Bank

neoliberal views about reform and opening. In addition to these informal denunciations, there were also officially organized criticisms of neoliberalism and the Washington Consensus.[26] Finally, nongovernmental and governmental forces converged to oppose the market-oriented reforms and to strengthen the government's driving role to harness[27] and control over the market.

As demonstrated above, interference in microeconomic activities by the official powers established the institutional foundation for corruption. Efforts to curb corruption by increasing government control over the market only served to entrench this institutional foundation.

11.3 Corruption Spreading Throughout the Society

The expansion of the institutional basis for rent-seeking led to a rapid spread of corruption.

Based on the World Bank's Control of Corruption Indicator,[28] corruption in China worsened noticeably after 2000 (Fig. 11.1).

Rampant corruption in the early twenty-first century can be measured by three dimensions.

First, the scale of corruption expanded sharply. According to "Gray Incomes and the National Income Distribution Report, 2013," compiled by the Income Distribution Task Team of the China Society of Economic Reform,[29] beginning in the

[26] See CASS Neoliberalism Task Team, *Assessment of Neoliberalism* (Beijing: Social Sciences Academic Press, 2004).

[27] The Report to the 16th CPC National Congress, "Build A Well-Off Society in An All-Round Way and Create A New Situation in Building Socialism with Chinese Characteristics," states that all Party committees and leaders should "continuously enhance their capability to harness the market economy."

[28] The Control of Corruption Indicator is one of six worldwide governance indicators (WGI) published by the World Bank. The indicator is a percentage: the smaller the value, the lower the strength of governance or the higher the level of corruption.

[29] Wang Xiaolu, "Gray Incomes and the National Income Distribution Report, 2013," *Comparative Studies*, no. 5 (2013).

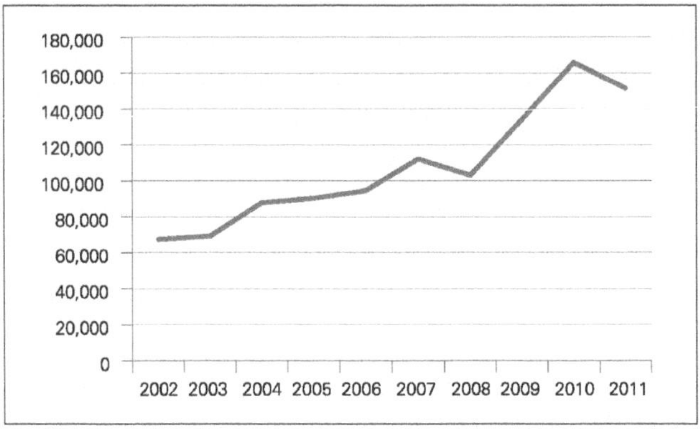

Fig. 11.2 China: illicit capital outflows (2002–11, USD million). *Source* Estimates based on Data from Dev Kar and Brian LeBlanc (2013): "Illicit Financial Flows from Developing Countries: 2002–2011

Table 11.2 Household disposable income and gray income (RMB trillion)

	2005	**2008**	**2011**
1. Household income (National Bureau of Statistics Flow of Funds Matrix)	11.29	18.59	28.50
2. Household income (Estimates by the Income Distribution Task Team)	13.73	23.24	34.74
3. Gray income (2–1)	2.44	4.65	6.24
4. GDP (Estimates by the Income Distribution Task Team)	19.95	34.19	51.03
5. Household income/GDP (Estimates by the Income Distribution Task Team, 2/4)	68.8%	68.0%	68.1%
6. Gray income/GDP (Estimates by the Income Distribution Task Team, 3/4)	12.2%	13.6%	12.2%

Sources National Bureau of Statistics; Wang Xiaolu team estimates

early twenty-first century, household gray income based on unknown sources[30] was growing faster than GDP. Total household gray income was estimated at RMB 2.44 trillion in 2005, RMB 4.65 trillion in 2008, and RMB 6.24 trillion in 2011 (see Table 11.2).

[30] Gray incomes refer to incomes without clearly identified sources that are not included in the official statistics. There are different views about whether gray incomes are mainly due to rent-seeking activities and corruption. Wang Xiaolu, in "Gray Incomes and the National Income Distribution Report, 2013," contends that "gray incomes mainly come from corruption, power for money deals, monopolies, and rent-seeking through institutional loopholes." Luo Chuliang, Yue Ximing, and Li Shi, in "Another Comment on Gray Incomes by Wang Xiaolu," *Comparative Studies*, no. 2 (2012), point out that Wang Xiaolu's data show the bottom income group also had gray income, weakening his argument that gray income mainly comes from corruption and rent-seeking.

Part of the vast wealth gained through corruption went abroad. According to various research reports, Illicit capital outflows rose from tens of billions of USD in the early twenty-first century to hundreds of billions of USD per annum in more recent years. For example, a report by Standard Chartered Bank reveals that the value of illicit capital outflows to casinos in Macao and from there to various places around the world reached USD 185 billion (the equivalent of RMB 1.2 trillion), an increase of 43 percent from 2010 and at least a doubling from 2008.[31] Global Financial Integrity found that in the ten years from 2002 to 2011, illicit capital outflows from mainland China due to tax evasion, corruption, and criminal activities totaled USD 1.075 trillion, ranking number one globally. In 2011 alone, illicit capital outflows reached USD 151.3 billion.[32]

Second, the number of people involved in corruption rose dramatically. This measurement increased in tandem with the expansion of the institutional base for rent-seeking. In 2010, *People's Tribune*, a journal under *People's Daily* (the mouthpiece of the CCP Central Committee), organized a cover feature discussion on the nouveau riche. The journal's commentary highlights that, according to a relevant organization's report, "China's 3000 Richest Families in 2009," the wealth of these families amounted to RMB 1,696.3 billion, or RMB 565.4 million per family. The list includes ten thousand families whose combined wealth totals RMB 2,105.7 billion, with an average of RMB 200 million per family." The commentary points out that with their deep political and funding connections, these "red families," the main source of the wealthiest families, enjoy a high starting point and can quickly amass social resources. In a survey organized by the journal, the top response (75.56 percent) to the question "What are the main factors affecting the image of the nouveau-riche families" is "the power-for-money deals between government officials and businessmen."

According to the White Paper, "New Progress in the Judicial Protection of Human Rights in China," issued by the State Council Information Office on September 12, 2016, in the four years from 2012 to 2015, courts at various levels concluded 94,900 cases of corruption and bribery and they sentenced 100,200 criminals.

Third, corruption crept into Party, government, and military organizations and spread to the top agencies. Corruption in the economic field inevitably led to political corruption. Since unchecked administrative powers possess a strong allure for creating wealth, there will inevitably be those willing to pay a high price to acquire it. In the mid-1990s, people began to buy and sell official positions in Party and government agencies, and this phenomenon became widespread and commonplace by the beginning of the twenty-first century. In 2005 an outrageous money-for-official-position case occurred, involving Han Guizhi (deputy provincial Party secretary of Heilongjiang province) and Ma De (municipal Party secretary of Suihua

---

[31] Wang Zhihao (Stephen Green), "China: Warm Money, Hot Money, and Red-Hot Money," Standard Chartered Global Research, December 28, 2011, retrieved from Wang Xiaolu, "Gray Incomes and the National Income Distribution Report, 2013."

[32] Dev Kar and Brian LeBlanc, "Illicit Financial Flows from Developing Countries: 2002–2011," (2013), http://iff.gfintegrity.org/iff2013/2013report.html.

city in Heilongjiang province). More than 900 people were implicated, including several provincial-level officials and more than 100 prefectural-level officials. This was "the largest money-for-official-position case since the establishment of the People's Republic." But corruption became more severe, as revealed during the anti-corruption movement initiated by the 18th Party Congress in 2012. The corruption cases involving many people, found in Party, government, and military organizations at the national, provincial, and lower levels, were called "nest (clique) cases." Among senior officials sentenced for corruption, there was a Politburo member, a vice chairman of the Party Central Military Commission, and even a member of the Politburo Standing Committee. The extent of corruption was shocking.

In this context, a series of provincial vote-buying cases occurred, the first ever such high-level cases in the history of the People's Republic.

In Liaoning province, large-scale, illegal vote-buying activities took place during the election of members to the Provincial Party Standing Committee in 2011, and during the election of members to the Provincial People's Congress Standing Committee and the election of provincial delegates to the National People's Congress in 2013. "After the case was exposed in 2016, it was found that among the 102 deputies elected to the National People's Congress from Liaoning province in 2013, 45 had their qualifications revoked due to involvement in bribery, accounting for 44.1 percent. Among the 619 deputies elected to the Provincial People's Congress in the same year, 523 were involved in bribery scandals, accounting for 84.5 percent. Of the 62 members of the Provincial People's Congress Standing Committee, 38 had their qualifications revoked, representing 61.3 percent, leaving less than half of the Standing Committee members in office and thus rendering that term of the Provincial People's Congress Standing Committee unable to perform its functions.[33]

11.4 The Widening Gap between Rich and Poor and the Threat of Crony Capitalism

The bogged-down reforms and the macroeconomic policy mistakes led to a severe social consequence: the accelerated polarization of wealth. The problems discussed in the previous chapters, such as the monetary expansion, inflation, and delays in establishing a social security safety net, enlarged the gaps in household incomes. Moreover, the spread of corruption allowed corrupt officials who controlled the allocation of resources and people with rent-seeking channels to plunder the general public, quickly accumulating an enormous amount of personal wealth and becoming billionaires.

As noted in a previous chapter, a survey by the People's University in 1995 reveals that China's household income Gini coefficient reached 0.46 in 1994, exceeding

[33] "The Political and Business Ecosystem as Shown by the Vote-Buying Cases during the Liaoning Provincial People's Congress Election," *Anbang Consulting Daily Economics*, no. 5297, September 20, 2016.

the widely accepted cutoff value of 0.40.[34] According to two household surveys conducted by the Income Distribution Task Team under the Institute of Economics of the Chinese Academy of Social Sciences, the Gini coefficient was 0.382 in 1988, but by 1995 it had risen to 0.452.[35] According to the World Bank's 2006 *World Development Report: Equity and Development*, the Gini coefficient for Chinese residents' income had risen from 0.16 prior to the reform and opening to 0.45 in 2001.[36]

Before the reform and opening, poverty was widespread in China, but it was still not an equal society. The widening gap among hierarchical levels in terms of monetary distribution and in-kind benefits strengthened the bureaucratic system and elevated the benefits for a very small number of people.[37]

In the early 1980s, after the onset of the reform and opening, Deng Xiaoping said, "Let some people get rich first."[38] The policy was intended to allow hardworking people and those knowing how to run businesses to get rich first. Under the premise that everyone could enjoy a decent standard of living, income differences arising from varying abilities and opportunities were considered normal.

What was abnormal is the following. On the one hand, corrupt officials who controlled resource allocations and people with channels for rent-seeking became rich overnight because of their power. On the other hand, working people, including SOE employees and especially ordinary farmers, received limited benefits from the reforms, and their lives did not improve significantly. In the worst cases, their basic livelihoods could not be secured due to a lack of social security. Furthermore, inflation devalued the incomes of wage earners who lived from hand to mouth. Skyrocketing prices of goods and assets, like stocks and real estate, did not hurt the financial market manipulators and those with political backing; instead, such skyrocketing prices provided good opportunities for those people to get rich. Employees in monopolized sectors could easily secure high incomes due to their special market status. All these factors exacerbated the wealth gap caused by unequal opportunities.

[34] Li Qiang, "Analysis of the Gaps between Different Income Groups in China," *Kexue daobao*, no. 8 (1995).

[35] Zhao Renwei and Keith Griffin, comps., *A Study of China's Household Income Distribution* (Beijing: Social Sciences Academic Press, 1994); Zhao Renwei, Li Shi, and Carl Riskin, *A Second Study on China's Household Income Distribution* (Beijing: China Financial and Economic Publishing House, 1999).

[36] World Bank, "World Development Report 2006: Equity and Development" (Chinese translation. Beijing: Tsinghua University Press, 2006).

[37] Yang Kuisong, "From an In-Kind Provision System to a Graded Salary System: Evolution of Income Distribution for Party and Government Officials Before and After the Establishment of New China," *Historical Research*, no. 4 (2007).

[38] "We should allow some people to get rich first in the rural and urban areas. Becoming rich through hard work is legitimate. This new approach has received widespread support, i.e., to let some people get rich first, and to let some regions become prosperous ahead of others. The new approach is better than the old way." See Deng Xiaoping, "All Tasks Should be Conducive to Building Socialism with Chinese Characteristics," 1983, *Selected Works of Deng Xiaoping*, vol. 3, p. 23.

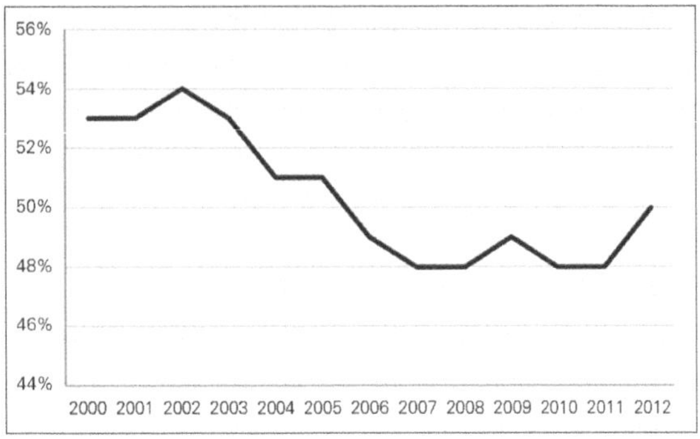

Fig. 11.3 Share of Worker Remuneration in National Income Since 2000 *Source* NDRC, Beijing Normal University

According to the National Bureau of Statistics (NBS), the share of labor compensation in national income decreased from 2003 to 2010 (Fig. 11.3).[39]

When addressing the issue of equality, it is essential to distinguish between inequality of opportunity and inequality of outcome. Under current conditions in China, the primary focus should be on opposing and eliminating inequality of opportunity. Inequality of outcome has dual consequences: on the one hand, it can stimulate labor and business activity, thereby increasing efficiency; on the other hand, however, for individuals with congenital disabilities, the government must assume responsibility by establishing a social security system that ensures basic welfare for low-income groups, creating an effective "safety net" for residents. Unlike inequality of outcome, inequality of opportunity distorts the allocation of resources under competitive conditions, leading to misallocations and negatively impacting efficiency. Eliminating inequality of opportunity is positively, rather than negatively, correlated with improved efficiency. Achieving equal opportunities will benefit efficiency rather than harm it.[40]

In China, the gulf between the rich and the poor exceeded the cutoff line in the 1990s, and it further expanded in the early twenty-first century due to severe inequality of opportunity and rent-seeking activities by those connected with power.

Beginning in the late 1980s, the rich-poor polarization worsened rapidly. According to the NBS, the Gini coefficient of household incomes was around 0.3 in the early 1980s, but it rose to 0.479 in 2003 and it reached 0.491 in 2008. The coefficient decreased after 2008, but it was still as high as 0.474 in 2012 (Fig. 11.4).

According to income disparity indicators based on data from the NBS, in 2011 the ratio of per capita disposable income between the top 10 percent highest-income households and the bottom 10 percent lowest-income households in urban and rural

[39] Department of Employment and Income Distribution, NDRC and China Institute for Income Distribution, Beijing Normal University, *Annual Report on Household Income Distribution (2014)* (Beijing: China Financial and Economic Publishing House, 2014), p. 5.

[40] Wu Jinglian, "Appropriately Handling the Excessive Income Gaps," *China Economic Times*, July 5, 2006; Wu Jinglian, "There Must Be a Due Date for Equality of Opportunity," *Caijing*, no. 2 (2005).

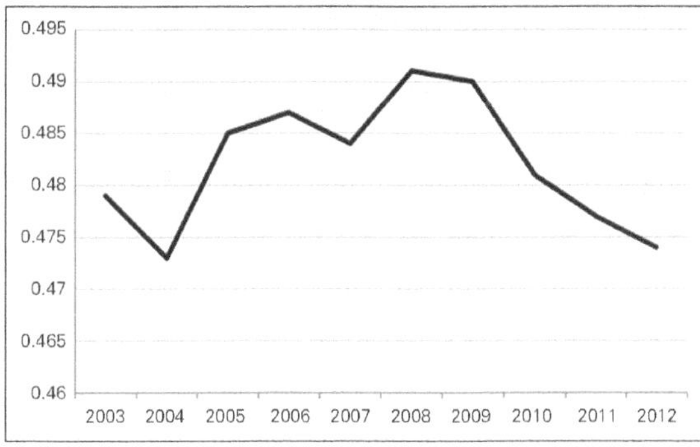

Fig. 11.4 Changes in China's Gini coefficient, 2003–12. *Sources* NDRC; Beijing Normal University

areas was 23.6, exceeding that in all developed countries as well as that in most developing countries. Estimates by Wang Xiaolu from the National Economic Research Institute of the China Economic Reform Foundation suggest that this disposable income differential was as high as 67.0.[41]

Closer attention should be paid to the pace of the widening gulf in family wealth during the last ten years, which far exceeded the speed of the widening income gap. According to the China Family Panel Studies of the Institute of Social Science Survey, Peking University, the Gini coefficient of net family wealth was 0.45 in 1995, rising to 0.55 in 2002 and reaching 0.73 in 2012. In 2012, the top 1 percent of households owned 34.6 percent of the nation's wealth, while the bottom 25 percent of households owned only 1.2 percent. The continuous expansion of the gap between the rich and the poor will inevitably cause severe social tensions, thereby threatening social stability.[42]

In *The Rise and Decline of Nations*, American economist Mancur Olson introduces and thoroughly analyzes the concept of special interest groups. He argues that these groups, which represent only a small segment of the population, are essentially parasitic "rent-seeking coalitions." Their focus is not on competition but on dividing up resources, disregarding the enormous damage their actions may inflict on the society as a whole, with the sole aim of reaping profits for themselves.[43] Today, enlightened people are deeply concerned about the influence of such special interest groups in China. If this problem is not resolved, people will have no "sense of gain" or sense of security, regardless of how high the economic growth rate may be. Unfair growth might even become a catalyst for social unrest.

During China's reform process, the special interest groups in the society were constantly being reshuffled. New interest bodies, classes, and groups continued to emerge. Some people took advantage of the vast powers of government officials to allocate resources, and they colluded with these officials to become overnight

---

[41] Wang Xiaolu, "Gray Incomes and the National Income Distribution Report, 2013."

[42] https://www.isss.pku.edu.cn/cfps/en/index.htm.

[43] Mancur Olson, *The Rise and Decline of Nations,* 1982 (Chinese translation by Lu Yingzhong. Beijing: Commercial Press, 1999), p. 52.

billionaires. Meanwhile, the general public was resentful of the market-oriented reforms because they felt exploited and mistreated. It is safe to say that it was the lag in political reforms that gave rise to these special interest groups, which have since become an enormous obstacle to social and economic reforms.

China's "semi-market, semi-command" economy that had come into being by the end of the twentieth century is a transitional economy composed of two systems. It may advance to a sound market economy or it may return to the old command economy. If various reforms are obstructed, the tendency for state capitalism to return will become increasingly likely.

State capitalism refers to a set of market-controlling political and economic institutions formed through competition between state capital, which relies on its political power, and other capital types. In China's historical context, where democracy and the rule of law are lacking, state capitalism is highly likely to evolve into crony or bureaucratic capitalism, which was described by Mao Zedong as "feudal, comprador, state monopoly capitalism." Without firm economic and political reforms to redirect this trajectory back to a market-oriented, rule-of-law, and democratic path, such a system risks becoming entrenched. Once a path is locked in, as Douglass North suggests, it will be difficult to deviate from it without significant social upheaval.[44]

[44] Douglass C. North, *Institutions, Institutional Change and Economic Performance,* 1990 (Chinese translation by Hang Xing and reviewed by Wei Seng. Shanghai: Gezhi Publishing House, 2014); Wu Jinglian, "Path Dependence and Chinese Reform," 1995, in *Where to Seek Great Wisdom* (Beijing: SDX Joint Publishing, 1997), pp. 351–358.

Chapter 12
Only a Comprehensive Deepening of the Reforms Will Ensure a Bright Future

During the first decade of the twenty-first century, China faced the increasingly severe situation of outstanding achievements but apparent defects in social development under its transitional system. This triggered intense debates in which two opposing assessments of the situation were presented, leading to sharply divergent policy recommendations for the future.

When the debates first began, the proponents of the so-called "China model," i.e., high economic growth driven by an assertive government, held the upper hand. By their own description, a primary characteristic of the China model was a strong government guiding market activities and driving economic growth. They believed that this model would be copied by other countries and become a beacon for world development. However, further into the debate, an increasing number of people, as they examined the facts, began to take an opposite view. They came to realize that during the first thirty years of the People's Republic, overall development had been slow under the control of the dominant government; in contrast, the reform and opening, beginning at the end of the 1970s, had greatly motivated the general public, releasing their creativity and resulting in high annual economic growth of nearly 10%. They pointed out that in recent years, pauses in the reform trajectory had caused worsening developmental imbalances, a lack of coordination, unsustainability, and aggravated social tensions. Therefore, according to their thinking, the only way out was to restart the reforms and to accelerate the development of a uniform, open, competitive, and orderly market and to expand the rule of law to maintain fairness and justice in the country.

In November 2012, the 18th Party Congress, conforming with the will of the people, adopted a decision to comprehensively deepen the reforms. During the following two years, the Third and the Fourth Plenary Sessions of the 18th Party Central Committee adopted a top-down design and an overall plan to establish a uniform, open, competitive, and orderly market economy and to develop the country based on rule of law.

W. Jinglian, *China's Economic Reform*, Understanding China,
https://doi.org/10.1007/978-981-96-9607-9_12

China's next task was to overcome the strong resistance and formidable obstacles to implementing the comprehensive deepening of reform. Whether this can be achieved will determine both China's fate and its future.

12.1 Two Different Assessments and Opposing Policy Proposals

The previous chapters have analyzed China's tremendous achievements driven by reforms. In addition, the chapters have discussed the pauses in the reform process during the early twenty-first century due to opposition from both old and new vested interest groups, thereby increasing social and economic tensions.

There were sharply different assessments about the co-existence of the outstanding achievements and the conspicuous drawbacks to the reforms thus far. One group believed that the triumphs and the difficulties were due to progress, or the lack thereof, in carrying through with the reforms. On the one hand, the market-oriented reforms empowered the rise of the Chinese economy. On the other, the slowing down and pauses in the reform process, and the legacies of the old system, e.g., continuous state dominance in resource allocations and widespread interference in microeconomic activities, hindered transformation of the growth mode and the containment of corruption, leading to worsening problems. In contrast, the opposing view suggested that the market-oriented reforms had been the root cause of all the social problems, and China had still been able to make astonishing achievements only because it had a solid and robust authoritarian government that had a strong capability to mobilize resources and exert social controls. As a result, the government could "concentrate resources on big things" to achieve high GDP growth. Proponents called this economic development mode with command economy characteristics the "China model."

In the early twenty-first century, the latter view that advocated a dominant government, massive investments, and high economic growth prevailed in public forums. Under these circumstances, the previous mainstream position calling for the primary role of the market in resource allocations, which was criticized as neoliberalism, was abandoned.

At first, the China model was presented as the "Beijing Consensus," the opposite of the Washington Consensus that was based on a free-market doctrine.[1] Criticism

[1] In 1990, the Peterson Institute for International Economics sponsored a seminar in Washington, DC, with participants from the International Monetary Fund, the World Bank, the U.S. Treasury Department, and representatives of some Latin American countries. The focus of the discussions was on addressing the severe inflation and debt crises in the Latin American countries and exploring ideas for economic reform. British economist John Williamson, summarizing the discussions in ten policy prescriptions, called these prescriptions the "Washington Consensus." They included: (1) strengthening fiscal discipline and avoiding excessive budget deficits; (2) redirecting public expenditures from subsidies to pro-growth and pro-poor services, such as primary education, primary healthcare, and investments in infrastructure; (3) expanding the tax base and reducing the marginal

of neoliberalism and the Washington Consensus surged in China in multiple waves.[2] Meanwhile, Joshua Cooper Ramo, director in the office of John Thornton[3] of the Brookings Institution (an American think-tank), published a lengthy report titled "The Beijing Consensus" in May 2004. Ramo, who later would become a vice chairman and co-chief executive officer of Kissinger Associates, found that some countries had cast aside the Washington Consensus because of the high social and economic costs. Ramo's report indicated that China was the sole country to present an alternative model that could be emulated by the rest of the world. According to Ramo, China was forging a new development path toward prosperity known as the Beijing Consensus. This approach emphasizes driving change through innovation and experimentation, prioritizing improving the people's livelihoods, and safeguarding national sovereignty with an asymmetric defense strategy. Ramo pointed out that China was becoming a challenge to the United States because of its increasing strength and because of Beijing Consensus' appeal to the rest of the world.

As soon as it appeared, the Beijing Consensus was highly appreciated both within and outside of China. However, Ramo's description of China's development path under the Beijing Consensus was too abstract and generalized, often based on half-baked knowledge about what had really transpired. This gave birth to a more localized proposition about the "China model." In contrast to the view that reform and opening drove China's rapid economic growth, advocates of the China model attributed China's economic rise to the country's unique institutional model. They maintained that the model was worthy of being copied by other countries, particularly by the developing countries. According to this view, the main characteristics and strengths of this model were its "strong government" and "government-driven development."

Professor Zhang Weiwei of the Geneva School of Diplomacy and International Relations was an influential advocate of the China model. In his *China Shock Trilogy*, he writes that the Great Unity ("da yitong") political system had prevailed in China ever since the Qin and Han dynasties. In other words, "The dynasties following the Qin all adopted the Qin's political and legal systems." This legacy of a strong and active government lives on in contemporary China today. According to Professor Zhang, China succeeded in reform because "government authority evolving throughout history and the political party's authority formed over its long revolutionary period are used to promote China's modernization, to organize and implement the reform measures, and to coordinate the contradictions during the reform process. ... Government mobilization, persuasion, and guidance have significantly

---

tax rates; (4) letting the market set interest rates and maintaining low positive rates; (5) liberalizing the foreign exchange regime; (6) liberalizing trade; (7) removing restrictions on foreign direct investments; (8) privatizing the SOEs; (9) reducing government controls and abolishing regulations that obstruct market entry and competition; and (10) ensuring legal protection of property rights.

[2] He Bingmeng, "Neoliberalism and Its Essence: A Dialogue about Neoliberalism," *Journal of Chinese Social Sciences*, November 13, 2003.

[3] John Thornton, an American lawyer, had served as co-CEO of Goldman Sachs International, chairman of Goldman Sachs Asia, and chairman of the Board of Trustees at the Brookings Institution. After retiring from Goldman Sachs in 2003, Thornton became an adjunct professor at Tsinghua University in Beijing and set up the Thornton China Center at the Brookings Institution.

reduced the costs of solving complex problems. … China has also developed a 'macro-consolidation capability.' This capability is based on state control of land, the financial sector, and the large backbone enterprises. It is comprised of concentrating resources on big things and making macroeconomic adjustments. Such a capability also includes promoting the leapfrog advance of the private sector in development. … The combining of this macro-consolidation capability with market mechanisms has resulted in the world's most extensive urbanization, largest real estate market, most extensive high-speed train network, and second-longest highway network. The rate of homeownership rate in China is higher than that in the developed countries, and housing conditions for most farmers have significantly improved. … In this super-large country, the central government provides macro guidance and maintains stability and balance, while the local governments use tax revenue, land, and policy resources to attract investments and to increase local employment, income, and social prosperity. All these features contributed to the country's rapid rise. It can be said that both the central authorities and the local governments are the engines behind China's economic development. … Today, China has the world's strongest administrative capability, as evidenced by its success in holding the Olympics and the World Expo and its response to the financial tsunami. … [In the future, China will] continue to improve its system, and it will eventually exceed the Western model in all dimensions, just like Shanghai surpassing New York today."[4]

Advocates of the China model often cited Chongqing municipality as evidence of the government's magic power. At the time, Bo Xilai, CCP Politburo member who was later sentenced to life in prison for bribery, corruption, and abuse of power, had been Party chief of the municipality, and Chongqing's political and economic performance was called the "Chongqing miracle."[5]

For instance, after a field trip to Chongqing in 2011, Zhang Weiwei published an article in *Hongqi wengao*, a semi-monthly publication put out by *Qiushi* magazine (a journal under the CCP Central Committee). In his article, Zhang claims, "I have stated several times that China is exploring a political, economic, and social system that will surpass the Western model. …. Chongqing's exploration has formed a comprehensive set of practices in broad areas. … Chongqing is a place of miracles because the leader is tackling the big things with far-sightedness and courage, and he has a well-thought out, feasible plan, and the ability to implement the relevant policies."[6]

When Bo Xilai still held power over the life and death of the people in Chongqing, several serious scholars, based on detailed evidence collected from meticulous studies, exposed the secret of the so-called Chongqing miracle.

---

[4] Zhang Weiwei, *China's Shock* (Shanghai: Shanghai People's Publishing House, 2011); Zhang Weiwei, *China's Impact* (Shanghai: Shanghai People's Publishing House, 2012); *and China's Leap* (Shanghai: Shanghai People's Publishing House, 2014).

[5] Zhang Weiwei, "Observations from a Visit to Chongqing," *Hongqi wengao*, no. 2 (2012).

[6] Tong Zhiwei, "Research Report on Chongqing's Anti-Crime Social Management Model," in *Collection of Papers Presented to the Association of Constitutional Law Meetings*, vol. 2, October 22, 2011.

But in March 2012, Bo Xilai was removed from his position as Party secretary of Chongqing municipality, and in April, his membership on the Party Central Committee as well as on the Politburo was suspended. In October of that year, the Supreme People's Procuratorate launched an investigation into his activities, and his dirty secrets were slowly revealed.

The state apparatus controlled by Bo Xilai and other Party and government officials in Chongqing had created a chilling effect through the so-called gangland crackdowns. People no longer dared to openly criticize public affairs because they feared criminal allegations or other punishments by either the authorities or those holding power.

During the crackdowns, Chongqing Municipal Government confiscated the property of private enterprises and entrepreneurs under the guise of fighting organized crime. According to a *Chongqing Daily* report in September 2010, the municipal government destroyed 14 criminal organizations, investigated 364 gangs involved in organized crime, and seized RMB 2.9 billion in associated assets. But the actions by the Public Security Bureau, which led to the confiscation and seizure of the involved assets, lacked external oversight. During the execution phase of these actions, the Public Security Bureau effectively replaced the courts in leading the criminal enforcement of property assets. According to an interview in *Caijing* magazine with lawyers representing the involved entrepreneurs, before the final verdict, the implicated individuals, fearing for their lives, dared not claim their property rights. After the final verdicts, they were unsure how to assert these rights. In addition, which parts of their assets were connected to criminal activities and which parts were unrelated became a blurred issue. How the relevant assets were handled by the Chongqing Public Security Bureau was almost "impenetrable," leaving the involved parties with no way of knowing the full details.

In the spring of 2012, the fallacy in the China model were exposed, and the so-called Chongqing miracle was debunked politically. The atmosphere once again began to warm up for reform as an increasing number of people sought to return to the reform agenda. Many pointed out that instead of being confined to economic reforms, the next round of reforms should combine market-oriented economic reforms with reforms of the governance structure based on rule of law and democracy to establish an inclusive economic and political system. Thus, a new consensus on reform gradually emerged among insightful individuals in various fields.

Meanwhile, some local governments and a few central government agencies carried out experimental reforms to address some of the practical problems they were encountering.

For instance, the People's Bank of China adjusted its policies to gradually liberalize its lending and deposit rates. In addition, the China Securities Regulatory Commission (CSRC) shifted its regulatory approach from substantive approvals to compliance-based regulation centering on mandatory information disclosures.

In the Opinions on Deepening the Economic Reform Priorities in 2010, issued by the State Council in May 2010, the National Development and Reform Commission required "an appropriate withdrawal of state capital from the general competitive fields." Based on this requirement, the Shanghai Municipal Government prepared and implemented a plan to reduce the number of industrial sectors covered by state-owned capital enterprises from 79 to 50 within a period of five years.[7]

Guangdong province in particular stood out for its institutional innovations. (1) Shenzhen municipality allowed civic organizations to be independent of administrative agencies. This was followed by a province-wide move in the same direction. Guangdong took the first but essential step to "properly handle the relationship between the government and society, accelerate separation of the role of the government from the role of the enterprise, and clarify civic organizations' rights and responsibilities, support their self-governance by law, and allow them to play their respective roles."[8] (2) Beginning in 2012, with the agreement of the State Administration for Industry and Commerce, Guangdong province implemented a business-registration reform. This reform aimed to address the issues of excessive administrative control, overly stringent entry requirements, numerous pre-approval processes, and an emphasis on approval over management. This shift involved moving from a "administrative permit first, then licensing" approach to a "licensing first, then administrative permit" approach [for activities subject to administrative review]. Subsequently, in October 2013, the State Council decided to adopt the pilot experience from Guangdong and promote nationwide business registration system reforms. This marked the beginning of replacing the "universal administrative approval system" with a "negative list system" based on the principle of "freedom unless prohibited by law" and setting the stage for the operation of a free enterprise system.

The above progress paved the way for significant breakthroughs at the 18th Party Congress in November 2012 and at the Third Plenary Session of the 18th Party Central Committee.

12.2 The Significant Breakthroughs of the 18th Party Congress and the Third Plenary Session of the 18th Party Central Committee

The 18th National CCP Congress, held in November 2012, lived up to expectations by deciding to "deepen reforms in key areas with greater political courage and wisdom at the opportune moment." This signified the CCP's decision to restart the reform agenda. In terms of the economic reforms, the goal was to "adhere to the reform direction of a socialist market economy," "properly manage the relationship between the government and the market," and "allow the market to play a fundamental role in resource allocations to a greater extent and with a broader scope." In terms of political

[7] Ding Bo and Liu Ying, "How State Capital Exists in Shanghai," *Liberation Daily*, December 8, 2012.

[8] Decision of the CCP Central Committee on Major Issues Concerning Comprehensively Deepening the Reforms, adopted by the Third Plenary Session of the 18th Party Central Committee, November 12, 2013.

reforms, the aim was to "accelerate the institutionalization of socialist democratic politics" and "achieve rule of law in all national work."

Following the determination of the 18th CCP to comprehensively deepen the reforms, various sectors discussed the top-level design, implementation roadmap, and timeline for the new round of reforms. The China Economic 50 Forum, a think-tank composed of 50 senior Chinese economists, proposed detailed recommendations about how to formulate and about the key content of the top-level design and the roadmap for a comprehensive deepening of the reforms.[9] In addition, some research institutes offered their suggestions as well. Based on these broad consultations, the drafting group for the 18th Central Committee's Third Plenary Session, led by General Secretary Xi Jinping, worked for six months to draft the Decision of the CCP Central Committee on Major Issues Concerning Comprehensively Deepening the Reforms (Draft for Discussion). The decision was approved by the Third Plenary Session of the 18th Central Committee in November 2013, providing a top-level design and overall plan for comprehensively deepening the reforms, especially the economic reforms.

The decision made judgments on major reform issues that had been hotly debated in recent years and made arrangements for specific measures for the future comprehensive deepening of the reforms based on these judgments.

The decision explicitly stated at the outset: "The goal of comprehensively deepening the reforms is to perfect and develop the socialist system with Chinese characteristics, and promote the modernization of the national governance system and governance capacity." This grand goal is to be achieved through a comprehensive deepening of the economic and political reforms.

The decision identified economic system reform as the focus of the comprehensive deepening of the reforms, pointing out that the "core issue of the economic reforms is to properly handle the relationship between the government and the market, allowing the market to play a decisive role in resource allocations and better utilizing the role of the government. … Market-determined resource allocations are a general law of market economies; to perfect the socialist market economy system, this law must be followed, focusing on resolving issues of an imperfect market system, excessive government intervention, and inadequate supervision." General Secretary Xi Jinping, in his explanation of the Decision of the CCP Central Committee on Major Issues Concerning Comprehensively Deepening the Reforms, pointed out that "further managing the relationship between the government and the market is essentially about managing whether the market or the government plays the decisive role in resource allocations."

This clarified the direction for the comprehensive deepening of the economic reforms.

After clarifying the core requirements of the economic reforms, an important task was to establish certain systems and mechanisms to achieve these requirements.

[9] Wu Jinglian, "China's Reform: The Overall Plan and Present Measures," 2013, in Wu Jinglian, *Facing the Era of Great Transformation* (Beijing: SDX Joint Publishing, 2014), pp. 247–252.

From this perspective, another crucial assertion of the Third Plenary Session decision was its re-emphasis on the judgment of the 1993 Third Plenary Session of the 14th CCP Central Committee[10] on "building a unified, open, competitive, and orderly market system," indicating that "building a unified, open, competitive, and orderly market system is the basis for the market to play a decisive role in resource allocations." This statement is significant because a unified, open, competitive, and orderly market system reflects the essential characteristics of market institutions, addresses the current problems in China's economic system, and sets forth the basic framework for the systemic goals of the comprehensive deepening of the reforms.

This provision addresses the prominent problems and major defects in the current economic system. These problems and defects are manifested in five areas: first, the fragmentation by sectors and regions and the market fragmentation necessitate the establishment of a unified, integrated market; second, differential treatment and excessive investment entry restrictions for enterprises of different ownerships and in different localities, make it difficult to achieve fair competition in the market and necessitate equal openness for all market entities; third, excessive government administrative intervention, industry and local protectionism, and widespread administrative monopolies that lead to a loss of the indispensable competitive nature of the market require implementation of competition policies to restore and maintain market competition; fourth, market disorder, collusion between officials and businessmen, market interventions, and the proliferation of malicious competition practices, require the establishment of orderly competition based on rule of law; fifth, uneven development of various markets, with satisfactory commodity markets but with underdeveloped and disorderly factor markets require accelerated construction of a market system.

To build a market system with these characteristics, reforms in multiple areas are needed. In the discussions following the 18th National Congress, scholars suggested various reform proposals, and the subsequent decision of the Third Plenary Session put forward several specific requirements.

First, a modern property rights system with clear ownership, defined responsibilities, and strict protection is the foundation of a market system. To establish such a foundation, the decision of the Third Plenary Session states: "Both the public and non-public sectors are important components of the socialist market economy and are important foundations for the development of China's economy and society, … Property rights in the public sector are inviolable, and property rights in the non-public sector are also inviolable, …[and] the state protects the property rights and legitimate interests of various ownership economies, ensures equal access to production factors, open, fair, and just market competition, and equal legal protection." Adhering to equal rights, equal opportunities, and equal rules, abolishing unreasonable regulations on non-public sector economies, eliminating various hidden barriers, and

[10] The D*eci*sion of the CCP Central Committee on Certain Issues in Establishing a Socialist Market Economy System, adopted at the Third Plenary Session of the 14th Party Central Committee in November 1993, points out that "to let the market play a fundamental role in resource allocation, it is imperative to foster and develop the market system. … [to form] a uniform, open, competitive, orderly, and broad market."

formulating specific measures for non-public sector enterprises to enter the franchise field" all must be earnestly implemented. Currently, the land property rights system has significant flaws, restricting farmers' property rights and obstructing advances in new urbanization. A unified construction land market for urban and rural areas should be established based on land empowerment and confirmation. Therefore, "Under the premise of compliance with planning and land use control, rural collective operational construction land should be allowed to be transferred, leased, or invested, and to enter the market with the same rights and prices as state-owned land."

Second, a pricing system formed through market competition is the core of the entire market system. Only through competitive pricing that reflects resource scarcities can the two fundamental functions of a market economy—effective resource allocations and the formation of incentive-compatible mechanisms—be realized. Therefore, a necessary precondition for establishing a market system is to achieve market-based pricing, allowing prices to flexibly reflect market supply and demand conditions. To this end, the basic principle set forth by the Third Plenary Session decision is: "Anything that can be priced by the market should be left to the market, and the government should not interfere inappropriately." Specifically, this involves achieving market-based formation of the RMB exchange rate mechanism, accelerating the marketization of deposit and loan interest rates, advancing price reforms in the water, oil, natural gas, electricity, transportation, and telecommunications sectors, and freeing prices in the competitive (non-natural monopoly) segments. Government pricing should mainly be limited to important public utilities, public welfare services, and network-type natural monopoly segments. Administrative prices should also be more transparent and subject to social supervision.

Third, advancing state-owned enterprise reform. Many major measures of state-owned enterprise reform identified at the turn of the century have not yet been implemented. For example, reforms such as opening the competitive segments of the electricity sector and competitive bidding have not been realized. Some departmental reforms, like those in the railway sector, have stalled since 2005. These reforms must be resumed. Additionally, the decision proposed shifting national management of state-owned enterprises from the current "enterprise management" (management of people, affairs, and assets) to "capital management" as the main approach. This is a particularly important principle that must be diligently implemented.

Fourth, competition is the soul of a market system. Competition policies must be improved to constrain market monopolies and unfair competition. One of the biggest obstacles to implementing competition policies is government regulations, with the current Anti-Monopoly Law making exceptions for administrative monopolies.[11] Clearly, such regulations that do not meet the requirements for competition should be revised. Even for natural monopoly industries where state capital continues to hold a controlling interest, the decision requires "implementing reform mainly focusing

[11] Article 7 of the Anti-Monopoly Law, effective in 2008, states: "the state protects the legitimate business activities of firms operating in the state-dominated industries related to the lifelines of the national economy and national security and to the franchise monopoly industries." Many jurists believe this provision opened the door for administrative monopolies.

on separating government and enterprise, government and capital, franchising, and government supervision, and, according to the characteristics of the different industries, implementing separation of network operations and opening up of competitive businesses, and promoting marketization of public resource allocations."

Fifth, following the market economy and the rule of law principle of "anything not prohibited is allowed," implement a negative list system for market entry. For areas not listed on the negative list, all types of market entities should be able to enter equally. At the same time, it is necessary to promote the facilitation of the business registration system, reduce qualification certification projects, switch from "certification before registration" to "registration before certification," and gradually replace the paid-in capital registration system with a subscribed capital registration system, among other changes. According to the decision of the Third Plenary Session, Party and government leadership should further streamline administration and delegate powers and deepen the reform of the administrative approval system. Economic activities that can be effectively regulated by market mechanisms should not be subject to approvals, and the remaining administrative approval items should be regulated by more efficient approvals.

Regarding management of the relationship between government and market, the decision also points out the importance of better utilizing the role of the government.

The decision adds the modifier "better" before "utilizing the role of the government," which is significant. The key issue here is how to overcome the problems whereby government roles are inadequately performed—for instance, the government's "excessive intervention" and "inadequate supervision," as pointed out in the decision, in order for the government to better play its role. In the past, Chinese government leaders have repeatedly stated in reports to the National People's Congress that over the years, various levels of Party and government leaders have taken on many responsibilities they should not handle or cannot handle well; while many areas that the government should manage were either not managed or not managed well. Extensive government administrative intervention and direct involvement, as well as administrative monopolies by state-owned large enterprises, have suppressed the initiative and creativity of enterprises as market entities and technological innovators. This has made it difficult for the market to effectively allocate resources and establish incentive-compatible mechanisms. Therefore, to properly play its role, the primary task of government is to define its tasks and to change the past situation whereby the government was "reaching too far." It is necessary to "substantially reduce the government's direct allocation of resources" and for it to be transformed into a limited and effective government under constitutional and legal constraints.

Accordingly, the decision clearly defines the government's functions and roles, stating that "the responsibilities and roles of the government mainly include maintaining macroeconomic stability, strengthening and optimizing public services, ensuring fair competition, strengthening market supervision, maintaining market order, promoting sustainable development, advancing common prosperity, and addressing market failures." In summary, the government's roles and responsibilities are to provide public goods that the market cannot provide.

First, maintaining economic stability through macroeconomic management is a fundamental responsibility of the government. However, China's economic management system, evolving as it did from a planned economy system and selective industrial policies, still bears the marks of a planned economy system. "Macroeconomic management" originally referred to managing the total monetary and fiscal quantities, but many people also refer to government intervention in individual microeconomic activities as "macroeconomic regulation." This has led to a distortion where the implementation of macro-management by Party and government agencies is transformed into micro-level intervention. Another issue is the conflating of the prevention of inflation and stabilization of the general price level under conditions of an excessive money supply with price controls and administrative pricing. As a result, not only has the general price level not been controlled from the source but this has also undermined the basic mechanism of market-based resource allocations through price changes reflecting relative scarcities and supply–demand conditions, replacing market allocation of resources with administrative power. The Decision clarifies, fundamentally, that macroeconomic regulation is to use fiscal and monetary policies as the primary tools to maintain an economic balance, stabilize market expectations, ensure the functioning of the market, promote major economic structural coordination, optimize the layout of the forces of production, mitigate economic cyclical fluctuations, and prevent systemic risks. This aligns with the management concept of a modern market economy. By following these principles for macroeconomic management, the government can avoid any misalignment or overreach in economic management and enhance the relevance and effectiveness of its macro-stability policies.

Second, strengthening and optimizing public services is another fundamental responsibility of the government. Among the various public services that the government must provide, creating a favorable institutional environment for the effective functioning of the market is crucial. The decision requires, on the one hand, "minimizing central government management of micro-level affairs and eliminating approvals for economic activities effectively regulated by market mechanisms," and, on the other hand, "ensuring fair competition, strengthening market supervision, maintaining market order," and "establishing fair, open, and transparent market rules," reflecting the need to further reinforce the functioning of the market.

The Decision of the CCP Central Committee on Major Issues Concerning Comprehensively Deepening the Reforms does not limit reform to the economic domain. Since the "overall goal of comprehensively deepening the reforms is to improve and develop the socialist system with Chinese characteristics and to advance the modernization of the national governance system and governance capacity," political system reform naturally becomes an essential part of the agenda.

Based on the goals set by the 15th and 16th National Congresses of the Communist Party of China[12]—"developing socialist democratic politics," "building a socialist

[12] Jiang Zemin, "Hold High the Great Banner of Deng Xiaoping Theory for an All-round Advancement of the Cause of Building Socialism with Chinese Characteristics to the 21st Century: Report at the 15th Party Congress," *People's Daily*, September 12, 1997; Jiang Zemin, "Build a Well-off

rule-of-law state," and "enhancing socialist political civilization"—the decision devotes five out of its sixteen chapters to the most important political system reform issues: Chapter 4, "Accelerate the Transformation of Government Functions"; Chapter 8, "Strengthen the Construction of a Socialist Democratic Political System"; Chapter 9, "Advance the Construction of a Rule-of-Law China"; Chapter 10, "Strengthen the Constraints and Supervisory System in the Operation of Power"; and Chapter 13, "Make Innovations the Social Governance System."

To advance the construction of a rule-oflLaw China, the 2014 Fourth Plenary Session of the 18th CCP Central Committee issued the CCP Central Committee Decision Concerning Several Major Issues in Comprehensively Advancing Governance According to Law, further elaborating on rule of law and construction of a rule-of-law state.

The Fourth Plenary Session decision first points out: "Compared to the requirements of the Party and national development, the expectations of the people, and the goals of modernizing the national governance system and governance capacity, there are still many issues in rule-of-law construction that have not been adapted or do not meet expectations." The main issues are: "Some laws and regulations fail to fully reflect objective laws and the people's will and lack relevance and operability, with a prominent tendency toward departmentalization and blame-shifting in legislation; there are severe issues of non-compliance with laws, lax enforcement, and lack of accountability, with problems of disconnected enforcement systems, multiple enforcement bodies, and selective enforcement, and a lack of standardization, strictness, transparency, and civility in enforcement and judicial practices, leading to strong complaints from the public about injustices and corruption in enforcement and judicial processes; some members of society have a weak awareness of respecting, trusting, and using laws to protect their rights, and some state staff, especially the leaders, have a weak awareness of acting according to the law, with occurrences of breaking the law, substituting the law with words, using power to override the law, and personal favoritism."

The decision states: "These issues violate socialist rule-of-law principles, harm the interests of the people, and hinder the development of the Party and the country, and they must be addressed with great effort."

The decision also clarifies some important content of the reforms, including: First, improving the system whereby the Constitution is at the core of judicial and prosecutorial powers. Courts and procuratorates should independently and impartially exercise their powers in accordance with the law, ensure fair justice, and improve judicial credibility. Second, emphasizing "that adhering to rule of law must first adhere to the Constitution, and adhering to law-based governance must first adhere to the Constitution." The system of constitutional supervision by the National People's Congress and its Standing Committee should be improved, and the construction of a rule-of-law government should be accelerated.

Society in an All-Round Way and Create a New Situation in Building Socialism with Chinese Characteristics: Report at the 16th Party Congress," *People's Daily*, November 18, 2002.

The Decision of the CCP Central Committee on Major Issues Concerning Comprehensively Deepening the Reforms requires: "Concentrate the wisdom of the entire Party and society to the greatest extent, mobilize all positive factors to the greatest extent, dare to tackle tough problems, and be brave in facing risks. With greater determination, break through ideological constraints and solidified interests, [and] promote the self-improvement and development of the socialist system with Chinese characteristics. ... By 2020, achieve decisive results in important areas and key reform links, complete the reform tasks proposed in this decision, form a systematic, complete, scientific, and effective institutional system, and make the various systems more mature and well-defined."

12.3 Overcoming Obstacles to Comprehensively Deepening the Reforms

The 18th Party Congress embarked on "comprehensively deepening the reforms with greater political courage and wisdom." The Third and the Fourth Plenary Sessions of the 18th Party Central Committee provided the top-down design, road map, and timetable for the reforms. These inspirational decisions point to a clear direction with effective measures. However, the experience from over thirty years of reform and an analysis of the current situation show that making proper decisions is merely a first step. It does not guarantee that all will be smooth sailing thereafter. The reform is destined to encounter resistance and obstacles, and only with perseverance can we achieve our final objectives.

First, there has been resistance from the old ideology. Since the establishment of the Qin empire in 221 BCE, the Chinese state has fundamentally relied on autocratic imperial rule. For over two thousand years, the political system upheld "Qin legalism." Although Emperor Wu of Han, Liu Che (r. 141–87 BCE), promoted Confucianism, in practice what he was promoting was still a blend of "a Confucian facade and a Legalist core," exercising the Way of the Hegemon (ba-dao) and the Way of the King (wang-dao) in turns. [13] After the People's Republic was established, the conventions of the so-called feudal Qin dynasty were not systematically criticized or uprooted.[14] Later, the government embarked on the "Soviet path," using the Soviet economic and political system as the basis for training cadres. During

---

[13] Once, when scolding his crown prince Liu Shi (later Emperor Yuan), who revered Confucianism, Emperor Xuan (Liu Xun) (91 BC–49 BC) made the following statement: "We Han emperors have ruled with a mixture of force and benevolence. Why do you want to bid ado to that Zhou dynastic system and to rule by teaching moral characters?" (*Annals of Emperor Yuan, Book of Han*). Tan Sitong (1865–98), an outstanding philosopher in the late Qing dynasty, pointed out that "the political conventions of the past two millennia follow the Qin dynasty, but they are illegitimate. The learning that prevailed in the past two millennia is that of Xun Zi, but it was hypocritical. The illegitimates took advantage of the hypocrites, and the latter curried favor from the former" (Tan Sitong, "The Learning of the *Ren*").

[14] *Selected Works of Deng Xiaoping* (Beijing: People's Publishing House, 1994), vol. 2, pp. 328–338.

the Cultural Revolution, there was also prolonged indoctrination of the so-called "theory of continuing revolution under the dictatorship of the proletariat," leading to an erroneous ideological consciousness that to this day has a profound impact on the people. The reform, a great undertaking, requires effectively addressing the resistance from such outdated ideologies and forces of habit.

In his August 18, 1980 speech, "On the Reform of the System of Party and State Leadership," Deng Xiaoping points out: "From old China, we inherited a strong tradition of feudal autocracy and a weak tradition of democratic legality. [During the new democratic revolution,] we did not complete the task of eliminating the surviving feudal influences in the ideological and political fields because we underestimated their importance and because we quickly proceeded to the socialist revolution. … [The leadership system of the Party and the state] bear the stamp of feudalism to one degree or another. … Therefore, the following task should be established: to continuously eradicate feudalism's ideological and political legacies and effectively reform the relevant institutions. … In endeavoring to eliminate these influences, we must stress the need to effectively restructure and improve the systems of the Party and state in such a way as to ensure institutionally the practice of democracy in political life, in economic management, and in all other aspects of social activity, and thus to promote the smooth progress of modernization."[15]

Second, another source of resistance has been the special interest groups and corrupt forces. Whereas the ideological obstacles can be overcome by popularizing the humanities and the social sciences and correctly guiding public opinion, the opposition on the part of the special interest groups will be much more difficult to break.

Since the 18th Party Congress, the anti-corruption campaign has revealed that enormous corrupt forces exist in Party/government/military organizations, the business world, and even academic circles due to the expansion of the institutional foundation for rent-seeking. These forces are unwilling to let the market and democracy-oriented and rule-of-law–based reforms uproot those institutions that allow them to amass great wealth, and they will desperately fight back.

Apart from the high-ranking corrupt figures (*menghu ju'e*), many officials and businesspeople consider that corruption is commonplace. The banality of evil exists because of the omnipresent institutional distortions, corrupt bureaucratic conventions, and hidden rules. Therefore, any reform affecting these special interest groups' opportunities to abuse their powers and to peddle their influence will encounter their resistance and opposition.

Third, a modern market economy is a precise and immense system that evolved over hundreds of years (some say over a thousand years). Instead of going through a natural process of evolution, the reform in China has been a deliberate process to establish an efficient market-economy system during a period of several decades. This requires broad and adequate theoretical preparations and multi-disciplinary expertise. In his significant work *Toward a Comparative Institutional Analysis*, Professor

[15] Ibid.

Masahiko Aoki points out that individual institutions are interrelated and interdependent within the overall institutional arrangements: Only mutually consistent and complementary institutional arrangements have vitality and can be sustained.[16]

Although challenging to operate, various segments of the old system were interlinked and complementary, a characteristic formed during an extended period of adaptation. When one component was modified, even if the change was progressive, it could lead to systemic functional problems. For instance, some local governments previously relied on large-scale urban development for financing. When the land market assigns more property rights to farmers and ensures that farmers can share the benefits of the increase in the value of land, local governments will have trouble maintaining their financing model that depends on the income from land transactions. As a result, some local governments will have difficulties servicing their debts. An overarching design considering all of these links based on China's experience and the advanced social sciences is needed so that the new system will operate smoothly.

Comprehensively deepening the reforms is a complex project, with hundreds of institutions requiring replacement. What tasks should be carried out first, and what tasks should be put on the back burner? Which reforms can be undertaken separately, and which reforms need to be done in coordination with other reforms? These matters should be carefully thought through. Success will require skilled political decision-making based on adequate professional expertise throughout the process, from the planning of the reform to its implementation. The participation of high-quality professionals is a prerequisite for success.

Fourth, maintaining a stable macroeconomy within a supportive economic environment is essential to successfully undertaking the challenging task of comprehensive reforms.

China's reform experience shows it is risky to launch significant reforms when the macroeconomic environment is strained by the excessive issuance of currency and when aggregate demand far exceeds aggregate supply.

At present, China's economy faces three overlapping challenges (the downshift in economic growth, the pains of the structural adjustments, and the consequences of the earlier economic stimulus policies): GDP growth is slowing down, the defective economic structure is pending adjustment, the monetary expansion has not yet been addressed, and the leverage ratio remains high. These problems mean that the comprehensive deepening of the reforms will face strains in the macroeconomic environment.

The stimulus policies aiming to boost the short-term growth rate as well as the loose credit policy and the large-scale investment programs should be halted to alleviate the strains and to facilitate the initiation of the forms. Furthermore, to maintain macroeconomic stability and support a smooth start to the reforms, resolute measures should be undertaken to reduce the leverage ratio, e.g., the existence of zombie enterprises that rely on loans to survive for a long time but have no hope of being recovered.

[16] Masahiko Aoki, *Toward a Comparative Institutional Analysis*, 2001 (Chinese translation. Shanghai: Far East Publishing House, 2000), pp. 19–20.

To sum up, comprehensively deepening the reforms requires that Party and government leaders at all administrative levels break down the barriers, overcome the difficulties, and push for comprehensive reforms with extraordinary political courage and wisdom. Great political courage refers to a determination to unwaveringly defend the banner of reform and opening and to overcome the resistance and obstacles from the old ideologies and special interest groups. Greater political wisdom calls for working with professional talents and applying high operational skills to avoid any risks and to resolve the inevitable difficulties during the transition.

Only in this way will China be able to overcome the hardships and challenges in deepening the reforms and to comprehensively reenergize the economy.

12.4 Ensuring that Comprehensively Deepening the Reforms Will Be Fruitful

Since the 18th Party Congress, the CCP central leadership has attached unprecedented high importance to countering corruption. Firm implementation of the policy to punish both senior- and low-level corrupt officials ("tigers and flies") led to in-depth disciplinary inspections and a resultant high-intensity and rapid crackdown on corruption. As a result, the spread of corruption was contained. During its term, the Eighteenth Central Commission for Discipline Inspection (CCDI), after receiving approval from the Party Central Committee, investigated 440 senior Party members (at or above the provincial government and military corps commander levels or other senior officials managed directly by the Party Central Committee). Among these people, 43 were members or alternate members of the 18th Party Central Committee and nine were CCDI members. Nationwide, the disciplinary inspection and supervision agencies received 12.186 million petitions, responded to 2.674 million tips, launched 1.545 million cases, and punished 1.537 million officials, over 8,900 of whom were central government department–level officials and 63,000 were county government and division chief–level officials. In addition, cases of 58,000 criminal suspects were handed over to the judiciary bodies.[17] The anti-corruption efforts achieved noteworthy results and won praise from the general public, who had long been resentful of such corrupt officials. The morale of the people within and outside the Party was raised.

Having already achieved meaningful results, the anti-corruption efforts should pay more attention to the institutional problems that have led to such corruption. The institutional foundation for rent-seeking should be eradicated and the democratic monitoring of public officials should be strengthened. Because of the widely existing legacy of the planned economy, government officials still control enormous resources, which provide them with vast opportunities for rent-seeking. This is the root cause of the perennial corruption. Therefore, there should be no hesitation in

[17] "Report of the Work of the Eighteenth Central Commission for Discipline Inspection to the 19th Party Congress," passed by the 19th Party Congress on October 24, 2017.

implementing market and rule-of-law–based reforms to establish a modern market economy and to reduce the opportunities for corruption and rent-seeking. Meanwhile, oversight of political power should be enhanced based on the principles of democracy and rule of law. Only by undertaking comprehensive measures to address the institutional foundations can an effective mechanism be established under which people dare not to, cannot, and do not want to engage in corruption.

Beginning in 2014, comprehensively deepening the reforms entered the implementation phase. On January 24, 2014, the Central Leading Group for Deepening the Reforms in charge of overall coordination held its first meeting. The meeting passed three sets of work rules (for the leading group, for the sub-groups, and for the administrative office of the leading group), publicized the lists of members of the six sub-groups that are charged with systemic reforms related to the economy and the ecological environment, democracy and rule of law, cultural affairs management, social management, Party construction, and disciplinary inspections. The meeting also issued the division of labor among the central Party and government agencies for implementing the Decision of the Third Plenary Session of the 18th Party Central Committee, specifying the responsibilities of these organizations regarding 336 reform measures. At this meeting, Xi Jinping, Party general secretary and head of the leading group, required that the six sub-groups become operational as soon as possible. He also instructed that the provinces establish their own leading groups for comprehensively deepening the reforms. Furthermore, the relevant central government agencies were asked to set up accountability mechanisms to act in coordination with the leading group. This signaled the official launch of the comprehensive reforms.

Following the leading group's first meeting, implementation of several priority reforms began and plans for other reforms were issued. Many reform plans pointed to a clear direction with effective measures.

In October 2015, the Party Central Committee and the State Council issued Several Opinions on Advancing Reform of the Pricing Mechanism. This document points out: the pricing mechanism is the core of the market system, and the market's decisive role in resource allocations depends on whether it can determine prices. As laid out in this document, this reform is fundamental because the market's efficient allocation of resources and incentive compatibility mechanism depend on a free pricing system. Prices in the competitive fields and in the competitive sections of the supply chains should be substantially liberalized by 2017, and a market pricing mechanism should be established by 2020. However, the pricing reform should be implemented cautiously and with determination because it will affect the administrative powers and interests of some agencies and individuals, and it will directly impact businesses and the people's livelihoods.

The opinions on price reform require gradually establishing the primacy of competition, a task that is crucial to the overall reform. For decades, China's economic policies focused on selective industrial policies under which the government directly allocated resources. In June 2016, the State Council issued an important document, Opinions on Establishing a Fair Competition Review System to Develop the Market Economy, replacing the selective industrial policy with a competition policy as the policy foundation and requiring fair competition reviews for normative documents and other policy measures with respect to the economic activities of market entities. The first step was prior fair competition reviews for all new policies. Any violation of the fair competition principle was to be addressed before the new policy was to be issued. The next step was to conduct fair competition reviews of the existing policies and institutional arrangements. Rules and practices contrary to the principle or hindering competition were to be abolished. These steps would facilitate the establishment of a uniform, open, competitive, and orderly market, which is a basic institution in a market economy.

The Opinions of the CCP Central Committee and the State Council on Improving the Property Rights Protection System and Lawfully Protecting Property Rights, issued in November 2016, laid out a critical reform to improve the property rights foundation for the market economy.

This document clearly states that "a property rights system is the cornerstone of the socialist market economy, and protecting property rights is a necessary requirement for upholding the basic socialist economic system. Stability in property ownership leads to stability in governance; effective protection and realization of economic entities' property rights are the foundation for sustained and healthy economic and social development." The document then outlines five fundamental principles for property rights protection: "equal protection," "comprehensive protection," "legal protection," "joint participation," and "addressing both the symptoms and the root causes."

The opinions on property rights protection have several essential implementation requirements: (a) improving the legal framework for equal protection of property rights, (b) identifying as soon as possible wrongful convictions that generated strong public resentment, and (c) when dealing with historical property rights cases, strictly adhering to and observing the principle of non-retroactivity of the law and applying the principle of "following the old law and adopting a lenient approach" between the old and new laws. These challenging tasks require close cooperation among the agencies in charge of communications, legislation, and justice.

At the New Year's tea party hosted by the National Committee of the Chinese People's Political Consultative Conference at the end of 2016, Xi Jinping announced that with the completion of 419 reform plans, the main framework for key structural reforms in major areas had been essentially established.[18]

In this context, it is important to strengthen the capability to act and overcome the various obstacles to effectively implement correct policies, sound top-down designs, and specific plans. From the 20th meeting of the Central Leading Group onward, all leading group meetings have called for specifying the relevant agencies' responsibilities, tightening the responsibility requirements, and improving the mechanism to supervise and inspect those agencies and to hold them accountable. Moreover, personnel decisions should reflect the strengthened accountability; General Secretary Xi Jinping pointed out at the 25th meeting of the Central Leading Group that the

[18] "The New Year's Tea Party Hosted by the CPPCC," Xinhua, December 30, 2016.

policy should "promote those people who implement the reforms and demote those people who do not."

From its beginning, the reform and opening process experienced many twists and turns as well as setbacks; still, following the logic of historical determinism, China will advance toward a market economy, rule of law, and democracy. The central theme of the economic reforms has evolved from "a dominant planned economy and supplemental market adjustments" to "a decisive role of the market." Socioeconomic development accelerated when the market-oriented reforms made substantial breakthroughs and, as a result, the people's livelihoods registered noticeable improvements. However, hesitations and setbacks sometimes occurred due to the influence of the old concepts and the old political slogans. At other times, the reform process became stalled, and people did not realize that they had turned in the wrong direction or had even retreated backward. Such behavior must be changed. When adverse phenomena occur, perseverance is needed to unwaveringly carry out the reforms and to overcome the institutional obstacles to socioeconomic development. Only in this way can we hope to achieve improved efficiency, better structures, and sustained development.

There are enormous challenges ahead in implementing the overall economic reform plan adopted by the Third Plenary Session of the 18th Party Central Committee.

First, establishing a modern, uniform, open, competitive, and orderly market system remains the central task. Achieving this goal requires political, economic, and legal efforts, including protecting property rights and practicing rule of law. The existing administrative protections, collusion among government officials and businesspeople, and abuses of market dominance should be eliminated through a better competition policy and a more robust law enforcement system.

Second, the leading agencies of the Party and the government should perform their duties to establish a sound business environment and provide efficient public services. Progress has been made in lowering market entry bars, innovating oversight mechanisms, and improving service efficiency. But there is a need to prevent any U-turns. Therefore, the reform should go deeper in expanding uses of the negative list for market entry and the positive list regarding government duties. This will ensure compliance with the following principles: "Everything which is not forbidden is allowed" for both enterprises and individuals, and "no one can wield power without authorization by law" for Party and government organizations.

Third, the reform of state-owned enterprises must strive to overcome the difficulties and navigate through the deep waters. Currently, state-owned enterprises still control a significant amount of important economic resources and hold monopolistic positions in many industries. Maintaining and strengthening these structures inevitably reduces the survival space for other economic sectors, obstructs the formation of a fair competitive market, and makes it difficult to improve the overall efficiency of the national economy. How can the ownership structure be adjusted in line with the principles of "advancing in some fields and withdrawing from others" and "there are things to do and things not to do," as based on the requirement of the Fourth Plenary Session of the 18th Party Central Committee? How can the role of the

SOEs be transformed from making personnel decisions, running day-to-day operations, and controlling assets to mainly managing capital, as required by the Third Plenary Session of the 18th Party Central Committee? These and other conceptual and practical issues remain to be addressed.

Fourth, the external opening should continue in the context of building "a community of a shared future for mankind." China's experience offers a good lesson: using the opening to promote the reform. At present, an anti-globalization trend is popular among certain groups. In response to the call of those supporting anti-globalization, China should counter all forms of protectionism, lower the market entry bar for foreign investments, promote fair competition, and develop a high-standard free trade zone network. The pilot free trade zones are meaningful for the overall reform because, in addition to the preferential policy treatments for specific regions, the pilots seek to establish a market-oriented, internationalized, and rule-of-law–based business environment to further reap the "dividends of the opening."

China's socioeconomic reforms are a continuous and ongoing process. The experience gained since the onset of the reform and opening demonstrates that the obstacles to socioeconomic development can only be overcome by persisting with the reforms and rigorously implementing the measures for comprehensively deepening the reforms. It is only through such a commitment that the Chinese nation will be able to secure a bright future.

Postscript

This book is a reflection of my observations and ideas about the process and experience of China's reform and opening.

I began teaching a course on the Chinese economy for Ph.D. students in the Graduate School of the Chinese Academy of Social Sciences in 1995. Later, I introduced the same course to MBA and EMBA students at the China Europe International Business School. The course was continuously updated in tandem with China's ongoing reforms and economic development. Based on my teaching notes for the course, I wrote *Economic Reform in Contemporary China: Strategy and Implementation.* That book, published in 1999 and using a modern economics analytical framework, offers my observations on China's economic reforms and social development. It has attracted the attention of readers both at home and abroad who take an interest in China's economic development. Published in English, Japanese, and traditional Chinese characters, it is a reference book intended for use in higher education courses on the Chinese economy.

Even though the 1999 book still attracts attention among academics, it was, after all, published almost twenty years ago. With many new lessons learned, China's reform and opening has advanced further, thus requiring additional theoretical summaries and policy analyses. Therefore, since its publication, the book has been updated with additions and corrections in various editions. However, these are only partial updates rather than comprehensive systematic thoughts on China's reform process. So, in early 2014 I began to prepare a new book, entitled *China's Economic Reform Process*, to cover a more extended time period and to include the recent years.

At first, I thought it would be relatively easy to pen a new book: the 1999 book could provide the basic structure, and it would only be necessary to add some supplementary material. However, after beginning the draft, I realized it would be necessary for me to learn from past experiences, update my knowledge, and develop some new theoretical analyses and summaries. But unfortunately, day-to-day teaching and research was more demanding of my time. As a result, I stopped and started the drafts on several occasions, and it thus took me three years to complete the manuscript.

During the initial drafting, Ms. Zhang Xinwen, my China Europe International Business School assistant, managed the text entry and formatting, verified the data,

W. Jinglian, *China's Economic Reform*, Understanding China,
https://doi.org/10.1007/978-981-96-9607-9

and prepared the tables and charts. She also contributed to Chapter 7: The Turn of the Twenty-first Century: Market Forces Driving China's Economic Rise. At the invitation of the Encyclopedia of China Publishing House, Dr. Qiu Yuefang checked the citations and formatted the final text.

Wang Xian, Liao Qiang, Huang Shaoqing, and Wu Suping reviewed the first draft of the text and provided comments. Based on their recommendations, I made some modifications to several chapters.

Ms. Liu Yaping at the National Institute of Finance, Tsinghua University, provided much support in editing the text and entering the data. Director Guo Yinxing of the Encyclopedia of China Publishing House devoted much time and energy, with maximum tolerance and understanding of my rounds of revisions, to edit and publish the book.

My sincere gratitude goes to all these people for their cooperation and support.

Wu Jinglian

August 2018

Index

W. Jinglian, *China's Economic Reform*, Understanding China,
https://doi.org/10.1007/978-981-96-9607-9

N

O

P

The manufacturer's authorised representative in the EU is Springer Nature Customer Service Centre GmbH, Europaplatz 3, 69115 Heidelberg, Germany. If you have any concerns regarding our products, please contact ProductSafety@springernature.com

Printed and bound by CPI Group (UK) Ltd, Croydon, CR0 4YY
21/09/2026
02219983-0010